SPEAKING OF SPAIN

SPEAKING *of* SPAIN

THE EVOLUTION OF RACE AND NATION IN THE HISPANIC WORLD

Antonio Feros

Harvard University Press

Cambridge, Massachusetts
London, England
2017

Printed in the United States of America

First printing

Library of Congress Cataloging-in-Publication Data

Names: Feros, Antonio, author.
Title: Speaking of Spain : the evolution of race and nation in the Hispanic world / Antonio Feros.
Description: Cambridge, Massachusetts : Harvard University Press, 2017. | Includes bibliographical references and index.
Identifiers: LCCN 2016050810 | ISBN 9780674045514
Subjects: LCSH: National characteristics, Spanish. | Nationalism—Spain—History. | Cultural pluralism—Spain—History. | Racism—Spain—History. | Spain. Constitución (1812) | Spain—Colonies—America—History.
Classification: LCC DP52 .F47 2017 | DDC 946—dc23
LC record available at https://lccn.loc.gov/2016050810

Para Moncho

CONTENTS

MAPS

SPEAKING OF SPAIN

Introduction

THE YEAR 1492 was a momentous one in Spain, a year that challenged the very notion of what was Spain and who was Spanish. The marriage of Isabella and Ferdinand in 1468 and the subsequent dynastic union of the crowns of Castile and Aragon—the two main states in Iberia—meant that, for the first time since antiquity, inhabitants of the Peninsula could think of themselves as part of one polity and subjects of one monarchy. Even as they conquered the last remaining Muslim state on Iberian soil (the Kingdom of Granada) and nurtured a fragile unity, the new monarchy turned outward to initiate the process of imperial expansion in Europe, Africa, America, and Asia. The coincidence of political unification and imperial expansion under the aegis of the Catholic Kings of Spain forced on the inhabitants of the peninsula, and the subjects of the Spanish monarchy generally, troubling and enduring questions about national and racial identity. This early confrontation with the world and its unknown others is also what makes Spain the key case for historical questions about race and nation in the making of the modern western world.

With Spain only ever provisionally unified and Catalonia threatening to regain its sovereignty, with constant debates about the meaning of Spain and Spanishness and about the presence in the country of "foreign" populations (Jews but especially Muslims and Latin Americans), it is evident that many of the questions Spaniards discussed in the past have resurged prominently in the early twentieth-first century. Although the main subject of this book is not contemporary Spain but the early modern period (sixteenth to early nineteenth centuries), it is all but impossible to understand some of modern Spaniards' main preoccupations without looking at the past and our ancestors' views and decisions. We need to understand how our ancestors promoted the idea that Spain was a nation while also developing ideas about the characteristics of a Spanish race and ideas about human and cultural diversity within the peninsula and overseas territories under the control of the Spanish monarchy. These are the main subjects of this book.

Hispania, the name used by the ancients to refer to the Iberian Peninsula, is of uncertain origin. However, it has been sufficiently well established that this southern European territory was first settled by peoples from other parts of the Mediterranean and North Africa and later by the northern European Celts. Greeks and Romans recognized that this was a region somewhat isolated from the rest of Europe by one of the continent's most imposing mountain chains, the Pyrenees, which meant that access to it was mainly by sea. Impenetrable by land, its internal geography also posed significant challenges, impeding communication to the extent that at various times the regional communities of Iberia were almost completely cut off from one another. Until the medieval period, the impetus to unification invariably came from foreign arrivals (Greeks, Phoenicians, Carthaginians, and especially Romans and Visigoths), who were drawn to the peninsula by its easy maritime access, its natural resources, and the climate in its southern regions. The Romans were the first to gain control of the entire peninsula, or most of it, first as a mere colony and later as an imperial province. Over the course of centuries, from 218 BCE to the fifth century CE, the Roman presence would leave a profound mark on Hispania—its language, culture, political discourse, and laws. The Roman period also witnessed the settlement in Hispania of Jews from the Roman province of Judea. This was another community of outsiders who would come to play a central role in Iberian history.

The crisis of the Roman Empire also engulfed the Iberian Peninsula, as Gothic peoples from central Europe began to arrive in the early fifth century. The Gothic occupation was completed when one of the branches, the Visigoths, consolidated their power in the closing decades of the fifth century. At least in the symbolism that it later acquired, the period of Visigothic domination, which lasted until the early eighth century, was one of the most important in Iberian history. During this era the various peninsular territories were politically unified for the first time, and Christianity was proclaimed as the official religion, a move that has profoundly marked Spanish history until the present day. Modern historians have questioned the stability of the Gothic regime, and the strength of the Gothic influence on the native population of the peninsula, but nevertheless, the Visigothic period would be invoked from the Middle Ages onward as a sort of model, albeit a mythic one, of an Iberian Peninsula unified in politics and religion.

The Visigothic reign in Hispania ended the way it had begun, with the Visigoths this time on the receiving end of a new foreign invasion, originating in North Africa and representing the tidal wave of an expansionist Islam. The new invaders, known to Spaniards under the generic designation of Arabs or Moors, crossed the Straits of Gibraltar in 711 and within a matter of months had overrun virtually the entire peninsula. Later generations of Spaniards constructed a myth that eighth-century Iberian Christians resisted the Arab invasion to the last breath and stoutly rejected conversion to Islam, but the reality was somewhat different. Many of the Visigothic elites died in military clashes or went into exile in France, large numbers of Christians chose to convert to Islam, and the Jewish minority collaborated with the new invaders. For at least a century and a half following the invasion, there was every indication that Iberia would become yet another province in the orbit of the powerful Abbasid Caliphate with its seat in Baghdad, with the remaining Christians a tolerated minority. Gradually, however, in spite of rather unpromising beginnings, various Christian statelets in the north were consolidated and began making tentative inroads to Al-Andalus in the south. By the fifteenth century, all the elements that would characterize early modern Iberia were in place: the existence of various independent Christian kingdoms that were a product of the struggle against the Arab power but also the presence in the peninsula of three communities—Christians, Arabs, and Jews—that were sharply distinguished by their ethnic origins, religion, and culture and each with a significant presence in every region of the peninsula.

Other developments central to understanding the early modern period may also be traced to the late fifteenth and early sixteenth centuries. The closing decades of the fifteenth century saw the dynastic union between the two most powerful Christian powers in the peninsula, the crowns of Castile and Aragon, represented by Isabel of Castile and Fernando of Aragon respectively. This was a dynastic union, but it would have important unintended consequences in the politico-constitutional sphere. For the first time ever, because the impulse towards unification resulted now from internal forces, the great majority of the inhabitants of the peninsula could think of themselves as members of a unified political entity, subjects of the same monarchy and of rulers born in the peninsula, even though regional identities and political autonomy endured.

As a result of three seminal events, 1492 was a particularly significant year. The first of these was the conquest of the sole remaining Muslim state on Iberian soil, the Kingdom of Granada, by the armies of Isabel and Ferdinand, and its integration in the Spanish monarchy as part of the crown of Castile. One of the consequences of this conquest was the forced conversion of all Muslims in Spain in the immediately following decades. The same year, Ferdinand and Isabel ordered the conversion of all the Jews in the peninsula and the expulsion of those who refused. The most important outcome of these parallel processes was the imposition of a single religion, Catholicism, on the entire Iberian Peninsula, now seen as the bond that would force all its inhabitants to see themselves as members of one community. The voyages of exploration and the conquests that would duly transform the Spanish monarchy into a global power also began in 1492. Spain's expansion initiated the Spanish migration to the Americas and elsewhere, the conquest of overseas territories, and with it the opening of debates on the characteristics of non-European peoples, especially the Africans and Amerindians, and the possibility of their political and cultural integration in the Iberian world.

The coincidence of political unification of most of ancient Hispania, and imperial expansion under the aegis of the Catholic Kings of Spain in Europe, Africa, America and Asia, provoked peninsular inhabitants, and the subjects of the Spanish Monarchy generally, to begin to reflect on what was "Spain" and who was "Spanish." The span of time covered by this book, between the end of the fifteenth century and the start of the nineteenth, witnessed profound changes in the meaning of nation and the characteristics of its people. In 1500, few were able to articulate clearly what it was that constituted Spain or "Spanishness." Some insisted that the Spanish monarchy was not a unified state but a monarchy composed of distinct regional communities, constituted as politically autonomous kingdoms, and that there was no such thing as a Spanish nation or even Spaniards. There were people who might be identified as Castilians or Catalans or Aragonese or Valencians but no people who could be properly called Spaniards. In the seventeenth century, some but still not very many felt able to argue confidently that it was possible to speak of a Spanish community, a Spanish nation, inhabited by people with shared ethnicity, culture, and religion. By the early nineteenth century, the end point of this study, the situation had changed dramatically. It was now claimed, by a majority of the cultural and political elite, that Spain was a nation and that a majority of those born in Spanish territories, whatever their ethnic origins, could be considered "Spanish citizens."

These transformations and processes are the subject of this book, which in turn is centered around two prominent concepts, nation and race—perhaps the two most polemical concepts in scholarly studies. A desire to understand nation and race in the history of the Iberian world was my original motive for writing this book. To be sure, there are studies of nation and race in given historical periods or regions within the Spanish world. In general, the national question, or the development of the idea of the nation in the Hispanic world, tends to be restricted to peninsular Spain. The question of race, meanwhile, is of primary concern in studies of the Jewish and Morisco questions in Spain but above all in works dealing with Spanish visions of non-European peoples under Spanish sovereignty in the Americas. However, no one has dealt with these subjects in a connected, systematic fashion during the entirety of the long early modern period and the implications of both for the political, constitutional, and cultural structuring of Iberian society.

There is clearly a very large literature on nation and nationalism to which this study properly belongs. The subject of the nation has attracted the passionate interest of a wide range of scholars.[1] The nation is, to borrow a tremendously apt notion, "imagined," created not as a result of the observation of verifiable realities but as the outcome of processes of ideological, political, and cultural constructions. Modernization arguments, which count Eric Hobsbawm among their most lucid proponents, are also invaluable. "Like most serious students," Hobsbawm wrote in his *Nations and Nationalism since 1789*, "I do not regard the 'nation' as a primary nor as an unchanging social entity. It belongs exclusively to a particular, and historically recent, period," with a start during the French Revolution.[2] As other scholars have suggested, however, modernist theories deny the possibility of understanding the processes of the creation, or of the invention, of national identities before the eighteenth century. For these authors, led by Anthony Smith, nations are "primordial," which is to say that nations "generally evolve rather organically out of pre-existing substrata of ethnicity," territory, language, and religion.[3]

Before the late eighteenth century, no clear sense of Spanishness or a "Spanish nation" existed. Those who make this claim are trying to argue that nations were already fully conceived and understood as such from the Middle Ages or even, in the Spanish case, from the Visigothic period onward, which is clearly erroneous. Nevertheless, the principal idea behind this study is that nations have origins, that they develop from and in specific contexts, and that they cannot be understood without taking into account what the population of the territory in question thought about themselves as a community in each particular period. In this light, it is argued here that the Iberian Peninsula experienced a prolonged contest between distinct visions of the nation and the patria (fatherland). It was a contest over whether all peoples under the Spanish monarchs' sovereignty should view Spain as their fatherland or believe instead that their true patria and nation was Catalonia or Valencia or Castile. Nations are indeed imagined, but we need to understand their historical evolution, the memories, cultures, traditions, and beliefs shared, and sometimes violently imposed, by the inhabitants of the Spanish monarchy.[4] We need to understand, to use Linda Colley's term, the "forging" of the nation, in this case throughout the entire early modern period.

The national question, or, more precisely, the debates on whether one or several "nations" lived within Spain and whether its people shared certain characteristics or diverged from one another in nature, history, culture, and language, has gone on unabated since the late fifteenth century. One of the objectives of this study is to assert the specificity of the Spanish case within the literature on the processes of national formation. Nations, as we understand them today, were constructed on a foundation of ideologies and sentiments developed over long periods of time, and this book contends that debates on the nation in early modern Spain were fairly precocious in comparison to other European regions. One of the peculiarities of the Spanish case is that the debate has been going on so long, since at least the late fifteenth and early sixteenth centuries, precisely because of the concurrence of dynastic unification of most of the peninsula and "Spain's" projection as an imperial power in Europe. Similar debates—and the emergence of the idea of a nation—can also be found in England more or less in the same period, perhaps because it went through similar processes—dynastic union, expansion and occupation of other territories in the British Isles and beyond, and increasing perceptions of English as a nation apart dating from at least the English reformation in the early sixteenth century.

The construction of a nation called Spain was contested throughout the entire early modern period and into the nineteenth century. In the Spanish case, unlike Britain and much of the rest of Europe, the reason for contestation was not religion—Spain remained Catholic during the entire period—but politics and culture. Debates in this period encompassed at least two main themes. The first concerned whether the union of the various kingdoms was going to result in the creation of a joined polity and nation called

Spain or whether the Spanish monarchy, even if politically united, was going to remain a dynastic state composed of several nations—Castilian, Catalan, Valencian, Navarrese, and others. Second, Spaniards debated whether this was the formation of a single "Spanish" nation, people, and identity or instead the superimposition of a "Castilian" identity on distinct regional identities. A comparable process has been observed in Great Britain, where the notion of Britishness was composed of myths, institutions, values, and a language that were essentially English. Among other things, this book analyzes how the different communities that coexisted in the peninsula responded to the creation of a dominant Castilian or Spanish national identity. In more than one sense, and at various points in time, this was a violent process, one in which the regional communities with a sense of their own separate identity—especially Catalonia—were forced to abandon or at least postpone their own national yearnings.

A majority of early modern Spanish intellectuals and politicians, as well as their nineteenth- and twentieth-century counterparts, believed that a Spanish nation or race had existed since the Iberian Peninsula was populated by Tubal, the grandson of Noah, and his descendants. The pervasiveness of this theory explains the other fundamental concept in this work: race. In the nineteenth century, race acquired a similar meaning in all European languages: "any of the (putative) major groupings of mankind, usually defined in terms of distinct physical features or shared ethnicity, and sometimes (more controversially) considered to encompass common biological or genetic characteristics."[5] From at least the early nineteenth century, race became generally linked to racism, or the belief that some races are superior to others and that these inferior races could endanger the ethnic purity and cultural identity of the superior races if allowed to live among them.

A central analytical tenet of this work is that, as in the case of the nation, the term *race* also evolved from the fifteenth century onward, parallel to dominant theories about the existence of distinct human groups (races) or explanations of the causes and consequences of human diversity. Viewed from this long perspective, it is clear that the modern concept of race did not appear until the eighteenth century, and this is also true of theories associated with so-called scientific racism. In the Spanish case, the definitions of race and racism as we understand them today first required the invention of one's own group as the ideal nation or race, with laudable origins and exemplary physical and mental characteristics, preserved immaculately across time and space. Spanishness was the combination of features and characteristics that distinguished the Spanish from other nations—other Europeans but especially other nations (Jews, Arabs, Americans, and Africans) who lived in territories controlled by Spain.

The transition in the eighteenth century toward the definition of Spaniards as members of a "white race," and the exaltation of this race as morally and physically superior, was the prerequisite to the categorical representation of the rest of humanity as members of naturally inferior other races—no longer just nations. Race and nation were concepts linked from the outset and developed in conjunction with one another. And, once again, the Spanish case appears exceptional and instructive, for it was in Spain that the debates on "nation" and belonging were from the start influenced by debates on whether the Spaniards were all those born in Spain and its territories (the civic idea of the nation) or only those who could demonstrate that they descended from pure Spanish ancestors (the ethnic idea of the nation).

In part, this is an intellectual history of the evolution of the concepts of nation and race in Spain, as found in the writings of the educated elite—theologians, jurists, explorers, and naturalists. But more importantly, it is a history of the politics of race and nation over a very long stretch of the Spanish Empire. The history of Spain and the Spanish world, like that of other peoples and nations, is marked by continuous ideological and political debates, by the rise of a dominant national project, but also by the resistance, at times violent, of those who wished to defend their rights and identities, national or ethnic. The aim of this study is to link intellectual processes with contemporaneous social and political practices and contests. The intellectual debates and political shifts marked, and with time changed, the social perceptions and the laws that ordered enormously complex societies on both sides of the Atlantic. These discourses and laws developed in the Hispanic world during the early modern period were used, to paraphrase Edward Said, to dominate and exercise authority over peoples originated in the Americas and Africa but also over minorities in Spain itself (the descendants of Jews and Arabs).[6]

Like other societies of the time, Iberian society was socially divided, and this social hierarchy determined how an individual was viewed, what laws affected the individual, and an individual's access to public offices, power, and authority. Spanish society was also, to use Charles Mills's words, divided following a racial hierarchy, by which some individuals suffered discrimination because they did not belong to the main or dominant nation or race, whatever its definition in each period.[7] A link between the emerging sense of the nation and the development of racialist ideas of the social body is not in itself unique to the Spanish case, but its specific circumstances and timing are unique. In the Iberian Peninsula, society was structured based on social hierarchy but also on a racialist basis due to the presence of ethnic groups perceived as non-Spanish. For example, converted Jews and Muslims were all subjects of the Spanish king but not always entitled to the same rights as those identified as Spaniards by origin and blood. In the overseas territories, the dominant criterion for social organization was fundamentally racial, with Spaniards and their American descendants as the dominant group and the rest—Native Americans, Africans, and individuals of mixed blood—as subordinated. As in the case of the nation, the structuring of the society based on racial criteria was also a contested terrain throughout the entire period under consideration.

This is above all a study of Spaniards' perceptions of self and others, within and outside of Spain. This is not an analysis of European perceptions of Spain and Spaniards. Countless works have been dedicated to that topic, in the belief that understanding what foreigners had written about Spaniards would help explain the reactions and concepts developed by Spaniards about themselves. Certainly, during some of the periods covered in this study, especially the 1700s, Spaniards were often responding to images of their country, history, and character promulgated by foreigners. Spaniards, like any other community, cultivated their own sense of identity based on their own traditions and experiences. The European narrative of Spain and Spaniards in the early modern period is no doubt interesting, and diverting, but it is far less complex and compelling than the history of Spaniards' visions of themselves.

The thematic and chronological division of this book mirrors its major questions and lines of analysis. The first four chapters cover the sixteenth and seventeenth centuries, tracing out the emerging definitions of Spain and its people in the peninsula and the Americas in the early formative period. Chapter 1 analyzes the political composition of the Spanish monarchy during this period, while Chapter 2 discusses contemporary theories about the existence of a Spanish ethnotype. The third chapter considers the predicament of the converted Jews and Muslims in Spain during this same period, while the fourth looks at Spanish visions of non-European peoples, above all the Africans and the Amerindians. Chapter 5 moves to the eighteenth century and analyzes the processes of national and ethnic creation in Spain, while Chapter 6 looks at these topics in the Spanish-American context. The seventh and last chapter focuses on the political processes and debates that in the early nineteenth century led to the first liberal constitution in Spanish history, known as the Constitution of Cádiz (1812). The constitution gave a new, concrete form to the modern meaning of nation, citizenship, gender, slavery, and race. Yet the "discovery" or "invention" of the Spanish nation was not simply the outcome of these parliamentary debates or the contemporaneous struggle against the foreign French invader. It was the product of political processes and ideological fashioning that had been occurring since the beginning of the sixteenth century. This book is an attempt to understand those primordial ideas about the Spanish nation and the contexts that shaped them—on their own terms but also because these concepts and ideas in some vital ways continue to inform the identities and struggles of modern Spaniards.

1

Spains

In October 1469, two young princelings—Isabel, eighteen, and her cousin Ferdinand, seventeen—married in a small Castilian town in virtual secrecy. As members of the same Trastámara dynasty, their marriage was an attempt to establish order and stability in the peninsula following decades of conflict, regicides, rebellions, and civil wars.

Isabel became queen of the crown of Castile in 1474 when she succeeded her brother Enrique IV. Five years later, in 1479, Ferdinand became king of the crown of Aragon. This was strictly a union of heads, not bodies: the marriage accords did not call for, or envisage, a true political and juridical union of the two crowns and their kingdoms. Nevertheless, the practical result of the marriage was that for the first time in centuries, the two most powerful states in the Iberian Peninsula were dynastically amalgamated.

Many nineteenth- and twentieth-century historians claimed that this fateful union of the crowns of Aragon and Castile stitched together a territorial unit rent asunder by the eighth-century Arab invasion of the peninsula and also unquestionably marked the birth of Spain as a nation and state. In the past few decades, however—at least since the establishment of democracy in Spain in the 1970s—historians have challenged this interpretation. In their view, the marriage of Ferdinand and Isabel did not forge a nation, and the old kingdoms survived as autonomous entities with deeply entrenched "national" identities that have endured until the present day. Alternatively, a growing number of early modern historians have observed that one of the key if unintended consequences of the marriage between Isabel and Ferdinand was not the creation of a nation-state so much as the emergence of a well-defined Spanish national identity. They find evidence of this process in cultural and juridical concepts and practices that reveal an increasingly widespread sense among early modern Spaniards of belonging to a "Spanish" nation and in a growing popular tendency to self-identify unambiguously as "Spaniards."[1]

Rather than engage in an extended, polemical discussion of this voluminous historiography, this chapter intends to explain political and territorial involutions in sixteenth- and seventeenth-century Spain and to inquire along the way into the meaning for contemporary Spaniards of terms such as *Spain*, *nation*, and *patria*. This study departs from both the old and new interpretations. Its goal is to analyze how sixteenth- and seventeenth-century Iberians viewed and understood Spain and whether they believed that the marriage of Isabel and Ferdinand fundamentally changed the structure of the Spanish state. To answer these questions one must turn to political initiatives; to the cultural and social strategies launched from the writing desks of government ministers, advisers, and intellectuals; and to the debates and sometimes violent conflicts over what kind of Spain should prevail.

As a case study, Spain can usefully be compared to other European polities. J. G. A. Pocock exemplifies the comparative approach. He characterizes the British Islands in the sixteenth and seventeenth centuries as "multinational: a history of nations forming and deforming one another and themselves. . . . No nation's history can be understood without that of its interaction with other histories; that national histories have been shaped in the process of shaping others."[2] Likewise, a history of the various kingdoms that coexisted as parts of a larger entity called the Spanish monarchy must also consider the increasing attempts to create a united kingdom of Spain.

The history of the Iberian Peninsula in the sixteenth and seventeenth centuries must be viewed as a multinational history, the history of *Spains* in the plural rather than the singular. The axis of this chapter is the continuously shifting balance between the regions and the center or, to be more precise, between the various regions and the one that ended up becoming dominant among them: Castile. Perhaps there was one Spanish monarchy, but there was not one Spanish nation. However, this should not be read as a history of a failure but as one of experimentation: it is a history of copious debates, recurrent uncertainty, and struggles to define what Spain was.

Over the course of these two centuries, erudite Spanish writers—or, to use the term of the day, *letrados* ("the lettered elite")—developed an obsessive interest both in Spain and in each one of its constituent kingdoms, their history, their formation, the origins of their peoples and communities.[3] Many sixteenth- and seventeenth-century Spaniards from various professions—historians, poets and theologians, legal experts, medical doctors, diplomats and military commanders, rulers and vassals—contributed to the construction of varied theories and concepts that help explain how Spaniards saw themselves. It is nevertheless important to keep in mind that this obsession with Spain did not result in a consensus about Spain, its history, or its composition. In retrospect, some common threads can be found in these disparate theories and political initiatives—a coherence and certitude that they often lacked: the scholarly and literary production of this period was, before all else, fluid and polyvalent.

Like the book overall, this chapter is a history strictly of those territories that contemporaries thought of as "Spanish"—the kingdoms of the Iberian Peninsula and the American territories under the sovereignty of the Spanish king. The Spanish Habsburgs also held possessions in Italy and in the Low Countries; however, discussions, reflections, and conflicts over Spain and its future composition transpired almost exclusively in the Iberian Peninsula and Spanish America. A few Italian authors contributed to these debates, but they were solitary islets in a Hispanic sea. One of the central arguments of this book is that it is important to distinguish between the history of a dynasty—the Habsburgs—and the history of a territorial community identified from time immemorial as "Spain" (Hispania). The Habsburg kingdoms in the Iberian Peninsula were part of a global monarchy. But these peninsular kingdoms, along with the Indies, configured themselves not only as the principal part of this global monarchy but also as a part that was clearly differentiated from the rest of the Habsburg possessions.

In the struggles for diplomatic precedence during the sixteenth century, English and Spanish writers debated about which of the two monarchies was the more ancient, stable, united, and centralized. For the English the answer was obvious: the English monarchy was more ancient, the only one of the two that could claim to be administratively and territorially united and that had remained free of foreign domination for more than 500 years. The Spanish monarchy, in contrast, was internally divided into autonomous kingdoms. The history of Spain had been one of glaring dynastic discontinuities. Even more significantly, for almost 800 years parts of Spain had been subject to a foreign power, the Arab followers of Muhammad who invaded the Iberian Peninsula in the eighth century.

Spanish writers had a radically different view. First, they argued that there was ample evidence that Spain had been a united monarchy from the Visigothic invasion in the fifth century until the present. Although the Arab conquest of the Iberian Peninsula in the eighth century had led to the establishment of several independent kingdoms, it should not obscure the fact that since the eighth century "there have been 68 (Spanish) kings succeeding each other in legitimate order." The 1492 conquest of Granada, the last remaining Muslim stronghold, had made it possible to reunite the kingdom of Spain, reverting back to the time of the Goths, who had ruled over the "whole" kingdom of Spain as had Ferdinand and Isabel and their successors during the sixteenth century.[4]

Neither interpretation advanced by English and Spanish writers was entirely correct. However, both highlighted the great complexities in the juridical and political evolution of Spain and anxieties felt by many Spaniards and Europeans at the time. Indeed, for many sixteenth- and seventeenth-century Spaniards, it was no secret that the Spanish monarchy was composed of a number of kingdoms with contrasting juridical-political realities and that, rather than designating a single polity, *Spain* was the name given to a geographical region occupied by several communities.

To be sure, the Iberian situation and history was not unique in Europe. The fifteenth century in most other European polities was characterized by instability and conflicts between neighboring kingdoms, some intent on expansion, others equally committed to a vigorous defense of their independence. This was certainly true in the British Isles, where the independent kingdoms of England, Scotland, Wales, and Ireland had been competing for territory. In France, which is often thought of as a relatively unified monarchy since the Middle Ages, the political-territorial reality in the fifteenth century was actually one of divisions, conflicts, and kings able to lay claim only to portions of the territory identified by the old chronicles as the lands of the Franks. Alongside a throng of duchies and counties were independent or quasi-independent territories—Navarre, Brittany, Flanders, Béarn, and Burgundy. In all cases, unification, or territorial agglomeration, occurred militarily or through matrimonial alliances between ruling houses.

Around 1450, some two decades before the marriage of Isabel and Ferdinand, the Iberian Peninsula was divided into a number of competing independent kingdoms. Various territories in the north, northeast, center, south, and east of the Iberian Peninsula—the old kingdoms of Galicia, Leon, Asturias, Cantabria, Old and New Castile, Extremadura, Murcia, the so-called Basque provinces, and all of Andalusia with the exception of Granada—had coalesced earlier to form the crown of Castile. This was the most powerful peninsular crown in terms of size, population, and economic resources. Between 1400 and 1700, the population in the crown of Castile amounted to nearly 80 percent of the total population of the peninsula. Castilian monarchs had belonged to the Trastámara family since the mid-fourteenth century, and Isabel had held the crown since 1474.

The other important crown was Aragon, composed of kingdoms and territories in the eastern part of the Iberian Peninsula. They included Aragon, a kingdom since the early twelfth century; Valencia, constituted as a kingdom in the mid-thirteenth century; the principality of Catalonia, formally founded in the twelfth century (in the seventeenth century it would become one of the most powerful and wealthiest territories of the peninsula); and the Balearic Islands, established as a kingdom in the fourteenth century. The territories of the crown of Aragon had a long history of expansion in the Mediterranean, which accounts for the Catalan presence in Sicily and Naples from the fourteenth century onward.

These two powerful crowns shared the peninsula with smaller independent kingdoms. To the south was the Emirate of Granada, the only remaining Muslim kingdom in the Peninsula after 1250, which would remain independent until 1492. Portugal occupied most of the western Atlantic seaboard. It was a kingdom already constituted by the thirteenth century within its present borders, independent until 1580 and again after 1640. Finally, straddling the northeastern fringes of the peninsula and present-day southwestern France was the kingdom of Navarre, the first Christian realm established following the Arab conquest, in the tenth century, and governed since the fourteenth by a French royal family.

The marriage of Isabel and Ferdinand made it possible to establish peace between the crowns of Castile and Aragon and between them and the kingdom of Portugal. This territorial unification continued in the coming decades. In 1492, the armies of Isabel and Ferdinand conquered Granada, the last remaining Islamic kingdom. In 1512, eight years after Isabel's death, Spanish armies conquered the territories of the kingdom of Navarre in the Iberian Peninsula. Almost seventy years later, in 1581, Philip II became the king of Portugal. Charles I was Ferdinand and Isabel's grandson and the first Habsburg ruler of Spain. His enthronement in 1517 as king of both crowns transformed the monarchy created by Ferdinand and Isabel into a pan-European monarchy. Charles inherited jurisdiction over extensive territories scattered throughout the continent. In addition to the Iberian kingdoms, he ruled over a number of Italian territories—Sardinia, Naples, Sicily, Genoa, and Milan—the Low Countries, and French Lorraine. The situation did not change much after Charles resigned in 1556 and left the Spanish and a majority of his European possessions to his son Philip II.

The immediate political and military consequences of the union of Ferdinand and Isabel irreversibly changed the course of Iberian history. Their contemporaries were apparently convinced that, virtually overnight, a new political entity had been created, the start of a definitive reunification of the peninsular kingdoms. In 1492 the humanist Antonio de Nebrija, author of the first grammar of the Castilian language, declared that, with the dynastic union of Ferdinand and Isabel and their great triumphs, "the limbs and the pieces of Spain, which had been scattered over many parts, were

MAP 1. Spain in 1600: A composite monarchy
The crowns of Castile and Aragon were united in 1474. The kingdom of Granada was conquered in 1492 and annexed to the crown of Castile. The kingdom of Navarre was conquered in 1512 and annexed to the crown of Castile. The crown of Portugal joined the union of the crowns in 1581.

brought together and joined as one body and kingdom."[5] Royal officials recognized the merits of reuniting the various peninsular kingdoms under the authority of one monarch. At the start of their joint reign official circles talked approvingly of Ferdinand and Isabel proclaiming themselves "kings of Spain, now that they were [rulers] of the major part of the peninsula." The monarchs rejected the temptation and held on to their separate titles.[6] As equal partners, both Isabel and Ferdinand were in agreement that they were not going to promote the dissolution of all extant kingdoms in order to create one, and only one, Spanish kingdom.

The monarchy's strategy in the 1500s was to transform the figure of monarch and religion, king and God, into foci of loyalty and union instead of forcing the total dissolution of the various kingdoms. At this time, monarchy, not republic, was widely considered the system that could unite disparate kingdoms through the person of the ruler. Few individuals, and then only in times of acute crisis, seriously questioned the monarchical nature of the state, and in fact monarchy was perceived as the ideal, and God's ordained, political order. God was lord of all creation, without rival or equal; the sun dominated the other planets; and man was supreme among all God's creatures on earth. Descending from the macrocosm, and the natural world, to the microcosm of man, order and hierarchy prevailed. The soul ruled over the body; within the body, the head, as the superior organ, dominated the rest. This image of perfection led many political commentators to believe that subjects of monarchical states lived better than others—their lives, property, and liberties were better protected than those of inhabitants of republics and other types of states.[7] The king was generally represented as a father and, as such, the main focus of obedience, love, and respect for all his Iberian subjects. The sixteenth-century Valencian political writer Tomás Cerdán de Tallada reminded his contemporaries that the king or the monarchy was "the common homeland of all the inhabitants of these kingdoms," the bond that could keep diverse peoples together.[8]

There are clear signs of the "hispanization" of the Habsburg monarchy as a Spanish common identity was being constructed among many of the territories under their sovereignty from the mid-1500s onward. This was even more so following the union with Portugal in 1581. Although the Spanish Habsburgs never completely shed their pan-European identity, their Iberian subjects distinguished between the monarch's strictly "Spanish" possessions and all the rest, increasingly seen by peninsular subjects as "foreign." If Iberia was a territory clearly delimited and separated by the Pyrenees and the seas, then the peninsular kingdoms must also differ from other European Habsburg territories and should therefore be treated as a discrete part of the whole—linked to yet apart from the rest. An early seventeenth-century Portuguese observer, Lourenzo Mendoza, divided the Spanish king's subjects into two groups. One was composed of "Spaniards," born of Spanish parents, whether or not residents of the Iberian Peninsula. All others were "foreigners"—whether natives of the Low Countries or Italians. The latter were subjects of the king by law. But in culture and ethnicity, they were Italians and comprised the "Italian nation"—in contrast to the inhabitants of Iberia who were members of the "Spanish nation." The latter included the Portuguese, Catalans, and Castilians, all of whom were "natural and true Spaniards, and true and loyal vassals of the king."[9]

Loyalty to one and the same ruler, increasingly viewed as Spanish, was just one of the forces that unified all Spaniards in the early modern period. The other was religion—in the Spanish case, Catholicism. As Catholics, Spaniards felt part of a single family. Religion itself bound people and communities with distinct political identities. By law and birth, the inhabitants of the peninsula were Catalans or Castilians or Aragonese or Portuguese, but all were Catholics and as such shared certain sentiments, desires, obligations, and loyalties. Under Catholicism, the Portuguese Bartolomé Filipe wrote, "there were no differences between peoples or nations or kingdoms . . . Those who are Christians, are brothers as Jesus' adopted children. Those who are not, are aliens and foreigners."[10]

The profound religious divisions of sixteenth- and seventeenth-century Europe inspired Spaniards to reflect on the role of religion in the formation and destruction of countries. Abandoning the true faith produced divisions, crises, the fall of rulers and dynasties, and changes in political systems. Nations could come under the sway of tyrants or, even worse, foreigners.[11] The conservation of the true faith, on the contrary, created nations and empires and allowed them to conquer and unite other peoples under the aegis of religion. The best example was Rome, chosen by God to be the seat of the Christian church and therefore allowed to gather together "all the kingdoms hitherto divided, to domesticate customs . . . to become the homeland of the whole world and all its peoples."[12]

This period saw the rise of "sanctified patriotism" in Spain, an amalgam of the defense of religion with the defense of the homeland and king.[13] Histories of Spain written in the sixteenth and seventeenth centuries told of a people that had endured moments of great peril and gradually been revealed as a providential people. They were imbued with passion and principles, profoundly Christian, and relentlessly engaged in the defense of its liberties, land, and people against invaders or enemies—whether Phoenicians, Romans, or "Africans," as the Arabs who had occupied the peninsula since the eighth century were frequently called.[14] To prove this narrative, Spaniards, and especially Spanish elites, became obsessed with collecting relics of martyrs and saints and publishing accounts of Spaniards who defended and died for their faith against Romans, Muslims, European heretics, Asians, or Native Americans. On the peninsula, this search for Spanish saints, martyrs, and holy places may be seen as an attempt to create a Christian genealogy for Spain but also to give Spaniards the sense that they were united by religion.[15]

We see most clearly the gradual crystallization of the view of Spain as a distinct and united country in military and diplomatic affairs. Individuals born in the various Spanish kingdoms filled many of its diplomatic posts, and the same was true of the army. As in other contemporary European countries, armies were often composed of mercenaries, members of various nations who sold their services to the highest bidder and, at times, volunteers who wished to help the cause of their coreligionists in other parts of Europe. Many soldiers in the Spanish armies, and especially those who formed their spine, the *tercios*, were natives of the peninsula. Those born in Spain, in any one of its kingdoms, were privileged when it came to promotions and leadership positions.[16] And in the prescriptive literature on military affairs or in dramatic works celebrating Spanish victories abroad, readers and viewers were presented with an army, or, rather, a nation in arms, prepared to sacrifice everything in defense of the Spanish motherland, religion, and the king.[17] In these texts, Spain was imagined as a united nation surrounded by enemies, ancient and modern, fighting heroically against all.[18]

Like some other Europeans, Spaniards saw the French as their greatest enemies, even though both monarchies were officially Catholic. From the early 1500s until the end of the 1600s, most of Spain's international conflicts were against France. This antipathy between the Spanish and French went beyond geopolitical rivalry. It became something more tangible, a radical clash of characters and personalities, with each nation influenced by its territory, climate, and, especially, fundamentally contrasting, divergent histories. Indeed, we might reasonably analogize relations between Spain and France to those between England and France. In both cases, confrontations between the two nations clearly served to consolidate a common identity. If France tacitly reinforced the English identity as Protestants and Englishmen, then likewise conflicts with France helped to construct an identity as Spaniards and the only true Catholics.[19]

Actually, it was easier for Spaniards to recognize themselves as members of one united Spanish community or nation when they were living abroad or when facing other countries in war. Carlos García wrote in 1617 that the Spanish "have a remarkable trait that sets them apart from other nations, in that when they happen to meet away from their country, they love, honor, and respect one another greatly, even if back there [in Spain] they had been mortal enemies."[20] The seventeenth-century author Benito de Peñalosa y Mondragón, a Benedictine monk born in the Basque Provinces, best summarized these tendencies. In a work published in 1629, Peñalosa insisted that, although Spaniards were in some ways divided—a reference to their separate kingdoms—it was no less true that "whenever required they would rally with promptness to succor and aid their sweet and dear Spanish *patria*, the stem and the root whence they proceed, where their relations and friends are, and their ancient homes and estates, and the bones of their venerable ancestors."[21]

The fictional character Don Quixote, who would come to be considered the quintessence of Spanishness, demonstrates the existence of ideas in other venues that promoted greater unity. Cervantes's famous eponymous work was published at the start of the 1600s—the first part in 1605 and the second in 1615—but many of the ideas and attitudes it expressed predated those years. In one of his numerous extended commentaries, Don Quixote argued that "prudent men and well-ordered republics take up arms and unsheathe their swords and risk their persons, lives, and fortunes for only four reasons: first, in defense of the Catholic faith; second, in self-defense, which is [in agreement with] natural and divine law; third, in defense of their honor, their family, and their fortune; fourth, to serve their king in a just war." But Don Quixote added a new reason to fight: "If we wish to add a fifth, which can be considered the second, it is in defense of their *patria*," a concept that for Don Quixote meant the region or kingdom where one was born, not Spain.[22] For Cervantes and his contemporaries the local *patria* was second only to faith in God, which speaks volumes about Spain's internal politics.

The foundations of this regional identity and autonomy were rooted, in the case of Spain, in the history of resistance against the Muslim occupiers that helped to create diverse and independent Christian kingdoms. But there was also a political culture preeminent in Spain and the rest of Europe that helped to sustain separated kingdoms. The model was the Aristotelian understanding of how humans organized themselves. For protection, they created fairly small communities in which everybody knew each other, with all the naturals collaborating in the defense and ruling of their community. It was possible, certainly after 1500, to think about the creation of bigger communities—monarchies and empires—but they were created in the interest not of the various peoples but of royal families. If this happened, the shared belief was that the ruler should keep intact the regional communities, allow their inhabitants, or naturals, to be in charge of ruling and administrating their own communities, and permit them to decide their own destinies within the political frame of the monarchy created by Isabel and Ferdinand.[23]

Throughout this period, the Spanish monarchy that resulted from the marriage of Isabel and Ferdinand endured as what has been called a composite monarchy, in which a single monarch governed various, not fully united kingdoms. In the Iberian kingdoms, the marriage accords between Isabel and Ferdinand stipulated that the union of the kingdoms would be based on the principle of *aeque principaliter*, "under which the constituent kingdoms continued after their union to be treated as distinct." This model would be followed in all future cases, with the exception of Navarre and Granada, which were treated as conquered kingdoms and incorporated into the crown of Castile.[24]

Although each one of the kingdoms was part of the same body, the Spanish monarchy, this did not "compromise the identity and autonomy" of each kingdom.[25] Each had its own parliament (the crown of Aragon boasted three assemblies—one each for the kingdoms of Aragon and Valencia and one for Catalonia, the latter indisputably home to the most vibrant institutional life in the peninsula).

Without a joint parliament, the various peninsular kingdoms did not share the same laws. Each one also had its own currency and customs duties to control the passage of people and goods from one kingdom to another. Some of the kingdoms, especially Portugal and those comprising the crown of Aragon, had their own governing authorities and institutions. Their officials had to be natives of that particular kingdom, which they administered based on its own laws, using its official language—Portuguese, Castilian, Catalan, or Valencian. The vast majority of the inhabitants of the Iberian Peninsula came into contact with these authorities and not central organs of the monarchy. These were the institutions that most saw as truly representative of the community and "fathers of the commonwealth, to whom belong the right to defend and increase the honor of the *Patria*."[26]

With very few exceptions, the Spanish rulers did not have at their disposal institutions whose authority extended over all the kingdoms. Beginning with Charles I (1517–1554) and particularly during the reign of his son Philip II (1554–1598), monarchs were advised by something akin to a dynastic council, the Council of State, which provided an overview on all the king's possessions but largely confined itself to advising the monarch on policies in relation to other monarchies. A few institutions did have wider jurisdiction that stretched across the borders of various kingdoms. The Council of the Inquisition, for example, was authorized to pronounce judgments on questions of religious orthodoxy in all the monarchial territories precisely as a response to the idea that religion was the main bond between the various kingdoms. But generally the king was assisted in the governance of individual kingdoms by institutions specific to each one—the Councils of Castile, Aragon, Flanders, Italy, and Portugal—and as a rule the members of these councils were natives of the kingdoms they helped administer. These councils did not concern themselves with the health of Spain as a whole; instead, "they look after the welfare of each one [of the kingdoms], they speak for them, and defend and watch over them."[27] The monarchs also had their representatives in each of the kingdoms—viceroys or governors, depending on the importance of the territory—but their powers were limited because nothing could be done without the consent of the representative institutions and sociopolitical elites of various kingdoms.

Further attesting to the kingdoms' autonomy, nearly all had preserved the juridical principle of the right of "nativeness" *(derecho de naturaleza)*.[28] Briefly, the right of nativeness stipulated that only natives of each one of the kingdoms could hold secular and ecclesiastical offices, collect rents, purchase property, establish entailed estates, and inherit or bequeath property. In the parlance of the day, natives were citizens *(ciudadanos)* of a community, native born or naturalized, and as such enjoyed the privilege of participation in the governance of the community and in the discussion of "public affairs."[29] Those who were not natives or had not been naturalized were considered foreigners—and the requirements for becoming officially naturalized were often quite rigorous.

To determine who was legally a "native," kingdoms used a combination of the so-called *ius sanguinis* and *ius solis:* one had to be born in the kingdom *(ius solis)* and descended from parents who were also natives *(ius sanguinis)*. From this perspective, foreigners in Catalonia included Castilians, Navarrese, Basques, Andalusians, and the Portuguese but also those born in other kingdoms of the crown of Aragon. The same was true in Castile, where foreigners were considered to be all those born in Catalonia and the other kingdoms of the crown of Aragon or Portugal but not natives of the other component kingdoms of the crown of Castile.

In the 1500s and 1600s, there was not a Spanish patria, and neither existed a Spanish "nation." That word has its origins in the Latin *natio*, or "birth." Guido Zernatto observed in the 1940s that *natio* was a term that designated a group of people of limited size: "It was larger than a family (a family was never designated as a *natio*) but smaller than a clan *(stirps)* or a people *(gens)*. The Romans never designated themselves as a *natio*. There was a *populus Romanus*," not a Roman *natio*.[30] Given the existence of autonomous kingdoms in Spain, it is therefore unsurprising that the term *nation* in the sixteenth and seventeenth centuries was used primarily in one of two senses: either in reference to communities of foreigners in a particular city, university, or even army or, and more relevant here, to describe a group of people "who belonged together in some way because of similarity of birth" in the same city or land. With very few exceptions, when referring to the peninsula, Iberians used the term *nación* to refer to the Catalans or the Castilians or the Aragonese or the Galicians or the Cantabrians. In Antonio de Nebrija's words, the Spanish people or *gens* included not one but several "nations . . . Castile, Aragon, Navarre, Portugal . . ." each structured as an autonomous kingdom.[31] They almost never used *nación* to refer to Spaniards—more a people, or *gens*, than a nation. The rare examples of its use to connote Spaniards typically came from Castilian authors.

From a juridical-political standpoint it was impossible to be a native of "Spain" or a "Spanish" citizen. Obviously, one could be a subject of the Spanish king, but by law one was Catalan or Castilian, Aragonese or Valencian, Portuguese or Navarrese, and never Spanish. This idea of "naturaleza" was linked to the idea of "patria," unanimously understood as "the land of one's birth," as Sebastián de Covarrubias indicated in 1611, and this meaning persisted throughout the sixteenth and seventeenth centuries.[32] Therefore, Catalonia was the patria for the Catalans, and Castile was the patria for the Castilians. The existence of these particular *patrias* helps explains the surge, especially in the late sixteenth century, of particular patriotisms based on the notion that only natives "are familiar with the laws of their motherland and its ways," the only ones who could be expected to defend and protect it, and as such the only ones fit to govern and worthy of full rights.[33] More importantly, these *patrias* were the primary recipients of their inhabitants' loyalty and service, hierarchically positioned above parents, family, and even monarchs.[34]

The only partial exception to this was in the Americas. The Indies—legally referred to as "the Indies of Castile"—were conquered territories annexed officially to the crown of Castile. Since the sixteenth century, however, all peninsular subjects, whatever their kingdom of origin, had the right to migrate to the Indies, obtain lands and offices. The result of this opening of the New World to all peninsular subjects of the Spanish king, is that they and their Creole descendants were from the beginning called "Spaniards", and therefore it was possible to speak of a de facto, not a legal, Spanish nativeness *(derecho de naturaleza)*. This should not be taken, however, as proof of the increasing strength of a Spanish collective identity among all of the king's subjects. Neither in the peninsula, nor in the Americas was there a simple and clear path to the creation of a Spanish nation. The situation in the Americas was mostly an unintended consequence of special demographic and political circumstances. Despite the opening of the right to migrate to all inhabitants of the peninsular kingdoms, in fact virtually all migrants to the Americas were Castilians (at least until the eighteenth century), as were the absolute majority of the royal officials who served there, and as we shall see, Castilians were the ones who most often spoke about the need to create a community of Spaniards. This process was easier to sustain in the Americas, because unlike in the peninsula, there were no other competing kingdoms or crowns, no communities of non-Castilians that defended the rights and freedoms of their own kingdoms, no people who identified themselves not as Spaniards but as Catalans, or Valencians, or Aragonese.

Histories of the kingdoms written during this period explicitly described the patriotic and national sentiments within each. In their structure and content, these histories followed the conventions for all history books of the time. Invariably, they emphasized the salubrious and fertile natural environment of the place or land and made references to ancient history, including the early kings, the original settlers, and the history of the Visigothic period. Above all, they highlighted the struggle against the Arab occupiers and the gradual construction of an autonomous kingdom until the moment of its incorporation into the Spanish monarchy. Cumulatively, these histories suggest that each one of the kingdoms possessed a measure of self-awareness—a sense of its own history, its particular role in the construction of the monarchy, and its idiosyncratic institutions and characteristics. Even more importantly, all of these works treated their subjects as quasi-independent communities endowed with unique natural, historical, cultural, and, in some of the Basque provinces, demographic characteristics that were distinct from other kingdoms or communities.[35]

Catalonia and Portugal are two paradigmatic cases in the early modern era. Catalonia was undoubtedly the kingdom with the most developed sense of its own political, cultural, and historical identity. More local or regional histories were published in Catalonia than in any other Iberian kingdom, and they waged the most vigorous defense of their native language, traditions, rights, and liberties. They also staged the most important and open discussion of the proper relationship between each one of the kingdoms and the monarchy as a whole. These histories of Catalonia had an obvious aim: to place Catalonia and all its attributes on an equal footing with those of Castile, as the latter had been presented in similarly laudatory works. Perhaps the most important aspect of these histories, and their inevitable focus, was the history of the creation of Catalonia as an independent kingdom in the struggle against the Arabs.

In their writings, Catalan historians and scholars generally wanted to prove that Catalonia was a kingdom in its own right, with privileges and liberties acquired during the wars of reconquest and with its own language that sustained a distinct culture. Catalan historians thus defended a vision of Spain as a politically and culturally diverse monarchy.[36] The idea consistently promoted by Catalan authors during this period and beyond was that Catalans wanted to be part of the union as long as their cultural idiosyncrasies, distinct political identity, language, and liberties were respected. Catalan representatives continuously repeated that the original union signed by Ferdinand and Isabel was between equal partners. This helped sustain a pluralist vision of the monarchy that complemented a similarly pervasive current of opposition to what they viewed as the progressive "Castilianization" of the political and cultural peninsular worlds, or at least the increasing power of Castile within the monarchy.[37]

The Portuguese case was in many respects similar to the Catalan, with some important differences. Here, it was precisely the process of political integration within the Spanish monarchy that drove many Portuguese to look inward and contributed decisively to the growth of their own historical, cultural, linguistic, and particularly imperial identity. To some extent, although these sentiments predated the union with Spain, it was only after 1600 that the Portuguese began to define themselves as a separate and independent people throughout time. Perhaps more important, Portugal also started to define itself more clearly in opposition to Castile, which had been designated, as it would be later, as the "national" enemy *par excellence*. The union did not produce any discernible change in the self-perception of a majority of the elite Portuguese. With a few exceptions, there was no apparent surge of "Spanishness" among them or a sense that they belonged to a wider community.[38] One of the best historians of Portugal, Pedro Cardim, found that "the number of chronicles narrating the separate history of the Portuguese rose significantly" beginning in the 1590s. These works emphasized the "circumstances that distinguished the territory from the rest" of the peninsular kingdoms. Their authors insisted on the separate origins of the Portuguese from other Spaniards and on the existence since antiquity of a "Lusitanian Monarchy," distinct and independent from the Spanish. They referred repeatedly to the existence of a territory, a language, and a history that were not "Spanish" and certainly not Castilian but distinctly Portuguese.[39]

Castile presented arguably the most complex case. There are many indications that the kingdom developed a sense of its own Castilian identity. It became clear that Castile wished to maintain its autonomy and separate identity during the Revolt of the Comuneros (1519–1521), a movement headed by Castilian urban elites against the new monarch, Charles I (1516–1556). Charles I's election as Holy Roman Emperor in 1519 had an immediate and explosive impact in Castile, whose urban elites took it as a sign that their kingdom would lose its pivotal position in the new order in addition to its identity as a kingdom in its own right. Charles had been educated in Flanders, did not speak Castilian, and was surrounded by counselors who were natives of the Low Countries. In short, there was every reason to believe that Charles saw Spain in general, and Castile in particular, as little more than a territory to be drained of its capital and resources in pursuit of imperial ambitions elsewhere. The defeat of the Comuneros in 1521 did not signal the disappearance of Castile as a separate kingdom but, to the contrary—and paradoxically—its gradual transformation into the nerve center and unifying agent of the monarchy. From this point on the vast majority of the highest officials of the monarchy would be Castilians (natives of one of the various territories that formed the crown of Castile), and the centers of royal authority would be established in Castile. This was especially so during the reign of Philip II (1556–1598), who chose a small Castilian town, Madrid, situated near the geographic center of the Iberian Peninsula, as the seat of his court and capital.[40] After overcoming a few relatively minor crises in the later sixteenth century, Castile would become the most loyalist and royalist kingdom in the Spanish monarchy. And, more importantly, the kingdom of Castile gradually came to see itself as synonymous with Spain and, as we will see, tried to transformed its Castilian identity into the genuine Spanish one.

The most problematic region or territory was undoubtedly the Indies—the Americas, or the New World. Virtually from the outset, the Spanish, clearly confident in the legitimacy of their claim to their overseas possessions, declared the Americas a part of the Spanish monarchy and started to variously style themselves as kings of the Indies, much as they had been called kings of Castile or of Aragon. Nevertheless, the Indies were incorporated into the Spanish monarchy under different circumstances and fashion than the peninsular kingdoms.[41] For a start, the Indies were never legally constituted as a kingdom. As part of the crown of Castile, these territories certainly did not have their own parliament, and their cities and communities were not represented in the Castilian Cortes, although in the sixteenth and seventeenth centuries there would be numerous debates on the possibility of including at least the largest colonial cities, Mexico City and Lima. The king even authorized assemblies of the representatives of American cities, although these never came to fruition.[42]

Everybody tended to refer to these territories as the "Kingdoms of the Indies," which conveyed the relative size and importance of America rather than its legal status.[43] This vision of the New World as an important part of the monarchy helps us understand some of the royal policies and initiatives, especially its decision to create the Council of the Indies, founded in 1524. This council was very similar in structure to existing councils that assisted the king in the governance of his kingdoms. Unlike the other territorial councils, however, the members of the Council of Indies were all born in the peninsula, and almost all of them were naturals of the crown of Castile.

Aside from these central institutions, Spanish rulers created others in the Indies themselves, which gave them a feel of autonomous kingdoms. The most important in this respect were the viceroyalties, one with its seat in Mexico City and the other in Lima, which persisted until the 1700s. The two viceroys, named by Spanish kings as their lieutenants in the Indies, held executive power, and their most important function was to defend royal interests and those of

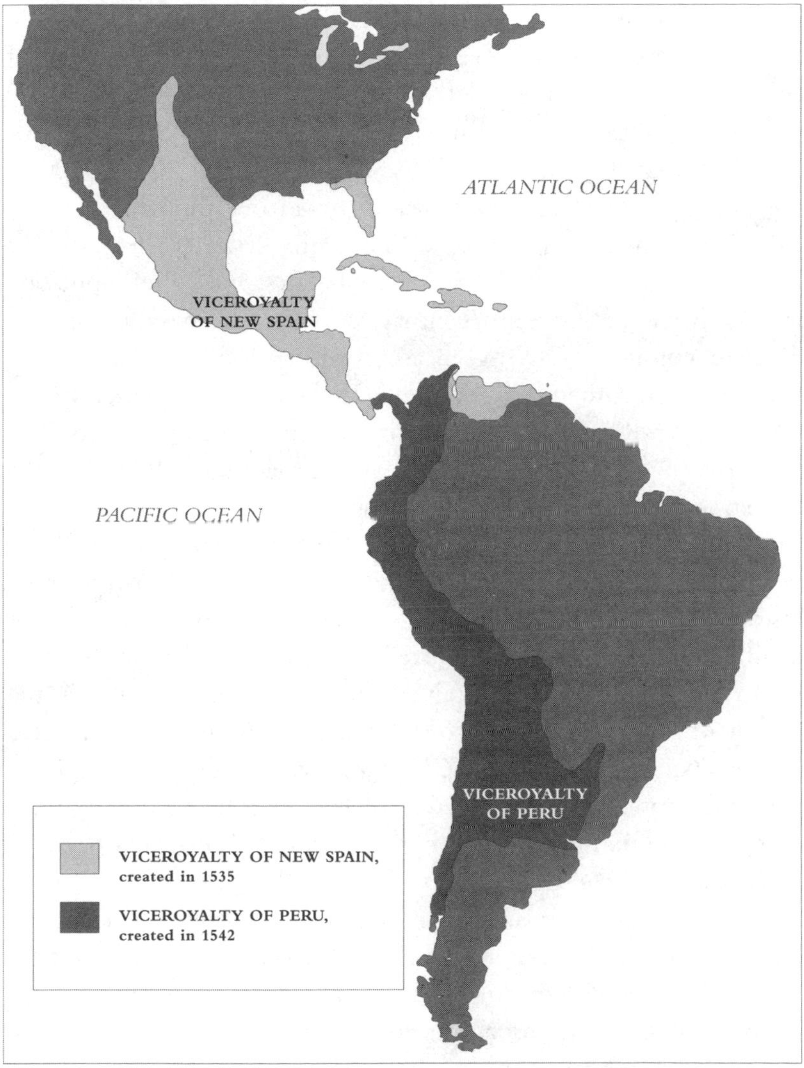

MAP 2. Spanish America in 1700

Government and administration of the Spanish American territories through two viceroyalties.

indigenous peoples. In addition to the viceroyalties, monarchs ordered the creation of a number of Audiencias, high courts of justice to deal with cases and complaints presented by both Spaniards and natives (twelve were created during the first two centuries of Spanish sovereignty) and a series of posts for the administration of economic matters, military defense, and local government.[44]

More significantly, Spanish writers and the monarchy both promoted the transformation of the Americas into a continent that, if not by origin then certainly in reality, was to be thought of as yet another part of a greater Spain. To be sure, histories of the native inhabitants and their traditions, customs, rites, and beliefs appeared frequently in the sixteenth century, but with the passage of time America was increasingly seen as a continent created by and for Spaniards. Until their arrival, Spaniards believed that America had been an entirely incoherent land without a name or history. Its peoples were not only savage but also unaware that they belonged to the human species and lacked any sense or memory of their own history and origins. Spaniards had discovered America or, as Hernán Pérez de Oliva insisted, had "invented" it. They had given it a name and a history and had reintegrated the continent into the great human family. From the perspective of the late seventeenth century, the historian Antonio de Solís maintained that the key personalities in the history of America were not Montezuma or any of the other pre-Hispanic kings but Columbus, Cortés, Pizarro, and the conquistadors and colonists who followed in their wake. These men and their deeds, and the foundation of cities, should fill the opening pages of every history of America. It was truly a new Spain, which was said to be populated by "the Spanish"—not Galicians, Basques, Catalans, or Castilians but *Spaniards*. Few expressed this as succinctly as Fernández de Oviedo who, in dedicating the second part of his natural history of the Indies to Emperor Charles, insisted that his compatriots were entitled to boast of his peninsular origins "for our Indies were discovered by . . . Spaniards, Your Majesty's vassals."[45]

Yet it is in this period, and especially from the end of the sixteenth century, that something resembling an "American" *patria* began to develop, one that extended as far as the hope that the Indies would become a kingdom in their own right, in which the

Creoles—Spaniards born in the Indies—would have access to the highest administrative offices and become the guardians and defenders of their motherland. After all, the conquistadors and their Creole successors "considered themselves to be the founders of a new kingdom" and thus demanded greater political autonomy of the sort enjoyed by the peninsular kingdoms.[46] At no point during this period did Creoles choose to defend their privileges as an "American nation" but rather as Spaniards. It is of both great interest and significance that in the Americas, a conception of nativeness emerged that was clearly defined as Spanish, "a common Spanish nativeness," rather than allied to one of the separate peninsular kingdoms. This Spanish nativeness occurred here precisely because, as Tamar Herzog has shown, the basis of sociopolitical organization in the Americas was neither kingdoms nor viceroyalties but cities. Here, the salient division was between Spaniards and the "true outsiders: the Indians, mestizos, mulattos, and, to a certain degree, non-Spanish Europeans."[47] With time, however, these Creoles would start to view themselves as a different kind of Spaniard as well.

Throughout the sixteenth and seventeenth centuries, many of the king's subjects acknowledged the need to foster the feeling among Spaniards that they were united through the person of their monarch and a shared religion, a common history and enemies, and perhaps a shared future. For some of these subjects, the possibility of creating a united *patria*, one to whom all owed their absolute and superior loyalty and in which there would be no distinctions based on place of birth, was undoubtedly the *sine qua non* to ensure Spain's future as a superpower in the European context and, more important, internal political stability. After all, until the marriage of Isabel and Ferdinand, the major conflicts had been fought between the various Christian kingdoms in the peninsula, and the persistence of conflicting identities and loyalties could lead to disintegration, disunity, and an ominous new round of "civil" wars between distinct kingdoms. In the early seventeenth century, the official chronicler Pedro de Valencia noted that the central problem of the Spanish monarchy was its division into kingdoms, the result of the failure at Ferdinand and Isabel's marriage to unite "all the reigns . . . in one crown, in one commonwealth, under the same laws, without divisions and differences, not even the names of Castilians, Aragonese, Portuguese, Navarrese; all should be called Spaniards, as they are, speaking one language, sharing in the enjoyment of the same common goods and comforts" but also cooperating in the preservation of the monarchy.[48]

These anxieties about political disunion were not unique to Spain. In the early decades of the 1600s, other monarchies were dealing with problems caused by internal territorial divisions. France in the sixteenth and seventeenth centuries was also divided into more than twenty provinces and sovereign territories, such as Navarre-Béarn, but there, at the turn of the seventeenth century, territorial unification was proceeding apace. This was not an outcome of deliberate talk of unification so much as the incidental result of the progressive expansion of the "domaine royale" through marriages with French aristocrats of royal blood or the imposition of royal sovereignty over rebel subjects, as in Béarn in 1620.[49] This consolidation of royal authority coincided with the resurgence of France as the preeminent power in seventeenth-century Europe, a revival that contemporary Spaniards attributed to its internal unification. For many, France became the archetypal modern state, due to "the uniformity of laws, affinity of customs, one language and Climate, (which) at once bind them to each other, and separate them from foreigners."[50]

The situation in the British Isles was much more complicated, if only because it was the lone monarchy that seriously contemplated the union of different kingdoms. The processes resulting in territorial integration over the course of the sixteenth century were evident in the case of Wales, stripped of its juridical independence by Henry VIII in the early sixteenth century, and the Kingdom of Ireland, violently conquered by England roughly by the end of Elizabeth I's reign. This expanded English kingdom had to contend with, and at various times struggle against and invade, a restive and independent Scotland, not unlike the situation on the Iberian Peninsula in the 1400s. Things changed when James VI of Scotland succeeded Elizabeth as James I of England. From the start of his reign in England, James clearly signaled that he wanted to see a union of all the kingdoms over which he ruled, creating a "united kingdom," and to change his official title to King of Great Britain.

In his 1604 speech to Parliament to propose these changes, James underscored the benefits of unification. These kingdoms "joined into great Monarchies; whereby they are become powerful within themselves, to defend themselves from all outward Invasions, and their Head and Governor thereby enabled to redeem them from foreign Assaults, and punish private Transgressions within." He also reminded his audience that each one of these kingdoms—England itself but also Scotland—was in turn the product of a union of smaller territories and that ultimately this new union had been preordained by God: "Hath not God first united these Two Kingdoms both in Language, Religion, and Similitude of Manners? Yea, hath he not made us all in One Island, compassed with One Sea, and of itself by Nature so indivisible, as almost those that were Borderers themselves on the late Borders, cannot distinguish, nor know or discern their own Limits?"[51]

James's hopes and designs were to be disappointed, however, largely due to the opposition and distrust of the English Parliament, Scottish fears of being swallowed up by a monarchy in which England would be the principal part, and a parallel anxiety among the English, fearful of losing their ancient constitution and identity.[52] Whatever the reasons for this failed union, the problem of division into kingdoms confounded British rulers for the remainder of the seventeenth century and was a key element in what traditional historiography often referred to as the English Revolution, now generally known as the age of Wars of the Three Kingdoms (1639–1651). More to the point, however, the arrival of James, a Scot, on the English throne marked, perhaps paradoxically, the beginning of a period in which England became the dominant kingdom, initiating what has been termed the anglicization of Great Britain. Historians continue to debate whether this anglicization ultimately led to the creation of a common British identity or simply the marginalization of others and a forced superimposition of an English identity on the kingdoms of a composite British monarchy.[53]

The British and Spanish cases have a number of similarities and differences. In Spain, unlike Britain, unification and its relative advantages did not become the subject of parliamentary discussion.

However, there were numerous debates and proposals related to the union of kingdoms that closely resembled those on the British Islands. Similarly, along the way, there was a general awareness that altering the politico-juridical structure of the monarchy would be extremely difficult if not impossible. In Pedro de Valencia's words, these "Kingdoms . . . cannot be reduced to one republic and a single set of laws (for who would persuade Portugal and Aragon?)."[54]

A significant number of Spaniards, however, nevertheless believed that it was important to create a union of bodies and minds. They gave many reasons and proposed many methods, yet since the end of the 1500s there had been no lack of clamor in political and intellectual circles for the restoration of a truly united Spain—in language, culture, religion, demography, strategic interests, and political objectives. Tommaso Campanella, the eccentric Calabrian friar and a subject of the Spanish king, advised the latter to adopt measures that would render his monarchy more powerful and even invincible. "Every stable dominion," he wrote in *The Monarchy of Spain* at the beginning of the seventeenth century, "necessarily requires a natural affinity between the subjects, and between the subjects and the prince . . . and a multitude of families brought together under the same sky, laws, customs, uses and aims, a shared tongue and one and the same manner of dress" as well as a single religion. "Where many of these ties are found at once," Campanella continued, "society is stronger and the dominion of authority more readily affirmed."[55]

Some Spaniards also reminded their contemporaries of the already extensive and long history of unions within the Peninsula and that these unions brought enormous benefits to the king's subjects. Baltasar Álamos de Barrientos, one of the most interesting political commentators of the seventeenth century, reminded Philip III (1598–1621) that the kingdoms of Leon and Castile had become independent following the conquest of their territories from the Arabs and, over subsequent centuries of separation, had developed distinct cultures and forms of government. Their union in the thirteenth century, however, had enabled a gradual assimilation between the inhabitants of the two kingdoms, such that all now considered themselves citizens of the same, indivisible kingdom, with a shared culture, language, customs, and laws. More interesting still was the fate of the northern provinces, the region known today as the Basque Country, whose inhabitants, in spite of having their own language and perhaps even different ethnic origins, had been absorbed by the crown of Castile and were considered to be fully integrated within it. The dynastic union of the crowns of Castile, Aragon, and Portugal presented a similar opportunity for the Iberian Peninsula as a whole. "They are all neighbors," Barrientos continued, "and nothing stands between them but a brook, a sierra, an earthen boundary-mark in [the same earth]." With time, proliferating contacts, the promotion of a single body of laws, a common language, intermarriage, and educational curricula, Barrientos argued, "these many provinces . . . would soon become one kingdom of many provinces. But only one [kingdom], and one king of all, and everything."[56]

We do not know whether these feelings were widely shared on the entire peninsula or expressed only by Castilians. All who wrote about these matters, however, tended to underscore that the great problem was to establish the terms on which this union should occur. Was it a question of bringing together all the various kingdoms as equals, or did union imply a fundamental inequality, the imposition of the dominion of one of the parts over the rest? Did it require the creation of a new identity, Spanish, or simply the imposition of a Castilian identity over all others?

Fear of the latter was growing among inhabitants of the non-Castilian kingdoms by the end of the sixteenth century. They feared that in practice, this was not the creation of a common identity or a hispanization of *all* of the peninsular kingdoms but the imposition of a Castilian identity on its neighbors—in effect, the castilianization of Spain, not unlike the contemporary anglicization of Britain. Perhaps the root of the problem, some reflected, was that the original union of Castile and Aragon had not been as equitable as it was claimed from the very beginning—which would promptly become evident as each of the territories conquered after Isabel and Ferdinand's marriage (Navarre, Granada, and the overseas territories) was incorporated into the crown of Castile. The relationship grew even more unequal after 1550, when kings and their advisers began to see Castile as "the head and the heart of the Monarchy," in the words of the early seventeenth-century royal chronicler Pedro de Valencia.[57]

The castilianization of Spain was evident in historical writing and the transformation of the Castilian language into "Spanish." From the early sixteenth century until the early seventeenth, contemporary histories of Castile were not so much, or not only, histories of the kingdom but appeared as proxies for a general history of Spain. Although the titles of these works usually purported to narrate histories of Spain, in fact they focused mainly on Castile and did not reflect Spain in its totality. Many of these histories did concentrate on Spain as a whole until the Arab invasion in the eighth century. But after that cataclysmic watershed, in describing the long process of reconquest and even the events following the marriage of Ferdinand and Isabel, a majority of historians tended to trace the fortunes of the kingdom of Castile as synonymous with the history of Spain. They usually minimized, and on many occasions simply ignored, the history of the formation of the other kingdoms, their contribution to the struggle against the Arabs, and their own political constitutions, legends, and myths. The title of the most important official historian was not "royal chronicler of Spain" but "royal chronicler of Castile."[58] It is also suggestive that once a royal library was created under Philip IV, history books were organized under the following sections: "Universal chronicles of the world," "Histories of Spain and Castile," and "Histories of the kingdoms of Aragon, Valencia, Catalonia, Sardinia, Navarre and Biscay."[59]

Everybody associates Spain with one language, Spanish.[60] Spanish as such, however, did not exist in the sixteenth and seventeenth centuries. Or, rather, it was a language in the process of being created, precisely in connection with the castilianization of Spanish identity. The linguistic map of the Iberian Peninsula at the end of the fifteenth century—the time of dynastic union—was highly diverse. In addition to Castilian, there were several other official languages—Catalan, Valencian, Portuguese, Galician, and Basque.[61] As the humanist Juan de Valdés explained, in Spain there were "as many different tongues as there are lords and masters."[62]

Many began insisting that to ensure the success of the new monarchy, facilitate its expansion, and unite the hearts of all its subjects, it was necessary to impose a single language. The biblical narrative of the Tower of Babel demonstrated that languages were divisive forces in empires and nations, while a shared language promoted peace and friendship among different communities.[63] Few made such a compelling case for the creation of a new language or, more precisely, the transformation of Castilian into the language of the new monarchy, as did the Andalusian Antonio de Nebrija. A historian, humanist, and Latin scholar, Nebrija was ahead of his time when he published the *Grammar of the Castilian Language* (1492). In a preface in dedication to Isabel, he offered a number of noteworthy reflections on the subject. First he affirmed that language and power walked hand in hand, as the history of Rome and Latin had clearly shown. Castilian was destined to follow a similar path, having sprung from and developed parallel to the expansion of the crown of Castile. Nebrija was convinced that Castilian would spread even further after the union of the crowns of Castile and Aragon.

The second claim appeared to be of the highest importance in 1492, when the conquest of Granada coincided with the beginnings of Spanish expansion in the Mediterranean and north Africa and the transformation of Castile into the dominant kingdom within the new monarchy: "Once your Highness has subdued many barbarian peoples and nations of itinerant tongues . . . they will have to receive the laws that victors impose on the vanquished, along with our tongue. It is quite plain that not only the enemies of our faith will have need of knowing our Castilian language, but also the Vizcayans, Navarrese, the French, Italians, and all those with some business to transact, or the need to converse in Spain, thus requiring our language."[64] A century later, Pedro de Valencia also viewed the existence of a common language—once again, Castilian—as key to the creation of a true union of all Spaniards.[65]

Neither Isabel and Ferdinand nor their immediate successors, however, tried to impose Castilian as the only official language, and linguistic diversity was generally accepted along with juridical and institutional plurality. It was considered to be an inevitable part, and reflection, of plurality. The official attitude was summed up perfectly by Philip IV in a work best described as an intellectual autobiography. He recalled that a part of his education was learning languages. Some of them were foreign—such as French and German—and useful for understanding enemies and allies alike. But especially useful were languages spoken by his vassals: "For I could never countenance obliging them to learn another in order to understand me," and so, he says, he learned Italian and "the languages of Spain, [which is to say] my own [Castilian], Aragonese, Catalan and Portuguese."[66]

Even without an officially prescribed linguistic uniformity, Castilian began to expand throughout the peninsula from the late fifteenth century onward, replacing completely or in part all of its rival languages. In some regions it transformed vernaculars into purely oral languages, used only in isolated rural areas or in the private sphere of family life. Or it gradually condemned them to secondary status. Surveying the linguistic map of the peninsula around the year 1600, Bernardo de Aldrete claimed that, although in some areas "two tongues together" were still in use, with the gradual introduction of Castilian in many places, "the other [was] being forgotten, and if in those kingdoms no language but Castilian were to be allowed in the courts and tribunals, it would end up being introduced all the more rapidly, and even in the absence of this [measure] it is growing every day."[67]

Experts have tended to see this process as a case of diglossia, when "two or more languages or varieties of language are used by the same speakers in different 'speech domains,' addressing different people or introducing different topics."[68] Castilian was therefore a language spoken by all, recognized at least unofficially as the language of the monarchy and one that would quickly begin to gain acceptance, in Spain and beyond, as the new, Spanish language. It was associated with all the communities on the peninsula. Nobody yet spoke in terms of Spanish as the language of a new Spanish "nation," but many were beginning to notice the confluence and confusion of both terms—Castilian and Spanish. For example, Sebastián de Covarrubias's encyclopedic dictionary, one of the most popular works ever published in Spain, had the revealing title *Treasury of the Castilian or Spanish Language* (1611).

The confluence of Castilian and Spanish characterized Galicia, Valencia, the Basque provinces, Aragon, and Navarre.[69] The situation was more complicated in Catalonia and Portugal, which were the most consolidated kingdoms culturally and politically. As in other territories, Castilian was frequently used in both kingdoms in printed works, theatre, and sermons and as the language of erudite debate and political commentary.[70] In contrast to other kingdoms, however, Catalan continued to play an important and influential role in the principality, above all in times of conflict, and especially in the 1630s and after, when the defense of the Catalan language and its use were linked even more closely with the defense of Catalonia and its identity, institutions, rights, and history.[71] The situation was similar in Portugal, where Castilian became the language of intellectual life, especially after 1580, but Portuguese remained the language of internal administration, the official language of the kingdom, and the dominant tongue in the cultural sphere.[72]

Another sign that the monarchy was being castilianized, despite avowals to the contrary, was that the vast majority of public offices dependent on royal patronage were ending up in the hands of Castilians. The common opinion against this was clear: if all were subjects of the king, if all owed the same loyalty to the monarchy, and if their political involvement was crucial to maintaining the commonwealth, then it was the king's obligation to make it possible for natives of every one of the Iberian kingdoms to participate in their own government at all levels. Campanella defined this as the "union of bodies." He felt that this union had been attained by the French and Ottomans, which explained the greater political unity of these monarchies. Among other things, a union of bodies entailed support for marital unions between individuals from different geographic regions, equal education for elites, linguistic uniformity, and access to government posts for all, regardless of place of origin.[73] Despite these views, the sheer numbers seem to indicate that the king was steadily transforming himself into a manifestly "Castilian" ruler, since the vast majority of royal officials were indeed Castilians, in both the Iberian Peninsula and the overseas territories under his sovereignty. Even the Count Duke of Olivares, prime minister under Philip IV and one of the foremost promoters of this union of bodies, acknowledged that Spanish kings had shown a flawed tendency to favor individuals from the crown of Castile (Castile, Navarre, the Basque provinces, Galicia, and Andalusia), while Catalans, Aragonese, Valencians, and the Portuguese were essentially marginalized.[74]

In the late sixteenth century a growing number of non-Castilian subjects became convinced that, whether planned or not, Castile was not only increasing its political and territorial preponderance but also transforming itself into the model for a new monarchy and a new nation, both defined as Spanish. Toward the end of the sixteenth century, non-Castilian kingdoms were restive about what they perceived not as a process of genuine "Spanish" unification but as the elimination of the autonomy and rights of kingdoms, with the help of Castile, to augment the king's power. This growing resistance first became apparent in the "Alteraciones of Aragon," a 1591 revolt that erupted in several Aragonese cities and particularly in the capital of Zaragoza to defend the laws and liberties of the kingdom that were seen to be under threat from institutions and troops in the service of the Spanish king Philip II.[75] Equally evident was the continued refusal of the non-Castilian kingdoms to contribute to the upkeep of the monarchy and to accept a share of the swelling costs of the defense of the Catholic faith in Europe and the government of Spain. By the late 1500s, the king and his closest ministers were frustrated about the constitutional frame of the monarchy, in which kingdoms were only nominally under the king's authority.[76]

The Count-Duke of Olivares, prime minister of Philip IV (1621-1665), best articulated this monarchical frustration with the non-Castilian kingdoms, using truly paradigmatic concepts: "Damned be the nations, and damned are the *hombres nacionales*," a reference to non-Castilian subjects who were fundamentally loyal to their own nations or commonwealths.[77] In response to these sentiments, Olivares offered proposals for unification of the kingdoms. He did not intend to transform the Spanish composite monarchy into one that resembled the French, with more integrated regions and royal authority. Instead, he and his allies most desired to unite the various kingdoms behind their king, thus transforming Philip IV into a great and powerful monarch. The problem, or fatal flaw, in his strategy was that the model for his new monarchy could only be Castile. His frequently cited words addressed to Philip IV still best summarize his objectives and strategy: "Your Majesty should regard the question of making himself King of Spain as the most important affair of his Monarchy. I mean to say, Sir, that your majesty should not be content to be King of Portugal, of Aragon, of Valencia, count of Barcelona, but to work and consider with mature and secret counsel to the end of bringing these kingdoms which comprise Spain into conformity with the laws and style of government of Castile . . . which, if we could find the proper way to encompass it, would make your majesty the most powerful prince in the world."[78]

Once again it should be emphasized that Olivares did not espouse anything that might be construed as a Castilianist ideology or even a Hispanic one. His only ideology was a defense of the king and the monarchy. He did not seek the creation of a Spanish nation so much as an extension of royal dominions and authority. He wanted to furnish his king with political structures that would enable him to maintain Spain's power in the world. Olivares was clearly prepared to negotiate with kingdoms over the implementation of this new policy, and moreover he was convinced that these negotiations would be fraught. He surmised that ultimately, the use of force would be required, and the king's armies would have to occupy the most recalcitrant kingdoms.[79] Under the circumstances, the king and his first minister initially tried to impose a rather less ambitious scheme, unveiled by Olivares in 1625 and baptized as the Union of Arms. It was a "program for mutual defense" of sorts, to which all kingdoms—peninsular, European, and American—would be obliged to contribute. Each kingdom would be committed "to providing and maintaining a fixed number of paid men, who would constitute a common military reserve for the monarchy as a whole." Each individual kingdom's quota of men was also enumerated (Castile and the Indies, 44,000; Catalonia, 16,000; Aragón, 10,000; Valencia, 6,000; and so on).[80]

The king, his ministers, and many Castilians did not conceive of the Union of Arms as a disguised project of territorial unification, whether juridical or cultural. Nor did they perceive it as a diminution of the rights and liberties of the various kingdoms. However, the growth of regional patriotism in the previous decades spurred many non-Castilians to interpret the Union of Arms and similar initiatives as direct attacks on the their kingdoms' autonomy.

Undeniably, many of the kingdoms that comprised the Spanish monarchy remained loyal throughout the seventeenth century, even during its most conflict-ridden decades.[81] Nonetheless, the tension between kingdoms' rights and attempts to create a united monarchy was very pronounced in Portugal and Catalonia. Even by 1600, the Catalans, or at least their elites, began to see the Spanish monarch as an absentee ruler (Spanish kings generally did not visit kingdoms other than Castile and lived mostly in Madrid or the Escorial) as well as a Castilian one, surrounded by Castilian advisors and steadfastly intent on castilianizing the monarchy overall. As Pedro de Valencia wrote in 1605, these subjects felt "lorded over by Spaniards or Castilians," and consequently they "are not [the king's] subjects from the heart," a situation that might potentially incite rebellion and conflict.[82] And that is what happened in 1640 in Catalonia. A movement that had begun as a peasant uprising against the royal troops stationed in the kingdom, in anticipation of a French invasion, was quickly transformed into a struggle to defend the kingdom and its liberties against a king accused of acting tyrannically.[83]

Not all Catalans dreamt of independence, and even in the years following the 1640 revolt, many Catalans publicly displayed their loyalty to Philip IV and Spain in terms that a modern historian has described as "royalist Spanish patriotism."[84] Plainly, however, the crisis of 1640 crystallized opposition to the crown's centralizing policies and encouraged the idea that the most important civil conflict was kingdom against kingdom. Perhaps more importantly, even if heretofore scarcely conceivable, it became possible to imagine a separate Catalan community, distinct from the other communities in the peninsula. This imagined community enjoyed unique political rights and freedoms and was also increasingly conscious of being a *nation* of Catalan people, not just a kingdom.

Portugal was in many respects similar. Following its union with the Spanish monarchy in 1580 due to an internal dynastic crisis, Portugal never felt completely at ease within the larger polity. Many Portuguese natives were in the service of the Spanish kings, but even after the union of Portugal, none of the initiatives designed to foster a sense of concord and common purpose succeeded. These included efforts to integrate the elites and Portugal's overseas empires and to make the Portuguese feel part of the Hispanic family. During the Iberian union, between 1580 and 1640, many Portuguese thought of their position as akin to captivity. They felt themselves increasingly oppressed—the term *enslaved* was sometimes used—by the

"Castilian government and nation," which had acted similarly toward the "Aragonese, Galician and other kingdoms of Spain."[85] Following the death in battle of king Sebastian in North Africa, many believed that Portugal had been taken hostage and would remain so until the return of "the hidden one," either Sebastian himself or one of his Portuguese descendants. From 1640 onward, the stakes in the conflict between Portugal and the Spanish king were readily apparent. If Philip IV were to reconquer Portugal, this would mean "the suppression of the Portuguese kingdom's laws and freedoms and its being reduced to the status of a 'province.'"[86] The fact that the Portuguese revolt of 1640 was referred to as a "restoration" (of an independent Portuguese monarchy and empire) indicates the Portuguese rejection of integration within the Spanish monarchy.[87] Portugal became a de facto independent monarchy in 1640 and officially in 1668 when the Portuguese and Spanish rulers signed a peace treaty.

The situation in Catalonia was different. The most consequential outcome of the revolt in 1640 was the separation of a significant part of the kingdom and its immediate integration into the French monarchy. Although militarily defeated and reconquered by Spain in 1652, after several years as a French province, Catalonia was reincorporated into the monarchy without formally losing any of its privileges, rights, or institutions. In practice, however, the crown persecuted all those implicated in the revolt, circumscribed the powers of the kingdom's institutions, and tried to prevent the dissemination of separatist ideology.[88] Equally important, from 1640 on, internal divisions began to appear between Catalans who wanted to protect the rights and separate identity of the kingdom and those who opposed any suggestion of independence and were prepared to publicly demonstrate their loyalty to Philip IV and Spain. The Catalans, or at least their elites, drew another lesson from this experience: the French monarchy was far more centralizing and homogenizing than the Spanish. This memory undoubtedly influenced their decision, and that of other Aragonese kingdoms, to support the Habsburg over the French candidate in the War of the Spanish Succession.[89]

The revolt of the Catalans, the separation of Portugal, and the growing number of voices proclaiming the distinctiveness of the Basques in relation to other peninsular kingdoms provoked a great deal of reflection on the past and future of the monarchy. The main thread of this discussion was whether all inhabitants of the Iberian Peninsula belonged to a nation called Spain and whether this nation was led by a unified state. The majority of commentators leaned toward the model of the state established by the Catholic monarchs. The arguments might be political, such as those articulated by the Aragonese Baltasar Gracián. In his book, written as an homage to Ferdinand and published in the same year as the Catalan and Portuguese revolts, Gracián drew attention to what he perceived to be the betrayal of the principles that presumably underlay the union of the crowns in the late 1400s. These principles were originally designed, he wrote, to avoid "making one nation—the Castilian—the head, and the other—the Aragonese—the feet."[90]

Others went even further and considered the existence of separate kingdoms not as a problem that required a solution but as a natural, almost divinely ordained state. For example, in the seventeenth century, some started to believe that the differences between Catalans and Castilians were complex. They were political but also cultural, historical, demographic, and natural, with each region influenced by differences in climate and food. Catalans, Castilians, Valencians, and so on, were essentially distinct and different from each other. This was the opinion of bishop Juan de Palafox y Mendoza (1600–1659), a native of Navarre and one of Olivares' supporters. Surveying the Spanish situation in the 1640s, Palafox criticized not the rebel territories as much as those intent on destroying or reducing the legal-political diversity of Spain, including his own patron, Olivares. In his view, Spain was, and should remain, a plural community—a sentiment he undoubtedly shared with many of his contemporaries, especially non-Castilians. Olivares' policies were "born of good intentions, to make the government uniform and thus exclude diversity which is often the mother of discord." His goals, however, were impossible to achieve because "God, as the Creator capable of making all lands after the same fashion, [nevertheless] created them different . . . , it is furthermore necessary that laws should, like dress, follow the contours of the body, and be different in each Kingdom and Nation."[91]

Palafox's words should not be read as evidence that the possibility of a Spanish nation was forever precluded. What they reveal instead, as do the Catalan and Portuguese revolts, is that the peninsular subjects of the Spanish kings had yet to confront the question of creating a modern nation-state. Neither the available concepts nor the prevailing political attitudes permitted such a debate at this time. It is true that in these processes and events one may observe much of the drama that would be enacted by Spaniards in later centuries. Yet, despite what has been frequently argued of late, events in the sixteenth and seventeenth centuries neither predetermined modern conflicts nor did they foreclose the various paths that Spanish history may have taken. The events of these turbulent decades preordained neither the failure nor the success of Spanish nationalism in the future.

2

Spaniards

THE CHRONICLER of the New World, Gonzalo Fernández de Oviedo, referring to the diversity of populations and kingdoms in the Iberian Peninsula in his *General and Natural History of the Indies* (1535), was frustrated by the lack of unity among Spaniards: "Who could reconcile the Biscayan with the Catalan, hailing from such different provinces and tongues? How might the Andalusian find common cause with the Valencian, the [native of] Perpignan with the Cordoban, the Aragonese with the Guipuzcoan, the Galician with the Castilian (suspecting the former of being Portuguese), and the Asturian or *montañes* with the Navarrese, etc.? And so, in this fashion, not all the vassals of the royal crown of Spain have kindred customs nor [do they speak] similar languages."[1] The pro-Spanish Piedmontese Giovanni Botero implied as much in his famous *Relazioni Universali* (1591–1598). He explained that the Spanish monarch exercised sovereignty over a multitude of lands and peoples, and in the Iberian Peninsula alone, his subjects included "nations who differed greatly *(naciones diferentísimas)* in laws, inclinations, humors, and customs, namely the Castilians, Aragonese, Vizcayans, Portuguese" in addition to Italians, Germans, and inhabitants of the New World.[2]

It is slightly paradoxical, then, that early modern authors who wrote on the Spanish from a demographic perspective imagined a single family or lineage, with common ancestors and similar physical and mental characteristics. For sixteenth- and seventeenth-century Spaniards, there was not a Spanish *natio,* although there was a *populus Hispanorum.* To put things more bluntly, given the existence of legally autonomous kingdoms, it was utterly impossible to speak of a Spanish nation and Spanish patria; however, everything indicates that Spaniards truly believed that there was a Spanish people. This idea inspired Covarrubias to close his essay on Spain with a laconic phrase, pregnant with meaning: "Spaniard, the native of Spain."[3]

Yet the natural conditions of this Spanish land, the origin of its inhabitants, their physical and mental characteristics, and their similarities or differences to other Europeans remained ambiguous and murky. Was there in fact a Spanish people? Was it possible to speak of a Spanish *gens* (lineage) or, in other words, a demographic strand to which all the inhabitants of the peninsula belonged? Were Catalonians, Basques, Galicians, or Andalusians different from some perspectives—culturally, for example—but essentially similar in others? Were the differences between them purely politico-cultural or grounded in variant natures? Was there something essential about being Spanish, or was there an essential quality to being Catalan, Castilian, or Galician?

The self-perceptions of sixteenth- and seventeenth-century Spaniards reveal an emerging sense of demographic "Spanishness": their recognition that all inhabitants of the Iberian Peninsula were in some sense "Hispanic," biologically, and shared common origins, customs, physical, and mental characteristics. This is not a study of "race" or "racialism," however. To be sure, Spaniards like other Europeans of the time used the term *race (raza)*, but its connotations differed from those it would begin to acquire in the eighteenth century. In the trilingual dictionary of Girolamo Vittorio, published in 1609, "raça" in Castilian was associated with the (French and Italian) words "race, lignee, generation, prole, stirpe, lenaggio"—words pertaining to lineage, family, and ancestry.[4] In general usage, race was an indication of "quality," with reference to animals and especially cloths but also social groups—as in, for instance, belonging to a noble lineage or "race" or to a good or bad lineage ("buena y mala raza"). In his dictionary Covarrubias defined race as "the breed of thoroughbred horses, which are branded with iron for identification. Race in cloth, the yarn that stands out from the rest in the weft or woof," but he also mentions that when referring to humans, the use of the term *raza* implied the negative characteristic of "belonging to a vile lineage, like the Moorish and Jewish raza."[5] The concept of ethnicity in recent decades has tended to take the place of racial terminology. But until the nineteenth century, as Covarrubias once again explained, it referred to "the same as gentile or pagan." This definition was congruent with contemporary English and French usage.

In the documents of the period, there is no mention of a black, red, or yellow race. Even references to a "white race," which were beginning to appear in other European countries, especially in the English world in the late 1600s, are not found in the Spanish world until the 1700s. One could be designated as belonging to the Spanish people, and in this sense it was possible to speak of a Spanish lineage or a French or an English one, and so on. In the case of Jews and Arabs, or Moors, in Spain, they would come to speak of a Jewish and Moorish lineage, raza, or nation. The debate over whether there were clearly different human lineages was the most important one in the early modern period and certainly in early modern Spain. Was there a Spanish lineage, meaning that all Spaniards had a common origin and therefore had shared and permanent physical and mental characteristics, whatever region they inhabited, and could this lineage be used to establish a hierarchical "racial" division within the society?

Sixteenth- and seventeenth-century Spaniards had to confront the presence in Spain, throughout its history, of many foreign and native peoples. Spaniards of this period constantly wondered about whether they were descendants of the original Iberian natives or, to the contrary, the product of recurrent biological mixing between different peoples in the past and present. Europeans certainly had a tendency to view Spaniards as a mixed people, the product of successive commingling between Iberian natives and numerous ethnic groups that had settled in the peninsula over the centuries—Celts, Carthaginians, Phoenicians, Romans, Goths, Arabs, and Jews.[6] In these Europeans' eyes, it seemed clear that the demographic history of the Iberian Peninsula made it virtually impossible to determine whether a native Spanish lineage had emerged at some point and had managed to endure to the present. Various peoples in the course of its history had invaded the peninsula, and furthermore it was hardly a secret that on the peninsula Spaniards, Muslims, and Jews had mixed. In the Americas, Spanish had mixed with Indians and Africans from the very beginning of the conquest. If all this was true, then what was the effect on the people of Spain and their characteristics? Were they members of a pure Spanish lineage, or were they all the result of the mixing of many lineages?

Spaniards' answers to foreign and internal views on the origins and purity of Spaniards was to construct idealized images of themselves and their demographic history while developing theories and laws to determine who was and was not a real Spaniard. In so doing, they developed theories to support their superiority over others, which are the focus of some of the following chapters. What seems relevant here is that concepts and theories developed by Spaniards to describe themselves, as well as other peoples in their orbit, would form the bedrock of Spanish racialist discourses developed in later centuries. These theories were also important because not all Spaniards agreed on what type of nation they wanted to construct. Some wished to base the construction of a Spanish nation privileging those who could demonstrate they were "pure" Spaniards. But others viewed the Spanish people or race as resulting from a combination of geographical conditions and biological mixings throughout history and that it was possible instead to build a Spanish nation based on shared civic and political values.

Like other Europeans, early modern Spaniards were steeped in the biblical account of human origins and the evolution of different nations or lineages. According to Genesis, God had created the world and everything in it, including human beings. In this interpretation, all humans had the same origin and were descended from common primogenitors, Adam and Eve (monogenesis). For Christians of every denomination this was a fundamental tenet of dogma, not merely another theory about the origins of humanity. At least in the Spanish world, until the nineteenth century if not later, to suggest that there had been various creations of man, that not all humans shared common ancestry, and that they might therefore be distinguished by radically contrasting characteristics (polygenesis) was impossible to accept on theological grounds and also would have been grounds for persecution by the church and secular authorities. Official doctrine, or what might be called theological reasoning, led to the belief that all were inherently equal, all possessed a rational soul, all had the capacity for distinguishing between good and evil, and all possessed the faculties required to improve their lot.

The axiom that there was a certain essential similarity and equality between all humans makes clear why it was so hard to account for what was demonstrably obvious and fiercely debated by the mid-sixteenth century: the reality of human diversity. In 1556 the Spanish translation of one of the most popular books of Renaissance Europe, Joannes Boemus's *Mores, leges, et ritus omnium gentium (The Manners, Laws, and Customs of All Peoples)* was published in Antwerp. The book was originally published in 1520, in Latin, but the Spanish version prepared by Francisco de Támara was based on an Italian edition published in Venice. The Castilian edition included an additional section on the Indies *(The Book of the Customs of All the Peoples of the World and the Indies)* to make it more attractive to the Spanish reading public.[7] As the title of Boemus's work indicated, what had impressed him and his contemporaries was the sheer multitude of heterogeneous peoples, with different customs and in various phases of cultural development. Támara referred to this in the prologue to his translation: "Such diversity of peoples so different from one another, not only in their color and features, dress, and adornments, but in their customs and ways of life, rites, ceremonies, laws, statutes, ordinances, sects and forms of administration and government."[8] López de Gómara, one of the most important historians of Spanish expansion, shared this opinion. He described the Americas as the most suitable laboratory for the studious to pry into the secrets and vagaries of nature as well as the infinite variety "of the complexions of man."[9]

What interested them far more than describing these differences and human diversity was understanding their reasons. Spaniards and other contemporary Europeans had various theories at their disposal that purported to explain human diversity. The first was climate theory, or the belief that natural conditions in each region—climate, soil, the influence of the stars, and so on—affected the physical and mental constitution of the humans who settled in each territory. This theory had been popular in ancient Greece and Rome and continued to exert a powerful influence in medieval and early modern Europe. It is relatively straightforward and relies on the belief that all bodies are made up of form and matter. In the case of human bodies, their basic constitution was the product of a combination of the four humors (blood, black and yellow bile, and phlegm), which were linked to the four natural elements (air, fire, earth, and water) and the four seasons (spring, summer, autumn, and winter). Different combinations of these elements helped to determine character and the mental and physical qualities of each individual in a particular territory. Changes in the natural conditions, resulting from planetary movements and the climate, effected changes in inhabitants' constitution. Conversely, if an individual or an entire community were to relocate to a different climatic region, their physical and mental characteristics would change over time.

The basic division of the world into climate regions was already very clear in medieval times, thanks to the work of the Arab scholar Ibn Khaldun (1332–1406). He divided the earth into seven regions. Occupying the center was the so-called fourth region, where humans "are more temperate in their bodies, color, character qualities, and general conditions. They are found to be extremely moderate in their dwellings, clothing, foodstuffs, and crafts." The countries in this region were Syria and Iraq (the most temperate and perfect) but also the Maghreb, India, China, Al-Andalus (Spain), and the European countries north of Spain. All of the other regions were either too hot or too cold and as such produced humans who were weaker, less moderate, and less civilized. Inhabitants of the most extreme regions of the earth, Khaldun explained, possessed characteristics that were "similar to those of the dumb animals, and they become correspondingly remote from humanity."[10]

In the early modern era the Frenchman Jean Bodin (1530–1596) was one of the foremost exponents of this theory, which he discussed in a number of his works. Spaniards knew him primarily through one of his most important texts, the *Six Books of the Commonwealth*, originally published in 1576 and translated into Castilian in 1592.[11] Like his predecessors and contemporaries, Bodin was baffled by the great diversity of peoples and sought explanation in the natural conditions and the location of each one of the inhabited regions. Essentially, he posited the existence of a temperate zone (France, parts of Spain, parts of Italy, and Macedonia), torrid zones (the south of Spain, Sicily, North Africa, some of the sub-Saharan regions, and parts of America), and a frigid zone (England, Scotland, northern Germany, and Denmark, among others). Bodin argued that knowledge of the location of each community was sufficient to predict their characteristics with almost unerring accuracy, a viewed shared by Spanish authors.[12]

According to Bodin, the peoples of the north would be blond and green-eyed, Africans black and black-haired. The residents of Seville, however, though situated in the torrid zone, were white, while other peoples in this zone, such as inhabitants of the Cape of Good Hope, would be black, and the people of the River Plate chestnut-colored. More important were the characteristics of those who lived in the temperate zone, where inhabitants of different countries, the French and the Spanish, for example, might also be dissimilar in certain respects. By nature, the Spaniard, although more southerly, would be more contemplative, moderate, and ingenious than the Frenchman. The latter was naturally more choleric than contemplative, which rendered him more active and diligent. With these characteristics in mind, Bodin believed that some biological mixings were positive. The descendants of a mix between the French and Spaniards would be more perfect than their French and Spanish predecessors, for example, and would resemble in some respects the Italians, who inhabited the most temperate region of all.

Based on these theories, Spaniards also tried to understand the natural conditions of the peninsula and how these helped to make "the Spanish people distinct from other nations."[13] This perceived link between Spanish territory and Spanish people is evident in many of the *laudes Hispaniae* (praises of Spain), which first appeared in the Middle Ages, and in numerous examples of the genre in the sixteenth and seventeenth centuries. These usually began by situating Spain geographically and clearly demarcating its physical limits. Spain was always located in the temperate zone yet as a peninsula perfectly isolated and delimited from its neighbors. Its only land frontier, with

France, was formed by the Pyrenees mountain range, which made it virtually inaccessible. Quevedo summarized the effects of felicitous natural conditions on the Spaniards: "Neither cold makes us phlegmatic and lazy like the Germans, nor excessive heat renders us useless for work like the blacks and the Indians; rather, one quality tempered by the other produces well-adjusted customs."[14]

For some Spaniards, however, climate theory—although certainly useful—could produce incorrect answers to the questions posed in the Introduction. Climate theory helped to sustain the idea that in the Iberian Peninsula there was not a single nation but several: Catalans, Castilians, Galician, Portuguese, or Andalusians. It was believed that each kingdom had different climate conditions, and this could explain the diversity of peoples, cultures, languages, manners, and dress among the Spaniards. This internal diversity was among the most frequent literary subjects of the era, from political treatises to plays, novels, and poems. Debates over who was better, more intelligent, harder workers, or better Christians in the various kingdoms were staples of literary production and scholarly works during the early modern period. And based on the theories discussed earlier, these differences were viewed as permanent and unalterable by rulers because a combination of climate and history had helped to developed different peoples and nations among the Spaniards. This was one more obstacle in any attempt to create a unified Spanish nation.[15]

Climate theory also supported the claim that all those born in Iberia, regardless of their ancestors, were genuine Spaniards. Some would espouse this theory to defend the integration in the Spanish society of the descendants of the Jewish and Arab populations that had first settled in the peninsula in medieval times. Climate theory also complicated matters for those who insisted that the Spanish character and features endured under all climates and anywhere on the globe. This would become clear in the debates about the characteristics of Spaniards born in the Americas.

For those attempting to demonstrate that there was indeed a Spanish people with shared and permanent characteristics, many authors complemented climate theory with others, especially the theory on the divine origins of human lineages. The crux of these theories was clear: God had created humans, and He ultimately conditioned the character, history, and specific role of each people. More importantly, God had determined the region that each lineage or family would settle.

Spaniards, like many Europeans, believed the theory that all individuals carried in their blood the unique characteristics of their lineage and that through blood these characteristics—physical, moral, and mental—were transmitted to their descendants. The basic principle was relatively straightforward: "The children inherit from their parents the inclinations and customs because they inherit their blood and temperament" during gestation. A man's blood is transformed into semen, which mixed with the woman's blood in the womb to produce a fetus, nourished in the womb with the mother's blood and later transformed into milk to feed the newborn.[16] The consanguinity of parents and offspring meant they were perfectly aligned with one another physically, mentally, and spiritually, as Pedro de Mexía assured readers in an essay included in his extraordinarily popular *Silva de varia lección (A Miscellany of Various Lessons)*.[17]

Early modern Spaniards, like their European contemporaries, could also point to concrete examples and social practices that seemed to confirm this interpretation. Since the medieval period, theories had been circulating that linked nobility and blood, and in fact *race* was a term originally associated with the nobility, whose blood, after all, granted them natural—social and political—preeminence.[18] This superior quality of the nobility passed from fathers to sons and distinguished those of noble blood from those who had obtained their titles thanks to royal favor or patronage, education, or wealth. Just as important, this quality imbued those who possessed it with an immutable character, akin to those of their ancestors, regardless of their upbringing.[19] No one framed this belief in such stark pedagogical terms as the Archpriest Alfonso Martínez de Toledo in *Corvacho* (1438), when he tells the story of the son of a peasant and the son of a noble, both educated in the countryside by the peasant boy's parents. Although raised under the same conditions, their natures were radically different:

> You will find the laborer's son still pleased with things of the village, such as plowing . . . while the son of a knight is not cured save by galloping around on a horse, and bearing arms . . . This is the work of nature. You will witness this every day wherever you may live: that the good man, of good race, returns to whence he came from, and the wretched man of vile race and lineage . . . will always revert to the vileness from which he descends.[20]

Spaniards extended these theories to entire lineages or peoples and not just the nobility. For them, each people or lineage acquired its own distinct personality, from the first moment each lineage was created: "For men's natures have not altered with different names and times; rather the same effects today correspond to those seen in ancient times."[21]

Among the knotty problems they tried to untangle were the origins and age of this community, the various lineages or *gens* that had populated Spain, and the precise moment in which these peoples had been transformed into *hispani*, or Spaniards. They also debated these peoples' physical and mental characteristics and the extent to which they were the result of a particular confluence of natural and genetic conditions. In trying to unravel these questions, many indeed discovered a Spanish people and the existence of an intrinsic nature that characterized the ancient Spaniards no less than those of the 1500s and 1600s.

Sixteenth- and seventeenth-century Spanish authors turned to history to account for the singular characteristics of peninsular inhabitants. The Spaniards' origins were part of a narrative that had its beginning in prehistory, close to the biblical origins of mankind. Starting with the work of the first-century historian Josephus and certainly since Isidore of Seville in the sixth century, the story of the origin of the Spaniards, or Iberians, had acquired a familiar and enduring form: they were the direct descendants of Tubal, the son of Japheth and Noah's grandson.[22] This was also the origin of the Basque or Cantabrian people, whom many in sixteenth- and seventeenth-century Spain believed to have been the original occupants of Iberia. The settlement of Spain thus belonged to the "second age" of the world, according to a chronology by the Spanish humanist Pedro Mexía. He was Charles V's chronicler and the author of some of the most popular works of sixteenth-century Europe, including the *History of the Roman Emperors* and especially *Miscellany*, or *Silva de varia lección*.[23]

As in other European countries, this early settlement was important as a badge of antiquity and therefore a basis for preeminence over neighbors and rivals. At the very least, Spaniards could say that their civilization was older than those of Greece and Rome and the land no less cultured from the dawn of its history. As Pedro de Medina put it, echoing Strabo, "Spain has possessed letters and sciences since it was settled by Tubal . . . And so one finds that among all the nations under the sun, there is not one that has produced as many writers as Spain."[24] No one but God had determined the Spaniards' history, having decreed that Tubal's progeny would inhabit the Iberian Peninsula, a region chosen for its extraordinary natural conditions and propitious for the development of a chosen people. Because of these divine origins, the character of Spain and its people was predetermined and constant through time.[25]

Spaniards believed that as with all communities past and present, a nation is formed over time, through natural growth, but also the influx of new peoples seeking shelter in its bosom. In the history of Iberia, Spaniards also discovered that almost from the very beginning several diverse peoples settled in the region, which provoked a serious question: had Spaniards been mixing with other nations from the beginning of their existence, and, if this was the case, how had this affected the characteristics of the primordial Spaniards? Certainly the biological mixing that was assumed to have taken place in Spain was unfailingly invoked by foreigners to question the European character of the Spanish lineage.

Sixteenth- and seventeenth-century Iberians certainly understood the consequences of so many nations coexisting in their midst, including the possibility that this coexistence would change, perhaps even corrupt, Spaniards' original character. They had the concepts to understand the consequences of miscegenation: "to mix lineages . . . when one is confounded with another, not of the same quality; and a thing is said to be without mixture when it is pure."[26]

Sixteenth-century official historian, Ambrosio de Morales, also cited the Romans' negative opinion of those who mixed with Iberians. He claimed that "it was an ancient Roman custom to enslave these *mestizos*, whom they called Hybrids"—and there is every reason to believe that this opinion was shared by many of his contemporaries.[27]

Spaniards were certainly aware that the Iberian Peninsula had attracted many peoples throughout its history. Dozens of groups of invaders or immigrants are mentioned in contemporary chronicles. *The First Five Books of the General Chronicle of Spain* by Florián Ocampo, royal chronicler under Charles I, asserts that from its very beginning in Spain the "people had always lived divided in so many nations, differing in customs, names, and condition."[28] The way to address these questions and problems was simply to claim that all the nations that settled in Iberia—Celts, for example, and also peoples coming from the Mediterranean region—were all descendants of Tubal and all together had constituted the original population of the peninsula, the ancient Spaniards, or *hispani*.

The vast majority of authors were inclined to brush aside the importance of later mixtures of their Spanish ancestors with many peoples who settled in or invaded the peninsula in the so-called historical period. There are numerous references to biological mixtures between Spaniards and Carthaginians, Spaniards and Phoenicians, Spaniards and Romans, but these are generally seen as superficial and incidental and without notable effect on the most prominent characteristics of the original lineage. For many, these mixtures had happened because of the "corruption" or "degeneration" of particular groups of Spaniards, above all in the southern parts of the peninsula, rather than a desire for intermarriage.

Spaniards struggled more to make sense of the Visigoths' arrival and its impact on the primordial Iberian population. Some authors gave the impression that Visigoths and Spaniards eventually formed a single *gens* by mixing throughout the peninsula. Others saw it in radically different, more "nationalist" terms, if the concept might be applied here. No one doubted that some mixing had taken place, but the majority of writers insisted that it had been very selective and affected only small groups of Spaniards—primarily a section of the native nobility. In a sense, they were describing the creation of a sociopolitical elite through mixtures, which had left the majority of the Spanish population untouched and its purity preserved. By this reasoning, the Spaniards were still in a pristine, pre-Visigoth state, especially in the northern regions of the country (Cantabria, Galicia, the Basque provinces, Catalonia, and Castile).[29]

The perceived role of the Visigoths shifted in accounts of the Arab conquest of Spain. The dominant view was that most Visigoths had perished during the invasion, while many others had simply fled the peninsula and sought refuge in France. Only a few remained, including the mythical king Don Pelayo, the instigator of the resistance against the Arabs, and some of his followers, although even they were considered to be mixed descendants of Visigoths and Spaniards. Beyond this political elite, most contemporary historians agreed that the majority of those who had defended the Iberian Peninsula from the Arabs had been the descendants of the original native Spaniards.[30] The Basque Benedictine monk Benito de Peñalosa summarized this opinion when he insisted on the untainted purity of ancient and modern Spaniards in a passage that is worth quoting in full: "All the settlers of the north—the ancient Vascones, some of the noble Catalonians, Galicians and Aragonese as well as other *Montañeses* of the North and West of Spain did not mix with the Goths, or the African Moors, or other nations that at one time possessed these kingdoms." From these "ancient Spaniards" descended all "the Spaniards who inhabit Spain and the Provinces and Kingdoms of this Monarchy." They are the chosen people, to whom God had "promised the Empire of the World." They did not descend from the "Phoenicians, Greeks, Carthaginians or Romans, who settled these kingdoms before the birth of Christ. . . . That stock of men, made up of different nations, has perished, and so little remains of it that we may truthfully affirm that Spain has been newly populated . . . Spaniards conserve the pure blood of the first settlers of this Kingdom, grandsons and sons of Tubal."[31]

But what about Jews and Moors? Certainly Europeans believed that Spaniards, at least an important part of them, had been mixing with Jews and Moors for centuries. A German traveler who spent years living in the Iberian Peninsula was very explicit about it and claimed that because Spain had been "lorded over" for more than

700 years by the Arabs and due to the presence of a significant Jewish community, a great majority of Spanish nobles—the nation's elite—had a mix of Christian, Arab, and Jewish blood in their veins.[32]

Spaniards in the sixteenth and seventeenth centuries, however, wanted to ensure that Europeans knew they did not have any natural tendency to mix with other peoples, even less so with members of the Jewish and Muslim nations that had inhabited the peninsula for centuries. Starting in the sixteenth century, one of the main arguments in favor of Spanish as a separate and distinct lineage was to demonstrate that through the centuries, Spanish authorities and individual Spaniards had viewed sexual relations with Jews and Muslims as illegal and criminal and that their intention was to conserve the "purity" of the Spanish *gens*. Spaniards who argued thus could cite numerous medieval laws that prohibited Christian Spaniards from cohabitating with, marrying, and having sexual intercourse with Muslims and Jews. Many recognized that perhaps some Spaniards did disobey these laws, but, again, they believed them to be a corrupted minority.[33]

The political implications of these ideas became abundantly clear in the mid-1500s, when purity of blood became the criterion not for being a Spaniard but for membership in the Spanish elite—the ones who would hold public offices, help the king to administer the kingdoms, access high education, and obtain the corresponding honors of nobility. By virtue of being born in the Iberian Peninsula *(ius solis)*, a Christian, the offspring of Spaniards, and a subject of the king, an individual was entitled to certain political and civic rights. In order to realize these rights, however, it was necessary also to belong to the right lineage—the Spanish lineage—and be able to claim the right of pure blood *(ius sanguinis)*.

Uniquely, these were not simply theoretical lucubrations in Spain. They had practical implications for the definition of the so-called purity of blood statutes, introduced in the early sixteenth century.[34] These statutes were a tool of social discrimination: aspirants to the honors and offices in question had to be hidalgos. This meant that their predecessors had not engaged in artisanal trades or, in the parlance of the time, the mechanical occupations, but their particular targets in the peninsula were the descendants of Jews and Muslims, considered to be religious enemies as well as descendants of foreign lineages. One of the questionnaires to determine whether a candidate was suited to receive a habit of Military Order, an honor designed exclusively for genuine Spaniards, specified that he had to derive from the "native caste of the kingdom" (the Spanish lineage) and had to be rejected if he belonged to one of the "foreign castes."[35] Significantly, these origins, pure or otherwise, were to be traced as far back in history as possible or as far as surviving documents and the memory of the place would allow.[36]

The most famous although not the first of these statutes was proposed by Juan Martínez Silíceo for the Cathedral of Toledo in 1549. In the course of the sixteenth and seventeenth centuries, many institutions adopted statutes of purity of blood, with the approval of the king and pope. Among them were many ecclesiastical corporations, including the cathedrals of Toledo, Badajoz, Seville, Cordoba, Granada, Jaén, Murcia, Burgo de Osma, Leon, Sigüenza, Avila, Santiago, and Oviedo; several religious orders, such as the Hieronymites, Dominicans, and Jesuits, three of the most important and influential; notable secular institutions, including the three Military Orders—Calatrava, Alcántara, and Santiago; educational institutions, such as the Colegios Mayores of Santa Cruz of Valladolid, San Clemente of Bologna, San Antonio of Sigüenza, San Ildefonso, and Alcalá; and various provinces and cities, such as Guipúzcoa, Vizcaya, and Villa de Espinosa de los Monteros as well as the royal institution charged with policing religious orthodoxy, the Inquisition. Many institutions adopted these statutes, but just as crucially, the desire to conserve the purity of the Spanish blood was shared by a majority of Spaniards. It was [embraced] by Catalans, Castilians, Basque, Galicians, and Andalucians and also Spaniards born in the Americas.

The requirements for membership in the Toledan ecclesiastical administration were straightforward. The first was that the aspirant should be an "Old Christian" without the admixture of Jewish or Muslim blood in any generation, as well as an *hijodalgo*, meaning that his ancestors had been of noble blood, even if they had held no title. If successful, candidates were obliged to swear to uphold the statute. All members of the cathedral chapter at the time of the statute's adoption who had Jewish or Muslim ancestors were to be stripped of their offices.[37] Leaving no room for doubt that his objective went beyond regulating membership in his cathedral chapter, Silíceo requested that converted Jews and Muslims also be prohibited from practicing as medical doctors and from marrying Old Christians, lest the blood of the latter be "debased and corrupted."

But what were the characteristics of this pure Spanish lineage? The combination of the origins of the Spanish people and the natural conditions in Spain resulted in the formation of a people with distinctive and unique features. In general, all contemporary authors tell us of a frugal people, imbued with a profound sense of justice, prepared to sacrifice their lives in defense of their homeland, family, and freedom. The Spaniards' character reveals them to be very strong in body and spirit and very much inclined toward arms.[38] Courageous in war yet merciful in peace, the Spaniard was said to love political stability and was intensely loyal to authorities who ruled without passion or violence. To recall, the Spaniard was also extolled as profoundly Catholic and prepared to lose everything in defense of his faith.

These narratives contain only scattered references to some of the physical characteristics of the common Spaniard. For instance, many authors mentioned that Spaniards were white, although not to the same extent as northern Europeans. A Catalan Jesuit at the end of the sixteenth century assured his readers that the native of Catalonia "is not so very white as the Fleming, the German and the Englishman, but a middling white, like the main part of the Spanish people."[39] Another seventeenth-century author, Carlos García, noted that Spaniards were "a shade brown," while the French were "white" with blond hair, in contrast to Spaniards who were dark haired.[40] The German author of the "Description of the Qualities of the Spaniards" ("Relación de las calidades de los españoles"), although he never refers to the color of the Spanish men, nevertheless insisted that the women—with the exception of those from the Basque provinces, who were "white and beautiful"—were "not very beautiful because they were tawny *(morenas)* and short."[41] To recall, however, these references to skin color did not carry the same significance in the sixteenth and seventeenth centuries as they would later or when they would be used to describe non-European peoples.

Although comparatively little was said regarding Spaniards' physical characteristics, rather more was said about their good customs and the great intellectual production of the "Spanish," clearly in response to foreigners' accusations to the contrary. From the early 1500s until the end of the 1600s, numerous texts appeared that testified to the sheer size and originality of Spanish intellectual production in all spheres. It was not until the end of the seventeenth century, however, that these disparate ideas and tendencies coalesced in a work with clear objectives and sense of purpose, which appeared in two volumes, prepared by the Sevillian scholar Nicolás Antonio (1617–1684)—first the *New Hispanic Library* (1672) followed by the *Ancient Hispanic Library* (1696).[42] The former was intended as an intellectual portrait of Spain and the Spanish, broadly and flexibly defined. Thus, Spain was represented not only by a few of the most famous literary figures but as the sum of many parts, of hundreds of "Spaniards" who had written or published something, though it may have been only a minor work, in many cases completely forgotten in its day.

These two volumes covered an extensive span of time, more than any previously published work. In his *Ancient Hispanic Library*, Antonio included all Spanish authors up to 1499, although his main purpose was to write an intellectual history of Spain in the Roman, Visigothic, and medieval periods. The *New Hispanic Library* was organized as an encyclopedia of writers who had published between 1500 and the 1670s. Entries included their names, titles of works, and, in case of those considered sufficiently important, a description of their works, occasionally a short biography to highlight the most noteworthy events in their lives, and their intellectual contribution.

The *Hispanic Library* was explicitly conceived as a collective homage to Spain and to the intellectual production of Spaniards throughout their history rather than a celebration of individuals. To be sure, its vision of Spain was broad and inclusive, demonstrated by the author's decision to include Portugal and the overseas possessions, although at the time of publication Portugal was once more an independent monarchy. *Spain (Hispania)* is a term that permeates the *New Hispanic Library*, a voluminous tome of more than 2,000 pages that cites hundreds of authors and works. Antonio's was a Spain composed of regions, provinces, and cities yet all of them part of the same nation, Spain—"the most enlightened region of the world." His work was addressed to all those born in Spain or in the territories under Spanish sovereignty. This Spain would be organized according to "regions" or "provinces," not nations or kingdoms, as the list of the "patrias" included in the *New Library* demonstrated: "Americans, which is to say, from the Hispano-Castilian Indies; Alavans; Aragonese; Asturians; *Baetians*, or Andalusians; Canarians; Cantabrians, that is to say, from the provinces of Guipúzcoa and Biscay; Castilians; Catalonians; Extremadurans; Galicians; Portuguese; Portuguese from the Asiatic Indies; Portuguese from the African Colonies, Brazil and the Islands; Murcians; Navarrese; and Valencians." All diverse in languages and places of birth but with a common characteristic: all sons and daughters of Spain.

The most consequential aspect of the theories analyzed thus far was the idea that Spaniards' traits and characteristics were the product of a combination of climatic influences and certain inherent attributes transmitted through their blood, which rendered them permanent and natural. Although the place of one's birth (the village, town, or region) was not completely irrelevant, a majority believed that all Spaniards carried the seeds of this common identity in their blood.

But one problem only became more urgent with the passage of time: were the descendants of Spaniards who settled in non-European regions, and especially the Americas, genuine Spaniards? Did they still possess the same characteristics of their peninsular compatriots? Were they affected by the different climate in the Americas, or was the Spanish gene so resilient that their defining characteristics remained unchanged? Equally important was the question of what kind of Spaniards they were: Catalans if descended from Catalan parents, for example, or was identity no longer determined by the place of birth, or *patria*, of their ancestors? Was it possible to think of a uniform Spanish lineage or nation, even when its components were dispersed all over the world? Were they connected to each other politically and institutionally, or were they more powerfully connected through their blood?

The crown never encouraged emigration to the Indies, if only because it was anxious about the progressive depopulation of Spain itself, but it tried to regulate the passage of those who wished to leave. Judging by the traits of those officially permitted to migrate, the royal authorities wished to settle the Americas with the sort of stereotypical Spaniard described above. Spaniards who applied for permission to emigrate to the Indies, a process tightly controlled by the monarchy through the Casa de Contratación, came from every one of the peninsular kingdoms. Although initially Isabel tried to reserve this right of passage for subjects of the crown of Castile, from the earliest days of exploration and conquest the Aragonese and Castilians exercised the right to emigrate, trade, or settle in the Indies. This right was extended to the Portuguese from 1580 until the independence of Portugal in 1640. It is equally true, however, that during the sixteenth century the vast majority of emigrants originated from the territories of the crown of Castile and above all Andalusia—nearly 40 percent of the total—although by the seventeenth century there was greater diversity in their provenance.[43]

Prospective migrants to the Indies had to fulfill other requirements, too, once again designed to reproduce exactly the Spanish lineage in the Americas. From the very beginning candidates were required to present sworn testimonies of witnesses from their native region. They needed to provide a detailed description of their physical characteristics—hair and skin color, stature, distinguishing marks such as scars—presumably in order to prevent successful applicants from giving or selling their permits to others.[44] The descendants of Jews, Muslims, and gypsies were prohibited from emigrating under any circumstances, as were individuals condemned for heresy and other crimes, a prohibition that extended in this case to their children and grandchildren. Nonetheless there is evidence that converted Jews and Muslims, especially the former, did make the crossing, as demonstrated by waves of persecution directed against them by the Inquisition in the Indies.[45]

Generally, the monarchy encouraged the emigration of families or of married couples, yet even so the majority of outbound passengers were single men, although many married men also made the journey (in order to emigrate, they had to present proof of their spouses' consent). In the 1500s, women never constituted more than 25 to 30 percent of the total number of emigrants, and the proportion of women leaving for the colonies further dwindled in the next century. The emigration process was filled with obstacles. The majority of emigrants processed by the Casa de Contratación shared the physical characteristics of their compatriots, invariably described as *brown (morenos)*, and although it appears that some passengers began to identify themselves simply as *white* starting in the late 1500s, we have already seen how both terms were used to describe Spaniards throughout this period.[46]

It is hard to know exactly how many Spaniards migrated to the Indies, but most scholars seem to agree on a figure of roughly 250,000 in the sixteenth century and around 100,000 in the seventeenth. The demographic crisis on the peninsula itself explains the steep seventeenth-century decline. Around the end of the sixteenth and the opening years of the seventeenth century, the Iberian Peninsula lost more than a million inhabitants to a series of plague epidemics that arrived from other parts of Europe, swept over the entire region, and resulted in endless petitions from local and royal authorities to stem the tide of emigration.

Many emigrants came from the lower classes, tantalized by the path to social mobility that the promised riches of the Indies seemed to offer. Evidence indicates that at least 50 percent of emigrants were from the laboring or menial classes, while some scholars have suggested that, at least in the sixteenth century, only 5 percent of emigrants would have been members of the gentry (hidalgos).[47] Although there were hidalgos and some nobles among Spanish colonizers, the general impression of the authorities was that the vast majority of conquistadors and colonists were of the humbler sort or drawn from the middling classes. The chronicler of the Indies, López de Velasco, maintained in the 1570s that a large number of Spaniards wanted to cross the ocean for the opportunity to improve their lives in America but that those who actually realized this ambition were "men who are enemies of work, of excitable spirit, and greedy for quick riches rather than maintaining themselves on the land."[48]

The Spanish population of the Americas was and remained relatively small in comparison with the rest, certainly when compared to the native population, which in spite of the demographic collapse precipitated by the conquest had recovered to no less than 6 to 8 million by the late sixteenth century. López de Velasco, in a 1574 report sent to the Council of the Indies in his capacity as cosmographer and chronicler, mentions some 200 Spanish towns, made up of around "thirty-two thousand Spanish households."[49] Extrapolating from these figures, the Spanish population in the Americas has been estimated between 118,000 and 140,000 around this time, or 1.25 percent of the total population. Based on later censuses and other data, the Spanish population was 450,000 in 1620 and around 655,000 in 1650 and rose to 750,000 by 1670. Given that emigration from the Iberian Peninsula had fallen dramatically in the seventeenth century, scholars conclude that the difference was the natural growth of the Spanish population in America, with rates of fertility apparently much higher than in contemporary Europe. In spite of their rapid growth, Spaniards still comprised only 8 percent of the total population in the mid-seventeenth century.[50]

Their relatively low numbers notwithstanding, Spaniards dominated the economy and natural resources of the continent, profited from Indian labor, owned slaves, controlled trade networks, governed the most important cities, and monopolized the membership of ecclesiastical and political institutions. Compared with other demographic groups, they enjoyed immense privileges, and regardless of their status or wealth they were all exempt from taxation, which distinguished the social elite in early modern Europe. Solórzano Pereira saw an analogy for this phenomenon in the history of Spain: "When the Goths conquered Spain, even the Plebeians among them were esteemed and valued by our Spaniards, so now among the Indians the vilest Spaniards are thought more worthy of honor and esteem than the most noble Indians."[51] A significant proportion of the Spaniards who emigrated to the Indies stayed poor, many were illiterate, and the Spaniards who settled on the frontier or peripheral regions, especially, were closer to indigenous populations in their cultural habits and mores than to the model of

Spanishness that was meant to be replicated in the New World. All considered themselves, however, as members of the colonial elite.[52]

Almost from the beginning of Spanish settlement, these individuals and families saw themselves as natives of the new land, and many of them chose to stay permanently. As a rule these were not individuals who planned to get rich in the Americas before returning to Spain. To be sure some, referred to as "indianos" in Spain, did choose this path—a few of them finding wealth and riches, many others only ruin. They were the exception, however, given that the overwhelming majority established themselves in the Americas, never to return, and the same was true of their descendants. For many of them life in the New World was good, or better than on the peninsula, and rich with previously unavailable opportunities. By the 1600s, especially after 1620, many saw the Americas as a land of promise and relative stability—and by then it had become common wisdom in Spain that the Indies were the most stable and politically loyal part of the monarchy.[53]

The Spaniards in America, at least the elite, lived a thoroughly hispanized existence. Those who sought higher education found it largely in universities and colleges founded in the American continent's most important cities. They read the same books as their peninsular counterparts, followed similar career paths, built their houses and cities in the Spanish style, and maintained strong links with their relatives in Spain.[54] At least officially these individuals in the Americas were categorized as Spaniards, not as Castilians or Galicians or Basques. Migrants tended to congregate in areas where relatives or neighbors had settled, and certain provinces were given names evocative of their home regions in the peninsula—New Granada, New Navarre, New Galicia, New Andalusia, New Castile—but this was more symbolic than legal and political. For all intents and purposes, and whatever their peninsular regional origins, all were classified under the same rubric of "Spanish."[55] A common language, Castilian, united them. As the great expert in the evolution of Castilian, Bernardo Aldrete, explained, the Castilian "spoken today by Spaniards in the colonies and their settlements in Africa, in Oran, in Melilla and Peñón de Vélez de Gomera, it is the same Castilian as in Mexico and all the cities of New Spain and Peru. The language of Spain and of these remote parts, and of the islands of the Philippines, is one. Those who travel from these kingdoms to those [overseas] do not find a different language, but only some words and dialects, just as they would in Cordoba, Toledo, Seville, Granada, and in every city and village, but the language is one."[56]

American Spaniards' self-perception was important, but it was not necessarily how their peninsular brethren perceived them. Rarely has a colonial population been the object of such attention as that of the sixteenth- and seventeenth-century Americas. From at least the end of the sixteenth century, by which time conquest had more or less fully given way to pacification and settlement of the Americas, the Spaniards living in the colonies were generally considered by the Spanish authorities as "natives," not by origin, like the Indians, but "by birth, as Spaniards whose home and residence [was there]."[57] Of even greater interest to many was the manner in which Spaniards adapted to life in the Indies and whether they were "going American" and thus losing some of the physical traits—their complexion, for instance—characteristic of Spaniards.

In this context, climate theory really rose to prominence for some Spanish observers. Spaniards born in America or who had lived in the colonies for some time and were thus labeled as *Creoles*—a term initially used to refer to the children of African slaves born in the Indies—were analyzed through the prism of theories that accounted for human characteristics based on the influence of climate, soil, and the natural environment. From an early stage many were convinced that the Americas lacked some of the natural attributes of the Iberian Peninsula and that its animals and humans were inferior.[58] These impressions were especially prominent in contemporary assessments of the Amerindians but were also applied to Creoles. Cosmographer López de Velasco wrote of the Creoles in a 1570s report: "The Spaniards who journey to those parts and remain there a long time, with the mutations of the skies and the temperament of the regions do not exhibit any change in the color and quality of their persons; but those born there . . . are known to be different in color and size, because they are all large and their color deepens declining to the disposition of the land; . . . even if the Spaniards had not mixed with the natives, they become like them, and they change not only in their bodily qualities, but the condition of their soul tends to follow the body, and as the latter changes so the former alters as well."

There was also a possibility, in light of the social origins of the vast majority of emigrants to the Americas, that their personal qualities and intelligence were deficient to begin with, thus exacerbating the effects of climate, "so many restless and lost spirits having gone to those provinces, the ordinary intercourse and conversation being depraved, affecting more readily those in whom the force of virtue is lessened; and so in those parts there are, and have always been, many calumnies and great discord between men."[59] This vision was shared by peninsular writers like Cristóbal Suárez de Figueroa, who in his famous work *The Passenger* denigrated Creoles as deficient in virtue and being very "different, nay the opposite" of peninsular Spaniards.

Yet in spite of the persistence of such ideas, the consensus opinion, and certainly the official stance, was that the Spaniards in America, the emigrants as well as the native-born, were no different from other Spaniards and had the same rights as their compatriots in the peninsula. Perhaps they were vulnerable to the influence of the American climate, which modified some manners and characteristics, but from the late sixteenth century onward, Creoles themselves also responded to these views, claiming that the climate in America had no degenerative effect on the Spaniard but, to the contrary, improved him.[60] But, for the most part, there were no significant differences between Spaniards, wherever they were found.

Once more, the dominant theory maintained that a Spaniard by lineage never ceased to be Spanish regardless of birthplace. One of the most interesting commentaries on this theory came from Benito Peñalosa y Mondragón, discussed earlier, who observed that in spite of the diverse geographic and climatic conditions in the Iberian Peninsula itself, the Spaniard was the same whether he lived in Aragon or Castile, America or Africa. The reason he gave is that Spain contained a variety of climates that made Spaniards easily adaptable to all the existent climates in the world. Everywhere they go or are born, Spaniards "find themselves as if at home, so that their perseverance and robust strength should see them carry through the heroic and admirable enterprises that are being witnessed and celebrated by all."[61]

The official view on the Creoles' Spanishness came from the pen of the great Spanish jurist, Juan de Solórzano y Pereira, born in the peninsula but who served as a judge in the Americas for several years, and the author of *Política Indiana* (1647), without doubt the most influential contemporary text on the American reality. No one should doubt, he wrote, that the Creoles "are true Spaniards, and should enjoy the same rights, honors, and privileges [than those born in Spain] . . . These children of Spaniards are and remain natives of Spain, even if they are found in parts so remote from her . . . , and [they] retain and conserve the quality derived from [the paternal source]." It was time to let go of the notion, Solórzano continued, that climate and the natural environment seriously affected these Spaniards' nature. To be sure, certain changes were manifest in the men living in different regions, but none of these were strong enough to eradicate the "blood of Spain" and its nature. The Creoles could not be discriminated against because the American environment had supposedly rendered them distinct and inferior. It was a far too common practice in Solórzano's time "to rashly attribute vices to [different] Nations for the hatred and envy of those who write [thus]," but this could not apply to Creoles because they, along with other Spaniards, "together form one body and kingdom, and are vassals of the same king."[62]

Debates among Spaniards over the nature and characteristics of Creoles did not end with the seventeenth century, notwithstanding the spirited and convincing arguments presented on their behalf by Solórzano, among others. In fact, the critiques only became more virulently hostile in the eighteenth century. These critiques created an ideological context in which Creoles were transformed into yet another group of colonial subjects along with the Indians and Africans.

But, starting in the first decades of the occupation and settlement of the Indies, something else had an impact on the image of the Creoles as well: the presence in the Americas of individuals with mixed blood. We cannot be sure how many there were or this population's growth over time, since colonial authorities did not keep consistent records on the ancestry of those who were baptized. Although with a hint of exaggeration, contemporaries were under the impression that hundreds, even thousands, of mestizos were born "every hour" and were "continuously multiplying," so that very soon "they would amount to more than the Spaniards."[63] Censuses in the Americas were always unreliable, but it has been estimated that in the mid-1600s mestizos numbered roughly 350,000, in addition to some 250,000 mulattos in the Indies.[64] These numbers seemed to many Europeans a confirmation that Spaniards as a result of their history, and perhaps even their natural proclivities, were prone to engendering "a mongrel sort of people," for generally "Spaniards love better the negro women . . . or the tawny Indian females, than their own white European race."[65]

Spaniards' tendency to mix with other communities in America was attributed by some to extenuating circumstances—"the shortage at first of [Spanish] women to marry," according to viceroy Marques of Montesclaros.[66] Others, at least among the Spanish, saw it as a kind of universal law. The early seventeenth-century writer Gregorio García, author of the most important book on the origin of the Indians, opined that mixing was inevitable whenever different nations shared the same territory. After all, this had already occurred on the Iberian Peninsula, "where we may observe today the presence of a mixture of all the nations that have settled there." But this mixing was taking place with unprecedented intensity in "our Indies, where we find Castilians, Indians, Portuguese, Galicians, Vizcayans, Catalans, Valencians, French, Italians, Greeks and blacks, and even secret Moriscos and Gypsies, or those with some remnant or fragment of this caste, and there is no lack of descendants of Jews—all of whom, living in the same provinces, are forced to mix through marriage or illicit unions."[67]

Of interest here, however, are not so much the reasons or justifications for this biological mixing as the extent and manner in which it helped to shape the concept of Spanishness that predominated in the Americas. Rather than the causes or consequences of miscegenation, commentators essentially wanted to determine who was Spanish or, more precisely, the characteristics of Spaniards in the New World. We have noted their defensiveness in response to allegations that the American climate weakened their physical and mental characteristics, but it is equally obvious that the Spanish in the Americas wished to assert their purity no less than their peninsular peers. The historian María Elena Martínez has reminded us that, starting in the late sixteenth century, nearly all American institutions, secular and ecclesiastical, royal and local, adopted purity of blood statutes that followed peninsular models.[68] In their original form, which applied for the better part of two centuries, the American *limpieza* statutes clearly stipulated that people requesting offices or honors had to demonstrate the purity of their social and religious background. As was the case in the Iberian Peninsula, they had to be free of any trace of Jewish or Morisco blood, be the offspring of a legitimate marriage, and not have exercised any mechanical trade.[69]

Although not all of the documented proceedings and investigations have been analyzed—a vast number survives from the sixteenth and seventeenth centuries—in the majority of cases examined by historians, rejection for ecclesiastical and secular offices was due to unresolved doubts over the aspirant's religious background (usually Jewish), illegitimacy, or social status.[70] These were the same criteria for discrimination already well established in peninsular practice, and they were clearly transplanted to America, virtually unchanged. Few mestizos (descendants of Spaniards and Native Americans) and even fewer mulattos (descendants of Spaniards and Africans) had the economic means, social clout, or contacts to seek public offices or honors, and this might explain why the American purity-of-blood statutes remained very much similar to the ones in the Peninsula.

Until virtually the end of the seventeenth century, the self-perceptions, assumptions, and beliefs of peninsular and American Spaniards were quite similar, but in the Indies physical characteristics became key to being seen as a Spaniard. The fear of being taken for a mestizo, mulatto, or illegitimate eventually resulted in a number of laws that cut against the grain of Spanish legislation, intended to distinguish the pure Spaniards from other American populations, including their own mestizo sons. On the Iberian Peninsula, all of these regulations were aimed at discriminating against those with Muslim or Jewish heritage.[71] In the Indies, on the other hand, more and more Spaniards wanted to distinguish themselves not from descendants of converted Jews and Muslims but from Native Americans and, especially, Africans. The local circumstances in the Indies made Spaniards believe that they needed to create a different social hierarchy, one that helped them claim their purity not in contrast to Spaniards with Jewish and Muslim ancestors but from people of other nations—Africans and Native Americans. The source of power, once mulattos and mestizos started to claim political and economic privileges, could no longer be social and economic. It also had to be "racial." Other chapters will explore how this discourse based on the old tradition of purity of blood transformed into a fully developed racialist discourse.

The distinguished historian Thomas Holt has written that in Spain and Spanish America, "anxieties over [its] racial mixture, made racial purification the basis of its national formation."[72] Other historians, including Maurice Olender, have similarly suggested that while purity-of-blood statutes should not be interpreted as proof of unambiguously racialist theories at this early date, they undeniably did posit a biological element—an inheritance passed on through blood—as one of the main criteria in thinking about and governing the nation. The coalescence of a national community, the statutes asserted, should not be based on certain acquired virtues and characteristics (conversion to Catholicism, loyalty to the same monarch, or Spanish birth) but rather on certain innate, natural characteristics and therefore "virtues attributed to a timeless nature prevailed over societal and historical change."[73]

However, the politics of "race" in the sixteenth and seventeenth centuries, and also later, were complex. More than witnessing the division of the Spanish people into two, with "pure" Spaniards on one side, enjoying access to public offices and benefits, and those perpetually marginalized because of their Jewish, Muslim, Indian, or African blood on the other, we are witnessing the establishment of the criteria to identify, first, who could be defined as Spaniard and, second, the conditions one should have to become a member of the Spanish political and social elite. The key to understanding the politics of race in early modern Spain is not so much the existence of these purity-of-blood statutes in general but how they were variously applied against so-called "internal others"—individuals with Jewish and Muslims ancestors—and descendants of "external others"—Native Americans and Africans.

3

The Others Within

Muslims, Jews, and their descendants (known as Moriscos and conversos, respectively, in the sixteenth and seventeenth century) occupied a special place in the collective imagination of Spaniards, as demonstrated by the vast number of publications and documents devoted to both. Undoubtedly, the presence of these communities was a growing source of moral, social, and political anxiety for many Spaniards, and they became the propitiatory victims of forced conversions and violent persecutions. This is not a study of the repression of conversos and Moriscos before and after 1500 or the complex social realities of these communities. Some inevitable reference will be made to these issues, but the focus is on the role of Jews and Muslims in the construction of the Spanish nation. The anxieties these communities provoked and responses to them—social, literary, and institutional—revolved around the question of belonging. They spoke of overcoming the obstacles imposed by history to construct a coherent sense of the nation. They considered who could, or could not be, part of the nation, on what grounds, and what this meant for the excluded.

Spaniards of the sixteenth and seventeenth centuries were convinced of the possibility of forging a united Spanish people. They believed that a natural and essential Spain existed despite politico-juridical divisions. It existed primarily and fundamentally not in the laws or institutions or state but in its people—in the descendants of the original inhabitants of Hispania. The great debate in this period concerned the disposition of those groups and individuals who, although sharing many of the characteristics that defined Spaniards in general (Catholicism, loyalty to the king, and peninsula-born), were nevertheless not descended from the original Spaniards, even though in the majority of cases their families had lived on the peninsula for several centuries.

Beginning in the early sixteenth century, if not earlier, all Spaniards were legally equal. All were citizens of one of several territorial communities. All the same, many on the peninsula did not see the conversos or the Moriscos as true "Spaniards." They insisted that Jewish and Muslim converts and their descendants should be barred from government posts or honors. Granted, they were Catholic subjects of the Spanish monarch, and they might legally even be natives of various kingdoms, but for many they were still aliens, incapable of feeling like other Spaniards and certainly unable to become good Catholics. To paraphrase J. G. A. Pocock's concept, these two groups were "internal others": they were inhabitants of Spain and subjects of the Spanish king and yet denied full access to the higher echelon of Spanish society.[1]

Spaniards had begun to discriminate against lineages perceived as foreign in the course of debating the origins and evolution of the Spanish lineage and biological mixing throughout history. The kernels of the discourses against Jewish and Muslim converts, the internal others, were anti-Judaism and anti-Islamism. But this does not connote the invention of scientific racism. In the sixteenth and seventeenth centuries, the implications of these discourses were not so much "racial" as national. The argument here is that, in the process of creating an identity, Spaniards in the peninsula did not need to invent Jewish and Muslim races. Instead, they clearly distinguished these communities as belonging to lineages separate from the rest of the Spaniards as extraneous or foreign but also as bearers of impurities—especially religious—associated with those lineages.

At the same time, it is important to remember that not all Christian Spaniards perceived the conversos and Moriscos as "others." Some viewed them as Spaniards in nature and characteristics and wanted to integrate them into the Spanish community that germinated after the marriage of Ferdinand and Isabel. Once again, the Spanish case is demonstrated to be complex. Indeed, competing theories emerged in the early modern period on who should be considered Spanish and their attendant rights and social roles. Many Christian Spaniards undoubtedly thought of conversos and Moriscos as essentially foreigners—individuals who could never be part of the Spanish community or share their compatriots' Spanish identity. Others, grounding themselves in theories discussed earlier, believed that conversos and Moriscos were Spaniards by birth and by faith and therefore deserved to be fully integrated into their community.

Conversos and Moriscos also participated in these debates and offered alternative or complementary readings of the genealogy of Spanishness and the terms under which they could be integrated, or not, into Spanish society. Conversos and Moriscos confronted differently the question of who belonged to Spanish society. The former tried to hide as much as possible their Jewish heritage; the latter showed profound pride in their Arab origins and culture. Spaniards also viewed these two groups as different from every single perspective, and they designed policies and strategies based precisely on this perception of difference.

Collective memory in the sixteenth and seventeenth centuries was shaped by reconstructions of Iberian Peninsula history, by the inescapable presence of Jews and Muslims in that history, and by discourses generated against these groups in Christian Spain. Although the debates were quite different in many respects before and after 1500, the vocabulary used was already current in the Middle Ages. It was generally recognized that Spain was a very different place after 1500, not least because after that date, Catholicism was the only officially sanctioned religion in the peninsula. But it was just as clearly understood that in discussions of the descendants of Jews and Muslims, the relevant concepts, memories, identities, and, in many cases, laws were the legacy of the Middle Ages. Whatever the case, this section does not endeavor to describe the entire history of Spanish Jews before the late fifteenth century but to underline those moments and policies that would condition and influence Spaniards' images of Jews and Judaism in the sixteenth century.

Although it is unclear when the first Jews settled in the Iberian Peninsula, evidence suggests that they were already an important community in Roman Hispania (206 BCE–406 CE). After years of relative political and social stability, the Visigothic conquest of Spain inaugurated a more turbulent period for Jews, especially after 589, when King Recared made Christianity the official religion. From the early seventh century, the Visigoth rulers seemed to have taken it upon themselves to convert or expel all Jews under their authority. Many historians view the years between 650 and 715 as one of the most difficult periods in the history of the Spanish Jewish communities. Scores converted to avoid expulsion, while others decided to leave the Iberian Peninsula and settle in various areas of Northern Africa.

Persecuted by the Gothic kings, many Spanish Jews chose to collaborate, often actively, with Arab invaders who occupied almost the entire peninsula beginning in the eighth century.[2] With most of Iberia under Arab control, Jews were active economically, politically, and culturally. Some of the most famous and influential Iberian Jews—including Rabbi Moses Ben Maimon, or Moses Maimonides, as he is better known—lived during the first centuries of Arab domination, and from the eighth to eleventh centuries the Jewish community in the peninsula was able to forge a strong collective identity.[3] By the late thirteenth century around 150,000 Jews lived in a territory with a total population of no more than 4 million, almost all living in Christian kingdoms. While Jews were expelled from other European polities—from England in 1290, France in 1394, and several provinces in Germany, Italy, and the Balkans between 1350 and 1450—the Jewish community thrived in Spain during the fourteenth century, growing to 200,000 by 1450, which made it one of the largest in the world.[4]

Until late in the 1400s, Christian rulers condemned Jews' beliefs and religious ceremonies yet recognized their right to worship and to remain unconverted.[5] In everything else, Jews were treated as a separate nation (lineage) and eternal enemies to all Christian nations (despite the shared genesis of the two faiths) and condemned to perpetual servitude: "The reason that the church, emperors, kings and princes permitted the Jews to dwell among them and with Christians is because they always lived, as it were, in captivity, as it was constantly in the minds of men that they were descended from those who crucified Our Lord Jesus Christ." Jews could not own Christian slaves, hold public offices, or exercise professions that would give them authority over Christians. Christians in turn were forbidden from cohabiting with Jews, inviting them into their homes, bathing in the same spaces, or being treated by Jewish doctors. And more important, Jews were forbidden from having intercourse with Christian women. The penalty in such cases would be death for the Jew and a range of punishments for his Christian consort, including death if she had committed adultery.[6] So as to forestall temptations and any possible misunderstandings, given the physical similarities between Jews and Christians, the former were ordered to wear identifying marks in public "so that people may plainly recognize a Jew, or a Jewess."[7]

As in other parts of Europe, Spanish Jews were accused of and persecuted for a variety of lurid and heinous crimes—child murder, cannibalism (usually linked to child murder), desecration of the host, and well poisoning.[8] Again, pogroms against Jews were not unique to Spain, and they actually started much later on the Iberian Peninsula than elsewhere in Europe. The pogroms in Spain, especially those in 1391 and the mid-1400s, were just as devastating for the Jewish community.[9] Another major outcome of these riots and pogroms—one with far-reaching consequences for Spanish society—was the forced conversion of thousands of Jews and, with them, the first attempts to implement purity-of-blood statutes.[10]

This was the case, for example, in Toledo, one of the main cities in the crown of Castile, where members of the city's government implemented the so-called *Sentence-Statute of Pero Sarmiento* (1449) against the conversos. This lasted only a few days but set the precedent for purity-of-blood statutes implemented after the 1550s.[11] Conversos were accused of having allied themselves with those bent on destroying the city, following in the footsteps of their Jewish ancestors, who were said to have assisted the invading Arabs in the conquest of Toledo. As a result, conversos were forbidden to hold any public office, and only genuine Spaniards could hold power in the cities. Perhaps the conversos might have been born in Toledo, but they were portrayed as members of a community of outsiders, aliens to the Spanish lineage.

In response to the converso issue, another institution of more lamentable reputation appeared precisely at this time. Created by papal decree in 1478, the Inquisition was not, as some have argued, an instrument of a centralized state bent on imposing religious uniformity. Advocated by certain elements within the church—mainly some of the religious orders—and paradoxically by many conversos, the Inquisition was rooted in a similar ideology to the one that had inspired the Sentence-Statute of Toledo: the belief that conversos were naturally predisposed to relapse into their old religion. Such an attitude was "against the social order, the Church, and the state" and thus merited unyielding persecution, regardless of cost, lest the nation and monarchy perish.[12]

There is no doubt that the violence unleashed by Inquisitorial persecution in the final years of the fifteenth century was akin to a pogrom, in this case officially and legally sanctioned.[13] The Inquisition detained, interrogated, and tortured thousands of conversos from all social groups—rich and poor, educated and illiterate, and including royal councilors and confessors. It tore apart families by forcing those accused of heresy to point fingers at brothers, sisters, fathers, mothers, and even dead and buried family members, which in some cases led Inquisitors to exhume the corpses and bones of the deceased. Many were condemned to prison sentences or lost their goods and property, while many others were condemned to be burned at the stake. Those who managed to escape into exile were burned in effigy, which emasculated in perpetuity the victim's and his relatives' honor.

The Inquisition would reverberate culturally for many years, but what is important here is that the sheer number of conversos suspected of Judaizing drew the attention of the authorities back to Jewish communities themselves. This is because many secular and ecclesiastical authorities believed that the main obstacle to conversos fully assuming their new status as Christians was the continuing influence of Jews who resisted conversion. By this logic Ferdinand and Isabel signed an order in March 1492 to expel all the Jews who refused to convert to Christianity.[14]

That an entire community or nation should pay for the crimes of a few, an issue explicitly addressed in both decrees, was entirely defensible to Catholic monarchs and their contemporaries: "And because whenever a grave and heinous crime is committed by some members of a community, it is reasonable for that community to be dissolved and obliterated, and for youngsters to be punished because of the crimes of their elders." Isabel and Ferdinand's order also encapsulates the larger drama of the Jewish nation, which was once again being expelled from a territory its members viewed as their motherland: "It is agreed and resolved that all Jews and Jewesses be ordered to leave our kingdoms, and that they never be allowed to return." Jews were viewed by many as aliens to the land despite centuries of Jewish presence on the Iberian Peninsula, and Christians did not seriously oppose Jewish expulsion. We cannot know for certain how many Jews were forced to leave Spain, but historians believe that around 100,000 were expelled in 1492, a majority of them from Castile. Of these, more than 80,000 crossed the border into Portugal, at least until 1497, when they were once again presented with the stark choice of conversion or exile.[15]

The expulsion of such a vast number of individuals from the land where their ancestors had lived for centuries was doubtless one of the most dramatic events in the history of Spain. But of particular interest here is the effect of this expulsion on the peninsula. There is no doubt that from 1492 onward, the real "Jewish enemy" for Christians was no longer the proscribed Jews themselves but the thousands of conversos who remained in the peninsula, whom many Spaniards viewed as religious enemies and, more troublingly, as people who intended to corrupt the blood of the Spanish people. In David Nirenberg's words, the growing presence of converted Jews in secular and ecclesiastical institutions throughout Spain "transformed the old boundaries and systems of discrimination . . . Categories that had previously seemed primarily legal and religious were replaced by the genealogical notion that Christians who descended from Jewish converts . . . were essentially different from 'Christians by nature,'" or old Christians.[16]

These new discourses held that the nature and customs of individuals were wholly determined by their genealogy and blood, such that conversos could never become genuine Spaniards. Faced with this discourse, many of the first-generation conversos, along with their defenders and allies, championed a radically different idea: the creation of a Spanish nation as well as a socially and politically united monarchy, founded by fostering sentiments, identities, and ideologies that united the greatest number of Spaniards. The idea was to identify elements that would integrate the greatest number of peninsular inhabitants as possible and to eliminate, or at least attenuate, factors that sowed discord.

All those who took part in these debates—many of them pre-1492 converts—occupied positions of great power and influence, including bishops, such as Alonso or Alfonso de Cartagena (1384–1456); papal advisors, such as Juan Torquemada (1388–1468); administrators of religious orders, such as the Hieronymite Alonso de Oropesa (?–1468); royal confessors and councilors, such as Hernando de Talavera (1428–1507); and historians, such as Hernando del Pulgar (1436?-1493). The Inquisition persecuted at least one, Hernando de Talavera, even though he had served as Queen Isabel's confessor and archbishop of Granada. All of them had converted before 1450.[17] These authors offered three principal rebuttals to advocates of discrimination. The first recognized and reaffirmed the theory of human creation shared by all Christians: God had created Adam and Eve, the progenitors of all humanity, from whom all were descended. God's intention had been to create a single human family, not many. The creation of different lineages in the Tower of Babel was not intended as a permanent division of the human family but as punishment for those guilty of crimes or great sins.[18] Pulgar more directly accused promoters of anti-converso legislation of defying "the law of nature, for we are all born of one single mass and from noble beginnings, and [also] against divine law, which ordains that all are" of one church and one God.[19]

More important was the notion that God had decided to reunite the scattered human lineages through Jesus Christ. As a man, Jesus had been the product of a mix of lineages—gentile and Jewish—and thus symbolized the reunion of all humans: "The Israelites, like the gentiles, upon entering the Catholic faith through the gate of sacred baptism endure not as two peoples or two different lineages, but from the offspring of one and the other is created a new people."[20] Through Christ, Cartagena argued, "all differences between peoples and lineages were effaced, for in this second, pure Adam all reverted to the [original] unity."[21] Moreover, although many Jews had called for Jesus to be crucified, not all Jews had been present in Israel at the time, and Spanish Jews in particular were descended from those already living in the Iberian Peninsula at the time of Christ's death. Furthermore, from the legal and religious standpoint, the sins of the fathers could not be extended to the sons.[22] It was the converso from Cordoba, Juan de Lucena (1430–1506), who perhaps best summed up what we might call the converso ideology. In one of his writings he describes being told that he spoke like one of "your people" (in other words, like a converso), to which Lucena responded: "One law, one faith, one religion, one king, one homeland, one church and one God for all. Mine people is whoever partake more in this."[23]

These were self-assured arguments that would have a lasting influence in debates about the construction of a new Spain. In the closing years of the 1400s, these arguments opened a path to full integration for the conversos, or at least for those who belonged to the social elite. It was certainly the way forward suggested by authors discussed above: it was possible to feel Spanish, to love Spain, to be profoundly Catholic, and at the same time to feel proud of one's Jewish ancestry. In other words, love and loyalty to Spain, to *feel* Spanish, was a civic or political sentiment, and it did not require pure Spanish blood. For the next few years, members of the converso elite married their descendants to members of the nobility and occupied important secular and ecclesiastical posts.[24] At least until the early sixteenth century, some conversos could even be praised as model Christians, such as Pablo de Santa María, who was described by fifteenth-century historian Hernando del Pulgar as a "Jew of noble lineage" who had converted to Christianity because he believed it to be the true faith and was certainly a better Christian than many who were descended from generations of Old Christians. For Pérez de Guzmán, another historian and poet, the future was promising. It was only natural that the process of integration should take some time, perhaps two or three generations, but by then all would be firm believers and competent citizens.[25]

It is difficult to measure precisely the degree of integration among conversos. Inquisitorial logic insisted that many of them Judaized at some point of their lives and that various local converso communities continued to maintain strong links with one other. On the other hand, modern scholars have cast doubt on these conclusions. Few would deny that many of them maintained some of their ancestors' beliefs and customs, but with the passage of time these began to disappear or to lose their religious significance. Moreover, the pattern of the Inquisition's activities does not corroborate the view that the majority of the conversos were Judaizers. Or, at the very least, the pattern indicates that the attitudes of religious and secular authorities toward them were changing with time. We have the most detailed information for the Inquisition between the years 1540 and 1700. In the course of these 160 years, there were around 60,000 inquisitorial cases. Between 1540 and 1615, 7 percent of all cases involved individuals accused of Judaizing. This number rose to 18 percent between 1615 and 1700 as a result of the arrival in the crown of Castile of Portuguese New Christians, widely perceived to be the most tenacious in holding on to their former religion and beliefs. From 1540 to 1700, between 1,200 and 1,500 individuals were executed (roughly 1.8 percent of the total number of individuals prosecuted by the Inquisition), and among these, once again, the majority were converted Jews—one more indication that Judaizers were considered to be the most dangerous and universally reviled heretics.[26]

However, there is also evidence that members of the converso elite were able to marry their daughters and sons into the nobility, while many served as bankers to the monarchy and founded influential mercantile dynasties. And at least in some regions, modern scholars have shown that in daily life, descendants of converted Jews and Old Christians mixed and coexisted in relative harmony, since they saw each other as Catholics and Spaniards.[27] Toledo, institutionally one of the most anti-converso cities, is a case in point. Historian Linda Martz has noted that in Toledo "contacts and interaction between the two groups were numerous. This is true in the world of finance, manufacturing and commerce, dominated in large part by conversos."[28] The descendant of conversos, González de Cellorigo argued in a pamphlet in favor of integration of Portuguese conversos that so many of Spanish conversos had fully integrated into Spanish Christian society that many of their heirs had been ennobled, and the Jews as such had simply disappeared. "And if the same were to be done in Portugal," he continued, "the name of 'Jew' would also disappear from that kingdom, which is so dishonorable that the name itself is odious for this reason, and despised."[29]

Although exact measures of conversos' integration are elusive, we do know that the debate about the conversos' exclusion or assimilation into society helped to transform attitudes about the purity of blood statutes.[30] The generation of the Duke of Lerma and the Count-Duke of Olivares—in other words, those at the helm of the monarchy from at least 1595 until 1640—had a much more practical sense of politics and were more inclined to promote elements that united the people instead of those that separated them. They promoted ideas and devised plans conducive to the unification of the various kingdoms of the monarchy, and the same logic was applied to the population of Jewish origin.[31]

These royal officials requested a reevaluation of the statutes—rationales, practical implications, and means of reform. A standard criticism of the statutes was that they divided and separated the Spanish people into different "nations," contrary to the goal of creating a common homeland and a single, unified monarchy. The Augustinian Fray Luis de León, professor at Salamanca, prisoner of the Inquisition between 1572 and 1576 (accused by his Dominican colleagues of religious errors in his Castilian translation of the biblical text of the Song of Songs), and the son of converso parents, made this point in one of his most famous works, *The Names of Christ* (1587). He noted that the best kingdom is one "in which no vassal may be called vile because of his lineage or despised because of his family or social rank, and all are equally well born. . . . It is impossible to establish peace in a kingdom whose parts are opposed to one another, and differences made between them, one group with much honor, the other rejected and without honor . . . This is . . . a kingdom prone to illness, and on the brink of civil war on the slightest pretext."[32] Pedro Fernández de Navarrete, a writer who promoted economic and social reforms to improve the monarchy, pinpointed as Spain's greatest problem the fact that conversos, both Muslims and Jews, had always been treated as "separate members" of the society given the "name of strangers." Instead, Spain should be like the

Roman Empire, where laws had "permitted marriages between nobles and plebeians, so that through this bond all dissension should cease, which had so often agitated the republic."[33]

Perhaps even more important for our purposes, criticism directed at the statutes casts doubt on the very notion of a pure Spanish lineage. Fray Agustín de Salucio offered one of the most comprehensive critiques along these lines.[34] Like many authors of the period, Salucio did not call for the complete abolition of the statutes. He proposed instead that they should apply to the descendants of Jews and Muslims for only a very few generations and not in perpetuity. Thus, he claimed, at some point in time these antecedents would disappear, and all Spaniards would be one. More significantly, he questioned theories of a "pure" Spanish lineage. Salucio observed that counting only the previous six centuries, since the year 1000, each Spaniard would have around a million ancestors, which surely made it impossible to know for certain whether all the ancestors of any individual had been Christians. In virtually every case it was likely that these ancestors included "Moors, and many Jews, and many heretics, or perhaps their sons, or grandsons . . ." Since the Roman conquest of Spain, countless Jews had arrived in the peninsula, making it highly probable that all contemporary Spaniards had at least one Jewish ancestor. Those who had converted 400 years ago—that is to say, in 1200—should be considered Old Christians, even though all of them probably had some Jewish blood. Relying mainly on a narrative of the Muslim conquest written by a Morisco, Salucio also argued that thousands of native Spaniards had remained in their hometowns and cities when the Arabs invaded and conquered Spain and that many of them "became Moors."

If past intermingling made it impossible to distinguish between the various genealogies that intersected in each Spaniard, it might also be a model for the future. The humanist Pedro de Valencia was Philip III's official chronicler. In a memorial discussing the Morisco situation, he masterfully expounded the philosophical principles behind policies of hispanizing all the Iberian Peninsula inhabitants. For Valencia, as for Salucio and others, the best strategy was not to eliminate the statutes by decree but to eradicate the ideology and attitudes that supported them. In a 1605 memorial in defense of the

Moriscos, he urged support for biological mixing in Spain. This would eradicate different nations and castes and join them together in "one new body and name of commonwealth." With this biological mixing "the stain would spread quickly to all, and the Old Christians would cease to exist." In this context, Valencia advised the monarch to unite all the kingdoms of Spain and dispose of all the factors that separated Spaniards, and, "though it may be through lies, a way should be found to persuade the citizens of this commonwealth that all are brothers of one blood and one lineage, and natives of one and the same land, so that they may think of her as a mother, and should wish to die and suffer hardships for her."[35] In modern terms, it was nothing less than an explicit call to invent a Spanish nation, in which all would share common, mixed origins and in which all would love and defend only one *patria*, Spain.

The sources seem to indicate that with time, many conversos disappeared as such and were integrated into Spanish society with full rights because they lost a recognizable, distinct Jewish identity. Before and after 1492 a significant number of them chose self-imposed exile in the Low Countries, France, Italy, England, Turkey, or North Africa.[36] Yet the majority of the approximately 200,000 Jewish converts remained in the lands inhabited by their families for centuries and were left to confront directly the emerging problems and dilemmas.[37] To protect themselves against the Inquisition's attacks or against political and social discrimination, most did what they could to suppress public knowledge of their Jewish ancestry. In many cases they chose simply to disappear, become invisible, or pass as Old Christians by migrating to areas within the Spanish monarchy where their ancestors were unknown. Fearful of being seen as Judaizers and recognizing that, from the early sixteenth century on, the avenues to social ascent would be closed because of the purity of blood statutes, the great majority of conversos dealt with their integration into Spanish political society, and their cultural and religious assimilation, by believing that full integration was only possible if they eradicated all vestiges of their Jewish identity. Many contemporaries noted this general attitude, including the converso and seventeenth-century political commentator Martín González de Cellorigo. In a 1600 memorandum on the Moriscos he stated that the conversos had formerly not minded being identified as Jews but, once converted, repudiated this designation, since the term had become "the most injurious and offensive word that one might say to another."[38]

The path to integration was the renunciation of everything that made individuals different from what Spaniards were trying to promote: a Spanish nation with the features and characters of the Spanish people. It has been proved, for example, that hundreds if not thousands of conversos were able to access public offices—local, ecclesiastical and monarchical—even at those institutions with purity-of-blood statutes. But the main point here is that they were able to do so precisely by losing their identity as conversos, by creating for themselves false genealogical credentials as pure Spaniards.[39] Certainly by the mid-seventeenth century, and with very few exceptions, the conversos were appreciated as an integral part of Spanish culture because their works were Spanish and in many cases paradigmatic of "Spanishness."[40] This process is clearly evident in the work of Nicolás Antonio, author of the encyclopedic work that tried to encompass all "Spanish" writers from antiquity to the 1670s. In the prologue to his *New Spanish Library*, Nicolás Antonio praised the great contribution of the "Hebrews" to theological speculation during the Middle Ages, when Christian regions were mired in barbarism following the Muslim triumph.[41] All references to "Hebrewness," however, vanish once he turns to post-1500 authors. This was true even in the biographies of those who were known to have converso roots or who had been prosecuted by the Inquisition as a consequence. In each case Antonio claims that his subject was of noble origin or from a good family and highlights his contribution to the creation of a Spanish culture.

Certainly after 1600 discursive changes occurred in depictions of Jewish converts in Spanish literature, with the gradual disappearance of negative references so popular in the fifteenth and sixteenth centuries.[42] With growing frequency, those unduly preoccupied with their noble or pure genealogy are ridiculed in literary works, while some authors championed new ideals of nobility and virtue based on personal merits and conduct rather than inheritance. The debate surrounding the conversos and their integration into society was an opportunity to challenge the opinion that only those descended from the original lineages could be declared Spaniards and, conversely, to promote the idea that Spain should be a community actively forged by all of its members. That group included all those who possessed a number of shared characteristics—and especially those prepared to abandon their particular identities for the sake of only one identity: Spanish.[43]

To be sure, some Spaniards continued to claim that the presence of Jewish blood could provoke the corruption of the Spanish blood and lineage. The early modern historian and Benedictine friar Prudencio de Sandoval was one of them, suggesting that a Jew could not become a deserving Spaniard though he might be "three parts hidalgo, or Old Christian" because even one part of the bad Jewish lineage "infects and spoils him."[44] Francisco de Quevedo (1580–1645) was one of the most popular and prolific writers of the period and the author of one of the most eloquent contemporary apologies for Spain, *España defendida y los tiempos de ahora* ("Spain Defended and the Present Times"), in 1609. He made the same point in a pamphlet that attacked policies to integrate converted Portuguese Jews into Spanish society. Neither baptism nor conversion nor having being born in Iberia could transform Jews into genuine Christians and Spaniards, for "they have always been as they are now, and will always be as they had been," he wrote. He also expounded one of the elements that would later be a linchpin of "scientific racism": the notion that "bad blood" contaminated the good. "One drop of blood derived from Jews [is enough] to seduce one to revolt against Jesus Christ . . . it invariably spoils the good blood with which it is joined, and for this [reason] seeks it. It never improves with the good in which it is mixed, and for this it is feared."[45]

However, by the 1660s, very few wrote about the dangers of converso blood. Instead, some authors started to propose a much more anti-Semitic discourse now addressed against Jews. This inflection happened with the publication in the 1670s of the *Sentinel against the Jews* by Fray Francisco de Torrejoncillo. This book went through many editions in the seventeenth and eighteenth centuries.[46] Torrejoncillo was neither original nor particularly brilliant, but he had the foresight to compile all of the accusations and invectives directed against the Jews and transform them into a code of physical, moral, and ethical characteristics. This code was now used to define a separate and distinct lineage—no longer the race of noble origin mentioned in the *Siete Partidas* but a degenerate one. Jews were betrayers of Christians and, more specifically, of Spaniards, Torrejoncillo argued, and God had chosen to mark them with certain physical characteristics to make them more readily identifiable. Several of these physical characteristics were already part of the anti-Jewish repertoire of earlier centuries: some grew tails, others menstruated (men and women), yet others could not produce saliva. Many engendered worms that bit their tongues while they slept; their bodies exuded insufferable odors, and they had large noses. Jews, more importantly, were depicted as a race apart, disloyal, contemptible, oppressed, poor, repulsive, crude, vulgar, and destined to remain subjugated to other peoples. By then, however, this was not the race to which those already-integrated Spanish conversos belonged. Their blemishes and deficiencies had improved or in many cases been erased altogether through mixture with Spaniards, their contact with Spanish culture, and the influence of the unsurpassable natural conditions of the Iberian Peninsula.

The history of Islam in Spain is no less complex than that of Judaism, although its beginning is much easier to pinpoint. In 711 a combination of Arabs, Berbers, Syrians, and other North African peoples crossed the straits of Gibraltar, led by Tariq ibn Ziyad, the Moorish governor of Tangier, and defeated the Visigothic army in Andalusia. Other groups crossed the straits in their wake. After a series of battles and skirmishes, the troops, led by Tariq and his superior Musa ibn Nasayr, were finally halted when they reached the Pyrenees. Prevented from crossing into France and their advance in the Iberian Peninsula blocked by small groups of Christians in the mountainous north, the invaders began to occupy the land and organize the political, social, and economic structures of the new Spain, known to the victors as Al-Andalus.

With the exception of several small communities in the north, very few inhabitants of the peninsula opposed the invaders. Some members of the political and social elite left the major cities, but a significant number swiftly entered into political or matrimonial alliances with the victors, and a majority of Iberians remained in their homelands. Although early modern Spaniards cultivated the myth that a majority of Christians had abandoned their towns and villages to join the Christian forces in the north, very few did in reality. Many in fact converted to Islam and intermarried with the invaders and their descendants, while some remained Christians—known as Mozárabes or Mozarabs—under Islamic rule. Although the exact number is difficult to ascertain, scholars believe that from the beginning of the invasion until the fall of the kingdom of Granada in 1492, around 350,000 individuals crossed the straits of Gibraltar to settle in the Iberian Peninsula, most of them by the end of the twelfth century.[47]

This is not the place to narrate the entire history of Muslim Spain. Suffice it to say that by the thirteenth century the kingdom of Granada was the only independent Muslim kingdom in the peninsula.[48] The shrinking territory controlled by Muslim rulers rendered a majority of Muslims in Iberia—now known as Mudéjares—subjects of Christian kings.[49] The various Mudéjar communities in Christian territories differed in many respects, but they all recognized one another as followers of the prophet Mohammad. In the north of the peninsula and the Castilian territories, the Mudéjares were relatively well integrated, their Arabic use and religious practices fading perceptibly. At the end of the fifteenth century, for instance, the Mudéjar community in the crown of Castile numbered 20,000, or 0.5 percent of the total population.[50] Catalonia, like Castile, harbored relatively few Mudéjares, less than 3 percent of the population. In Aragon, to the west of Catalonia, they made up at least 15 percent of the population, the majority living in rural areas controlled by an aristocracy that relied on them as a valuable source of cheap labor.[51] The same was true in Valencia, where numbers were even higher. There were 100,000 to 150,000 Muslims in the fourteenth century, and they were scarcely, if at all, integrated, having conserved their language, their customs, and, especially, their religion.[52] All were allowed to keep properties and lands, to have justice administered according to Islamic law and by their own judges, to practice their religion and instruct their children in it, and to exercise a limited right to migrate. The Mudéjares of Valencia were the most Islamized in the Iberian Peninsula. They remained in active contact with Muslims in Granada and North Africa and seldom integrated into Christian society.

Legally, relations between Christians and Mudéjares before 1492 were relatively straightforward.[53] As adherents of a different religion, Mudéjares did in fact have special status: their communities were under the direct protection of the authorities (royal or aristocratic) that ruled over the areas in which they lived. Generally, and especially starting in thirteenth-century cities, Mudéjares, like Jews, were obliged to live in designated and segregated neighborhoods *(morerías)*. Regional variations notwithstanding, Mudéjares were allowed to practice their religion, maintain their mosques (but not to build new ones), have their own religious authorities, and have justice administered by their own judges in accordance with their own laws. Christians meanwhile were obliged to respect these communities' autonomy and privacy and to refrain from forcibly converting them to Christianity.

The most important difference between Jews and Mudéjares—and, after 1500, their descendants—is that the former tended to be urban dwellers and lived amid or in close proximity to Christian communities. In contrast, the Mudéjares lived mostly in the countryside, in communities with few if any Christians, who tended to view Mudéjares as a political threat—as individuals likely to enter into pacts with Muslim powers. The tone and concepts used for Mudéjares and Muslims differed from those used for Jews. In the *Siete Partidas* they were described not as members of a single nation with noble origins like the Jews, but rather as ignorant followers of a false prophet who had preached a false religion.[54] As with the Jews, authorities regulated sexual relations between Moorish men and Christian women, with serious penalties to those who disobeyed these orders.[55] Like Jews, Mudéjares had to wear distinctive identifying marks in public, and they could not practice certain professions, for example, apothecary or medicine. They were not allowed to eat, drink, socialize, and participate in public rituals alongside Christians. Likewise, markets in Moorish neighborhoods were closed to Christians.[56]

For the Muslims in Spain, 1492 was a pivotal year. After years of conflict, on January 2, 1492, Isabel and Ferdinand received from the king of Granada the keys to the city and acknowledgement of his defeat. It was the fall of the last Muslim redoubt in Iberia, and the kingdom of Granada was annexed to the crown of Castile.[57] The defeat of the last Muslim kingdom on Iberian soil did not have the same immediate consequences for Muslims in Spain as the expulsion of the Jews that same year. Perhaps surprisingly, the conquest of Granada did not signal the religious unification of the peninsula. The Capitulations of Granada, signed by Isabel and Ferdinand with their Granadine counterpart Muhammad XII, were not an expression of a religious victory so much as a political-military triumph over an independent kingdom. They allowed Granadines to choose either to remain in their homes and settlements or to emigrate. Those who decided to stay could keep their land and houses and their laws and judges, and neither Christians nor Judeo-conversos could hold any office with authority over them. They were allowed to maintain their religious rites and ceremonies as well as their mosques, customs, and language, and they were also permitted to migrate to North Africa at any time. None of them was obliged to convert to Christianity, and the concession was even made to limit Christian immigration to Granada, in the short term, to maintain the existing (Muslim) social composition of the kingdom.[58]

The magnanimity apparent in the terms of surrender soon waned, and attitudes toward the conquered population changed after 1500, first in Granada and then the rest of Spain. By the first years of the sixteenth century, many Christians in positions of authority were demanding the prompt conversion of all peninsular inhabitants without exception. The new mood was uncompromising: all were to become Catholic, immediately, through mass conversions. The first official decree appeared in the crown of Castile in 1502. All Mudéjares and Muslims living in its territories, including Granada, had to be baptized and were forbidden from leaving the peninsula—although many did so illegally. In 1525 the authorities in the crown of Aragon ordered the baptism of all Mudéjares in their territory—including Aragon, Valencia, Mallorca, and Catalonia. From that point on all inhabitants of the Spanish kingdoms were, at least officially, Christians. However, the Muslim communities of Granada made a renewed attempt to preserve if not their religion then at least some of their own characteristics, customs, and traditions. In 1527 they offered Charles I an enormous sum of money in exchange for a number of rights: exemption from being prosecuted by the Inquisition and the maintenance of certain cultural practices (dress, the use of Arabic, and marriage ceremonies, among others). The king accepted the offer and conceded these privileges only to the Granadine community of Muslim converts for a period of forty years, until 1567.

The plight of the Muslim converts in these first decades was not as dramatic as that of the Jewish conversos, primarily because they were spared the full wrath of the Inquisition until the mid-1500s, but the presence of such a large number of new Christians of Muslim origin inspired heated debates among Spaniards. The central issue was always more or less the same; namely, whether these individuals were part of the demographic history of the great Spanish family because they were born in Spain and influenced by its beneficial natural conditions and, if so, to what extent their presence in Spain brought into question the dominant view of the Spanish people. Should they be allowed to maintain what appeared to be a distinct identity from other Spaniards and an obvious group solidarity? In other words, should the Muslim conversos continue to be seen not as part of Spanish society but as members of a Muslim community scattered throughout most of Spain? Was it plausible to believe that with religious conversion and the acquisition of a common language they would be hispanized and would be transformed into loyal subjects of the Spanish king?

Until the mid-sixteenth century, these individuals were known simply as "new converts." This signaled their recent inclusion into the Christian fold but also a hope that they might swiftly become true Christians. Regardless of their origin or place of residence, however, after 1540 the Muslim conversos were referred to generically as Moriscos, recognized as a distinct people or nation. The word *morisco* or *maurisco* had been used in the medieval period mainly in reference to the Mozárabes (Christians living in territories under Muslim rule) or to designate the Arab invaders of the Iberian Peninsula who originated in Mauritania (*maurisco* was derived from *mauricus* or *mauritanio*).[59] Plenty of evidence suggests that the Moriscos readily embraced this designation, as a group self-identification that helped distinguish them from Christian Spaniards and Jewish conversos.[60]

Although the exact population figures remain elusive, we know that in the sixteenth century there were between 300,000 and 400,000 Moriscos in Spain. With the exception of the Castilian Moriscos, who were mostly well integrated into Christian-majority societies, the greater part of the Moriscos lived in small towns and villages with a minimal Christian presence. In Castile, the Moriscos had lost some of their cultural traditions and knowledge of the Koran, dressed according to local custom, and tended to speak Castilian. In Castile, where a significant number of Moriscos sought social, cultural, and political integration, we find more official requests from individuals and communities not to be treated or designated as Moriscos because they identified as Christians and Spaniards.[61]

On the other hand, in Valencia and Aragon, the vast majority of Moriscos were peasants, mostly serfs working on seigneurial estates. They generally dressed *a la morisca*, preserved Muslim traditions and customs, and did not speak Castilian or Catalan, and although their knowledge of Islam was limited, they knew even less of Christianity and its doctrines.[62] Granada, as the last Muslim kingdom to come under Christian suzerainty, was the region most obviously dominated by Moriscos, who possessed a collective consciousness unmatched elsewhere in the peninsula. Fully conversant with their recent history, the Granadine Moriscos tensely endured between two identities—a pattern repeated in many kindred peninsular communities. The conclusion based on a growing number of detailed analyses of written texts left behind by the Moriscos is that Islam in Spain survived in those regions where the Moriscos were able to preserve their communities and identities. It disappeared where this turned out to be impossible, usually owing to the repression of the Inquisition and other civil and religious authorities and Moriscos' progressive integration into Christian society.[63]

In contrast to the Judeo-conversos, numerous depictions of Moriscos have survived. Many of them are negative, though a few are more complex and subtle. Contemporary Europeans and Spaniards who saw the history of the world as a mixture of lineages and religions perceived Muslims not as members of a single lineage, like the Jews, but as followers of a particular religion descended from many lineages. Thanks to the Bible, European Christians knew that Mohammad and his first followers had been Ishmaelites, descendants of the slave Hagar and her son Ishmael, whose father had been the prophet Abraham. Pedro de Valencia pointed out that one of the root causes of the enmity between Spanish Christians and Moriscos was this "lineage and nation," "which since the time of Ishmael has professed and continues to profess genuine hatred for all the sons of Sarah, who is the Church, especially those from Europe, and above all the Spaniards."[64] Sixteenth-century Spaniards did not see this as a mark of demographic distinction but one of religious difference. As regards lineage, it was clear that Muslims were subdivided into a number of national groups because Islam, like Christianity, was an expansionist religion, extending from the Arabian Peninsula to Africa and Asia and, beginning in the eighth century, to Europe through Spain, Italy, and the Balkans. Consequently, Spaniards easily grasped that there were several ancestries within Islam, some of which originated in sub-Saharan Africa.

Spaniards could not even be certain that Moriscos were completely distinct from them. Although some described Moriscos as having an olive complexion, most observers thought they possessed similar physical characteristics to other Spaniards.[65] The reasons for this are to be found, once again, in theories about the influence of the natural environment on individuals' physical and mental attributes. The royal chronicler Pedro de Valencia clearly explained the relationship: "The Moriscos, with regard to their natural complexion, and therefore [also] their ingenuity, condition and spirit, are Spaniards like the rest who live in Spain, because for nine hundred years they have been born and raised here, and this may be observed in their likeness or uniformity of proportions with the rest of the inhabitants."[66] To cite another example, Inquisitor Martín García wrote in the sixteenth century that the Moriscos "*sunt hispani, nor armenii, nec africani*" ("are Spaniards, not Armenians, or Africans").[67] In the majority of cases, Moriscos were described as "white though dark-complexioned," which was no different from standard depictions of other Spaniards.[68] A census conducted in 1573 of several hundred Granadine Morisco residents in Cordoba also suggests that authorities recognized that Moriscos shared the same physical characteristics with other inhabitants of the peninsula.[69] Perhaps even more instructive is Fray Diego de Haedo's *Topography and General History of Algiers* (1612), which described various communities living in the city, especially three—"Turks, Moors and Jews." He divided the "Moors" into many different groups—"*baldis*, *cabailes*, *alabares* and Moriscos." The last were described as white and well proportioned, "like those born in Spain or originating from there."[70]

The Moriscos appear to have been underrepresented in proportion to their numbers in liberal professions, universities, and the nobility and were generally found among the lowest social strata.[71] Members of noble families from Granada who chose to become Christians and remain in the peninsula received titles and land, and many of them were integrated eventually into Spanish society. A typical case was that of Don Juan de Granada Venegas, a noble Granadine. Many refrained from calling him a Morisco, precisely due to his wealth and social prestige, and he went on to play important political roles, first as a member of the Valladolid city council and later as the royal governor of the kingdom of Galicia.[72] Perhaps even more exemplary was the case of his descendant, Pedro de Granada Venegas. Born in 1559, the younger Venegas held posts in the royal palace and was part of the Christian forces that fought against Granadine Morisco rebels, a commander in the royal army that secured Portugal in 1580, a city councilor of Granada, and the city's representative in the Castilian Cortes of 1608. He was the first Marquis of Campotéjar and an erudite figure whose personal library betrays his total integration into the Spanish cultural and intellectual world.[73] When asked whether Venegas bore any trace of the Moorish lineage, Luis de Valdivia, himself a noble and an Old Christian, responded that "as for the Moorish race, it may not be called a race in the case of one who descends from a Moorish prince."[74]

Such attitudes toward the Morisco nobility further illustrate that the Moriscos were not all seen as members of a single lineage but descendants of a national group in Spain, one that for centuries had formed political societies with royal and noble families among them. Spanish society recognized the descendants of these social groups, once converted to Christianity, as nobles with the same rank as their Christian counterparts. The great Jesuit scholar Francisco Suárez wrote in 1603 that there was a "civil or natural nobility" possessed by the descendants of "Moorish kings," their nobles, and elites who did not relinquish it upon conversion.[75] The Jews, on the other hand, might claim descent from a noble nation, but as Jews they did not possess civil nobility because, Sebastián de Covarrubias explained, they had never been permitted to create an independent commonwealth.[76]

The assimilated Morisco nobles were only a small minority, however. There were few Moriscos in the universities, with the possible exception of the University of Granada's school of medicine, and it would be no exaggeration to say that very few occupied posts in the government of the monarchy and not many at the local level, with the exception once again of Granada. Some Moriscos, albeit very few, became part of the cultural elite. Perhaps one of the most famous was the Jesuit Ignacio de las Casas, a fascinating figure according to a recent study. Alongside him one finds several medical doctors, translators, and, especially, soldiers.[77]

The Moriscos generally were thought of and treated as rustic philistines. They were represented as slovenly liars and criminals, lacking all civic virtues, and "vulgar people," according to Fray Agustín de Salucio, or "miserly, like all of [their] caste," according to Cervantes.[78] It was widely claimed that Moriscos were endogamous and that their aim was to have as many offspring as possible in order to become the majority population and once again take charge of the peninsula. Although it is fair to assume that mixed marriages between Moriscos and Christians were more common than contemporary authorities and many modern scholars believed, it is equally certain that such marriages would have taken place between individuals of the lowest social orders who have left by far the fewest traces in the documentary record, with the exception of some of the Granadine Morisco elites during the sixteenth century.[79] In those territories where the most cohesive Morisco communities survived, especially the crown of Aragon, mixed marriages were practically nonexistent, in spite of pressure from civil and religious authorities for whom this was a key element of Morisco integration.[80] Fray Agustín de Salucio was highly acerbic about Moriscos' desire to populate the peninsula: they were dangerous, he wrote, "because they multiply like rabbits and each thousand will bring forth more than a million within a hundred years."[81]

More important perhaps is that Spaniards never ceased to see Moriscos as an internal enemy, the natural allies of foreign Muslim powers, inclined toward conspiracy and treason. Disloyal to the Spanish king, loyal to the Turkish emperor, and associated with the North African Barbary pirates, Moriscos still dreamed of reconquering Spain for the Arabs and restoring the glory of Al-Andalus, Spaniards widely believed.[82] Pedro de Valencia explained, "They are annoyed with us too because they believe that all Spain is theirs, and belongs to them by the most legitimate and binding title they can imagine, which is having won her by force of arms for the propagation of their sect and in obedience of their Prophet."[83]

It has been claimed that Spanish society, or at least its governing class in the sixteenth and seventeenth centuries, was more anxious about Jewish than Muslim converts.[84] The reality seems to have been precisely the reverse, in some regions of Spain more than others. Jewish conversos did not represent a social or political threat. As we have seen, it was widely acknowledged that by the late sixteenth century the majority had been successfully integrated into society. The Muslims converts did not disappear as a group in 1492 or thereafter, they never shed their markers of difference or contacts with foreign powers, and they continued to feel that the founts of their culture, religion, and intellectual life were not to be found in the Christian society in which they lived but among their Eastern brethren. The significant point here is that the history of Muslim converts in Spain demonstrates that not all minorities were treated equally in the process of constructing a nation. More important, not all minorities responded in the same way to challenges presented by the dominant ideology. As a consequence of the anti-Jewish sentiment so prevalent in the Iberian Peninsula, the Jewish conversos sought integration as individuals, disguised their roots, and did their best to tread the path toward hispanization. In contrast, the great majority of Moriscos did not conceal pride in their origins and maintained their relations with other kin groups within the peninsula and with the wider, international Muslim community.[85] As the historian Mercedes García-Arenal has stated, "The common feature of all Morisco groups is the pride taken by individual members in their nature as such [i.e., Moriscos]. Far from trying to erase or dissimulate their origins, the Moriscos saw them as a measure of their worth, and resisted all efforts to absorb them and deprive them of their identity."[86]

Secular and religious authorities were aware of this situation, and beginning in the second half of the 1500s they attempted to break this group solidarity and self-identity. Philip II's decision to discontinue the agreement his father Charles had signed with the Moriscos of Granada in 1527 was a key development in this respect. In 1567, Philip instituted measures to de-Islamize and hispanize the Morisco community in the former kingdom of Granada. This decree was one of the clearest indications that, as far as the Spanish authorities were concerned, integration was only possible once Moriscos disappeared as a distinct group, just as Jewish conversos had. The royal order required the Granadine Moriscos to abandon their forms of dress, their traditions and language, and their books in Arabic and to stop being "Moors and relating to each other as Moors." Their goal should be to become Christians and Spaniards. Then and only then would "they would be honored, favored and respected, and would be able to serve the king like other vassals, and in time their sons and grandsons would be elevated to honors, dignities and offices of justice and government in the manner of the noble and virtuous men of the kingdom."[87]

The Moriscos' immediate response to this decree revealed their overall strategy but also their full awareness of what was at stake. They mounted an active, public defense of their rights and Morisco identity by presenting themselves as merely another one of Spain's various communities or nations. Núñez Muley, a Granadine Morisco noble, best expressed this view in a memorial sent to Granadian authorities. His main argument against Philip II's decree was straightforward: Spain, and Christendom in general, was essentially diverse, made up of different nations and kingdoms. The Moriscos were yet another one of these nations. They dressed differently, spoke Arabic, and retained certain distinctive rites and ceremonies, but this was nothing unusual on the Iberian Peninsula. Not all inhabitants of Spain spoke Castilian, the language that was being imposed on the Moriscos, not everyone dressed after the Castilian fashion, and not all shared the same public rituals. Moriscos, he claimed, were Spaniards and Christians in different guise and speaking a different language. What should matter above all to the royal and local authorities were not these outward manifestations of cultural diversity but the fact that Moriscos were Christians and the king's most loyal subjects, who had not risen in rebellion since the conquest of Granada in 1492. The root of discontent, Muley observed, was the fact that, despite being Christians born in Spain, the Moriscos were denied the rights given to Catalans, Valencians, Galicians, or Cantabrians. The implications of his petition were also perfectly clear: the Moriscos should be integrated into the great Spanish family on their own terms, as a nation, their distinctiveness respected within a monarchy founded upon the acceptance of diversity.[88]

Muley's petitions did not make an impression on the Spanish authorities, who proceeded with the implementation of the de-Islamization decree. Their intransigence in turn convinced the Moriscos that they had the right to resist, and during the first months of 1568 they held a series of clandestine meetings to plot a general rebellion of the old kingdom of Granada. After several failed attempts, the end result was a military conflict known as the War of the Alpujarras (1568–1570), the most important in the peninsula since the 1520s. It took a large army led by Don Juan de Austria, Philip II's half-brother and the victor of the battle of Lepanto against the Ottoman navy, to finally defeat the rebels.[89] The course of the conflict also revealed the profound hatred between the Morisco and Christian communities. All contemporary observers reported horrific atrocities against populations of both communities, the use of rape as a weapon of war, the burning of churches and mosques, and the murder of parish priests and imams. The insurrection and the War of the Alpujarras also appeared to reveal three important facts: the solidarity between the various Morisco communities in the different Spanish kingdoms and regions; the belief that the Morisco predicament, and their fate, was inextricable from the political and military conflicts in the Mediterranean; and, finally, the growing divisions among Moriscos themselves, between those who were integrated in Christian-Spanish society and others who insisted on the existence of and the need to protect a distinct and autonomous Morisco community.

The rebels were defeated toward the end of 1570, and by early 1571 Philip II ordered the resettlement of Granadine Moriscos throughout the territories of the crown of Castile. The intention was clear: to break Morisco solidarity, integrate the greatest possible number into Christian cities and towns, force them to speak Castilian, make them abandon their traditions and customs, improve their religious education, and turn them into individuals. In short, it was an attempt at forceful assimilation.[90] The Alpujarras revolt also created profound divisions among the Moriscos themselves. In the first place, the Granadine Morisco elite placed itself virtually *en bloc* at the service of the monarchy to defeat the rebels and even transported many Moriscos into exile. Although their exact number is not known—and based on the surviving record they may not have been very numerous—Castilian Moriscos served in the Spanish army that defeated the Morisco rebels, and more significantly, these Castilian Moriscos increasingly claimed a different status from the rest. After the 1570s, Castilian Moriscos began demanding that they not be treated or referred to as Moriscos, since they considered themselves Christians in every sense and even argued that no Granadine Moriscos should be resettled in their towns or neighborhoods, lest all of them be tarred with the same brush. They claimed that they desired to be part of Christian Spanish society, not the Morisco community.[91] The clearest evidence of these internal divisions comes from a priest of Morisco origin, Francisco de Torrijos, who was asked whether those Moriscos who had not taken part in the revolt should be pardoned. He responded in a memorial of 1580 that such a pardon would be unwarranted because all of them had taken part in the initial resistance to the royal decrees and because ultimately they were all "of one nation, of one name and one opinion."[92]

Some members of the Morisco elite meanwhile persisted with their efforts to maintain their own identity as a distinct community.

From the 1580s on they followed in the footsteps of Núñez Muley, who had claimed that the Moriscos were entitled to preserve their customs as much as any Christian community in Spain, but they changed their strategy. They would shun rebellion but wage a cultural struggle to inscribe their history and demographic origins within the political and genetic history of Christian Spain. Their central argument was that they shared a history and a *gens* with other Spaniards, and therefore theirs was not the history of "others" but part of the history of Spain and Spaniards.[93]

A series of archeological discoveries in the city of Granada shed light on these initiatives to vindicate the Moriscos as one of the original nations of Spain.[94] The first discovery was in 1588, during excavations underneath a minaret of the old mosque, which was to be the site of the new cathedral. A group of workers discovered a chest containing what appeared to be ancient parchments with text in Latin, Arabic, and Castilian, ostensibly from the time of the Emperor Nero (37–68). Discovered alongside it were several human remains, bones and ashes, which were said to have belonged to Saint Stephen, and some fabrics allegedly once owned by the Virgin Mary. In 1595 there was another discovery, of 22 lead fragments or books, in an area close to the city, a hill known as Valparaíso and re-baptized by the Granadines as Sacromonte (Holy Mountain). The books contained texts written in Arabic on many different subjects: the annunciation of the new Christian religion by the Virgin and Christian doctrines alloyed with Islamic elements (no references to the Holy Trinity, the divine nature of Christ, or the power of sacred images). The books claimed that Saint James, one of Jesus's apostles, had indeed preached in Spain and that human remains found nearby belonged to the first Christian martyrs in the Iberian Peninsula: They were all Arabs who had accompanied the apostle and been converted by him (including Cecilio, identified as the first bishop of Granada).

These discoveries had an immediate impact. To be sure, scholars were first incredulous. Several of those commissioned to report on the findings by the ecclesiastical authorities immediately raised concerns about these "crude" fables and falsities, modern forgeries, and thought they were probably the work of Moriscos themselves. Rumor had it that Alonso del Castillo and Miguel de Luna—two medical doctors trained at the University of Granada, official Arabic translators, and well integrated into society—were behind these falsifications.[95] Yet many others, not only Granadines but also writers and civil and religious authorities, accepted these discoveries as authentic. The ecclesiastical and secular authorities of Granada interpreted them as evidence that the city had played a key role in the history of Christianity in Spain, which conferred on Granada a clear primacy over other cities.[96] For others, these texts appeared to show that Castilian had been the original language of Spain and the first Spaniards. This proved the unity and continuity over time of the Spanish community.[97] The Jesuit of Jewish ancestry Jerónimo Román de la Higuera drew similar lessons. He was the author of the false historical chronicles that purported to demonstrate the antiquity of Spain and the Spanish and the presence of Jews and Arabs among the first communities that would eventually coalesce to form the great Spanish family.[98] The impact of these discoveries was so great, and their advocates so numerous among both Moriscos and Christians, that neither the royal authorities nor Rome dared to pronounce definitively on the subject of their authenticity until nearly a century later, when the Vatican declared them fraudulent in 1682.

Miguel de Luna, one of the suspected authors of these forgeries, was also the author of one of the great best sellers of the day, *The True History of the King Don Rodrigo, Which Treats of the Loss of Spain and Her Conquest by Miramamolín Almanzor.*[99] The aim of Luna's *True History* was fairly clear: to assign the Muslim invaders, and by extension their descendants, an important role in the political and demographic regeneration of Spain. The Visigothic elite were portrayed as cultural, religious, and political degenerates. Only their demise, along with the death and overthrow of the king, would pave the way for Spain's regeneration. Luna's plot was not so different from Christian histories of the Reconquista, though in Luna's version the regeneration is initiated not by the leaders of the Christian resistance but by the Iberian Muslim rulers invariably depicted as wise, educated, and enterprising. They had preserved the unity of the peninsula—and were probably the only ones who could truly reunite the Iberian Peninsula.[100]

Luna's other, more important purpose in his *True History* was to situate Muslims as one of the original communities of the peninsula. The second part of the book opens with a paean to Spain, which

Luna claims had been written by Muza, the ruler of Al-Andalus. Like similar panegyrics, it describes Spain as a quasi-paradisiacal land, with natural qualities perfectly suited to human life. But this is the only point of agreement with Christian-authored encomia. In Luna's version, Spain was from the very beginning a land inhabited by several nations, each with its own language. Luna's implication was that when Arabs occupied the peninsula they imposed themselves over not a single nation, as Christian historians had asserted, but various different ones. Before and after the arrival of the Arabs, these nations continued to change and evolve. They mutually influenced one another and were constantly getting reconstituted. Luna further insisted that Muslim Arabs were part of the biological fabric of the Spanish community. In the first part of his work Luna observed that to proceed with the conquest and colonization of the peninsula, the invaders' chieftains promoted conversion to Islam and intermarriage with Christian elites. Luna claimed that many men and women accepted this bargain. They married into the new ruling caste and became Muslims.[101] Although this narrative of the demographic history of the Iberian Peninsula did not modify the official version already discussed, it proved useful to many who opposed the purity-of-blood statutes. This group included Salucio—who explicitly referred to Luna's work when he argued that all Spaniards had Moorish or Jewish ancestry—but also many who wished to show that the history of Spaniards as a nation was more complex and less pure than earlier maintained.[102]

When the lead books of Granada were discovered and Luna's work published, attitudes toward Moriscos in Spain were beginning to change. In short, the experiment of integrating into Spanish society while preserving a collective identity as Moriscos was coming to an end. After the War of the Alpujarras, in the early 1580s, a number of writers began to insist that coexistence was impossible among people with different religious beliefs, political loyalties, and demographic origins in the same territory. It was indeed the case that following the defeat of the Granadan revolt, some civil and religious authorities first ventured the opinion that it was necessary to devise a final solution to the Morisco problem, which could only mean their expulsion.

At least initially, the debate on the Moriscos was contained within royal institutions, but after 1604 it became a public debate. The choices were clear: on the one hand, some believed that Moriscos were Christians and subjects of the king, regardless of the errors of their ways and ignorance. Therefore the king was obliged to protect them and devise policies that would ensure their total conversion and hispanization.[103] Yet by this time the majority of those engaged with the issue in state institutions were of the opinion that the only solution was the expulsion of all, or some, of the Moriscos. Philip III finally pursued this option on April 19, 1609.[104] The decision to expel all Moriscos may have been the result of a particular confluence of political circumstances. Yet whatever the case, by the first decade of the 1600s, a majority of Spaniards were convinced that it was impossible to hispanize and Christianize the Moriscos or persuade them to abandon their distinct, collective identity in order to integrate into the Spanish community as individuals. This conviction is evident in all the criticisms directed at Moriscos. They kept themselves apart from other Spaniards—still dreaming that instead of integration into Spanish society, they could achieve the Islamization of Spain.

The outcome, one that modern scholars view as the first ethnic cleansing in European history, was the expulsion from the Iberian Peninsula, often under tragic conditions, of nearly 300,000 individuals, young and old, women and men, and all of them officially Christian. The majority came from territories of the crown of Aragon (some 180,000) and the rest from Castile and Granada. The edicts ordering the expulsion, implemented regionally from 1609 to 1614, were intended to assure Spaniards that the country and its inhabitants would be saved. Three reasons in particular were given for such a dramatic course of action: Moriscos' resistance to genuine conversion, their rebellion and crimes against Spanish authorities and Christians, and their incessant conspiring with foreign powers, especially the Ottomans. The royal decree to expel the Moriscos from Andalusia read, "Not only have they failed to observe and comply with the obligations of our holy Faith, but have always shown aversion to it, with great contempt for, and offense to God our lord."[105]

An unknown number of Moriscos escaped the expulsion and returned legally or otherwise to the Iberian Peninsula, but at least by the 1630s, Spaniards no longer preoccupied themselves with the Morisco question.[106] Muslims were still a source of anxiety, but they were now external enemies—the Turks and the Barbary pirates—and not internal ones. Spanish writers continued to debate the influence of Moriscos in the history of Spain, but this became a marginal concern, and few were troubled by thoughts of the presence of Muslim blood in the Spanish body from the 1620s onward. To be sure, some authors still saw Andalusia as a region "Arabized, or Islamized" in multiple ways, yet, in contrast to the Jewish case, Spaniards do not appear to have made the leap, at least not in the seventeenth century, toward a racialist discourse about Muslims.[107] The Arab and the Morisco came to be considered as something extraneous and foreign to the Spanish, and so it was believed that the expulsion of the Moriscos had been the final act—the definitive end of the process of regeneration and thorough hispanization of Spain.[108]

4

The Others Without

Moriscos and conversos were not the only "others" that Spanish society had to comprehend and consider for assimilation in the great Spanish family. From the early sixteenth century, two other populations, or nations, as Spanish authors tended to refer to them, were Indians—the natives of the Americas—and Africans. To be sure, America—the Indies or the New World—was an integral part of Spain for Spaniards. Those who emigrated to or were born in America were both legally and socially accepted as compatriots. The problem, and the subject of heated debate throughout the period, was the Indians' and Africans' place in the formation of Spanish society in the Americas and how far they should factor into the ongoing elaboration of the concept of Spanishness.

The great debate of the day was over which of the king's subjects on the peninsula and in America could be part of Spanish society and considered Spaniards, whether in a legal or practical sense. From a legal perspective, the matter appeared fairly straightforward: all free and Catholic subjects, born in Spanish lands, were entitled to rights and privileges and might in principle be considered Spaniards. To be sure, in the peninsula the purity-of-blood statutes meant that certain rights and privileges were denied to the descendants of Jews and Muslims. In America the situation was rather more complicated, precisely due to the presence of two populations, subjects of the king and living under Spanish laws yet whose origins and complexion were clearly at variance with those of the Spanish settlers.

The first of these populations or nations, the true natives of America, were the Indians. They were by far the majority of the American population, but they also predominated in politics and culture and thus became the object of particular attention and debate among Spaniards. As we will see, Spaniards' image of and relations with the inhabitants of the Americas changed over the sixteenth century, but legally, starting in the mid-sixteenth century, the vast majority of Indians under Spanish sovereignty were considered free subjects, like the rest of Spaniards, and, as such, an integral part of the monarchy. The historian Serge Gruzinski has drawn attention to what seems to have been a unique phenomenon in the history of European empires in the Americas: "Everywhere except Castilian America, Amerindians were inevitably marginalized, excluded or exterminated."[1]

Yet another demographic group in the Americas further complicated the ideological equation of how to structure Spanish society and notions of "nation and race": the hundreds of thousands of Africans, the vast majority of them slaves or descendants of slaves. In the first decades of Spanish dominion in the Americas, the authorities limited themselves to legislation on the number of slaves, their roles, and their public activity. However, the growing presence of free Africans and numerous "mulattos," descendants of Spaniards and Africans—many of whom were also free—radically altered the situation. From at least the late 1500s, these free Africans were also at once subjects of the king, subject to the same laws, officially Catholic, members of artisanal crafts, and, beginning in the 1600s, the mainstay of the proliferating militias in all parts of the continent. In this context, albeit not to the same extent as the Indians, Africans were gradually encompassed within the debate on the nation, the rights of its members in the Americas, and their potential role in the construction of a new society under the direction of the Spanish minority. Like the Amerindians, Africans became a focus of interest. Various authors speculated about their origins, the causes or reasons for their physical differences, the relation between physical aspects and mental characteristics, and the reasons why Africans comprised the great majority of slaves in the Americas.

The presence of these non-European nations in a Spanish dominion could not help but intrude into debates over the

Spanishness of the king's subjects. In the peninsula, all were considered Spanish, albeit with rights conditioned on purity of blood. In the Americas, these rights were apportioned based on a hierarchy of distinct and separate nations. The Creoles and other Spaniards, regardless of wealth or social status, were superior to the Indians, categorically, even including the indigenous elites, all of whom were treated as subalterns, or "those which are inferior or subordinate to another thing."[2] The Africans, meanwhile, whether slave or free and regardless of occupation or relative wealth, occupied the bottom rung of the hierarchy of nations.

However, this configuration of American society did not develop without intense debate within Spain itself. These debates questioned the nature and consequences of the Spanish conquest of America but also the origins of different peoples, the geographic conditions in the New World, the physical and mental characteristics of its inhabitants, and the legitimacy of slavery. These were similar to questions Spaniards had previously asked about themselves or about Moriscos and conversos in the peninsula. In this case, too, they were interested in integrating all the nations of the Americas into the great Spanish family and in the most desirable fashion—whether through acculturation (as in the case of the hispanized conversos and Moriscos on the peninsula) or biological mixing. For, unlike in the Iberian Peninsula, contemporary Spaniards in the Americas were fully aware of the existence of numerous individuals of mixed blood—the product of marriages (in very few cases) and extramarital sexual relations (in the majority of cases) primarily between Spanish or Creole men and Indian and African women. The presence of these mestizos certainly entered into the debate over who should be considered Spanish.

The question of Spanish attitudes toward and treatment of the Indians and Africans in America had preoccupied historians for decades. The traditional narrative told of Spaniards' efforts to civilize, as they saw it, and Christianize the Indians and Africans but at the same time insisted that from the beginning of the conquest and settlement of the Americas, the Spanish exhibited no racialist prejudices. If anything distinguished the Spaniards from their European counterparts, it was their unscrupulous mixing with the Indians and Africans and their genuine desire to integrate both into their society.

In recent years, two American historians, experts on the racial systems created in regions colonized by the English, have drawn attention to the alleged peculiarities of the Spanish empire in America and the great contrast between it and other imperial systems. George Fredrickson has singled out Spain as the only European empire that did not discriminate racially against its conquered peoples, all of whom played some role, sociologically and legally, in the construction of the Spanish race and nation. Such practices are in stark contrast to the peninsula, he argues, where Spaniards discriminated against the descendants of Jews and Muslims based on theories about the purity of the Spanish race. In his words, "Spain and Portugal were in the forefront of European racism or protoracism in their discrimination against converted Jews and Muslims, [while in] the Iberian colonies manifested a greater acceptance of intermarriage and more fluidity of racial categories and identities than the colonies of other European nations."[3] Compared with the English, for whom racial intermingling "was ideologically repugnant," the Spaniards, Gary Nash has also suggested, influenced by long experience of "incessant contact with dark-skinned Muslims" on the peninsula, partook in "continuous racial blending" in the Americas, which resulted in "a mingled civilization. With no prohibitions against interracial contact and interracial marriage, Spanish, African, and Indian people became extensively intermixed."[4]

More recently, historians of Spain and Spanish America have questioned this interpretation. They insist that there were no significant differences between Spanish attitudes on the peninsula and in the colonies and that both the attitudes toward and discourses about Amerindians and Africans on both sides of the Spanish Atlantic were fully and self-consciously racist. On the peninsula, the racism directed against Jews and Muslims had been couched in religious language, while in America openly racist discourses and practices developed toward Indians and Africans.[5] In the words of the historian Jorge Cañizares-Esguerra, Spaniards became pioneers in the elaboration of a racist discourse, precisely because of their experience in the Americas. The "science of race," Cañizares-Esguerra argues in one of the most cited articles on the subject, "with its emphasis on biological determinism, its focus on the body as the site of behavioral-cultural variations, and its obsession with creating homogenizing and essentializing categories, was first articulated in colonial Spanish America in the seventeenth century, not in nineteenth-century Europe." This "scientific racism" was firmly grounded in the "sciences of the day, astrology and Hippocratic-Galenic physiology."[6]

Both interpretations assume too much coherence and consistency in the theories and attitudes of sixteenth- and seventeenth-century Spaniards. Many contradictory theories about human diversity and the human constitution continued to coexist throughout this period. Many turned to climate theory and environmental arguments to explain the different physical and mental characteristics of non-European peoples. Others continued to argue against the utility of such explanations and to insist that the characteristics of different peoples were intrinsic to each one of the human lineages. Instead of analyzing local conditions, they proposed, one should focus on the origins of each people. Many believed that, although the physical characteristics of each lineage were permanent, the same was not true of mental or intellectual traits, which were the product of education, customs, and government. Yet others were adamant that not all members of a single lineage were equal. Distinctions should be made, as they were among Europeans, between the nobility and the people, and each social group should be treated according to its station. Finally, some also distinguished between different Indian nations. What seems beyond doubt, Anthony Pagden has written, is that in Europe, "most of the classificatory schemes dreamt up before 1700 were not in any obvious modern sense 'racial.'"[7]

Spaniards did not possess a clear and coherent vision of humanity as divided into radically distinct races. This was true from the earliest contacts with Jews, Muslims, Indians, and Africans. If such a theory had been deeply internalized, it would have settled unequivocally the matter of who was Spanish and who could enjoy the rights associated with being Spanish. Nevertheless, a study of the debates in the Spanish world on the Indians, Africans, mestizos, and mulattos does support the conclusion that in the specific context of the Indies it is possible to speak of a gradual emergence of what we could designate as a proto-racialist discourse. However, the adoption of this discourse was not a linear process and depended on more than scholarly debates and theories. With regard to Indians and Africans, Spaniards were concerned not solely with unraveling the natural history of humanity and its diverse nations but also with the more immediate question of what kind of society they were constructing: one based on the inclusion of all those born in Spanish territories regardless of ancestry or one based on a narrow and exclusive definition of Spanishness.

"The greatest event since the creation of the world, apart from the incarnation and death of the creator himself, is the discovery of the Indies," proclaimed Francisco López de Gómara in the epistle dedicating his history of the Indies to Emperor Charles V.[8] The great Portuguese poet Luiz de Camões echoed these sentiments. He celebrated the explorations, voyages, and conquests of his compatriots in one of the most influential texts of the early modern period, *The Lusiads*, which was an ode to the history of his homeland and Portuguese discoveries.[9] The most influential historian of the early modern period, Juan de Mariana, also eulogized Iberian exploits. For him the year 1492 was unparalleled in the history of Spain, encompassing the conquest of Granada and the expulsion of the Jews as well as the "most memorable enterprise, the source of the greatest honor and profit ever undertaken in Spain . . . the discovery of the Western Indies, which as a result of their greatness are called the New World; a wondrous thing, among so many centuries reserved for this age," and this nation.[10]

Sixteenth- and seventeenth-century Spaniards celebrated their conquests in the Americas, or the Indies as they were called at the time, and other milestones of the Spanish monarchy's extraordinary territorial expansion since 1492. These included the deeds of Ferdinand Magellan, a Portuguese native in the service of the Spanish monarch Charles I, who attempted the first successful circumnavigation of the globe—eventually completed by Juan Sebastián Elcano, a Spanish sailor—and the claim of sovereignty over the Philippines in the 1560s. The union with Portugal in 1580 brought many more territories into the Spanish orbit: Brazil, on the American continent, but also colonies in sub-Saharan Africa and Asia. By the mid-1500s, Europeans were aware that Spanish and Portuguese explorations and conquests had ushered in the first period of globalization in the history of humanity.[11] "All mortals," wrote the French writer Louis Le Roy in 1577, "can now exchange commodities with one another and provide for each other's dearth, like residents of one city and one republic of the world."[12] Spain around this time appeared outwardly as a nation intensely proud of its feats of exploration and settlement of the new overseas territories. Spaniards thought of themselves as members of a nation chosen by God to remake the world in its primeval unity. The Spanish and Portuguese, as Portuguese friar Paulo Ferrer told Juan de Mariana, were helping to usher in that "glorious age promised by the heavens" in which the entire world will be governed by "one Monarch, one Empire, one Sword."[13]

This glorification of Spain and its conquests obscured the frequent irresolution, chaos, and confusion of the imperial enterprise. Starting in the mid-1500s, the royal propagandists aimed to give the impression that the objective had been clear from the outset: to create a global empire with the purpose of spreading Christianity to every corner of the earth. The reality was far more haphazard. Spanish overseas expansion was initially driven by a desire to create a new commercial route between Europe and the spice-producing regions of Asia, not to create an empire. The Portuguese already dominated the known route that traced the coastline of the African continent to Asia—the so-called eastern route. So Columbus proposed to Isabel and Ferdinand the opening of a western route that would allow them to reach Asia by crossing the Atlantic. He famously embarked on the first of his voyages in late summer of 1492, and by October, Columbus and his crew made landfall in a group of islands they believed to be close to the Asian mainland. Columbus returned to Spain with a handful of enslaved natives of the islands, various gold objects, and other gifts for the monarchs. This evidence convinced Ferdinand and Isabel to approach Pope Alexander, the supreme spiritual authority of Christendom, to legitimize their enterprise. The result was a papal bull *Inter caetera* (May 4, 1493), a diplomatic victory for the Spaniards that would resonate through the centuries. Alexander recognized Isabel and Ferdinand's, and their descendants', rights of sovereignty over all the lands and peoples discovered in the course of these exploratory voyages and monopoly over the new commercial route. However, he also imposed on the Spanish rulers an onerous responsibility: the obligation to convert all of the gentile and pagan peoples they encountered, to educate them sufficiently for them to become good Christians, and to care for and protect them against the aggression of rapacious explorers.[14]

The conversion of peoples encountered by the Spanish in these first, commercially motivated forays appeared desirable and eminently practical. "So far in these islands no monstrous men have been found as many had predicted," Columbus wrote on his first return voyage to Spain, "but rather these people are all wonderfully pliable."[15] If these were the first impressions of Caribbean islands inhabitants, however, they changed in subsequent voyages. Relations with the native population disintegrated rapidly and completely because of Spaniards' treatment of the natives in the first decades of overseas expansion. The conduct of the first colonists was a far cry from the sentiments expressed in the papal bull, and the exploitation of the natives included wholesale enslavement, the destruction of indigenous societies, untold violence, torture, and rape.

Justifying these practices required a change in laws as well as opinions of those who claimed knowledge of the natives. The vision of natural innocence conveyed by Columbus evaporated quickly and deferred to descriptions of the Indians as depraved, inveterate idolaters, polygamists, and sodomites, cruel to their own kind and, in some cases, cannibals. In the early stages of the expansion, the only intellectual authority that seemed useful in making sense of these peoples was Aristotle and his theories on natural slavery. The majority of Spaniards who reflected on the American peoples in this opening phase believed that Amerindians did not "have a rational soul, but were at best one step above apes or monkeys," perfect examples of Aristotle's "slaves by nature"—individuals destined from birth "to be ruled," bought, and sold by civilized nations.[16] They were portrayed as barbarians and savages in every sense, and according to Dominican Fray Tomás Ortiz, in a 1525 report to the emperor Charles: "like asses, dull-witted, sluggish, ignorant . . . ; in sum, God never created a people so immersed in vice and bestiality, with no hint of excellence or good government."[17]

Spanish colonists' practices in these first years of expansion, and the vision of the Indian as a slave by nature, came under attack beginning in the 1510s because of two related processes. First, some Spaniards, especially theologians, questioned the legitimacy of the conquest itself and, even more urgently, the colonizers' treatment of the Indians.[18] The first public outcry happened in Santo Domingo in 1511, when the Franciscan Antonio de Montesinos accused colonists on the island of Hispaniola of cruelty. He alleged that they treated natives not only as slaves but animals and subjected them to such extremes of violence that they endangered the expansion of Catholicism and even the Spanish presence in the New World. Montesinos and his supporters were aware of the demographic catastrophe that had followed the Spanish arrival in the New World and that would result in many millions of deaths among the natives. The main cause of this demographic tragedy was the introduction of illnesses against which native populations had no immunity, but the majority of observers at the time, at least those inclined to take a critical view, were convinced that the main responsibility for this catastrophe was the shock of extreme violence perpetrated by Spanish conquistadors.[19]

These critics not only objected to the violence of the conquest but also asserted that it was grounded in false claims and rights as well as a deceptive and unchristian view of Amerindians. The central argument here was that neither the Pope nor the Emperor nor any other ecclesiastical or secular authority in Europe had any right to grant exclusive privileges of exploration and colonization to the Spanish or to any other nation or monarch. According to the University of Salamanca professor and Dominican friar Francisco de Vitoria, no one had the right to interfere in the internal affairs of other communities, to say nothing of stripping them of their lands and property. His theory was founded on the idea that all humans, regardless of their level of development, their beliefs, or even their crimes and savage customs, had certain natural, inalienable rights (to property, life, the formation of societies, and self-government). In Vitoria's words, "the barbarians undoubtedly possessed true dominion" over their lands and persons, and "they could not be robbed of their property, either as private citizens or as princes." Vitoria and others concluded that Spaniards could not enslave the Indians, compel them to work for the conquerors or colonizers, or forcibly convert them to Catholicism.

An equally grave accusation was that the colonists and royal authorities had created or encouraged a false image of the indigenous peoples—as cannibals, savages, and natural slaves—so as to justify their use of extreme violence and natives' wholesale enslavement. The alternative proposed by these critics of the conquest was a return to the image of the Indian as a noble savage, who, while he may lack the customary European trappings of civilization, possessed the necessary intellectual capacity to acquire them. The Indians were divine creatures living outside the civilized order, but there was no reason to believe that they were incapable of shedding this Aristotelian natural state—in which they were "society-less creatures (who) had cut themselves off from the means which God had granted to every man."[20] As Vitoria saw it, the Indians may appear "insensate and slow-witted" to Spanish observers, but these were not intrinsic or immutable qualities. They were the result of "their evil and barbarous education," something equally true of many Spanish peasants who also seemed "little different from brute animals."[21]

Second, another series of developments shifted the course of Spanish expansion, just as the debate over approaches to the native populations in America was intensifying (1519–1535): Spaniards encountered impressive and complex civilizations on the American mainland, the Mexica in the north and the Inka in the south. They realized that it was no longer possible to speak of natives of the New World as simple savages. This was especially true as they received news of Mexico, especially Hernán Cortés' letters to inform Emperor Charles about his campaigns and dealings with the Mexica and other indigenous nations. These were no longer descriptions of unsophisticated tribesmen without culture—naked, uncivilized, and perhaps even lacking a coherent language. The Mexica formed a complex and hierarchical society and possessed a highly developed culture and a religion—a false one, to be sure, whose rituals, such as human sacrifice, induced horror and revulsion among Spaniards, yet a strongly institutionalized religion nonetheless. Although their monarchy seemed more like tyranny to Spaniards, the Mexica had established a political, judicial, and administrative system that seemed equally complex.[22] These views were later corroborated by Pizarro and his men and by other conquistadors who described their struggles against the equally impressive and, as it turned out, fabulously wealthy Inka Empire in South America.

The crown was quick to grasp that the existence of the Mexica, and later the Inka, altered the cultural and political landscape in the Americas and demanded a reassessment of attitudes and relations with indigenous peoples.[23] Royal authorities were also aware that reports of violence during the conquest were damaging Spain's reputation in Europe and were thus more sensitive to pressure from missionaries and theologians to start an official inquiry. They wanted to resolve the matter in a series of debates between defenders of the crown's rights and those who claimed to be protectors of the Indians, with Bartolomé de las Casas foremost among them. The most famous of these debates took place in Valladolid from 1550 to 1551, with arguments presented by Las Casas in favor of Indians' liberty and his opponent, Juan Ginés de Sepúlveda, humanist and Aristotelian scholar. He defended the crown's interests and the idea that the wars of conquest against the Indians should be seen as just wars, vindicated by the crimes against nature and abominable customs of the conquered.[24]

Because of these critiques, measures were implemented in the 1530s that seemed to suggest that the accumulated negative perceptions of the natives, and the violent treatment they had been subjected to until then, would soon disappear. In 1536 Pope Paul III declared that Indians were fully human, and in 1542 the monarchy officially rescinded all previous decrees that had allowed the indiscriminate enslavement of Indians. Henceforth only Indians living in specific regions could be legitimately enslaved—those designated as savages or barbarians, but in reality all those who resisted Spanish domination (and in later decades even these distinctions were abolished, leaving in place the right to enslave Indians identified as *Barbaros* outside the Spanish jurisdiction). Laws regulating forced labor and new territorial incursions accompanied the prohibition of Indian slavery and were all part of a legislative process of juridical and political stabilization that culminated with the publication of the "Ordinances for the Discovery, Settlement, and Pacification of the Indies," issued by Philip II in July 1573. There were to be no new campaigns of exploration without prior approval from the royal authorities, and officials and colonists were enjoined to "forego the word conquest, using instead pacification and settlement," to ensure that the Indians were never "assaulted, or aggrieved."[25]

The monarchy, again responding to the ideas and concerns voiced by Las Casas and his supporters, also assigned native communities a clear legal status within the monarchy, which resulted in the creation of two distinct republics or commonwealths in the Americas—the Republic of the Spaniards and the Republic of the Indians. The natives thus officially became subjects of the Spanish king but governed and administered by their own authorities and officials and in theory residing in *pueblos de indios* (Indian towns). In order to protect the Indians, they separated the two communities as much as possible and stipulated that Spaniards may not live in Indian towns, with the exception of missionaries entrusted with their conversion. It was nevertheless assumed that once the Indians were civilized and hispanized, they could live alongside Spaniards in the American cities, still under the protection of their own magistrates but with full recourse to the royal institutions and authorities.[26] The monarchy also created a number of bodies principally charged with the protection of Indians, a task also entrusted to viceroys, the highest public authorities in the Americas. According to Juan de Solórzano Pereira, the greatest seventeenth-century expert on Indian affairs, all of these measures were evidence that the Spanish monarchs had always intended that "the Indians should be safeguarded and maintained in their complete liberty, and full and free administration of their property, like all the rest of your vassals in other Kingdoms."[27]

The central issue after 1542 was not the determination of whether the Indians were free vassals, however. Legally, there was no doubt on that point. Rather, the central issue was the determination of what kind of vassals Indians were, their characteristics, and whether Indians were all members of one lineage or many distinct lineages and nations. This question was largely behind the debates on conquest and the laws implemented, as participants weighed the prospect of integrating Indians into the society Spaniards were creating in the Americas. In order to pose this question, however, it was first necessary to construct a distinct image of the Indian and the Indian nation or lineage, not so much to justify keeping the Indians separate but to determine the means necessary for their integration into the monarchy as subjects with full rights.

As was true after the conquest of Granada in 1492, Spaniards had no problem distinguishing between the bulk of the indigenous population and the elite, not only among the Mexica and the Inka but also other Indian nations, such as the Tlaxcalans and the Maya. After all, just years before, the Morisco elite had been successfully integrated into Spanish society on the peninsula. Although the indigenous elite in the Indies were forbidden from performing their religious functions, the crown allowed them to keep their status, property, and power within the native community as well as the hereditary nature of their titles, offices, and wealth. The laws and guidelines for the government of the Indies decreed that children, and particularly the children of indigenous elites, should be sent to school where they would learn to read, write, and speak Castilian. The monarchy, through religious orders, also supported the creation of colleges of higher education for the instruction of the sons of elites. At least in Mexico, an order of knighthood was created especially for the indigenous elite, and they were allowed to attend institutions of higher education.[28] Also mirroring the case of Granada, some members of the indigenous nobility married Spaniards, though such unions were rare, especially after the late 1500s.

There was some debate about whether the Indian elite should be allowed to play an even more important role in the American societies, no longer merely as intermediaries between Spaniards and native peoples but also as eligible candidates for public offices in the Republic of the Spaniards—in the church or high courts or as provincial governors and urban magistrates. The Mexican-born Jesuit Juan Zapata y Sandoval made this case, relying on the very logic used in the peninsula. "Because it has been more than ninety years since they had been converted to the faith," he claimed, and given their equally great knowledge and preparation, the Indian elite should be preferred to the Spaniards because the former were natives of the land, while the Spaniards were "guests and foreigners."[29] In reality, however, not a single one among them, at least not in the 1500s and 1600s, occupied any office with authority over Spaniards.[30]

We cannot be sure why the monarchy and authorities in the Indies did not appoint members of the indigenous elite to posts with political or administrative authority outside the Republic of Indians, but it is quite likely that the majority of Spaniards were opposed to being governed by individuals who were not of the Spanish nation.[31] In accordance with the law, as individuals, the indigenous elites who lived in the cities with a Spanish majority had the right to become citizens of those cities, with the same rights—again, as individuals—enjoyed by Spaniards. We know, however, that the municipal ordinances explicitly denied these rights to Indians, Africans, and mixed-blood individuals.[32] The treatment of the indigenous elites seemed to indicate that Spanishness in the Americas, as had happened in the peninsula, would be an attribute reserved for only one community of individuals: those who shared an unambiguously Spanish lineage and ancestry.

Regarding the nonelite Indians, the new political climate created by the strident criticism of the violence of the conquest and the enslavement of the natives meant that after 1542, the most negative assessments of the indigenous Americas were marginalized, at least in public. Juan Ginés de Sepúlveda, humanist, Aristotelian scholar, and indisputably the most persistent critic of Bartolomé de las Casas, was untiring in his opposition, but he was not alone. In his written defense of the Spanish conquest of the Indies, a text countering the opinions of Las Casas and banned from publication in Castilian, Sepúlveda had argued that "they [Spaniards and Indians] are to one another as savage and cruel peoples are to the most benevolent; the prodigiously intemperate to the moderate and continent, and I am even tempted to say, as monkeys are to men."[33]

In contrast to this image of the Indian as naturally inferior, the alternative, momentarily triumphant view held that Amerindians' objectionable characteristics—their barbarism, evil customs, and religious beliefs—were simply the by-product of temporal circumstances, bad government, and especially American natives' isolation from other, civilized societies. Sixteenth-century Europeans, and certainly Spaniards, were conscious of the fact that geographical discoveries and advances in knowledge of their own time had surpassed the achievements of the illustrious Ancients.[34] Neither the Greeks nor the Romans had any inkling of the existence of America or the great diversity of climates, plants, animals, and humans.

Yet it was difficult to know what to make of these people because no one had been aware previously of their existence. Who were the inhabitants of the Americas, and in what ways did they resemble or differ from other, known peoples? Those who took on the task of answering this question did so from an analytical perspective that Anthony Pagden has named "the principle of attachment," which means an attempt to account for the new—the American—by rendering it similar to the known—the European.[35] There is indeed plenty of evidence of this approach in various analyses of Indians and reports on the Americas produced by the widest range of Spanish observers—missionaries, colonists, and religious and secular authorities. We might be even more precise and note that the Spanish applied the same theories on human origins and characteristics—of all humans, regardless of their region—to the Amerindians in these years that they had already applied to understand the origins of Europeans in general as well as Spaniards in particular.

Once again, Spaniards' starting point was a fundamental and irrefutable principle: all humans shared a common origin, and all descended from Adam and Eve. These newly discovered nations, Lopez de Gómara wrote, "are like us, aside from their color, for otherwise they would be beasts and monsters, and would not, as they surely do, emanate from Adam."[36] The Italian Alessandro Geraldini, a subject of Charles I of Spain and bishop of Santo Domingo, where he would die in 1525, also insisted on this diversity among humans but on their common origin as well: "Some peoples are torpid; others work with sublime ingenuity; some are warlike; and some are more inclined toward zealously cultivating their talents; others are drawn to commerce; [yet] others to agriculture. . . . Some, more distant from the sun, are whiter, blond haired and blue eyed; others, in greater proximity to the solar heat, are tawnier, with completely black eyes and hair." All were, indisputably, human.[37]

It has been argued that in the Americas, climate theory was key in constructing a racialist discourse of the Indians, who were portrayed as inferior beings.[38] The problem with this explanation, as many contemporaries tirelessly pointed out, is that this purported "science" was rather imprecise, and the extent or nature of climatic influence was not easy to determine. Perhaps climate explained some physical features (skin color, for example), but it could not explain everything. That much was clear to most observers at this time. More to the point, although some believed that the prevailing natural conditions in the Americas produced animals and humans of inferior quality in comparison with their European counterparts, many others—Creoles and peninsulars—maintained precisely the opposite. They claimed that America, or some of its regions, afforded perfect conditions for the development of various human families.[39]

The most compelling evidence against climate theory was that America included many different climate zones and yet inhabitants of different regions of the continent resembled one another. This led many observers to conclude that peoples' physical and mental characteristics were not entirely the product of the natural conditions of their region but were perhaps something intrinsic to every human family or lineage.[40] To glean these original characteristics and understand their development, it was first necessary to ascertain the origin, or the original lineage, of each nation rather than its physical location and understand the history of each nation from the time of its first settlement in the land that it now inhabited. Spaniards had privileged this interpretation to emphasize their own singular origins, which, in combination with the natural conditions on the Iberian Peninsula, good government, and the Christian religion, had resulted in their virtually perfect physical and mental constitution.

From the very beginning, the problem was identifying the origins of American inhabitants, since neither the Bible nor any other known text seemed to acknowledge the existence of this continent or its peoples. Many solutions were offered to this mystery. They ranged from claims that American natives were descended from "Moors" or "Jews" or "Spaniards" (some indeed argued that Americans were descendants of Tubal, like Spaniards themselves) or Northern European nations or Africans, when the continents were still joined. Others, in order to account for diverse American nations, postulated separate origins: while the ancestors of some indigenous groups had allegedly emigrated from Asia by crossing a passage that had once united the two continents, others descended from nations that had arrived from elsewhere, having crossed the Atlantic or the Pacific.[41]

It was impossible to be sure about these peoples' origins—and many were inclined to concur with José de Acosta's assertion that Americans descended from Asian populations—but all agreed that the first settlers did not possess a highly developed culture. In Acosta's words: "I believe that the New World and the West Indies have not been inhabited by men for very many thousands of years, that the first men who entered them were savage hunters rather than civilized folk, and that they came to the New World because they had strayed from their land or because they felt cramped and in need of seeking new lands." When they arrived in these new lands, they began to settle "little by little, with no more laws than a bit of natural instinct (and even that somewhat clouded) and at most a few customs left over from their original country." Although perhaps "they came from civilized and well-governed countries, it is not difficult to believe that they forgot everything in the course of a long time and little use."[42] There was nothing original in these explanations. If all humans had the same origin, the dispersal of the various lineages after the Tower of Babel resulted in the gradual removal of each family from the cradle of civilization, in most cases before they had acquired the customs of civilized men. The dispersion of many of these peoples, Boemus wrote, "was very rapid and occurred before . . . the children . . . had appreciated the customs and ways of life of their parents. This was the source of so many diversities and differences."[43]

These differences in customs between peoples separated from each other in ancient times led some to propose a classification of all human groups on earth. Their criteria were physical characteristics, the region they occupied, customs, manners, religious beliefs or lack thereof, technological development, degree of civilization (in other words, the development of hierarchically ordered political communities with organs of government and justice), education, dwellings, dress, and diet. Once again Acosta offered the most complete and systematic version of this classification.[44] The Europeans were the ideal against which to measure others, and in fact his starting point was the belief that all non-Europeans were barbarians, both as pagans and because "they depart from true reason and the common way of life." Not all barbarians were alike, however. As Acosta himself said, "some barbarians are far ahead of other barbarians," a notion that would explain the existence of complex societies among the Indians. Their position in the hierarchy of nations was thus determined by a number of particular characteristics—"incapacity," "savagery"—invariably signifying "how distant they are from the common practice of other men, and how little wisdom and rational thought they possess."

In the first category of barbarians, and closest to Europeans, were those who "do not depart greatly from true reason and the common way of life." These peoples had established stable governments, laws, fortified cities, commerce, magistrates, "and what is most important, the use and knowledge of letters." This category included "the Chinese, the Japanese and a good part of the eastern provinces of India, who were at some point reached by Asiatic and European culture." The second category of barbarians included those who, "although they have no knowledge of writing, or written laws, or the philosophical or civil science, do have their own magistrates, system of government, fixed and frequent assemblies in which they conduct their political administration . . . and a certain splendor in their religious worship; they have, in other words, their own way of human life." Among these would be "our Mexicans and Peruvians, whose empires, systems of government, laws and institutions the whole world may rightly admire." These nations, which also included the Araucanians and other minor kingdoms ruled by *caciques*, or lords, "are nevertheless removed from true reason and the habits proper to human kind." They live in cities, not as savages, and have laws, magistrates, and a certain understanding of justice. Yet they remain naturally inclined toward many "monstrous deviations" and should thus be permanently "under the authority of Christian princes and magistrates"—although they would be granted certain civil rights.

The final category of barbarians were "savages, akin to the beasts, who scarcely have any human feelings, without law, without rulers, without agreements, without magistrates or a fixed system of government, moving from place to place, and even when they settle down their abode is more like the caves of wild animals, or stables. . . ." In this group Acosta placed the natives of the Caribbean islands, said to be extremely cruel and given to cannibalism, as well as other American peoples such as the inhabitants of Florida, Brazil, the *Mosca* of modern-day Nicaragua, the population of the Moluccas and other Pacific islands, and the majority of the inhabitants of sub-Saharan Africa, or Ethiopia, as contemporary Europeans often referred to this region. "All these are hardly men, or only half-men, so it is best to teach them to become men, and instruct them like children."

An essential feature of this classification, however, was the belief that barbarians were capable of changing, that their backwardness was not a permanent condition but the result of their lack of education and isolation from the centers of civilization and true religion. Their customs and beliefs were temporary, corrigible defects. José de Acosta set the general tone in claiming that the barbarism of native peoples was not innate, or the product of "birth or climate, but rather an inveterate education, and customs not very different from beasts." If genuine efforts were made to civilize and educate them, even the most barbarous peoples would show improvement. The proof was Spain itself, where many individuals born in Cantabria, Asturias, or Galicia "are taken for uncouth yokels so long as they remain among their own countrymen; but once placed in the schools, or the royal court, or the markets [of the great cities], their admirable skill and ingenuity comes to the fore, and they leave all others behind."[45]

The conclusions drawn from this, and from similar theories, by various interested observers were fairly obvious. In the first place was the apparent coincidence of more or less common characteristics in every region of the Americas. With few exceptions, it was generally accepted that Indians were physically weak, or at any rate weaker than most other peoples, and ill-suited to the hard physical labor Spaniards required. They further noted that Indians had some physical shortcomings (an egg-shaped head, for instance), but it was also recognized that the majority of these were the result of cultural practices rather than natural defects. Spaniards generally believed that Indians were of an intermediate hue, neither black nor white but "tawny" or "olive." Until the seventeenth century, however, many still believed there were several types of Indians distinguished by their skin color and physical characteristics: natives of the tropics were shorter, Patagonians were taller, Quito region natives were white skinned, and River Plate natives more hazel colored. Some natives were as white as Spaniards, with straight dark hair and very rarely curly hair, like the African.[46]

More important were their character, customs, and social and cultural practices. It was widely believed that Indians practiced polygamy, suffered from sexual incontinence, and abused alcohol and drugs. Before Spaniards' arrival they were prone to committing horrendous crimes—sodomy, human sacrifice, and cannibalism—yet most observers were convinced that the majority of the more grievous crimes had all but disappeared and that many Indians had become true Christians. They were obedient and loyal to their masters, missionaries, and royal authorities.[47] Until at least the mid-1600s, this was the dominant view of the Indians, who were described as good-spirited and quick and eager to learn. The Indians could be improved, even though some intrinsic traits still meant they were mentally inferior to the Spaniards. In the opinion of the vast majority of observers they were lacking in reason—able to master the mechanical arts, for instance, but not humanistic occupations. They were meek and introverted, indifferent to public affairs, and uninterested in general or individual economic improvement.

This image of the Indians as a people in the process of becoming civilized under Spanish tutelage helps to explain their juridical status within the monarchy. Solórzano Pereira summarized it in his seminal work, the *Política indiana*, where he gathered a vast trove of pertinent information, from theories on the origins of the Indians, the condition of the various Indian nations, the actions of the Spaniards in the early days of the conquest and after 1540, and the numerous efforts made to protect, educate, civilize, and convert the natives to Christianity. He saw the Spanish monarchy following the footsteps of the Romans who in antiquity had played a similar civilizing role among "barbarous and cruel nations" in Europe. But even more important was his elucidation of Spanish laws, which assigned to the Indians the condition of "*miserables*," or "wretched ones," a people "with whom we naturally sympathize on account of their [low] estate, quality and hardships [they suffer]." This is what "we find in our Indians, for their humble, servile, and prostrate condition," even lower and more miserable than "the condition of the Blacks, and all the other Nations of the World."[48] Yet this was, once again, a temporary state: Spaniards would elevate them from this lowly condition. The Indians, Acosta had argued, are "slow-witted and infantile, and should be treated like children or women, or rather, like animals."[49]

From the mid-1600s some authors began to modify these theories in ways that foreshadowed the more profound changes of the eighteenth century. However, this is not to suggest that by the second half of the seventeenth century the Spaniards had elaborated an unambiguously racialist discourse about the Indians. The argument here is only that certain concepts and theories were beginning to acquire new meanings. These new concepts were in turn developed or modified in response to another controversial question, which seemed to proceed from assumptions already discussed: was there reason to believe that Indians had changed—more specifically, improved—in the more than a century of Spanish dominion? Few were able to justify the confidence shown by their sixteenth-century counterparts. Fray Benito de Peñalosa y Mondragón, the writer, to recall, who defended the pure origins of the Spaniards, was pessimistic. He pointed out that Indians were still full of vices more than a century after the conquest and liable to revert to their sinful idolatry. Crucially, "even today, more than one hundred years having passed since their discovery and conquest, nearly all of the Western Indians are incapable of [governing] even their own households and families" and thus even less apt to rule their own republics.[50]

No one was more closely identified with this new, gloomier outlook toward Indians than the Jesuit Bernabé Cobo, who, unlike Peñalosa, had resided for some time in America. Born in Lopera, Andalusia, Cobo migrated to the Americas in 1596 and eventually settled in Lima. He joined the Jesuit order in 1601 after spending time in various South American missions. He lived in Mexico from 1630 to 1650 before returning to Lima, where he died in 1657. Cobo's major work, *Historia del Nuevo Mundo (A History of the New World)*, was probably written in the 1640s but was not published until the late 1800s.[51] The significance of Cobo's *History* here is not so much what it revealed about American plants and animals (Cobo has been lauded as one of the great naturalists of the Indies) but what he had to say about American peoples.

Cobo did not propose a completely new theory about the nature and condition of the Indians, not least because he was still indebted to dominant theories on human origins. Elements of Cobo's work suggested that certain epistemological changes were under way in the appraisal of Indians and human groups generally. Cobo insisted that climate did not change the physical and mental characteristics of Indians, Africans, or Spanish. After all, in any given part of the American continent, the children of Spaniards were still born "white," like those in the peninsula, while the offspring of Africans were as black as their ancestors in Africa. Indians differed in color from the Spanish and Africans, and this was one of their distinguishing features, certainly in contrast to the Spaniards. The color of the Indians ranged between "brownish *(algo moreno)*, dark brown *(loro)*, olive *(aceitunado)*, tawny *(leonado)*, fawn-colored *(bazo)*, the color of cooked quince, and that which sums them all up best, mulattoed *(amulatado)*." In addition to his more specific taxonomy of skin color, Cobo's portrait conveys the sense that all Indians, without exception, were members of the same nation. "In terms of their size, disposition and other natural properties," he wrote, "above all in terms of color, the inhabitants [of America] are so alike, and there are so many similarities between them, as one finds in Europe among men born in the same province and subject to the same climate."[52]

Colonists and many in the royal government were initially opposed to the creation of a Republic of the Indians because it might in theory limit their control over the indigenous population, but with time they would come to appreciate an arrangement that facilitated the continued exploitation of the natives in a more ordered and institutionalized form. The creation of a separate native republic became even more important ideologically, as it institutionalized and thus helped to entrench predominant views on the nature of the Indians. Its existence alongside of and in subordination to the Republic of the Spaniards seemed to confirm the premise and the narrative arc, historical and otherwise, that Indians could only be a subjected people. They would first be "conquered," then "pacified," "converted," and, finally, put under Spanish "tutelage," perhaps indefinitely.[53]

We know that, as with other non-Spanish groups, however, Indians also contested many of these perceptions. In the first two centuries various indigenous communities resisted Spanish domination, both passively and actively. There are countless cases of indigenous communities choosing to revert to their pre-Hispanic religious beliefs collectively. Many others chose to resist Spanish domination even into the eighteenth century, and others, such as the Mayas of Yucatan, did their best to remain beyond the reach of the crown and church's bureaucratic machinery. Many of the so-called "friendly Indians" violently resisted Spanish oppression and exploitation. Modern historians of Mexico have uncovered several dozen rebellions of note in the sixteenth and seventeenth centuries and likewise for the territories controlled by Spain in the southern parts of the American continent.[54] Indigenous communities also resisted peacefully; for instance, they used the Spanish judicial system to protect their lands and safeguard their rights.[55] These processes showed that, as modern historians have noted, Amerindian communities struggled against Spanish cultural hegemony and also exhibited a clear desire to keep their societies separate from the colonists'.[56]

Even more significant for understanding the development of concepts of race and nation were the attempts by some Indians to write alternative histories of the New World and Spanish conquest. They often took a similar approach to the Moriscos, although it is impossible to know if they directly or mutually influenced each other. These histories written by Indian or mestizo elites are not the histories of barbarous or savage peoples but rather of intrepid nations; expanding, well-ordered polities; and complex and advanced civilizations, comparable in many cases to the great empires of antiquity.[57] Moreover, in a manifest appropriation of the historical narratives that Spaniards had constructed about themselves, many of these histories suggested that natives of the Indies had been Christians from the time of Jesus Christ and, even more importantly, tried to show that their origins were as noble as those of the Spaniards.

The Peruvian native Don Felipe Guaman Poma de Ayala, for instance, wrote at the beginning of the seventeenth century that the inhabitants of pre-Hispanic Peru had not been "savage animals," as many claimed, for then "they would not have had laws or prayers or the habit of Adam, and would be as horses or beasts, and would not have knowledge of the Creator, nor would they have sown fields, or had houses and arms, fortresses and laws and ordinances, and knowledge of God." On the contrary, Guaman Poma proclaimed the preeminence of the Indians over nearly all other humans: "Of the sons of Noah . . . one of them brought God to the Indies; others say that he was [the son] of Adam himself. The said Indians multiplied, known to God, and being all powerful, He may have chosen to keep these Indians apart [from others]." Just as the Moriscos were said to have descended from some of the first Christians in the Iberian Peninsula, the same claim was now made on behalf of Indians, converted to Christianity by the "holy apostle Saint Bartholomew." Because they were descendants of Noah's noble sons and had converted early to Christianity, pre-Hispanic native society had been a well-ordered and peaceful one in which women were respected and crimes severely punished. If the indigenous peoples in Guaman Poma's own time had any vices, they resulted from the corruption introduced by external agents—Spaniards, Creoles, mestizos, blacks, and mulattos—all of whom were degenerate and intent on the exploitation of the Indians. Even more important was Guaman Poma's assertion that the Indians, as the only true natives of the land, were the legitimate proprietors of the Indies: "Given that the whole world belongs to God, and so Castile belongs to the Spaniards and the Indies to the Indians as Guinea does to the blacks. Each one is the legitimate proprietor . . . And the Indians are the natural proprietors of this kingdom, and the Spaniards, natives of Spain. Here, in this kingdom, they are foreigners, *mitimays*. . . . For [God] created the world, and the earth, and planted each seed, the Spaniard in Castile, the Indian in the Indies, the black in Guinea."[58]

In his denunciation of the excesses committed against the Indians, Guaman Poma pointed to the Creoles as the main culprits but also the "blacks" or "Guineans." This was not an original complaint.

Numerous missionaries and Spanish officials had also denounced what they saw as the exploitation of the Indians by Africans, slaves and freedmen, which resulted in the implementation of various statutes and laws to curtail these abuses. Nevertheless, Guaman Poma also condemned the living conditions of African slaves. What caught his attention was not their servile status—something that Guaman Poma probably accepted to the extent that slavery had also existed in pre-Hispanic indigenous societies—but rather what he saw as slaves' total lack of rights, their unprotected state, and their owners' and authorities' general contempt for them.

These blacks or Guineans constituted one of the largest social groups in Spanish America, and their presence and size—in many places outnumbering Spaniards—reopened the debate on the nature and meaning of belonging to a Spanish community. The Indians had been forced into, and some perhaps even desired, a community apart—the so-called Republic of the Indians—but Africans were never afforded the right to form their own republic nor to belong to the Republic of Spaniards. Regardless of their status, slaves and freedmen lived among Spaniards. They were part of the public life of cities and towns in the Americas as well as Spain. As slaves they were legally the property of their masters and as freedmen residents of cities and towns. Whether slave or free they were all subjects of the king and members of the Catholic church, but for the most part they had minimal rights. Transported in large numbers to the Iberian Peninsula and the colonies, Africans in the Spanish world occupied a sort of no-man's land, invariably seen as outsiders to the community—sometimes feared, always ignored and despised.

Early modern Spaniards certainly had opportunities to better understand Africans and their lands of origin. Europeans, especially the Portuguese and Spanish, began establishing colonies on African territory as early as the fifteenth century. This process accelerated in the seventeenth century and reached its peak in the eighteenth. Soldiers, explorers, adventurers, slave traders, and missionaries were among those who left some record of their experiences on the continent. Africa and its inhabitants featured in histories, chronicles of voyages, and missions and in pamphlets that described the legendary Christian kingdom of Prester John. These invariably claimed expert knowledge of the continent; in reality Europeans were no more than superficially acquainted with the land and its inhabitants and knew even less of sub-Saharan Africa. As Bernardo de Aldrete, a seventeenth-century Spanish writer, wrote, Africa was "a vast continent, all or most of it scarcely known since antiquity, and though at present knowledge of it is greater than before, I still think that the paintings of geographers and the things recounted in the histories are oblivious to a good portion [of what there is to know]. The scanty knowledge of the ancients gave rise to so many fables that were spun and written down by the Greeks and Romans, which some believed and affirmed, taking them for the truth."[59]

This did not prevent Spaniards of the sixteenth and seventeenth centuries from writing copiously about Africa and Africans, including their origins, physical and mental characteristics, potential for intellectual advancement, and place in the expansion of the Christian faith. In contrast to the inhabitants of the Americas, Europeans were thoroughly convinced that they understood the origins of these peoples and the reasons for their different physical constitution. Like other human families the Africans were descended from Adam and Eve and thus fully human, even if some authors, following ancient sources, still claimed that parts of Africa were populated by monsters, who occasionally resembled humans. The Bible supplied a relatively straightforward account of the provenance of black Africans for those who explained human characteristics by origins. It was generally accepted in the Islamic, Jewish, and Christian traditions that black Africans descended from one of Noah's sons, Ham, whose punishment for insulting his father was that his progeny would be slaves to the lines of his brothers, Shem and Japheth. The conclusion drawn from this narrative by many Christian and Jewish writers was that Africans descended from Ham were a type of natural slave. Their dark skin marked them as separate from the rest.[60]

The predominant explanation since medieval times for Africans' skin color, however, was climate theory. The medieval Muslim author Ibn Khaldun, for instance, argued that Africans' dark complexion was simply the product of the prevailing climatic conditions in the region. The story of Noah made references to slavery, he argued, not to blackness. Khaldun implied that the torrid, scorching African heat affected the intellectual capacity of those who lived in such regions: "Their qualities of character," in both cases, he wrote, "are close to those of dumb animals." Other humans who inhabited the frigid zones shared the same customs and limitations, but their complexion was an extremely pallid white. Skin color was liable to alter, just as the color of the skin changed along with living conditions and climate, which proved that it was not a reliable guide to the mental capacities of humans: "Negroes from the south who settle in the temperate [zone] . . . that tends toward whiteness, are found to produce descendants whose color gradually turns white in the course of time. Vice versa, inhabitants from the North of the fourth zone who settle in the south produce descendants whose color turns black. This shows that color is conditioned by the composition of the air."[61]

Not all Spaniards in the 1500s and 1600s agreed with this theory. Especially those authors writing on the peninsula, including López de Gómara, believed that skin color did not change when an individual moved to a different geographic region, which they took as evidence that skin color was a quality intrinsic to humans and not the result of environmental conditions.[62] An expert on the diversity of national characters, Juan Huarte de San Juan, made the same assertion. He claimed that "the blacks in Spain pass on their color to their descendants through the seed" and that the only way for blacks to change their skin color was to mix with whites.[63] The issue continued to be clouded by uncertainties and contradictions. The Jesuit Fray Antonio de San Román maintained that in Ethiopia "even though some are darker than others, their quality, according to the best opinions, proceeds from within *(ab intrinseco)* rather than from the great ardor of the sun, for in cold regions they are born with the same black color." And yet, in a later chapter, he claimed that all Ethiopians "are born white, but the mothers rub their children with some oils and keep them in the sun all day, so it's a miracle they survive, and as a result they turn black, which is encouraged by a certain intrinsic quality."[64]

No Spanish author of this period went as far as the Englishman Thomas Browne. In his *Pseudodoxia Epidemica,* Browne refuted both predominant theories in virtually all parts of Europe, that "blackness" in humans was accidental (the product of climate) or that it was the result of Noah's curse of his son Ham.[65] Likewise there was nothing in Acosta's writings, or those of other seventeenth-century Spanish authors, that indicated an affinity with the theories of the Frenchman François Bernier, the author of a text titled "Nouvelle Division de la Terre par las differentes Especes ou Raçes d'hommes" ("New Division of Earth by the Different Species or Races Which Inhabit It," 1684). In it, Bernier suggested that instead of dividing the earth into climatic regions, it should be divided according to the physical characteristics of its human inhabitants. For this purpose he used the term *race* for the first time to designate not lineages or qualities but human groups with shared characteristics. He spoke of the existence of "four or five Species or Races of men."[66] One of these races was European and inhabited the European continent—excluding Russia and including "a small part of Africa" (Northern Africa) and a "good part of Asia" (including parts under the control of the Great Khan, the "three Arabias," all of Persia, and others). Among these species or races, Bernier observed that the natives of India and Egyptians were "*noir* or very dark," but this was an accidental side effect of the sun. Those among their elites who did not have to expose themselves to the sun "are no blacker (noir) than many Spaniards," and although the Indians (of the Indian subcontinent) had different facial features from the Europeans, this did not mean that they constituted a distinct "particular species." If that criteria were applied in all cases, it would have been necessary to speak of a Spanish race and a German one, and so on, for every European country. The other species or races of men included all the inhabitants of Africa—with the exception of the Mediterranean coastal rim in the north—whose chief characteristics were their facial features (thick lips and flat noses), oily skin, sparse beards, hair that was more like a kind of wool, and teeth as white as ivory. But their "essential trait" was their black color, which was not the product of the climate or the sun, as demonstrated by the fact that neither they nor their descendants changed in color when transported to colder climates. Africans' color only changed when "they intermarry with white women," which proved that color was an inherent characteristic of this species or race. It was something present in their "sperm and blood," although these were the same color across races.

It should be noted that in his classification, Bernier "nowhere suggests that his division could be employed to impute different mental characteristics to his four races," and Spanish authors would have fully accepted that.[67] Spaniards also used black skin color—whatever the hue—to identify a number of nations around the world that shared the same or similar barbarous customs: sub-Saharans (mainly from Guinea, Congo, and Angola, from whence the majority of slaves in the peninsula originated); North African Muslims of sub-Saharan origin; individuals born in Spain or Portugal to sub-Saharan parents, all of them baptized and in most cases Castilian-speaking; Moriscos with sub-Saharan ancestors; the native inhabitants of the Canary Islands; Hindus or Tamils, brought to the Iberian Peninsula by the Portuguese; and blacks born in Spanish America, who accompanied their masters on their return to the peninsula.[68]

It seems there was something distinct from skin color that rendered all blacks alike. The Spanish Jesuit José de Acosta summed up the dominant discourse by defining black Africans as "the most remote and uncultivated human lineage *(genus humanum)*" and including the majority of sub-Saharan peoples among the so-called third class of barbarians; in other words, the most savage and primitive, though he never ceased to remind his coreligionists that, even as such, black Africans were deserving, perhaps even the most deserving, of spiritual salvation.[69] As with the Indians, many Spaniards were convinced that, at least in theory, Africans and former slaves would be transformed through education into model citizens. A case in point was Juan Latino (1518–1596), a former slave who famously became a poet and professor of Latin in Granada. Although "Ethiopian by homeland and parentage," he was rightly included in Nicolás Antonio's *New Hispanic Library* because he was "Spanish by education." Perhaps Latino had been "a servant in body," Antonio explained, yet the education he had received "returned to his spirit those qualities possessed by the natives [Spaniards]." In time, he became "the head of the grammar school," a post he would occupy for twenty years; took a Spanish bride, "an honest and noble woman, whose social rank was superior to his own"; and dedicated himself to writing verse, including a long and famous poem in praise of Don

Juan of Austria, leader of the Christian troops in the battle of Lepanto.[70]

Yet in the history of Africans in the Spanish world, the issue of slavery looms large, more so than prevailing notions of Africa and its inhabitants. In her analysis of racism and slavery, historian Barbara Fields called attention to the fact that "race as a coherent ideology did not spring simultaneously with slavery, but took even more time than slavery did to become systematic." Many scholars have suggested that the wholesale enslavement of Africans was the logical outcome of an ideology that postulated their natural inferiority. Fields actually believes the opposite: people "are more readily perceived as inferior by nature when they are already oppressed. Africans and their descendants might be, to the eye of the English, heathen in religion, outlandish in nationality, and weird in appearance. But that did not add up to an ideology of racial inferiority until a further historical ingredient got stirred into the mixture: the incorporation of Africans and their descendants into a polity and society in which they lacked rights."[71]

The history of slavery in the Iberian world is undeniably complex.[72] Slaves were already present in large numbers during the medieval period, and this was a practice common to all three peninsular communities—Christian, Jewish, and Muslim. Yet one would be hard pressed to find anywhere in the Spanish world a justification of slavery based on Aristotelian theories of natural servitude. Primarily this was because slaves in medieval Spain came from many continents and in a variety of skin colors. Slaves in the peninsula between 1400 and 1600 included Mudéjares (unconverted Muslims) living in Christian territories, inhabitants of the Muslim kingdom of Granada, Albanians, Greeks, Slavs, and other individuals of European extraction generally found on the Mediterranean slave market. To these were added Moriscos, Jews from Northern Africa, Amerindians, and Asians. They exhibited a great diversity of skin colors, from pallid white to black and all shades in between.[73] The justification of slavery had its roots in dominant biblical and Roman traditions, where slavery was seen as a civil condition, not a natural state.[74] "Servitude," or the loss of liberty and enslavement, was "contrary to natural reason."[75]

This well-established set of ideas and practices about slavery provoked some Spaniards to question the legitimacy of African enslavement. Critics recognized that perhaps some of these slaves were prisoners of war but were convinced that a majority were innocents illegally captured by slave traders in collaboration with African leaders. These authors demanded the total prohibition of slavery and the liberation of all those enslaved without just cause.[76]

In contrast to the Indian case, however, few religious or public officials were prepared to take the slaves' predicament into serious consideration or made any concerted effort to pressure the monarchy into ending the slave trade. In the eyes of many missionaries, including the self-styled protectors of blacks, slavery was a lesser evil. Given the choice between living in sin amid the barbarism of Africa, on the one hand, and slavery among Christians, on the other, the latter was considered preferable because it opened the door to salvation and some degree of civilization.[77]

The number of black slaves imported into the Iberian Peninsula and the Indies in the sixteenth and seventeenth centuries was astonishing by any measure. On the peninsula itself, including Portugal, there were perhaps 100,000 slaves of various origins around the year 1600. Many peninsula inhabitants owned slaves—no more than perhaps one or two per family or business, in most cases. Available data on the sale of slaves on the peninsula indicate that the majority were women and children, destined primarily for domestic service. Sugar plantations in Valencia and the Canary Islands and salt mines in the south relied on slave labor, but the vast majority of slaves on the peninsula worked the land or as servants in churches, convents, artisan workshops, or the homes of the wealthy.

The numbers were even higher, and living conditions more precarious, in the Indies.[78] The Spanish monarchy facilitated the arrival of approximately 2,100,000 slaves in its American possessions between 1501 and 1866, behind only Brazil (4,750,000 between 1550 and 1867) and comparable to the number of slaves disembarked in the British Caribbean (approximately 2,050,000). Between 1501 and 1581 only territories under Spanish sovereignty received African slaves—more than 100,000—while between 1581 and 1650 some 600,000 slaves arrived in Spanish America. This was double the number that arrived in Brazil. Between 1641 and 1700, however, Spanish territories received a smaller proportion of slaves than any other region of the Americas, at less than 75,000. Mexico and Peru witnessed a steep decline, with scarcely any slaves arriving after 1640. An indication that Spain was losing its preeminence in some economic sectors, more than 300,000 slaves were sent to the English territories in North America and the Caribbean during the same time period; more than 100,000 to the Dutch Americas; and more than 500,000 to Brazil, the territory controlled by newly independent Portugal.[79] In compiling population counts based on contemporary sources, scholars have estimated that in 1650 there were 700,000 Africans in the Spanish territories, free and slave, many of them born in the Americas.[80]

Most owners had between one and five slaves, and most of the plantations were not large, using between 50 and 100 slaves. Figures from different parts of the Americas seem to confirm that in some regions the African population exceeded the Spanish. Borucki, Eltis, and Wheat write that "for a century from around 1550, several of Spain's circum-Caribbean colonies would have been predominantly black long before the development of the export sugar complex. More Africans than Europeans arrived in this broad region, as well as along the Pacific coast from Panama to Lima, before 1600," with important "black populations in Mexico City and on the Mexican coasts, on the Pacific and Caribbean shores of Colombia, in coastal Ecuador and Peru, and in Caribbean Venezuela—regions where the Amerindian population had largely been decimated after contact."[81]

Once enslaved, their experience of servitude was similar regardless of where they ended up, in part because of legal uniformity across the Iberian world.[82] The slave system imposed on the Iberian Peninsula and in Spanish America after 1500 was based on laws and frameworks that dated back to medieval Spain. The monarchy and secular authorities in the colonies had no particular interest in promulgating laws to protect slaves, strictly regulating the actions of slaveholders, or limiting owners' property rights over their slaves. The laws on slavery included in the thirteenth-century *Siete Partidas* were supplemented by slave laws and regulations produced by public authorities in the Indies during the sixteenth and seventeenth centuries, almost all of which aimed at imposing limits on the few rights still enjoyed by slaves and even regulating the lives of free blacks.[83]

These laws also stipulated that masters were obliged to attend to the needs of their slaves, not mistreat them, and were certainly forbidden from killing them without cause or the consent of a judge, unless "he [the slave] is found with his [the owner's] wife, or his daughter, or had committed an equally grave error, in which case he may freely kill him." Mistreatment without just cause was grounds for slaves to take their complaints to judicial authorities, who could rule that the slave should be sold to another master. The slaves also had the right to marry—a right protected by the church—although there is evidence that masters did their best to impede these unions. Legally, masters could not break up a slave family unit or sell one of the spouses or married slaves' children. As in other slave systems, the children acquired the legal status of the mother. They were considered slaves if the mother was enslaved, free if she was not. Slaves had to be baptized as a matter of course and to receive some form of religious instruction, although as everyone hastened to point out, baptism was meant to free souls, not bodies. Masters were also obliged to impart the rudiments of the Spanish language to their charges and to allow slaves to set aside several hours a week to work for their own benefit.

The Spanish system also provided for a number of ways to secure liberty. A slave could demonstrate that he or she had been unjustly enslaved, marry a free man or woman (although in the colonies all possible measures were taken to close this path to manumission), become ordained as a priest or friar, secure his or her freedom in the master's will, or purchase his or her freedom.[84] It is unclear how many individuals were able to obtain their liberty in one of these ways, although it would appear that the numbers were not high, at least not in the first century of Spanish presence in the Indies. An exception seems to have been regions, such as Mexico and Peru, where few if any African slaves arrived after 1640 and where observers were beginning to remark on the increasing communities of free blacks.[85]

Nothing in these slave laws indicated, however, that Spanish authorities were introducing measures similar to those seen in other empires in the last decades of the 1600s. The first French Code Noir was promulgated in 1685, and although in many respects similar to slave laws in the Spanish empire, it also included clauses (Art. IX), that prohibited and instituted punishments for sexual relations between free men and enslaved women and limited slaves' freedom to marry.[86] Even more indicative of changing times were the laws passed by the Virginia General Assembly in 1691 (ACT XVI), designed to restrict interracial sexual relations; for example, by prohibiting intermarriage between free "English or other White man or woman . . . with a negroe, mulatto, or Indian man or woman," on pain of expulsion and punishment of "any English woman being free shall have a bastard child by any negro or mulatto." In response to the belief that the presence of freed slaves set a bad example for those still enslaved, it was also decreed "that no negro or mulatto be after the end of this present session of assembly set free by any person or persons whatsoever, unless such person or persons, their heires, executors or administrators pay for the transportation of such negro or negroes out of the countrey within six months after such setting them free."[87]

Something was happening in the Spanish empire, however, that we might identify as the racialization of slaves, or perhaps more precisely the Africanization of slavery, the convergence of "African" and "slave." The gradual disappearance of slaves from other regions, hastened by the prohibition against the enslavement of natives of Spanish possessions in America and Asia, left the African continent as the only source of slaves.[88] Consequently, the terms *black* and *slave* became confounded, almost synonymous, in the Iberian world. The very title of a play from the early seventeenth century clearly shows this link: *The Best Master's Black (El negro del mejor amo)*, a work that could have been titled *The Best Master's Slave.*[89] As one of the slave characters in Francisco de Quevedo's "La fortuna con seso y la hora de todos" ("Fortune in Her Wits and the Hour of All Men") observed, "No other cause exists for our enslavement but the color, and the color is but an accident, not a crime."[90] Perhaps no one expressed this conflation of enslavement and black skin more clearly than the Creole Dominican from Lima Fray Juan de Meléndez, who omitted "blacks" from his description of the inhabitants of America because this nation "and those descended [from it] on one side . . . are all servile, and people of such [base] repute, and no one takes any notice of them."[91] Africans carried the indelible stigma of their skin color, a mark of servitude, dependency, and a mental state that was said to affect slaves and all their descendants.

During the sixteenth and seventeenth centuries, peninsular Spaniards did not pay much attention to blacks and certainly not to their contribution or place in the construction of a national identity. With very few exceptions, blacks—even those who became free—were invisible and the quintessential aliens.[92] Black Africans, slave or free, were also seen as elements extraneous to the body social and politic in the Americas and thus not legally entitled to membership in the Republic of Spaniards. Even the attainment of liberty did not include any right to citizenship or access to higher education or secular and ecclesiastical offices. Torn from their homelands, Africans in the sixteenth and seventeenth centuries were considered to be a nation apart from the rest but with few possibilities to create their own communities and govern themselves. From the legal standpoint, black Africans, frequently including freedmen, were not seen as "part of the city, or having anything to do with it," and were considered permanently tainted by the color of slavery.[93]

However, some developments indicated that Africans, especially free Africans, could play some role in the social life of the Americas. "Towns of blacks," albeit relatively few, appeared in some American regions, with a structure and organization similar to Indian towns.[94] Many American and peninsular cities saw the creation of so-called "Confraternities of Blacks" in many American and peninsular cities as a means for blacks to partake in the ceremonial life of urban communities, formulate and advance complaints, and potentially move to higher positions in the Americas' social hierarchy. There were even a handful of celebrated black saints, such as the mulatto Martín de Porres.[95]

More significantly, from the 1500s on, reports sent back by authorities in the Indies as well as by individual colonists insisted that Africans had an inordinate ability to adapt to the natural conditions of the Indies. Rescued from diseases and perilous living conditions in Africa, the slaves in America grew strong and reproduced quickly. A colonist in Panama echoed these notions in the mid-seventeenth century, using language reminiscent of earlier denunciations of the Moriscos' supposed propensity for procreation: "From a single black woman, [the houses of Spaniards] have filled with blacks and mulattos, sons and grandsons, and if one were to look into their families it would be discovered that each one has procreated more than fifty pieces."[96]

These were obviously gross exaggerations, but there is no doubt that Spaniards in the Indies feared Africans. Most descriptions dwell on their physical strength, natural valor, and desire for liberty. Although slave rebellions were rare, the Spanish authorities reacted severely against any hint of discontent and issued repeated prohibitions against freed "blacks" or slaves carrying arms of any type, by day or night. Those who raised a weapon against "a Spaniard, albeit without wounding [him]," could expect harsh punishment.[97] All manumitted slaves, or, as they were legally referred to, "all free blacks and mulattos," were also obliged to live with known or declared masters to exercise greater control over them.[98] Although the number of slaves who escaped from their masters was not too high, the authorities constantly decried the existence of communities of runaways and feared that these free communities would expand to include freed blacks and Indians.[99]

In the social sphere, however, Spanish colonists tended to see Africans as more useful and superior to Indians. The former were strong and loyal and showed initiative, while Indians appeared pusillanimous, timid, and lacking willpower or any sort of ambition.[100] Indeed, many in the colonies relied on black Africans to run their estates and to organize and manage Indians who worked for them. Africans, slave and free, also played an important role in the economy of Spanish cities and became part of the social fabric. Military service in the so-called "black and free mulatto militias" was the only practical path to social advancement open to Africans but not yet a path to fuller integration into Spanish or Portuguese American society. These militias would proliferate throughout the Spanish territories in the eighteenth century, but they appeared earlier in regions most susceptible to attacks from rival European powers.[101] Africans, and the memory of them, were gradually disappearing from the peninsula, but in the Indies the situation was quite different. Here, especially in later periods, the rights of free blacks and the abolition of slavery became a central element in debates on the nation, Spanishness, liberty, and citizenship.

In 1681 the Lima-born Dominican friar Juan Meléndez published a chronicle of his order titled *Tesoros verdaderos de las Indias* ("Veritable Treasury of the Indies"), which included a chapter on ". . . who are the Indians, *Indianos*, and other nations of this kingdom" of Peru.[102] There is nothing novel therein with regard to the Indians or the *Indianos* (Creoles). The author's views resonated with official theories, and he was proud of his Creole and Spanish heritage. What does stand out in this part of Meléndez's work is his image of the demographic constitution of the Peruvian viceroyalty and of the Indies generally. "The Kingdom of Peru and the rest of the provinces of the Indies," writes Meléndez, "are composed of three nations—Indians, Spaniards, and Blacks." The former are the "natives," the other two "aliens *(forasteros)* and outsiders." Their numbers may vary from one region to another, but without doubt "these three nations make up the entirety of the populace of those Provinces."

Meléndez continued that these three nations "are rarely joined together in matrimony." If this happened on occasion, the explanation was fairly simple according to Meléndez: the "whites" who married "Indian or black women" could not in any case be Spaniards "but of another of the white nations of Europe, who perchance had crossed to the Indies with the title of Spaniard, and if [he is indeed Spanish], he is a low-class, and if he had wed an Indian or a black woman in the Indies, he would have done the same with a shameless Morisca in Spain." The conclusion drawn is that individuals of each nation, and above all Spaniards and Indians, prefer "not to mix through the Sacrament of matrimony with those of another nation, wishing for their blood to run pure, without mixture of any kind among their descendants." As a result, Meléndez believed that in the Indies, "the Indian is and always has been an Indian, the Spaniard, a Spaniard, and the black, a black."

Meléndez was right to the extent that few mixed marriages were recorded in the Indies. But his assessment was nevertheless at least partly inaccurate, probably because as a Creole he preferred not to acknowledge the American reality: by the end of the seventeenth century it was no longer clear that all the Spaniards were Spaniards or that the Indians were all Indian or that all blacks were black. Chapter 2 described the vast number of individuals of mixed blood in the Indies in the sixteenth and seventeenth centuries: around the middle of the seventeenth century, there were no fewer than 700,000 mestizos (Spanish/Indian mix) and mulattos (Spanish/African) and a not insignificant number of zambos (African/Indian). This large number of mestizos and mulattos affected the peninsular Spaniard's opinion of the Creoles. For the former, at least, it seemed clear that not all who referred to themselves as Spaniards were truly Spanish, or at least not with the purity of the peninsulars. Also in Chapter 2 we saw how Creoles began to create distinctions between Spaniards and all the other nations or groups, which prevented Indians, blacks, mestizos, and mulattos from being denominated Spaniards and enjoying the associated rights.[103]

As we will see, these efforts by the Creoles to constitute and imagine themselves as a community of Spaniards of pure blood would become more concerted, extensive, and urgent in the eighteenth century. All the necessary elements, however, were already present in the decades after 1650, including the collective affirmation by Creoles that neither they nor their ancestors had ever mixed with Indians or Africans or at most had done so in special circumstances and very rare cases. In other words, the progressive identification of Spaniard and white, and not just pure blood, surfaced in the Americas before the peninsula.

In spite of Creoles' denial of racial mixing, numerous individuals in the Americas had been described as mestizos at one point or another. In the American world of the sixteenth and seventeenth centuries, the mestizo designation was a complex one. As Meléndez indicates, basic demographic conceptualizations and classifications were elaborated based on three nations with distinct legal rights and obligations: Spaniards, Indians, and blacks.[104] In reality, biological mixing was an obvious part of the American phenomenon from the very beginning, reported even by the first observers, but few engaged in a discussion about it or its social and cultural implications before the mid-1600s.

In the first decades of Spanish presence in the Americas, especially in Mexico and Peru, the biological mixing of the conquistadors with the indigenous elite was accepted by the authorities and Spanish society. The fact that some conquistadors married while many others chose to live with elite Indian women was perceived as a way to integrate indigenous elites into the new society. It also allowed conquistadors to consolidate their position as the dominant class in the colonies. Most of the mestizo children of these first unions were not legitimized through marriage, but they were generally recognized by their fathers and eventually became part of the Spanish local elite.[105] When this happened, as it often did in the Caribbean islands, they were called "sons of Christians" and generally accepted and integrated into society as Spaniards.[106] Spanish colonists typically recognized their mestizo offspring, especially in the sixteenth century, and this accounts for the sometimes remarkable growth of the population classified as "Spanish" toward the end of the century. Clearly, many of these Spaniards, men and women, were of mixed blood yet socially accepted, consciously or unconsciously, as Spaniards.[107]

One of them, historian and soldier Gómez Suárez de Figueroa, better known as "Inca" Garcilaso de la Vega, recalled that "the sons of Spaniards and Indian women—or Indians and Spanish women—are called mestizos, which is to say that we are a mixture of both nations. It was a name introduced by the first Spaniards who had children in the Indies. And as a name imposed by our fathers, and for its significance, I use it with pride and I am honored with it."[108] A majority of mestizos and mulattos, however—most of them a product of violence and the unabated sexual exploitation of Indian and African women—ended up living with their mothers in indigenous communities or, worse, as slaves and in many cases as indigents. They became individuals without history, lineage, or a social identity. In the same chapter in which he boasted of his mestizo heritage, Inca Garcilaso drew attention to a process that was already accelerating in the middle of the sixteenth century: the pride felt by some about mixed Spanish, Indian, or African ancestry was turning to shame, as many of those terms were being transformed into insults, heavy with social opprobrium.

With few exceptions, there were no grand plans in the Spanish world at the beginning of conquest for ethnic assimilation or the fusion of different nations through mixed marriages. Neither the American authorities nor the Spanish Creoles seemed to favor a union of bodies. In contrast, seventeenth-century French royal authorities and missionaries in the Caribbean islands and Canada encouraged mixed marriages because they would make it possible, the king's chief minister Colbert argued in 1660, "to form one people and one blood."[109] In the Iberian world, marriages between Spanish men and Indian, black, mestizo, or mulatto women were not prohibited but were rare nevertheless. When Spaniards married, they generally wed other Spaniards or individuals socially accepted as Spaniards, and throughout the entire Spanish dominium, with the exception of a number of royal *cédulas* issued early on, the secular and ecclesiastical authorities made no special effort to promote matrimony between members of different ethnic groups.[110] The majority of the unions that produced mestizos or mulattos were temporary, episodic, and nearly always abusive; consequently, the offspring were frequently illegitimate. Depending on the region, in 50 to 90 percent of cases, especially in the first decades, these mixed-blood children were the product of the sin of concubinage *(damnato concubitu)*, in Jesuit José de Teruel's words.[111]

For Spaniards, the problem, of course, was social identity and status. "Few honorable Spaniards marry Indian or black women," wrote the jurist Juan Solórzano Pereira, the crown's official spokesman of sorts on the Indies. Solórzano conceded that the mestizos and the mulattos, so long as they were the offspring of legitimate marriages, should perhaps be integrated into Spanish society or at least given the right to exercise offices that would enable them, and especially mestizos, to assist Spaniards and local authorities with indigenous communities. But he added that marrying mestizos and mulattos, or Indians and Africans, meant that their progeny would be "blighted by the stain of a different color, and other vices they are born with or imbibe with the [mother's] milk."[112]

These kinds of opinions have led modern historians to observe that, in the American context, the term *mestizo* in the sixteenth and seventeenth centuries was virtually synonymous with *illegitimate* and *impure*. Hence, Stuart Schwartz and Frank Salomon write, *mestizo* "was not so much the name of a firm social category as a term meaning a weakly defined person, one who might occupy varied social roles depending on demand and opportunity, but who was not really entitled by his or her 'nature' to any of them."[113] From the Spanish viewpoint, to recall, biological mixings confused the matter of lineage, at a time when the establishment of a people's lineage was fundamental to the construction of identities. With purity and quality equated, effectively distinct lineages were of paramount importance to the protection of the social order. Fray Juan Meléndez suggested as much when he observed that in the Indies each nation should be treated according to what it was and the distinction made between the pure and the impure: "that the Spaniard should be looked on as a Spaniard, the Indian as an Indian, the black as a black, and the mestizo as a mestizo, and it should not be permitted or consented to for anyone to leave his place, and good order should be kept, in which everyone should be taken for what he is and not rise above."[114]

To protect themselves from this confusion of lineages, nearly all American institutions—secular and ecclesiastical, royal and local—adopted purity-of-blood statutes that followed peninsular models. As initially formulated and then adhered to for almost the entirety of the first two centuries, the American *limpieza* statutes clearly stipulated that people requesting offices or honors had to demonstrate social and religious purity.[115] Rejection of candidates to public offices was based on suspicions about the aspirant's religious background (usually their Judaism), illegitimacy, and lack of hidalguía. Most of those investigated were Spaniards.[116]

Nevertheless, there is sufficient reason to believe that already by the mid-1600s, many candidates were disqualified because of non-Spanish ancestry or because their complexion appeared to betray their mixed racial background more than their illegitimacy. Two cases from the 1630s illustrate the contradictions inherent in the system but also confirm that the ideology of exclusion was becoming increasingly entrenched among Creoles and the American authorities. One involved a certain Joseph Núñez de Prado. In 1639 Núñez applied for the post of *procurador* of the Audiencia of Lima, one of the minor offices put up for sale by the crown in order to replenish the treasury and for which Núñez had paid double the market value. The Audiencia's initial response was to deny him the title because he was a mulatto and thus prohibited by law from holding an office reserved for Spaniards. In his defense, prepared by the lawyer Antonio Maldonado de Silva, it was argued, first, that Núñez was not a mulatto but a quadroon, since his father was Spanish and his mother a mulatta; second, that he had already demonstrated his aptitude for public office, having previously served as a royal notary, with the authorities' approval; and, third, that the nobility and the great services rendered by his father were sufficiently and well established, the implication being that the son had inherited the same virtues. The viceroy's response to these affirmations was to award him the office of *procurador*, which he duly assumed.

The second case was Juan Ochoa, who had been an usher of the Lima Audiencia for some time before being dismissed, also on the grounds of being a mulatto. Once again, there were plenty of arguments in his favor. His father, a Spaniard, had previously exercised the office with distinction and had earned the admiration of all those who knew him; his mother was not black but a mulatta, the daughter of a black woman and a Basque father. However, the decision in this case went against the supplicant because the office had always been held by "honorable Spaniards" and, even more importantly, because the applicant's complexion "gives notice of that part which comes from his mother." In other words, he was too brown.

Another case is perhaps even more representative of the ways that physical characteristics associated with non-Spaniards were increasingly becoming an exclusionary criterion. The individual in question was Alonso Sánchez de Figueroa, born in Spain to parents who were both legitimately married and Old Christians. When he applied to the Casa de Contratación for a permit to emigrate in 1625, he described himself as being "yellowish brown" (or "fawn-colored," "bazo"), shading into dark brown. In the peninsular context of the Casa de Contratación this self-description did not raise eyebrows, and Alonso received his license to emigrate. In the Indies, however, "bazo" or yellowish brown was a color "commonly seen in mestizos, sons of a white [father] and black [mother]," and when in

1634 witnesses described him as a mulatto, he was duly stripped of the office of scribe and notary, a post he had occupied for several months.[117]

Self-perceptions of mestizos and mulattos have been much less thoroughly examined. Douglas Cope's study has revealed a measure of solidarity among the "plebe" in American cities but also the cleavages that sometimes developed among them based on their origins.[118] In analyses of marriages in different parts of Mexico in the last two decades of the seventeenth century, the level of endogamy among Spaniards was found to have been about 95 percent. Mestizos in general tended to marry other mestizos and mulattos, and mulattos also intermarried.[119] Mestizos considered themselves superior to both the Indians and Spaniards because they felt "that through their mothers the land belongs to them, and that their fathers had won and conquered it."[120] But, as Cope has demonstrated, mestizos kept a "close association with Indians" throughout the centuries, and Spanish Creoles and authorities tended to refuse in many cases to distinguish between them.[121]

The fate of the mulattos as a group seems to have followed a different course. In official ideology, the racial mixture of Spaniards and blacks was the most vilified of all the permutations. As Maria Elena Martínez has written, "although colonial Spaniards increasingly marked both native and African ancestries as impure and generally saw mixture with either group in negative terms, it was black blood that was more frequently and systematically construed as a stain on a lineage."[122] Solórzano confirms this for us. He noted that "the Mulattos, although for the same reason comprehended in that general name of Mestizos, take on this particular one when they are the children of a Black woman and a white man, or the other way round, for this mixture is understood to be the vilest [of all]." And "for being an extraordinary mix," practically against nature, "it has been compared to the mule," an animal known to be the progeny of two equine species and thus a "bastard" one, incapable of procreation.[123]

Already from the start of the seventeenth century, however, one phenomenon was clearly discernible: Spaniards' growing preference for mulattos over other mestizos and blacks. As the examples discussed above demonstrate, the chief concern for Creoles and the authorities was to remove any confusion over criteria for Spanishness, and this was especially evident in relation to blacks, whose mulatto descendants were subject to discrimination. Yet at the same time, for the Spanish, mulattos were an improvement on the blacks and could be considered, in a sense, more active and useful subjects for the preservation of Spanish society in the Americas. This was the basis for Cristóbal de Lorenzana's proposal in a 1640s memorial to Philip IV. He suggested that in order to make the Spanish Americas a productive land and to defend it from foreign attacks, it was necessary to create a "new man," who could only be the product of a mix between whites and blacks.[124]

Nothing left behind in the sixteenth- and seventeenth-century records of the Spanish in the Americas indicates that a conscious project was ever conceived or implemented to promote the improvement of blacks, and perhaps their integration, through biological mixing with whites. But this is what seems to have happened in practice in areas where the number of imported African slaves had dwindled to a trickle. In one of these areas, Mexico City in the second half of the 1600s, there were more "Spanish-mulatto marriages than Spanish-mestizos." By the start of the eighteenth century, mulattos became "the second most numerous of all groups" in the city and in some other regions such as Venezuela and Panama.[125] They were the most numerous and the population with the best prospects for social mobility and influence within American societies, thanks in part to the range of economic functions they fulfilled but above all because they formed the backbone of the militias.[126] Despite this social mobility—which continued and even increased in the eighteenth century—the burden for mulattos continued to be their black African ancestors and their historical connection to slavery, which in the end would determine or limit their possibilities to become citizens of the nation that Spaniards tried to build in the early nineteenth century.

5

A New Spain, a New Spaniard

THE EIGHTEENTH CENTURY was a tremendously complex and unstable period in Spain, as in other parts of Europe. This was true culturally but also politically. Passive and indolent monarchs alternated with others such as the model reformist ruler, Charles III (1759–1788). It would certainly be incorrect to think of this century as a uniform, consistent time when Spaniards were culturally distanced from Europe and Europeans or as the start of the inevitable, irreversible waning of Spanish influence that permanently excluded the country from great power politics. The decline was neither absolute nor unbroken. Spain in the 1700s was still a powerful polity that carried weight in the international balance of power. It continued to derive enormous profit from its American territories, instigated radical reforms in its system of education, improved its infrastructure, and devised ambitious plans for a general economic recovery. As we will see in this and the next chapter, Spanish government and society exhibited a dynamism comparable to other European nations in the eighteenth century.

It is beyond the scope of this book to detail political chronology or contrast the monarchs' accomplishments and failures. Of interest here is the contribution of the eighteenth century to the idea of the nation, Spaniards' self-perception, and how different political and cultural factors contributed to the creation of a common identity. Without a doubt, ideas and discourses inherited from earlier centuries significantly influenced these debates and reflections, but new ideas also made an impression, and new conceptual and discursive traditions emerged. This is because the long eighteenth century in Spain was a time of profound ideological debate over national character. It included debates over the need for political unification, the characteristics of various ethnic communities that comprised the Spanish empire, and the plausibility of thinking of a "Spanish race" that had emerged out of the long history of coexistence of various peninsular lineages and kinship groups.

The Spanish experience of the eighteenth century resembled other Europeans'. In Spain, as in contemporary Great Britain, a common identity began to develop among peninsular inhabitants. Linda Colley has drawn attention to the fact that the creation of this common identity among Britons was above all the result of interactions and confrontations with a foreign and Catholic "other": namely, France and the French: "Men and women came to define themselves as Britons . . . because circumstances impressed them with the belief that they were different from those beyond their shores, and in particular different from their prime enemy, the French. Not so much consensus or homogeneity or centralization at home, as a strong sense of dissimilarity from those without proved to be the essential cement."[1]

Spaniards developed similar discourses and identities, albeit in different circumstances and contexts. As in the British case, Spaniards' identity was the product of encounters with other Europeans and especially a reaction to their disparagement by some of their neighbors and rivals in the eighteenth century. When Spaniards responded to these criticisms they were able to define themselves as a distinct nation—bearers of unique cultural and religious values and the product of a singular history. Unlike Britons, however, Spaniards responded to European critiques less by insisting on their difference and more by insisting on their similarity to Europeans. Although distinct in many respects, the last thing that eighteenth-century Spaniards wanted was to portray themselves as fundamentally different from other Europeans. On the contrary, they were profoundly European, in culture, sensibilities, physical appearance. The peninsula tended to exaggerate similarities between Spaniards and other Europeans. Thanks to their membership in the European human family and their European geography, the inhabitants of the Iberian

Peninsula increasingly saw themselves as Spaniards who belonged to Europe and who were distinct from the rest of the king's subjects elsewhere, including those resident in the Indies.

The emergence of the idea of a Spanish nation was also the result of internal political and cultural processes. Eighteenth-century Spain had inherited a complex political structure and a plurality of identities characterized by various kingdoms with different customs, cultures, and even languages. Yet Spain at the end of the eighteenth century was in many ways different from its predecessor. The structure of the state had changed, and it was increasingly felt that the different kingdoms had at last been unified. Now, nothing separated Catalans, Galicians, or Basques, who were all one and all of them citizens of the same nation: Spain. However, it is arguably the case that this unification, as in the example of Great Britain, was achieved through "superimposition" of differences rather than "integration and homogenization."[2] Eighteenth-century Spaniards also had to face problems inherited from preceding periods—the continued presence of citizens with Jewish and Moorish ancestry, for instance—although, as we will see, the assumptions underlying this debate in the 1700s were radically different. There is no doubt that in the eighteenth century, the inhabitants of the Iberian Peninsula increasingly saw themselves as members of an ethnic nation or nations (Spanish and Portuguese).

This analysis of new theories about Spain and Spanishness is essentially top-down. The sources utilized were produced by the lettered elite, various governing bodies, and governors themselves. There is little about what the vast majority of Spaniards thought of these new ideas and concepts of Spain and Spanishness, although one gets the sense that they made a considerable impression. The theories and images created of Spain and Spaniards in the course of this century, primarily by those with cultural or political authority, became the overriding narrative that shaped the collective consciousness of the vast majority of Spaniards.

This may convey the impression that all who participated in these debates shared a certain basic ideology about the Spain they wished to construct and the type of political system they favored. Especially in the 1780s and 1790s, but in other cases throughout the century, historians have shown that in spite of restrictions on political dissent, a significant number of elites wanted a more open political system. The state was still a personal monarchy, with a weak representative assembly (Cortes), but groups within the elite demanded the dismantling of repressive structures such as the Inquisition or the creation of parliamentary institutions to constrain the king's power.

These alternative visions of the Spanish state became even more prominent after the French Revolution in 1789, which had a profound ideological impact among sections of the Spanish political elite, some of whom would later take the lead in transforming Spain into a constitutional state. However, these political differences did not affect the common desire to create a new nation and a new Spanish identity. There was a notable measure of agreement among traditionalists and reformists on key questions, including what was Spain and who were Spaniards. They differed substantially over the future of Spain and its political system but not when it came to the core characteristics of the Spanish or the need to create a more cohesive nation.

The extent to which eighteenth-century Spain was truly comparable to the most advanced European nations, however, remains unclear. The trend among historians today seems to be that Spain in the age of the Enlightenment made great strides in economics, the development of political structures, intellectual creativity, and the advancement of the sciences. This view is consistent with that of Enlightenment-era Spaniards. Yet there is sufficient reason to believe that Spanish intellectual, social, and economic advances did not quite measure up to those of neighboring European countries. Spanish universities and other cultural institutions were certainly no match for their Western European counterparts; the potential to question religious orthodoxy was negligible; no constitutional or institutional framework would have facilitated serious political debate nationally or more active participation by ordinary citizens in the political process. There was a feeling even by the very early 1800s that Spain had been left behind by the rest of Europe and that it would take decades to catch up.

Carlos II, the last of the Spanish Habsburg kings, died on November 1, 1700, at 39 years of age. He had never been favored by fortune. Sickly since birth, Carlos II had suffered from serious physical and mental disabilities throughout his life—a consequence of the Habsburg propensity for inbreeding. The problem was not that the king had died young, however, but that he died without leaving a direct heir. This precipitated an unprecedented dynastic crisis for Spain: the emergence of two foreign candidates for the throne and the outbreak of a military conflagration of more or less global dimensions known as the War of the Spanish Succession (1701–1713). It would leave Spain soaked in foreign and native blood. After years of bloody struggle, the contending parties signed the Peace of Utrecht in 1713, which recognized Philip V, the grandson of Louis XIV of France, as the first Bourbon king of Spain, on condition that he would renounce his right to inherit the French throne as well. The outcome was nevertheless largely unfavorable for Spain. Although she would keep her American colonies, Spain was deprived of her Italian possessions (the Kingdoms of Naples, Sicily, and Sardinia and the Duchy of Milan), Belgium, and two strategically important territories—Gibraltar (presently still under English sovereignty) and Menorca (recovered several decades later). It was widely held that, although once secure among the great powers of Europe, Spain had been reduced by the early 1700s to a second-rate power. She was subordinate to Great Britain and especially to France, the two states that emerged from the conflict with their great power status enhanced.

The War of Spanish Succession was undoubtedly one of the most violent and costly conflicts in European history. The main theater of hostilities was the European continent, but the war also affected the Americas (Queen Anne's War). Its reach and intensity were reflected in the numbers involved, with nearly 2 million soldiers mobilized and more than 1 million dead. The geopolitical outcome of the conflict was apparently clear: it consolidated Great Britain and France as two global superpowers and confirmed, finally, Spain's decline as a European superpower. Although important, these realities did not preoccupy Spaniards in the aftermath of the conflict. The War of Succession was clearly fought with political hegemony in Europe at stake, but for Spaniards it was also a civil war. This phase of the conflict, which developed parallel to international hostilities, lasted from 1705 to 1715 and was contested by two well-defined camps. On the one hand were the Philipists, who from the very beginning supported the French candidate, Philip of Anjou, the future Philip V; on the other hand were the Austracistas, who recognized the Austrian candidate, Charles of Habsburg, archduke of Austria and the future Emperor Charles VI.

The historic division of Spain into separate kingdoms is key to understanding the formation of these opposing camps and their violent civil war confrontation. The French candidate was backed by all the territories that formed the crown of Castile—Castile proper, Andalusia, Galicia, Extremadura, and Navarre—as well as the Basque and Cantabrian provinces. On the Austracista side were all the territories belonging to the crown of Aragon—Catalonia, Valencia, the Balearic Islands, and Aragon. The crown of Aragon territories had at first recognized the French candidate as the legitimate monarch, but their experience with the French monarchy after the 1640 revolt had engendered mistrust. They saw themselves as the last hope for the defense of the liberties of the crown of Aragon but also of Spain as a whole, which they claimed was in danger "of being subjected to a veritable slavery" under the dominion of a French king.[3]

Regardless of either group's ideology or political aspirations, both sides seemed to agree that Spain was broken—many thought irrevocably—in politics, culture, and economy. And now there were two kings, so even the monarchy was no longer a common focal point. No one spoke at this juncture of one nation or a shared sense of Spanishness. The inflamed passions, outpouring of hatred, and effusion of violence all indicated that during these years Spain had been embroiled in an "implacable civil war."[4] During ten years of continuous warfare, both sides appeared ready to die in defense of their ideals or to kill as many of the enemy as possible. The battles were exceptionally brutal, without quarter given or taken. Each side was apparently determined to erase the other from the map. Both sides destroyed cities, executed prisoners, slaughtered all those who resisted, and set fire to houses, neighborhoods, whole towns, and villages. All contemporary chronicles insist that women and children were the most tenacious and fierce combatants and the ones who suffered the most.[5]

The civil war was effectively brought to an end with the capture of Barcelona by troops loyal to Philip on September 12, 1714, although sporadic resistance continued in several parts of the crown of Aragon. The victory over the Aragonese was officially presented as a "conquest," and in its wake came repression of those designated as rebels and traitors to the king and nation. "It is a sure principle," wrote Macanaz, one of Philip V's ministers, "that for the crime of rebellion which they have incurred, the Catalans, Aragonese, and Valencians have been reduced to penal convicts, so that by the law of nations they have been subjugated, and their property confiscated; and by virtue of civil law they have been condemned to a sentence of death, and their possessions confiscated; by the laws of these kingdoms the mark of infamy extends even to their progeny and descendants."[6] As is often the case in these situations, we do not have completely reliable or precise information about the extent of the persecution or how many were affected, but there is no doubt that a policy of repression was carried out on a vast scale and that it was unrelenting and harsh, especially for the 30,000 individuals who were exiled, many of them never to return.[7]

The end of open hostilities created an opportunity for debate on the root causes of the conflict. For the inhabitants of the crown of Aragon, the explanation was simple: they had opposed Philip because they were convinced that he would not respect the rights and liberties of individual kingdoms and that he would try to impose centralizing and standardizing policies like those implemented in France by his grandfather, Louis XIV. The Aragonese thus may be said to have risen in defense of their history, rights, privileges, and autonomy and the integrity of their *patria*. The Aragonese wanted to preserve the unique constitution and laws with respect to the kingdoms of the crown of Castile that had prevailed under the Habsburgs. As far as Philip's supporters were concerned, the rebellion of the Aragonese could be more easily explained as an act of obstinacy. The Aragonese were clinging to an anachronistic political system based on political decentralization and the preservation of historic differences between kingdoms and provinces. The most unsettling realization for the victors was that the inhabitants of the crown of Aragon, and the Catalans especially, carried disloyalty in their blood, just as Jews and Muslims had inherited their religious intractability, and it would take years, great vigilance, and repressive measures to "purge their blood of this malignancy entirely."[8]

The War of Succession allowed the Bourbons to introduce political reforms that could be justified as a "right of conquest." The implementation of these reforms, known as the Nueva Planta decrees, began while the civil war was still raging: in the kingdoms of Aragon and Valencia in June 1707, in the Balearic Islands in 1715, and in Catalonia in January 1716.[9] The various decrees differed in some respects, but the overriding objective was already evident in the one issued for Aragon and Valencia: "I have deemed it convenient . . . to reduce all my Kingdoms of Spain to the uniformity of the same laws, uses, customs and Tribunals, to be governed by the laws of Castile, so admirable and befitting the whole World."[10] This "castilianization" of the peninsular law codes was accompanied by the abrogation of all the rights, privileges, and constitutions of the old kingdoms. In practice—albeit not legally—the old kingdoms were thereafter treated as provinces linked directly to the monarchy.

Modern historians, and more than a few contemporaries, have been struck by the apparent similarities, as well as differences, between the simultaneous events in Spain and the political unification process in the British Isles. In the latter, the Treaty of Union was signed in 1707, which declared that the kingdoms of Scotland and England were to be "united into one kingdom by the name of Great Britain." This treaty followed decades of unrealized projects for a union as well as conflicts and civil wars. Both the Scottish and English Parliaments were formally dissolved, and elected representatives from both kingdoms would thenceforth come together to form the new Parliament of Great Britain. In 1708 this Parliament abolished the Scottish Privy Council, the body that until then had overseen the government of Scotland.[11]

Some contemporary Spanish observers saw the British union as a model for their country. The Aragonese Count of Robres, for example, although a partisan of the Bourbon cause, favored

MAP 3. Spain in 1789: Bourbon reforms
Spain divided in 28 intendancies, still respecting the old division in kingdoms. Portugal separated from the Spanish monarchy in 1640.

maintaining the *fueros* and privileges of the kingdoms of the crown of Aragon and pointed to the unification process in Great Britain as a possible blueprint. True, both Scots and English initially lamented the union—because they all "greatly love their ancient patrias, and it is impossible to expect immediate and universal approval on seeing sepulchered the authority of the nation that considers itself independent"—but Robres was nevertheless convinced that this would change over time. "The equity of the [terms of the] treaty and the accrual of great profits," he wrote, "would soften any bitterness, and truly there is no reason to think the Scottish name any more sepulchered than the English in the union of the two nations, but rather [there is every reason] to see both confounded in that of the Britons, the common ancient name of both peoples, and the parliament no longer univocally English, or Scottish, but of Great Britain." Robres also believed that the British model was more conducive to a genuine sense of unity than the one imposed by the Bourbons in Spain:

"There is no lack of those who insist that lord Philip V would be better served if he were to reduce his dominions to unity by this means rather than the *proclama* of 1707, because [if it were done in this way] it would be achieved with the appearance of a voluntary act, being seen as a national covenant and not as a punishment."[12]

In Spain, the process of unification was founded upon the military victory of Philip V's armies and not parliamentary debate as in the case of Britain. Even so, the similarities between the two processes are more striking than the differences. As J. G. A. Pocock has observed, "The British single kingdom . . . had been created to safeguard its own stability and act as a power in Europe."[13] This had also been the prevailing attitude in Spain from the seventeenth century onward and would be even more so in the eighteenth. Contemporary political thought dictated that small polities were doomed to be swallowed up by larger ones. Internal division led to decadence at home and defeat against foreign enemies abroad and made it impossible to harness efforts and resources in the cause of economic progress. One of the supporters of Philip V's reforms, Francisco Ronquillo, was a Spanish general of Philip V's army. He rose to become the president of the Council of Castile and noted that the outcome of the Nueva Planta decrees had been to reduce "the whole of this peninsula to that same unity it had in the time of the Goths, and when there is no other national designation but that of Spaniards, its power will be all the more tremendous than it was amid the profusion of almost foreign influences . . . and at last the time of the Count Duke of Olivares arrived, long desired, when the kings of Spain were unbound" by any other law save their own.[14]

The reality of the British union was far more complicated than Robres believed. Many Scots were not merely unenthused but actively in opposition to unification, if only because they predicted—in many ways correctly—that the union would ultimately favor England. England's dominant position within the composite monarchy created by James VI and I at the start of the seventeenth century would eventually transform the United Kingdom of Great Britain into a thoroughly Anglicized state. In other words, a union agreed to after parliamentary debate, and the product of a vote in Parliament, was not all that different in practice from the union obtained in the Iberian Peninsula through the unilateral, authoritarian implementation of reforms by Philip V as the fruit of a war between kingdoms.

The Nueva Planta decrees and subsequent reforms brought many changes in the political and territorial structure of the monarchy. Military commanders replaced the old viceroys, one of the most representative symbols of the composite character of the Habsburg monarchy, and had authority over political, judicial, and financial matters. This new political structure would be extended eventually to the rest of the peninsula. Eleven general captaincies were created, based in the head cities of each region (Santa Cruz, Sevilla, Málaga, Badajoz, Zamora, La Coruña, Asturias, Palma, Valencia, Zaragoza, and Barcelona). Only Navarre, Guipuzcoa, and Vizcaya maintained some of their traditional institutions as a reward for their unwavering loyalty to Philip V during the War of Succession. State finances were now wholly under the control of royal authorities, who determined the taxes to be levied and expenditures. The courts of justice were also castilianized, as Castilian law prevailed in judicial decisions, and the judiciary was disproportionately Castilian. The local authorities were no longer representative. Aldermen and magistrates were no longer elected by the different social estates but appointed by royal authorities in perpetuity and presided over by the *corregidor*, the local governor named directly by the king. Moreover, from the first years of Bourbon rule, the monarchy created a number of intendancies following the French model, one intendant chosen by the crown for each of the provinces into which the monarchy was now divided.

Reforms included other elements that in the past had been construed as crucial for the promotion of genuine national unity. Internal customs barriers, an impediment to the free circulation of people and goods, were abolished. This enabled the creation of a national market that, perhaps paradoxically, allowed Catalonia to become the most economically advanced region of the monarchy.[15] Moreover, and more importantly, the laws that reserved public offices in each kingdom for its natives were abolished. The importance of this principle was emphasized by one of the most interesting thinkers of the century, Miguel Antonio de la Gándara (1719–1783), better known as the Abbot of Gándara. He maintained that "to give all vassals, without distinction, equal patrimony in all of the King's dominions, in the provision of jobs and offices heeding neither nationality nor origin except the common one, the Spanish," was the only way to promote "the unity of all, and to extinguish the spirit of resistance from the hearts [of all]."[16]

The Nueva Planta decrees now authorized Castilians to obtain "offices and employment" in the kingdoms of the crown of Aragon and for the Aragonese "to enjoy [the same rights] in Castile."[17] Legally, at least in regard to appointments to various offices throughout the monarchy, there were no longer any Catalans, Basques, Galicians, or Castilians: all were Spaniards, with the same rights to employment, land, property, or commerce. With the benefit of hindsight, the Catalan jurist Ramón Lázaro de Dou y Bassols observed that since the Nueva Planta decrees, all the vassals "of the provinces of Spain" had the same right to exercise offices in each one of the peninsular regions. What mattered above all else was merit rather than one's province of birth. These changes had been inspired not by a desire to repress the subjects of the crown of Aragon but by the confirmation that all "the natives of a kingdom should look upon one another as brothers, sharing an interest in the common cause, and the for the benefit of the whole body."[18]

Political centralization reforms continued after the Nueva Planta decrees. The old councils that had assisted the kings in the governance of each of the separate kingdoms survived (with the exception of those of Flanders and Italy, which were abolished), but they were shorn of much of their authority and responsibilities. Seen as symbols of a moribund political world, the councils were supplanted by ministers chosen by the monarch, who could thus be replaced by dint of royal prerogative. The character of reforms became even more pronounced with the order for the integration of the Council of Aragon into the Council of Castile, which had kept its name but was now transformed into a supra-regional council.[19]

Unlike monarchs of previous centuries, the Bourbons also promoted linguistic uniformity, and following the pattern in other spheres, Castilian became the official language of Spain. Until the eighteenth century Castilian had been the de facto predominant language due to Castile's irresistible cultural and political sway over the other kingdoms. But in the eighteenth century, the defense of Castilian as the national tongue became more explicit and more interesting. The case was summed up by the Valencian intellectual Gregorio Mayans, who explained that Castilian—"[the language] generally spoken in Spain today"—was the dominant language because it was the one that best represented the entire aggregate of peninsular communities. Castilian was a hybrid language because within it were congregated all the cultures and languages that had at one time coexisted in the Iberian Peninsula—in order of precedence, Latin, Arabic, Greek, Hebrew, Celtic, Gothic, Punic, and Basque. Because all were subsumed in it—not because it was the language of the dominant political community—Castilian could legitimately be called "Spanish" and lawfully established as the official language of the Spanish nation.[20]

In the eighteenth century, unlike in the past, the monarchy itself was committed to the promotion of Castilian as the official language of Spain. The first move in this direction was the 1714 creation of the Royal Spanish Academy *(Real Academia Española)* to safeguard and promote the use of Castilian. In 1768 it was officially decreed that Castilian was the official language of Spain and its inhabitants because it was deemed necessary "to propagate the common idiom of the Nation for its greater harmony and mutual intelligibility." In 1770 this order was extended to the Americas and the Philippines, with the injunction that the natives of these territories should also be spoken to and taught in Castilian and that all other languages be allowed to expire.[21]

As part of the Nueva Planta reforms, the separate parliaments of the various kingdoms were suppressed, with the exception of the Castilian, augmented with representatives of the cities of Aragon's old kingdoms. This was now in theory a Spanish parliament, but it had virtually no political role. In other countries representative institutions were the loci of political debate (the Parliament in Great Britain, for example, and the provincial high courts in France, known as Parlements), but Spain lacked any such apparatus for feedback.[22] The Cortes met on various occasions in the course of the eighteenth century—in 1701, 1709, 1712–3, 1724–5, 1760, and 1789—but its main function was ceremonial, such as swearing allegiance to successive heirs to the throne. Not even at the 1789 meeting of the Cortes, when news of the revolution in neighboring France must have been on everyone's mind, was there any discussion of issues related to the welfare of the kingdoms. This might have been a means to reclaim the assembly's role as the nation's representative body.

From the perspective of state building, it is not at all clear that the reforms introduced by the Bourbons created in reality a united kingdom or state. To begin with, the Spanish king was still not legally the head of a single kingdom, as was the case in Great Britain. The Nueva Planta decrees "did not expressly proclaim the union of Castile and Aragon in a single larger entity called Spain, nor were the Aragonese kingdoms integrated into the crown of Castile. Instead they limited themselves to merely indicating that those kingdoms [of the crown of Aragon] would thenceforth be ruled in the same manner as those of Castile."[23] In other words, there was no kingdom called Spain, nor was the monarch legally considered to be king of Spain. Rather, the Bourbons continued to use the rather cumbersome list of separate titles—some of them obsolete, others little more than symbolic—that their Habsburg forbears had amassed and made their own: "King of Castile, of Leon, of Aragon, of the Two Sicilies, of Jerusalem, of Navarre, of Granada, of Toledo, of Valencia, of Galicia." The conclusion to be drawn is that monarchs were not interested in creating a "united kingdom" or even a "castilianized" monarchy. What they wanted, in fact, was "to establish or assert [their] absolute and unfettered sovereignty, unrestricted by any condition or circumstance," with recourse in some instances to Castilian political structures and law.[24]

To many, it was clear that if "regions" no longer exhibited an active consciousness of themselves as nations and kingdoms, this was not because their feelings on the matter had changed but because the monarchy had curtailed opportunities for the nurture and public display of particularist claims and separate identities. They had eliminated regional institutions or filled them with Castilians. The Catalan elites, for instance, continued throughout the century to raise concerns about what they saw less as the "hispanization" of the monarchy than its "castilianization." In one statement of grievances presented during the Cortes of 1760—although the memorandum in question was never discussed by the entire assembly—Catalan representatives, armed with relevant data, made it known that only a scant few Aragonese occupied some of the most important public offices in the peninsula, either in Aragon or Castile. The confirmation was as obvious as it was lamentable, for "Your Majesty had intended that in both Crowns jobs should be distributed promiscuously, without distinction of nation and with regard only to merits. You had thrown open the doors between the two kingdoms, and in fact Castilians found them open and freely entered Aragon to take up the best appointments, and yet for the Aragonese, Catalans and Valencians the doors of Castile have been virtually shut."[25] Independent of the Catalans, the Valencian representatives in this Cortes also presented memoranda to request, among other things, some of the political rights abolished by the Nueva Planta decrees. The eighteenth century also witnessed the beginning of the process of "nationalization" in the Basque Country, when the Basques began to imagine themselves as an ethnic and political nation, the "Republic of the United Provinces of the Pyrenees" in the words of the Basque Jesuit Manuel de Larramendi.[26] In light of these and other developments it appeared that regional identities and patriotism were merely dormant and that they could be stirred when the political opportunity arose.

It was generally acknowledged in the eighteenth century that rulers such as the Spanish Bourbons were not interested in a nation of politically active citizens but a monarchy peopled by loyal subjects. Perhaps the king of England, whose prerogatives were limited by Parliament, could eventually be considered an active citizen at the service of a recently united nation. Not so the Spanish monarchs. While some were not averse to working for the good of their subjects—this was, after all, the official ideology, with the king presented as the devoted father of his subjects—their paramount goal was to protect, strengthen, and increase the dynasty's reputation. In the case of the Bourbons, their relationship with their subjects was further complicated because most of the members of the new ruling dynasty were barely Spanish. Philip V had been born in France, where he spent the first seventeen years of his life, and what he coveted above all else was to be crowned king of France. One of his successors, Charles III, the monarch most open to political reforms, was born in Spain, but from the age of fifteen and for more than two decades thereafter, he lived in Italy as the king of Naples and Sicily until his succession to the Spanish throne in 1759. The Bourbons were a French dynasty that had been the archenemy of Spain and its kings for centuries. In the 1700s the royal house tended to impose French fashions and language in the Spanish court and to affiliate Spain's international interests with the French branch of the family.

All the evidence suggests that the Bourbons neither pursued nor encouraged policies designed to foster a genuine unity of the different Spanish kingdoms or to create among Spaniards the sense that Spain was the motherland to which all owed their undivided loyalty. This is not to say, however, that we cannot discern in eighteenth-century Spain processes of the "forging" of a Spanish nation or of a consciousness among the inhabitants of the peninsula that they belonged to a Spanish nation. In practice, the key agents in this forging of the nation were neither the state nor the parliamentary institutions but a handful of individuals who, from various political positions, were acutely attuned to the subject of the nation and motherland. One of the great minds of the eighteenth century, the activist and intellectual Abbot of Gándara, expressed it clearly in what was perhaps the most fascinating text of the period, *Apuntes sobre el bien y el mal de España (Notes on the Virtues and Ills of Spain)*. In this work he proposed a number of initiatives to create a Spanish nation and a new Spanish citizen. He reminded his readers that, although the king undoubtedly had the most "love of motherland" *(amor patrio)*, the true protagonists and those who should exert themselves to create and strengthen the nation were its people, especially the Enlightened elites.[27]

This was a gradual process that engaged members of the political and cultural elites of all different regions of Spain. Implemented initiatives were mainly restricted to the cultural sphere and, less frequently, the political. The majority of these authors cleaved to some idea of Spain as a timeless "natural nation," a popular concept in earlier centuries as well. Others, in contrast, spoke of the need to actively create or invent the nation, in Benedict Anderson's terminology, through the government and the people. It should also be noted that debates on the need to create a Spanish nation affected that other prevalent eighteenth-century concept: *patria*. Catalan Antonio Capmany elucidated the relationship between the two concepts (nation and *patria*) and their mutual transformation in a text written in the early 1800s and published in 1808: "Where there is no nation, there is no patria." Italy and Germany, two countries divided and perpetually subject to foreign rulers, proved this to be true. "If the Italians and the Germans, divided and torn into so many states with different interests, customs, and governments, should have formed a single people, they would not have been invaded nor dismembered. These are vast regions, described and indicated on maps, but they are not nations, even though they speak the same language. The general cry, Germans!, Italians!, does not inflame the spirit of any individual, because not one of them belongs to a [single] whole."[28]

Certainly, those who were preoccupied with such questions at the beginning of the eighteenth century were fully aware of their precedents. There appears to have been no change in the concept of nation from that articulated in the first edition of the *Dictionary of Castilian Language (Diccionario de la lengua castellana)* in 1734, where *nation* was defined as "the collection of the inhabitants of a Province, Country or Kingdom" and *patria* as "the Place, City or Country of one's birth." Terms such as *nationalism* or *patriotism* did not yet exist.[29]

From within the confines of his monastery, the Galician Benedictine monk Benito Jerónimo Feijóo reflected upon these old terms and concepts of nation and patria and how they might have caused the recent civil wars. Spaniards had fought one another in the early years of the eighteenth century, and Spain was not recovering as quickly as it should because of the false love of the "patria chica," the "little patria," or the "natural patria." Feijóo would identify this malaise as "*paisanismo*" (parochialism), "that inordinate affection, not for the Republic as a whole, but one's own, particular territory," for each kingdom and region, for the town and village of one's birth. This *paisanismo*, and not a natural inclination toward rebellion, was the root cause of the numerous conflicts that Spain had experienced throughout her history: "The love of the particular Patria, rather than being useful to the Republic, is noxious on many counts: Whether because it induces divisions in spirits that should be mutually united, so as to give strength and constancy to the common society; or because it is an incitement to civil wars, and revolts against the Sovereign, so long as the inhabitants of any Province, believing themselves aggrieved, judge the vindication of this [little] Patria a duty superior to all others."[30]

Finding a way to loosen the grasp of *paisanismo* and replace it with a true sense of nation and *patria* was undoubtedly a central preoccupation for eighteenth-century Spaniards. Feijóo had outlined the ideal in his essay. The true *patria*—the one worth dying for and to which all should owe their loyalty—was the "common homeland" *(patria común)*, Spain, which was now defined as the "body of the State, where under a single civil government we are united by the yoke of the same laws." Spain—not provinces, kingdoms, or towns and cities—would thus be "the proper object of the Spaniard's affections, just as France will be for the Frenchman, and Poland for the Pole."[31]

All measures implemented by successive eighteenth-century governments, in addition to proposals made by a significant number of individuals from every region, were designed to advance the ideal and creation of a shared homeland for all Spaniards. It would be a "stable and firm body of the Nation" based on "the unity of religion, of language, laws, coinage, customs and government, with equal distribution of offices and favors."[32] Not that Spaniards were expected to forget their regional identities or eliminate them completely. On the contrary, these would be always present and vital, although the objective was to create a hierarchy of loyalties and identities with Spanish identity uppermost as the only shared one.

Forging the Spanish nation required its would-be architects to look anew at the country's history in the belief that a nation could not exist without a shared history of origins, laws, religion, culture, and exploits. This history, or the writing of this history, alone could transform a disparate collection of individuals and communities into a living, unified nation.[33] In this regard Spain was part of the historiographical revolution that so characterized the Enlightenment, by which greater importance was assigned to documentary sources and the need to analyze and not simply describe.[34] More important than epistemological shifts, however, were the initiatives undertaken by the state as well as private individuals to promote the shared history of Spain as a keystone for a unified nation.

In 1738 the monarchy supported the creation of the Royal Academy of History *(Real Academia de la Historia)*, akin to the language academy, which would instigate and oversee the promotion of Spanish history and publish a biographical dictionary of all Spaniards who had contributed to the development of the nation. In 1754 it also was charged with writing a new history of Spanish America.[35] The academy's achievements were negligible, but important histories of Spain were published in the eighteenth century. They included Juan de Ferreras' impressive *Sinopsis histórica y cronológica de las cosas de España (Historical-Chronological Compendium of the Affairs of Spain)*, published in sixteen volumes between 1700 and 1727; the massive history of Christianity and the Christian church in Spain, Enrique Flórez's *Sacred Spain (España sagrada, teatro geográfico-histórico de la Iglesia de España)*, published in twenty-nine volumes between 1747 and 1775 and continued by other authors until it had expanded to fifty-six volumes; and the even more important history of Spanish contributions to European culture since antiquity, the *Historia crítica de España y de la cultura española* (*Critical History of Spain and Spanish Culture*) written by the Spanish Jesuit exiled in Italy Juan Francisco Masdeu, which was published in twenty volumes between 1783 and 1805. Other milestones included the translation into Castilian of Nicolás Antonio's *Biblioteca Hispana* and the publication of Juan Sempere y Guarinos's *Catalogue of Spanish Writers of the Reign of Carlos III (Ensayo de una biblioteca española de los escritores del reinado de Carlos III)*, a sort of history of eighteenth-century Spanish literature. In keeping with the times, the activities of the academy and the works published in this period always privileged the history of the Spanish nation as a whole and marginalized regional histories, which would not truly resurge until the second half of the 1800s.[36]

Beyond the publication of erudite histories, however, the eighteenth century was notable for the popularization of the history of Spain. Visions of the country's history began to infiltrate works aimed at the general public (historical compendia), theatrical works, and paintings. The ultimate aim of, or the guiding principle behind, such efforts was expressed by the poet Tomás de Iriarte, the author of one of the most popular histories of Spain. Insofar as we are all part of one nation, "we are all obliged to know the history of our Patria."[37] All of these popular histories tended to foreground events and exploits that could unify Spaniards and inspire pride in their homeland and ancestors: Tubal and the origins of Spain; the strong attraction exercised by Spain on other peoples due to its favorable natural conditions; the indigenous resistance to the Carthaginians and Romans; the arrival of the Visigoths and the first experience of Spanish unity; the Arab invasion, once again emphasizing Christians' resistance, leading to the final and complete restoration of Spain; the discovery and conquest of America; and the transformation of Spain into the preponderant power in Europe, beginning in the sixteenth century. These histories illustrated Spaniards' ethnic continuity and their unity across centuries, immutable customs, greatest deeds, defeats and great triumphs, and kings. They also illustrated sacrifices made by individuals and communities for the glory of Spain.[38]

In the rhetorical construction of national identity, the movement is more perceptible. Although it is not easy to measure the impact of literature and literary efforts, there is some evidence from the mid-1700s, at least, of more frequent references to Spain as the nation and common motherland of all Iberian Peninsula inhabitants. And it is important to emphasize that these references come from individuals and institutions from all the disparate regions of Spain. The Abbot of Gándara summed up these new national and patriotic sentiments when he claimed, "I have no other patria, party, nationhood, or blood than Spain, Spain, and Spain."[39] Juan Pablo Forner, a more traditionalist thinker, agreed that the love of *patria*, of Spain, was the hub of everything else, a sort of "cement of the political edifice," and if this love were to dissipate and the union broken, "I say frankly that such a nation would degenerate into a brutal and barbarous one." Forner also pointed out that love of *patria* was not simply, or only, something natural but also to some extent created and reinforced when a community shared "the same laws, the same customs, the same interests, and [was bound] by ties of mutual dependence."[40]

The Catalan Jesuit Juan Nuix considered himself to be "as Spanish as the Castilians" who had conquered America. Like them he would defend Spain against the attacks of foreigners, guided, as they had been, by the "national spirit" and the "love of the patria."[41]

This new vision of Spain as the nation of all, and the emergence of a Spanish patriotism, is evident in the evolution of concepts such as *nation*, *patria*, and *patriotism* and even a term so ostensibly straightforward as *foreigner*. In the second part of the eighteenth century, these concepts had acquired a new layer of complexity. For example, in the *Castilian Dictionary (Diccionario castellano)* published in the 1780s by Esteban de Terreros y Pando, "Nation" was now "the collective name designating a great People, Kingdom, [or] State subject to the same Prince or Government," and so it may be said that one is of "the German, Swedish, [or] English nation." Meanwhile, "Patria" was "the Country of one's birth." Patriotism as the love of *patria* or nation also began to feature in the vocabulary of Spanish authors from at least the 1760s, although initially love of *patria* was still thought of as a natural sentiment common to all human beings.[42]

A more modern concept of patriotism is used in a 1799 work by Joseph López de la Huerta, who distinguished between "love of the Patria [on one hand], and Patriotism," the former being a natural sentiment, passively acquired to some extent, while patriotism amounted to "an ardent desire to serve her [the Patria], to defend her, to contribute to her advancement, her wellbeing, her prosperity."[43] The changing concept of *patria*, and its closer connection to the term *nation*, is clearly evident in a discourse penned by the governor of the Council of the Indies, Antonio Porlier, marquis of Bajamar, which distinguishes between the old conception of the "sweet love" that everyone feels for the place of their birth and upbringing and the love we all feel for "our Nation. This is the true Patria, the mother of all, our only protectress, the depositary of our collective happiness." The love of the *patria chica* is "personal and individual," while the love of the "Patria" is "universal and vital to the Nation at large."[44] The change is even more marked in the words *extranjero* ("foreigner") and *forastero* ("nonresident, visitor"). Prior to the War of Spanish Succession, a Valencian, Catalan, or Mallorcan living in Madrid would have been "as foreign [over there] as a

Russian" because he or she was not "of that land or country." All that had changed by the end of the eighteenth century. Now, "a foreigner is the vassal of another sovereign," while Mallorcans, Catalans, Valencians, or Basques are no longer "foreigners" ("extranjeros") in Madrid but merely nonresidents ("forasteros"), who were as Spanish as the Madrileños.[45]

This strengthening of a common Spanish identity did not obliterate regional identities, especially not the Catalan. These identities, as José de Cadalso explained, were hard to eradicate because each was the product of a unique history, which was the source of difference between a Galician and a Catalan or a Valencian and an Andalusian.[46] Others also insisted that these regional identities were compatible with a Spanish identity, so long as they were subordinate and constituted a cultural and not a political identity.[47] The establishment of Societies of Friends of the Country *(Sociedades de Amigos del País)*, or patriotic societies, was predicated on the persistence of these regional identities and the belief that to promote the idea of Spain, it was essential to appreciate the idiosyncrasies of each of its component parts. In any case, contemporary observers saw these regional patriotic societies in essence as "the abode of [Spanish] patriotism."[48] A great number of late eighteenth-century Spaniards concluded that although regionalist diversity and tensions had not disappeared, decades of the promotion of a Spanish identity had left them "reduced, and virtually annihilated."[49]

Eighteenth-century Spaniards were more preoccupied with the need to defend Spain and the Spanish character against scathing criticism from other European countries than with the persistence of regional identity. This obsession with the national character was not unique to Spaniards, or to the eighteenth century. In earlier periods there had been some interest in defining and comparing the character of each European nation. Yet in the eighteenth-century context, defining the "national character" increasingly meant isolating the physical and intellectual peculiarities of each nation. The intention was not to think of the Spaniard, Englishman, and Frenchman as members of distinct races, but perhaps inevitably many of the terms and concepts used were reminiscent of those utilized by contemporary natural historians to portray human diversity. In other words, Europeans, and especially the Spanish, discussed national characteristics in order to place themselves squarely within the bounds of the European family, which was increasingly identified as the white race.[50]

Writers depicted the character of a people to gain insight into their temperament and customs as well as the moral and intellectual characteristics of an entire nation. As in earlier periods, the elements that combined to create the "natural character of a Nation—the physical properties, the native disposition or nature, or essential quality that marks and distinguishes it from the rest"—were the product of natural conditions as well as education, laws, and government.[51] This diversity between nations was natural and ordained by God, the ultimate author of the variety of natural conditions, languages, and cosmic influences.[52] The national character—and here it resembled concepts that would shape racialist discourse—was conceived in terms that rendered it particularly important. It was permanent, immutable, and present from the very genesis of each nation in the post-diluvian dispersion. These essential characteristics were so profoundly ingrained in the members of a nation that they could only be altered or erased through biological mixing with other peoples.[53]

Spaniards were not reflecting on their national character in a vacuum. Other Europeans developed an exceptionally negative image of Spain and the Spanish in the 1700s. In Spain, as in other European countries, the forging of the nation was shaped through confrontation with an external "other." This was not (at least not until 1808) a case of military struggles against enemies in the Iberian Peninsula itself. From the beginning of the eighteenth century until the early nineteenth, Spain was involved in, and was affected by, various military conflicts with other European countries, but the majority of these took place beyond Spanish borders.

From the cultural perspective, the main antagonists were still the French—not the French state but French intellectuals, who were sometimes joined by other Europeans. From the beginning of the century, Spain had to face a growing tide of disparaging critiques from other Europeans, who, among other things, questioned whether

Spain should even be considered a European nation. Criticism of Spain was nothing new, but now the tone, scope, ideas, and impact of the critiques among Spaniards were all quite different. There was no longer talk of Spain's desire to dominate Europe and become a universal monarchy and nothing about Spaniards' unwarranted pride or their haughtiness toward other Europeans. Spain was not talked about as a land of conquistadors but as a place marked by religious fanaticism, cultural backwardness, and political despotism. It was now seen as a country repeatedly conquered and subjugated by outsiders and unable to advance apace with more progressive European countries.

Many Europeans had an image of Spain, one shared by many Spaniards, as an empire that had scaled previously unheard of heights, only to enter a period of equally unremitting, and perhaps irreversible, decline. It was hardly a unique historical case. Eighteenth-century Europeans found the decline and fall of empires, past and present, perennially fascinating. The Greek and Roman empires were two signal cases because both had shaped the course of European history and culture. Spain's decadence was not placed in the same category as the two great powers of antiquity. Rome and Greece had also suffered decline, but even in the 1700s, their influence was felt in every European nation. Regardless of their opinion of their Greek and Roman contemporaries, Europeans considered themselves the intellectual and cultural heirs of ancient Greece and Rome.[54]

Spain was not viewed on such lofty terms. To the contrary, Spain became the target of withering criticism from European scholars and travelers. It had acquired a far-flung empire but had left nothing of value intellectually, culturally, artistically or scientifically. This in turn was attributed to Spaniards' national character. The idea that Spain was a backward country due to the nature of its inhabitants, and not its adverse fortune, was made explicit in works such as Abbé Raynal's *Histoire philosophique et politique des établissements et du commerce des européens dans les deux Indes* (1770). Raynal and his collaborators' main goal was to criticize Spanish colonialism as the cruelest in the history of European expansion. But they also portrayed Spain as a foreign-dominated country throughout its history, internally divided and unable to make any progress in the sciences and letters.[55]

In book VI, for example, Raynal introduced his readers to the history of a semi-barbarous people unable to profit from the country's many riches or to build sound political structures. Their ignorance made possible successive conquests of the peninsula by the Carthaginians and Romans. Spaniards, he wrote, "debased themselves to become slaves of the Romans, in which state they remained until the fifth century." The Visigoths, one of "the savage nations of the north," followed the Romans and reduced "all the kingdoms of Spain to one; which, notwithstanding the defects in its constitution, and the unbridled extortions of the Jews, who were the only merchants, supported itself until the inception of the eighth century." At this point the Moors, the "masters of Africa," were able to conquer Spain, by then a completely corrupted country. Dominated by the Moors, much more sophisticated than the Iberian Peninsula inhabitants, Spaniards divided themselves into "many kingdoms and provinces," only provisionally reunited after the marriage of Ferdinand and Isabel. The conquest in 1492 of the last Muslim kingdom, Granada, the richest and most civilized state on the Iberian Peninsula, paved the way for the grand adventure of the conquest and colonization of the Americas. However, this conquest made Spain even weaker. With the riches coming in from the Americas, laziness replaced love of work, and superstition eclipsed intellectual curiosity: "Whilst Europe was daily improving in knowledge, and all nations were animated with a spirit of industry, Spain was falling into inaction and barbarism."

Nicolas Masson de Morvilliers, author of the essay "Espagne" in the *Encyclopédie Méthodique*, culminated this foreign appraisal of Spain with a devastating assessment. Morvilliers observed that all, or nearly all, European nations—France, England, and Italy but also Russia, Poland, Norway, Denmark, Sweden, and others—were contributing to intellectual discovery and scientific advances and progressing in the education of their inhabitants. But not Spain. Europe owed nothing to Spain, and Spaniards had not made any contribution to knowledge, collective intellectual endeavors, or the general enlightenment of European societies at the present time or in centuries past. Intellectually, Spain was a "colony" of Europe, dependent on the rest of the continent for its development and modernization.[56] The Dutch philosopher and naturalist Cornelius De Pauw described

Spaniards as idlers and fanatics, while Montesquieu insisted that the Portuguese and Spanish required tutelage because "properly speaking they were not Europeans."[57]

Spaniards had never been equipped to sustain the power they had acquired in previous centuries, and intellectually they had never contributed anything to Europe's cultural stock. Even more galling than these assertions, for the Spaniards, was the apparently widespread European belief that, although belonging to the European lineage, they showed clear signs of degeneration. The two most common explanations for this were the prevailing climatic conditions in Spain, generally more extreme than in the rest of Europe, and, alternately, biological mixing historically with other peoples. The result is that Spaniards were brown *(morenos)* instead of entirely white. In the past Europeans had described the Spaniards in similar terms, but in the eighteenth century the descriptions and underlying explanations became more sophisticated and more alarming for the Spanish. The Spanish edition of Comte de Buffon's work on the *Natural History of Man* described Spaniards based on theories to explain Africans' dark skin. Babies in Spain "are born fair and handsome," wrote Buffon, "but as they grow up their complexion changes surprisingly; the air and sun render them yellow and tawny; nor is it difficult to distinguish a Spaniard from a native of any other country in Europe."[58] In preceding centuries these could be dismissed as superficial elements, and as earlier noted, many Spaniards thought that a tanned complexion was preferable to being too pale. However, in the increasingly racialist cultural environment of the eighteenth century, skin color determined a people's position in the hierarchy of nations and lineages. Thus, although all human beings were naturally darker at the end of their lives than at the beginning, what mattered was that some peoples were generally darker than others: "a Spaniard more brown than a Frenchman, a Moor [tawnier] than a Spaniard . . . a Negro blacker than a Moor."[59]

Even more unsettling for Spaniards, an increasing number of authors from the mid-1700s onward insisted that skin color was an intrinsic, and therefore indelible, characteristic of a given people, not an artifact of climate. In the case of European peoples, the climate could only induce minor changes, and thus any significant variations in skin color were attributable to racial mixing. If a European people, such as the Spanish, appeared darker than the rest, this could only be the result of mixing with non-Europeans—Arabs, Jews, black Africans, or American natives. Many Europeans believed that even if Spaniards had once been of common, European stock, over time and as a consequence of intermingling, they had lost that original purity and were now closer to North Africans than to their French neighbors. In other words, Europeans appeared to echo a sentiment expressed in the late eighteenth century: "Spain is located in Europe only through a geographical error."[60]

Needless to say, not all Europeans shared this opinion of Spain and Spaniards. For many, Spain remained the cradle of the most orthodox Catholicism, a monarchy whose king was distinguished by his paternalism rather than despotism and with imperial traditions that were worthy of study and even emulation.[61] It also goes without saying that many Spaniards thought these criticisms ill-conceived, the product of ignorance and envy. The cultural and intellectual history of the Spanish eighteenth century is to a large extent a history of Spanish responses to such negative outside perceptions. This is not to say that the Spaniards themselves were unwilling to acknowledge their country's problems. A significant number of all those who reflected on Spain's predicament or tried to respond to foreigners' criticism took a sharply critical view of past governments. Many wrote simple apologies for Spain, but many others offered constructive responses and proposed profound political and economic reforms. Surveying the thousands of texts, memoranda, and pamphlets that appeared throughout the eighteenth century, one is struck by three recurring motifs: Spain's enormous, albeit dormant, strength; the many ills afflicting the country; and the remedies required for its complete recovery.

This is indeed what Spain represented for many of its domestic critics: a naturally strong body enfeebled by centuries of ill-advised government policies but whose chances of improvement and recovery were nevertheless great.[62] In eighteenth-century Spain, as elsewhere, reforms of all kinds were very much on the agenda. Spaniards wanted to create a new system of education and bring light to the most isolated regions of the peninsula and the colonies and engaged in a lively public debate on the future of the nation. The criticism became even more intense after the French Revolution, with many authors denouncing the Spanish political system as retrograde and not befitting a European state. They suggested reforms intended to limit the power of the monarch and endow the nation with truly representative institutions.[63]

Responding to European criticism, Spaniards insisted that their country was an integral part of Europe, which was in turn the most perfect region of the earth, and that, despite being divided into separate polities, Europe was in many senses "a single nation, in which the sciences and the arts are cultivated in emulation [of one another]."[64] Spaniards also insisted that they had always been, and still were, of European stock and, in essence, white. If they had mixed with others, it had always been with populations of similar "national character." However, it was no easier in the eighteenth century than before to determine with great certainty which peoples had given origin to contemporary Spaniards. This was not for want of trying, including ongoing efforts to uncover and analyze documentary and archaeological evidence.[65] Yet the information was so vague and the evidence so sparse to begin with that it was hard to ascertain precisely the identity of these first settlers or of those they would have mixed with over the centuries.

Lorenzo Hervás y Panduro was a Castilian-born Spanish Jesuit who was exiled to Italy in 1767, and he provided the best response to this conundrum. "These primitive settlers of Europe . . . ," he wrote, "had always maintained close ties to one another, for they are of the same immediate family, and had in all times been established in adjoining countries, and had always known each other, and shared their civic and scientific achievements."[66] All European lineages or nations were descended from Noah's son Japheth or, rather, from one of Japheth's sons—Gomer, Javan, or Tubal. In turn they had engendered the three primordial nations: the Celts (direct descendants of Gomer), who had populated France, Brittany, part of the British Isles, and other northern countries; the Ionians (descendants of Javan), who gave origin to the Greeks and Italians; and the Iberians (descendants of Tubal), who settled in the Iberian Peninsula.[67] It was generally accepted that these autochthonous nations had expanded beyond their original territories commingled. The Celts, for instance, were said to have once occupied large parts of the Iberian Peninsula—a theory that had been around for centuries—and had mixed with some of the native peoples to become the Celtiberians.[68]

All of these peoples shared certain characteristics from their very origins. To begin with, they were all white, thus staking claim for themselves and their descendants at the apex of the hierarchy of nations. This was indeed how the matter was perceived in the eighteenth century, when white peoples were identified as the most perfect in the physical sense and as paragons of moral and intellectual perfection. In Spain, this notion of the convergence of physical and mental perfection in the white-skinned individual was endorsed as early as 1726, in the *Diccionario de Autoridades.* It defined the "White man, white woman" as "a person of honor, nobility, and recognized quality. Because the blacks, mulattos, men of Barbary *(berberiscos)* and other peoples who amongst us are taken for frivolous and contemptible, are not normally white, unlike Europeans, who are nearly always so. Being a white man, or white woman, is seen as a natural prerogative, which distinguishes those who possess it as well-born."[69]

Eighteenth-century Spaniards certainly described themselves as white. Perhaps not as pale as the Germans or English, but that was all to the better, given that extreme whiteness was incongruent with the color of the great nations of classical antiquity, the Italians and the Greeks. Fernández Navarrete, for instance, described the Spaniard as a man of good stature, swarthy or *moreno* in color, more or less white, with chestnut or black hair, generally curly, not tinged with the red or light tones of other Europeans. Although well proportioned, the Spaniard tended to be neither too fat nor excessively tall. Spaniards were said to have other common features: they were religious, perhaps proud and too preoccupied with questions of honor, but also, and despite this, intelligent, frugal, brave, and tremendously loyal and obedient to authority.[70] Nicolás Antonio or Juan Francisco de Masdeu set out to demonstrate in their works the Spaniards' intelligence, which had produced great philosophers, theologians, and literary and scientific figures.[71] The Spanish were perhaps a less industrious European nation, but this was due to "the lack of regulations, of learning, method, and the encouragement and tolerance of idlers," and not their intrinsic nature. No "other [nation] in Europe would be more active with the right leadership and direction."[72]

In the eighteenth century women were also beginning to factor in to these reflections on national character. This was partly because contemporary Spaniards acknowledged that the biological reproduction of the nation depended on the qualities of "their" women, just as they were aware of other Europeans' generally unfavorable opinion of Spanish women.[73] Images of women in Spain, as in the rest of eighteenth-century Europe, were influenced by new biological theories on differences between the sexes, which purported, much like theories of race, "to define social and cultural differences between men and women as 'natural' and therefore right and inevitable . . . Increasingly, medical writings seemed to imply that women were virtually a separate species within the human race."[74] In Spain's case, however, views also persisted by which women were by nature equal to men, although they occupied very different social roles.[75] For Benito Jerónimo Feijóo, who wrote more on the subject than most, the Spanish woman was essentially no different from the man in her physical and mental attributes, which was evident from many examples of female scholars, religious women, queens, and above all those brave women, "Amazons," who had helped defeat "the enemies of the patria."[76] This new importance accorded to women in discussions of the nation and its propagation helps explain why for the first time the female sex is included in descriptions of the Spanish national character. Fernández de Navarrete, for instance, dedicated several passages to the demonstration that Spanish women resembled their menfolk in many ways and should thus be classified as "white" (more so than the men) and as such bearers of the same physical and mental attributes as male Spaniards. Perhaps they were not as beautiful as other European women (in counterbalance to the prevailing European image of Spanish women—dark and orientalized, which is to say, possessing a dangerous beauty), but certainly they shared their intellectual and physical qualities.[77]

There is no indication, however, of debates in the eighteenth century that would become so central in the next one, over whether women should be part of the process of nation building, which would imply a more prominent social and political role. In the eighteenth century, and setting political ideology aside, men had no doubt that the woman's role in nation formation was that of protective mother. As Inés Joyes y Blake pointed out at the close of the century, society reserved women "for the noble destiny of respectable mothers of the family, and wives whose affable manners would enable their consorts to bear the heavy burden of the cares of this world."[78] Men on the other hand should occupy political offices and be heads of families at the same time, which confirmed their sovereignty over both spheres, the private and the public. "For although [men and women's] talents are equal," Blake continued, "one of the two must be the supreme head in the government of the household, and the family; anything else would be confusion, and disorder."[79]

The idea that the *patria* (the motherland, in the Spanish case) was also a mother to all her inhabitants began to permeate political imagery. From this standpoint, the woman could no longer be seen exclusively in her reproductive role as the perpetuator of the nation but also as a role model for new generations of Spaniards. This dictated that she acquire education and good manners and customs. Perhaps as a result, some Societies of Friends of the Country were prepared to discuss the possibility of female members. Ultimately, only the Madrid Society actually inducted a number of women to oversee initiatives pertaining to their own sex, especially the education of girls. The author Joyes y Blake urged women to remember "that your souls are equal to those of the sex that would oppress you; use the light given to you by the Creator; if you so wished, you could bring about a reformation of customs, which will never arrive without you."

Eighteenth-century Spaniards still could not escape the fact that other Europeans saw them as members of a race that had mixed historically with Jews, Arabs, and perhaps other Africans. Although some Spaniards conceded that their original white color "has been bastardized through commerce with black or excessively dark nations" in the peninsula and the Iberian world generally, others insisted that this was more of a problem in Portugal than Spain.[80] Whatever the case, if in earlier times reflections on Africans as part of the Spanish racial heritage were few and far between, the eighteenth century witnessed the almost total effacement of Africans. Significant numbers of African slaves were present in Spain during the 1500s and 1600s, but in the 1700s their numbers dwindled considerably. In Cádiz, to cite one example, 300 slaves were baptized between 1700 and 1711, but only six throughout all of the 1790s.[81] By this point, and thereafter, no one was prepared to venture an "Ethiopian" contribution to the nation's cultural or biological heritage.[82]

It was much harder to dismiss the Arab and Jewish elements. Both were part of the collective historical consciousness and, as many Spaniards and Europeans believed, the nation's biological inheritance. The Spanish writer Hervás y Panduro called attention to the prevalence among Spaniards and Portuguese of the aquiline or "Jewish nose," as it was referred to at the time, and many others were convinced that the Spaniards' tawny color was the product of a combination of climate and centuries of mingling with Jews and Arabs.[83] Such assumptions of racial mixing elicited a number of entirely predictable responses from many eighteenth-century Spaniards, which drew on deep-seated traditions and attitudes. Foremost was the belief that Spanishness could not incorporate Jews and Arabs, not in the least because both were perceived as eternal enemies of the Christians and Spaniards and as foreign elements that earlier had been expurgated from the nation. Anti-Semitism of the kind developed since the late seventeenth century and analyzed in Chapter 3 remained a prominent ideological strand that would become especially obvious during moments of civil unrest. Spanish intellectuals in the eighteenth century liked to believe that anti-Semitism flourished only among lower classes, but we know that it was also prevalent among the elites. Perhaps the most compelling evidence for the continued vitality of these ideological traditions is that throughout the eighteenth century purity of blood was a prerequisite for access to public offices in Spain while the Inquisition was unrelenting in its persecution of individuals accused of Judaizing.[84]

Meanwhile, Arabs continued to be seen as a backward people and an African race. Although not as dark as sub-Saharan inhabitants, they had the additional blemish of being the bearers and propagators of the Islamic faith. In much of eighteenth-century historiography, and especially in the compendia, the image of the "Moors" was unchanged: they were African barbarians who had conquered Spain and perpetrated unspeakable atrocities.[85] The struggle against

Muslims was still presented as the defining feature of Spain, and of Spaniards, who were heroic, brave, invincible, and incorruptible in their religious beliefs. Indeed, it was precisely in the eighteenth century that one of most enduring national myths was first consolidated, that of the Reconquest.[86]

Cultural and intellectual attitudes toward Spanish contact with Jews and Arabs were more complex, however, and transcended the simple continuation of these older trends. The eighteenth century also witnessed attempts to reclaim the notion of "Spanish" Jews and Arabs or, in contemporary parlance, "*our* Jews and Arabs." It was also at this time that another enduring idea, in a sense the obverse of the myth of Reconquest, was first proposed: the theory of "convivencia" (coexistence) of the three religions, or peoples, of medieval Spain and the belief that this coexistence was undone by religious, not racial, reasons. Those who espoused such arguments did not exactly deny that Spaniards had mixed with Jews and Arabs but insisted that neither of these peoples or races were distinct from the Spanish, at least not those who had lived on the Iberian Peninsula for centuries.

One response to the accusation that the Spaniards were a mixed race was to declare that Jews who had lived in Spain, and especially those who remained after 1492, were not members of a distinct Jewish race. The argument held that although the Jews originally came from Syria and Palestine, the majority had gradually acquired the predominant physical characteristics of their adopted land as they dispersed. This was especially true in places, such as Spain, where they ended up mixing with the natives and integrating into local societies.[87] Many observed that Portuguese Jews had indeed kept many of their original characteristics because they were generally endogamous, but others, such as the German Jews, "are no darker than other Germans . . . The inhabitants of Judea [meanwhile] resemble the Turks, only they are even darker than those of Constantinople."[88] The same was said to be true of the Spanish Jews, the only difference between them and Spaniards in the fifteenth century being their religious beliefs.

This strictly religious difference, according to Feijóo, incited the persecution of the Jews in Spain, which, more precisely, was a response to obstinate Jewish (and in a few cases converso) loyalty to their faith.[89] But it was generally maintained that Spaniards had done everything possible to facilitate the integration of converted Jews. These issues and attitudes rose to prominence in the eighteenth century, in no small part owing to the existence of one converso community, the Chuetas of Mallorca, who continued to suffer persecution and marginalization despite their official conversion in the late fifteenth century. Following investigations undertaken by and debates in the Council of Castile, however, the decision was taken to suspend all the laws that impeded the Chuetas from holding public offices because once their conversion to Catholicism had been demonstrated, there could no longer be: "any distinction of lineages . . . And if equity, justice, and good politics all counsel equality between the vassals of the same prince, governed by the same laws, and natives of the same kingdom, albeit of different religions, how much more equal are those who upon conversion were united with the rest by baptism, and how much more those who, like these petitioners, were Christians from birth, as their parents and grandparents had been since the said year of one thousand four hundred thirty-five, although descended from converts."[90]

It was an argument reminiscent of the one championed by Jewish conversos in the second half of the fifteenth century in opposition to the purity-of-blood statutes: baptism and genuine conversion erased the old families and lineages and created a single nation of Christians and Spaniards. One was not worthy of respect, holding office, or pursuing social advancement because of blood or lineage but because of religious devotion, love of the *patria*, and political loyalty.[91] In this context of calls for the recuperation of the nation's Jewish heritage, criticism first surfaced of the expulsion of the Jews decreed by Isabel and Ferdinand in 1492 and proposals to allow descendants of the expelled Jews to return to Spain. The last idea was officially sanctioned in 1797, although it had little practical effect and was generally motivated by the belief that some of the most powerful bankers in Europe were Jews of Spanish origin. The message was clear: Spain had been the motherland of one of the most important and influential Jewish communities in the world, and numerous descendants of this Jewish community were still living in Spain, now as Spaniards and Catholics.[92] It is important to highlight that this was not a defense of Jewishness or of Jews but of Spanishness and of Spaniards' capacity for integrating, and in some measure improving, different or inferior groups.

The Arabs in Spain were discussed in very similar although far less pliable terms. Spaniards viewed Arabs, unlike Jews, as a people or nation, even a race, and not just as members of a religious community. These considerations would never be set aside, although the animating, real issue once again was the image of Spain, and Spaniards, and this dictated that Spanish Arabs be seen in a different light than inhabitants of North Africa. The crucial element in this vindication of Spanish Arabs was separating them, and elite Arab culture, from Arabs generally.[93] The last group lacked culture, stubbornly adhered to a false religion, and was unable to contribute anything to the arts and sciences. But everything changed once some of these Arabs had settled in Spain. The most prevalent argument held that the Arabs who lived in Spain had also been barbarians, but from that point onward "their literary splendor began to manifest itself... which is proof that Spain had shaped and perfected our Moors, partly due to the communication they had with the Arabs of Asia in times of peace, and partly as a result of dealings with, and the example of the Spaniards."[94]

The final years of the eighteenth century saw efforts to recover the literary, historical, and artistic heritage of the Arabs in Spain, precisely to show the Spanish effect on the Arabs and how they had been transformed until they were virtually Spaniards themselves.[95] Arguably more significant were the thoughts of the orientalist Diego Clemencín in 1800 on relations between Spaniards and Arabs and Arabs' descendants, the Moriscos. According to Clemencín, Spaniards never had any regard for the Arabs who had occupied Spain, and Arabs had never come to be considered "Spanish" simply because the "Moor" had always been seen as the paradigmatic enemy and Christians' hatred of these invaders "was imbibed with the [mother's] milk, and believed to be sanctified by religion." There was every indication, however, that the Arab presence had been beneficial for Spain and the Spaniards. Despite all arguments to the contrary, Arabs had contributed far more than the Visigoths to Spanish culture: a richer and more melodious language, a love of manufacturing and the arts, and a more sophisticated science of politics. Clemencín went so far as to suggest that it is in "the study of Hispano-Arab history that one should look for the seeds of those variations that have distinguished us so much, and for so long, from other peoples of Europe, great vestiges of which still remain."[96]

Clemencín also claimed that the fundamental problem of sixteenth-century Spanish society had been the total inability, or perhaps refusal, to integrate them. The Moriscos had been separated from the rest of society and allowed to exist as a people apart. The integrative power of Christianity and Spanish civilization had enabled the relatively smooth absorption of numerous Morisco noble houses and Jewish families. If these policies had failed with the Morisco population generally, the responsibility lay with the Christians, for the Moriscos "were forced [to convert], and therefore became bad Christians; as bad Christians, they were persecuted; being persecuted, they became [our] enemies, and as enemies, it became necessary to exterminate or expel them."[97]

6

Race and Empire

Although others aside from "white Europeans" were to be found in Spain, eighteenth-century Spaniards invented a nation pure in origin, white, and, by dint of nature and ideology, located in Europe. That last notion, as we will see, is key to understanding constitutional debates at the dawn of the nineteenth century and especially to making sense of how representatives of the different Spanish regions situated themselves in those debates. The central question addressed in this chapter is how these ideas affected the vision Spaniards had of the Americas, territories they were now beginning to think of as dependent colonies, but also of the inhabitants of these colonies and especially those who had earlier been unquestionably considered Spaniards.

The so-called Creoles would still be acknowledged as descendants of Spaniards but no longer as Europeans, or not totally Europeans and perhaps not even whites, two essential markers of Spanish identity as it had been emerging in the eighteenth century. This is not to say that in the process of converting the Spaniards into a European family, the peninsulars tended simply to "darken" the Creoles. At times this was evidently the intention, as when the Spaniards referred to the miscegenation occurring in the Americas, which was radically transforming the biological—or racial—map of that continent. Summing up in the early 1800s the opinions that the peninsular Spanish had formed of the Creoles in the previous century, one of the most well-known representatives of the latter, Servando Teresa de Mier, observed that among Spaniards it was commonly accepted that Creoles were all like "the Indians or the blacks," and if their skin was somewhat more on the fair side bordering on white, they believed them to be mulattos or mestizos.[1] Spanish attitudes toward Creoles were also shaped by political processes: they were shaped by the progressive redefinition of the "American kingdoms" as "dependent colonies" and the accompanying transformation of the Creoles into colonial subjects, no longer Spanish citizens with the same rights as their peninsular cousins. Indeed, as a consequence of these new visions that Spaniards had of themselves and Creoles, the Creoles themselves began to search for a new identity, as Americans—pure ones, too, as we will see—with the objective of differentiating themselves from Native Americans and Africans as well as from Spaniards in the Americas and Spain.

This is why Creoles are now discussed exclusively in the American context. Up until this moment, the Spanish settlers in the Americas and their descendants had been seen as a part—albeit a disjoined part—of the great Spanish family. They were Spaniards who lived outside the peninsula but who nevertheless retained all the characteristics of those left behind. Changes in self-perceptions among both—Creoles and peninsulars—now required them to be analyzed separately. Creoles, like Spaniards, must be analyzed as they embarked on the process of constituting or imagining themselves as a separate nation. At the same time, however, these were tentative and often inchoate steps, and the suggestion is not that by the end of the eighteenth century, there was a clear national "American" consciousness among Creoles.

In his enormously influential study of the origins and evolution of nationalism, Benedict Anderson assigned Creoles the role of "pioneers" in the development of "conceptions of their nation-ness—well before most of Europe." This was the result of their growing sense of oppression by the metropolis and the influence of liberal ideas transmitted through a vibrant, flourishing print culture.[2] This is not the place for a detailed analysis of the criticisms leveled at Anderson's model, including the lack of concrete evidence to support his conclusions. The important thing to note here is that in the process of conceptualizing "their nation-ness," American Creoles, like peninsular Spaniards, were, even as late as 1800, still far from imagining themselves as a nation apart.[3] Yet there is no doubt that debates among the Spaniards and Creoles on who was Spanish and who was American and the circulation of various opinions in print had a great impact at the time. They became the basis for parliamentary debates of the early nineteenth century and the movements for national independence in Spanish America in the 1810s and 1820s.

Furthermore, the increasing differentiation between European and American Spaniards was accompanied by the racialization of other population groups in the Americas: Native Americans, Africans, and mixed-blood individuals who continued to proliferate throughout the continent, whom the Spaniards began to designate collectively and with growing frequency as "castas." This part of the chapter is not concerned with the question of whether the Spanish were the first or the last to develop a racialist vision of humanity or the first to divide humanity into distinct races with separate origins and different physical and mental traits. Nor does it deal with these issues diachronically to determine whether the discourses developed in the eighteenth century, in Spain and elsewhere, might have provided a solid foundation for racialist theories—the so-called scientific racism—that would prevail in the nineteenth century. Rather, the goal here, as throughout, is to analyze these questions synchronically, that is, to try to understand the development of these theories and concepts in the period under study. In our case, this is not only a methodological choice that privileges the study of how ideas and concepts develop in their own, precise chronological context. It is also inspired by the desire to respond to those who still insist that Spaniards' visions of the Native Americans and Africans did not change significantly in the course of the eighteenth century. They hold that the dominant vision of Native Americans and Africans was still decisively informed by earlier paternalism or that the vision of the Africans in the Americas was shaped exclusively by slavery. However, this chapter also answers those who have interpreted to the contrary and maintained that the Spanish imperial world in the waning decades of the 1700s was the time and place when abiding theories about human diversity were wholly and definitively replaced by scientific racism.

Clearly, by 1800, Spaniards were conscious of theories that humanity was divided into essentially and radically distinct races, that the Native Americans were one of these races, the Africans another, and that their mental and physical characteristics were not only permanent and immutable but also fundamentally different from those of the so-called white or European race. Rather than simply embracing or endorsing these ideas as imports, Spanish authors themselves were key figures in their elaboration. These conceptions cannot be discussed in a vacuum. Spanish imperial policies were indeed partly shaped by racialist theories but also by other ideologies and concepts. Once again, it is important to underscore that images of oneself and of the other were not only the result of epistemological changes but also the product of specific social realities and policies.

Spanish America in the eighteenth century is a particularly fascinating and fruitful topic because it shows the coexistence of contrasting political and ideological attitudes. While a growing number of Spaniards were beginning to think of Creoles as racially contaminated colonial subjects, official policy insisted on seeing and treating them as Spaniards and blood relations. Although Indians were ever more likely to be seen as a race apart, stunted by physical and mental limitations, in the eyes of the authorities they were still "childlike," requiring protection and tutelage until they were ready to be admitted as full members of the great Spanish family. A similar attitude was displayed toward Africans, whose status as an inferior race was ascribed to a temporary civil condition—slavery, which could be dissolved through manumission and social integration into the Spanish community—and not as the product of nature.

The same contrast was evident in the treatment of the vastly growing numbers of *mestizos.* The presence of these individuals of mixed racial or national heritage was seen by some as proof of the genetic degeneration transpiring in the Americas, especially among Creoles. For others it was merely an exotic curiosity, and its pictorial representations were collector's items. For still others—including the monarchy itself, occasionally—the mestizos were the key to social integration through the peculiar process of "blanqueamiento" (whitening). Finally, for some others, the mestizos were the product of a sort of biological engineering that would eventually create a new type of human.

The long span of the eighteenth century encompasses many momentous events, wars, political transformations, and rebellions. Not all of these events are equally relevant for the study at hand. Some of these—the Seven Years' War, the Indian rebellions in the viceroyalty of Peru, the urban revolts in the viceroyalty of New Granada, the Bourbon reformist policies in the Americas, the Haitian Revolution, and the independence of the Thirteen Colonies from Great Britain—did have a significant impact on the political and ideological dynamics that interest us here and will be referenced in this chapter. It should be noted, however, that in the Americas the political waters were relatively undisturbed until the 1750s. This contrasts with Spain itself, where political reforms and surrounding debates had already begun with the new century. The most important reforms, the conflicts with the greatest resonance, and the most interesting debates on nation and race all took place after 1750, roughly coinciding with the beginning of the reign of the most reformist Bourbon monarch, Carlos III (1759–1788).

Eighteenth-century Spaniards were aware that Spain was moored to the old structures of the past and that many of the reforms introduced by the Bourbons had not produced the desired effect.[4] They were also increasingly aware of the political and economic crisis that was closely linked to the mismanagement of the colonies. It is no secret that many foreigners criticized the Spanish empire as a model of incompetent administration. Montesquieu led the way. He declared that the empire had impoverished Spain by making it dependent on other European countries and, even more shamefully, on its own colonies: "The Indies and Spain are two powers under the same master; but the Indies are the principal one, and Spain is only secondary."[5] Before the publication of Montesquieu's work (1748), Spanish governments had paid little attention to American affairs, either to diagnose the ills or suggest remedies. At the start of Philip V's reign, royal authorities created a viceroyalty, New Granada, with its capital in Santa Fe de Bogota and with jurisdiction over the territories of the modern states of Venezuela, Colombia, Ecuador, and Panama. The creation of the additional viceroyalty in 1717 was primarily a response to the new monarchy's need to protect American territories coveted by England and Portugal, two enemies of the pro-French alliance in the War of Succession. The lack of a clear strategy for the Americas, or any interest in implementing one, is evident from the fact that the new viceroyalty was abolished in 1723 and not reestablished until 1739.

Yet the situation began to change in the 1740s and even more so in the 1750s with a flood of economic, administrative, and military reforms. From this point onward, many Spaniards who wrote from the Americas and Spain were beginning to acknowledge that the Americas, and especially the Creole elite, were favored in the relationship with the metropolis. As early as the 1740s, two Spanish military officers and geographers, Jorge Juan and Antonio de Ulloa, had written about the Americas as rich in natural resources and potentially a source of great profit to Spain. Yet they were impoverished because of the absence of a productive mentality and had become a haven for Creoles who did not feel the weight of royal authority or pay taxes or contribute to the metropolis in any fashion.[6]

This was precisely the tack taken by many of the Spanish lettered elite, following Montesquieu. As early as the 1750s, Abbot Gándara summed up better than anyone the opinions of Enlightened Spaniards on America. France "obtains more benefit from two small islands . . . than Spain from two great empires, Mexico and Peru. . . . To be sure, we conquered the Indies; but we have become voluntary tributaries of England, France, Holland, Genoa," he lamented and added, paraphrasing Montesquieu: "The governments of Holland, England, and France, have always looked upon their fatherlands as the principal part, and their Indies as the accessory part . . . We have done the opposite, for the lack of good policy we have effectively come to think of the Americas as the principal part of our wealth, and, neglecting the best interests of the mother, have made her an accessory to her children."[7] Bernardo Ward, a royal minister under Carlos III, highlighted the snowballing problems and the previous dynasty's responsibility for the dire situation. In a memorandum written prior to his death in 1779 Ward argued that "our system of government is totally decayed" to such an extent that no one until now has been able to "remedy the damage and disorder" caused by previous governments, and "it shall never be remedied until the Government of those dominions is founded upon maxims different from those hitherto followed."[8] The problems faced in the Americas were obvious: Creoles had been allowed to monopolize the continent's wealth, and since the middle of the seventeenth century their control over local and regional political institutions had increased; the missionaries on the other hand had managed to convince the monarchy that their presence in the Americas was justified solely on the basis and for the express purpose of defending the rights of Indians.

The new dynasty, having lost many of Spain's European possessions, understood that it was imperative to reform the empire and make the colonies manageable and profitable. There was but one alternative: the centralization of power in the peninsula and the creation of an imperial monarchy in which the Americas would be treated as provinces or colonies instead of distinct kingdoms.[9] It is true that, legally, little had changed. When the new monarchs cast their gaze upon America, they did not see merely small territories or colonies of Spanish settlers, with Native Americans they were obliged to protect. Formally and informally, the American territories were still known as "the kingdoms of the Indies," but in the mid-1700s important semantic changes begin to happen, especially repeated references to the Americas as dependent territories that should serve to benefit the "patria." This was bluntly articulated, once again, by Ward, who in his *Projecto económico (Economic Project)* recommended that Spain proceed with her American territories just as the Europeans had done with their "colonies." The fundamental principle should be that "all the consumption of their Colonies has to consist of the products of the patria."[10] In other words, his was an attempt to recover the original rationale: the overseas territories should be a secondary part to the metropolis, the main part.[11]

The reforms were slow in arriving, but once implemented the intent was clear. The Spanish state was no longer interested only in extracting silver from the Americas, and the project became much more comprehensive: to bring already colonized territories under control, to extend and establish frontiers with other empires, to eradicate the opposition of those Indian communities who still remained beyond the monarchy's control, and, more important, to transform the Americas into the principal or main market for Spanish goods. Many of these reforms were institutional. They included the creation of new viceroyalties (New Granada and Rio de la Plata), new captaincies general, more *Audiencias* (high courts), and the imposition of new regional administrators such as intendants, who were more directly dependent on colonial authorities. The objective was to create more rational and manageable territorial units but also to extend the authority of the crown to every corner of the empire.[12]

The monarchy also bolstered colonial defenses against other European empires, especially after the Seven Years' War (1756–1763). During this conflict, in 1762, Great Britain occupied Havana and Manila for several months and at the end of the war received Florida when the British agreed to leave Havana. Spain also had to contain more frequent attempts by the Portuguese, allies of Great Britain in all the eighteenth-century conflicts, to expand their territories in South America. All of these events demonstrated that one of the weakest points in the imperial chain was the army in the Americas. The reforms were first implemented in Cuba and then extended to other regions, especially and most successfully in the viceroyalty of Peru, which was potentially one of the most vulnerable. Although results varied across the regions, it is still accurate to say, as Monica Ricketts does, that "reform of the military was perhaps the most successful of all Bourbon" reforms in the Americas and resulted in the creation of a "meritocratic, semi-professional, and highly centralized institution." Its primary objective was clearly the defense of the American territories, but the military also became a crucial locus of loyalty to the Spanish monarchy, especially in the viceroyalty of Peru and in Cuba.[13]

The Spanish crown also promoted the discovery of new silver and gold mines (and their more efficient and profitable exploitation) and encouraged the exploration of still unknown interior and coastal regions. In a process labeled the "second conquest," they occupied

MAP 4. Spanish America in 1797: Bourbon reforms

Bourbon rulers reformed the government and administration of Spanish America by creating two new viceroyalties.

territories abandoned or not fully settled during the preceding centuries, including California and the Yucatan.[14] Spanish authorities in the Americas signed treaties with Native nations that had remained beyond their control as late as the eighteenth century and attempted to conquer territories inhabited by native communities that they saw as mired in barbarism.[15] These new policies were preceded and accompanied by efforts to increase knowledge of the American continent and its inhabitants, and the century saw numerous "Enlightened expeditions," whose objective was to collect and analyze new information about human, plant, and animal worlds as well as the physical geography of the Americas.[16]

Perhaps most representative of this sea change in the metropolis' policies toward the colonies were three internal and diplomatic processes. The first was the decision to expel the Jesuits from the Indies and Spain in 1767, following Portuguese and French precedents. The crown suspected that this religious order tended to oppose its political measures, as in the other cases, but the decision also reflected the marked regalism of eighteenth-century monarchs, who sought control over their national churches.[17] In agreement with France, the Spanish monarchy contributed funds and support to the rebellion of the Thirteen Colonies against Great Britain, which led to the independence of the colonies in 1776 and Spain's recovery of Florida in 1783. Although not all Spanish ministers favored aid to the North American colonists, the government of Carlos III was convinced that this would demonstrate to Spain's enemies that it was still a force to be reckoned with in the Americas, and indeed it is around this time that the Portuguese monarchy (a traditional ally of Great Britain) and Spain finally came together to find a diplomatic solution to their frontier disputes in the region of Rio de la Plata.[18]

Although it would be going too far to say that the monarchy adopted a clear policy against naming Creoles to high administrative posts, it does appear that generally, the monarchy preferred to appoint peninsulars to the most important offices in the American territories. The most detailed studies indicate that between 1630 and 1750, the number of Creoles in the American administration grew steadily, but from 1750 onward, with the introduction of political and institutional reforms, the monarchy tended to bypass the

Creoles. It should be pointed out that this was the consequence of a more overtly imperialist approach and not the result of pressure exerted by a more populous peninsular community in the colonies. Although more studies are required, the Creole population in the eighteenth century seems to have become even more predominant in relation to peninsular Spaniards than in previous centuries. No more than 100,000, and perhaps fewer, Spaniards emigrated to America in the 1700s, which meant that only 5 percent of the Spaniards or whites were Spanish-born, although this population occupied as many as 95 percent of all higher administrative offices in the colonies.[19]

As we will see, eighteenth-century Spanish authorities still justified Spanish sovereignty over the Americas and their inhabitants by the obligation to civilize and Christianize the Native Americans, but they also proclaimed a more unabashedly imperial mission. It was still maintained, as it had been since the late fifteenth century, that its evangelizing mission sanctioned by the papacy justified Spanish sovereignty in the Americas. But in the eighteenth century there was much greater emphasis on the idea that the right of conquest legitimized Spanish sovereignty.

This required a retelling of the history of America as a story of conquest and the heroic deeds of a superior people. While few Spaniards denied that the conquest had led to much death and destruction, it was now celebrated as a great exploit of which the Spanish people could be proud. It should therefore come as no surprise that the two most popular works on the history of the Americas in the eighteenth century were Antonio de Solís's *History of the Conquest of Mexico*, which, although published at the end of the seventeenth century, enjoyed enormous popularity in the eighteenth, and Juan Bautista Muñoz's *History of the New World* (1793), in which the Indians were presented as a savage, naturally inferior people without history or culture. Many members of the Royal Academy of History also favored the Scottish historian William Robertson's *History of America* (1777–1796), which included a certain amount of criticism of Spanish imperial ventures in the Americas but presented Spain's conquest and colonization of the continent as one of the marvels in human history.[20]

Of greatest importance and relevance here, however, is not so much the political-institutional reforms or the new economic policy designed to more efficiently exploit the New World's riches but the elaboration of new discourses and ideas about the different population groups that coexisted on American soil. It is unsurprising that the Enlightened elite would have shown great interest and enthusiasm for developing theories about these human communities. After all, they had already turned an inquiring lens on themselves, the peninsulars, and logically they would be interested in other groups under Spanish sovereignty in the Americas. The Spaniards were not by any means the only community interested in the origins and characteristics of different peoples or nations. In all European countries, regardless of their position in the hierarchy of empires, there were significant movements toward what we now refer to as scientific racism, or at least important advances in what eighteenth-century authors called the science of man.

This is not to say that what would be referred to as scientific racism completely displaced theories developed in previous centuries. On the contrary, these were still essential to eighteenth-century Spanish thought, and numerous authors and royal ministers continued to rely on them and to defend the central tenets of these theories. Recent studies have demonstrated that the shift from the theory that all humans were fundamentally alike to one that divided the human species into races with radically different characteristics was gradual and protracted. Only in the nineteenth century did a distinctly racialist discourse became truly dominant.[21]

Scholars have drawn attention to the presence of terms such as *race* and *ethnicity* in the dictionaries of the largest European languages. The word *ethnic*, for example, in this era still had a clearly religious rather than racial signification—a reference more to non Christians and uncivilized peoples. This was the meaning of *ethnic* reproduced in dictionaries published by the Spanish Royal Academy, including the 1780 edition. Indeed, it should be emphasized that this was the primary meaning in all dictionaries up to the one published in 1884, when another was added, more consonant with the modern definition of the word: "Belonging to a nation or race. Ethnic character."[22]

The same is true of the word *race*. In the *Dictionary of Authorities* published by the academy in 1738, race continued to have the signification of lack of purity of blood or belonging to a vile lineage. It would not be until the dictionary published in 1869 that, for the first time, race was defined as "one of the divisions of humankind." This conceptual evolution would not be complete until 1884: "Race. Each one of the varieties into which the human species is divided, has certain hereditary traits and above all a specific skin color. They are known as the white [race], yellow, copper-colored, dark or brown, and black."[23]

There were two main reasons for this continuity of older meanings of ethnicity and race. The first reason, and a particularly important one in the Spanish case, is that the evolution of racialist concepts and theories was still mediated by religious conceptions. The second reason is that racialist terms and theories were still not fully defined. Numerous theories, some of them mutually contradictory, still existed despite the fact that by the eighteenth century there were clear indications of the general direction of all such theories in the near future. In sum, discourses that outlined so-called "scientific racism" developed in the Spanish world, too, but other considerations limited their evolution.

It has been proven that in eighteenth-century Spain, the dominant theory continued to be the one set out in Genesis: all humans descended from Adam and Eve. The enduring influence of this theory explains the drastic criticism of polygenesis in Spain, as it seemed to undermine this narrative of common origin. Feijóo openly broached the subject. He attacked Isaac de la Peyrère, a seventeenth-century philosopher and originator of the so-called pre-Adamite hypothesis, who explicitly argued in *Praeadamitae . . . quibus inducuntur primi homines ante Adamum conditi* (1655) that Adam was the progenitor of the Jews only. And he attacked Louis Armand de Lom d'Arce, Baron de Lahontan, who implicitly argued in his *Nouveaux voyages dans l'Amerique Septentrionale* (1703) that Adam was the progenitor only of the "whites." For Feijóo, and for the great majority of his Spanish contemporaries, the only valid theory was that all humans descended from Adam and Eve, which was "a dogma of Faith received by the Church, and revealed in Scripture."[24] The first translator of Buffon into Spanish was careful to note that, although throughout the text Buffon used the terms *races* or *castes* in plural, it was "necessary to warn the scrupulous reader, that when the author speaks of the differences between races and castes of the human species, these words should be taken in the vulgar or colloquial sense, which becomes obvious in the final paragraph of the work, where he explains that since the beginning of the world there has only been one human species, descended from the same trunk."[25]

In the eighteenth century, however, especially in its second half, changes occurred that would prove key to the development of what has been named scientific racism. At one point or another, all European empires developed what contemporaries called the idea of natural history, the basis for a new perspective on human diversity. For the editors of one Spanish journal, *Memorial Literario*, first published in 1801, the eighteenth century was a time when natural history reached previously unimaginable heights, thanks to the work of Albrecht von Haller, Petrus Camper, Félix Vicq-d'Azyr, Louis Jean Marie De Daubenton, Peter Simon Pallas, Carl Linnaeus, and especially, at least in Spain, George Louis Leclerc, Comte de Buffon. To these one might add Spanish authors—Jorge Juan, Antonio de Ulloa, Félix Azara, Isidoro de Antillón, Joseph de Gumilla, and many others—who in some cases contributed vitally to these new racialist conceptions.[26] Other fields were also essential in the formation of racialist discourses and ideologies, including craniology and the study of human and animal bone structures. These advances purported to "assuage the desire that wise men have harbored since ancient times of discovering in man's exterior clear traces of his interior faculties, of his passions, and his morals."[27]

Since the common origins of all humans was a universally accepted idea, at least in the Spanish world, debates focused on other theories. One of these, the least popular, posited the existence of human groups who occupied the lowest human stratum, akin to intermediaries between primates and humans. Defenders of this theory, among others, included historian of Jamaica, the Englishman Edward Long, and the Dutchman De Pauw. In his appraisal of certain peoples of the Americas, De Pauw described the continent as having generated all sorts of semi-human, degenerate species, an opinion shared by at least some Spaniards.[28]

For the greatest scholar of the subject in eighteenth-century Spain, the Jesuit Lorenzo Hervás Panduro, these theories could not have been more divorced from reality. In the first place, there could not be humans who were in any sense like monkeys. If that were so, they would clearly not be humans because God in his infinite wisdom would not permit such monsters. Hervás denied the existence of humanoid monsters and the widely popular myth in sixteenth- and seventeenth-century Europe that humans and certain animals (bears and monkeys) could procreate.[29]

Two other theories had much greater resonance in the Spanish world. These new theories shared with the older ones the belief in the common origins of all humanity. Human diversity was not the outcome of separate creations (polygenesis) but due to the scattering of Noah's descendants after the Flood. The first of these theories, proposed by the Comte de Buffon, the German naturalist Johann Friedrich Blumenbach, and many Spanish authors, was that white was the original color of humanity and that the appearance of different colors, from brown to black, was symptomatic of the degeneration caused by climate and other environmental factors. Variations in climate and soil were responsible for differences in skin color.[30] The main thrust of this theory was not that all humans were originally white but that once a nation or community had acquired certain physical characteristics, these endured into future generations, and nothing—not the climate, diet, or the environment—could thereafter change them. Only biological mixing with men or women of other races or communities could lead to some, albeit limited, changes. Supporters of this theory continued to believe that all humans were innately equal in their intellectual capacity and equally capable of progress and improvement: "All men are uniformly predisposed to acquire the greatest scientific knowledge, so that differences in climate, temperament, etc., have no bearing on differences in understanding," and that regardless of physical traits or physiognomy "man is always left with his free will, which must prevail over the actions of the material organs, whatever these may be, while morals must triumph over the force of the passions."[31]

Others claimed that these changes were not superficial but profound and clearly had an influence on the intellectual capacity of each one of the human races or species. It was not merely a question of skin color but also its thickness, bone structure, the size of the cranium, and other organs.[32] They characterized the process of change as evolutionary: "Scarcely had man emerged from the heavens and set off from one climate to another, when his nature began to suffer alterations that were minor in the temperate regions, which we suppose to have been close to his place of origin, and increasing as he moved away from it."[33] The Amazonian missionary José Gumilla wrote that regardless of why God had allowed it to happen, after being scattered from the Tower of Babel, "white fathers could [now] engender black children, and these married one another, and populated the countries they possess until today, and have filled them with Blacks over the course of time, in the same way as other peoples [have done in other] provinces."[34] In other words, the natural characteristics of human groups changed to adapt to new conditions, but once these alterations had taken place they were irreversible and permanent.[35] It hardly mattered if a white man were transported to Africa or an African to Europe, since each one preserved his original physical and mental traits.[36]

The great challenge for these new theories was to determine how many races, or human groups, existed and which physical and mental traits distinguished each one.[37] The Swedish naturalist Linnaeus had identified four races—white, black (African), brown (Asian), and red (American)—although in later works he introduced a number of sub-races, thus complicating what had initially seemed a clear and concise division.[38] The ambiguity was also evident in one of the best-known works by the Scottish philosopher David Hume, who would only go so far as to assert that "there are four or five different kinds or species of men." This imprecision was far from unusual, at least in works published in Spain.[39] The Frenchman de la Croix, for instance, spoke not in terms of races but of two great human groups—one composed of whites and their associates (brown, yellow, and olive-complexioned) and the other of blacks of different shades. But he also offered a parallel classification based on color as well as body structure and facial features: Europeans; Asiatic or Tartars; Lapps; and Africans, or at least "black Africans."[40] The Spanish liberal Isidoro de Antillón proclaimed in his *Lecciones de Geografía* that there were four "varieties or distinct races . . . the Arab-European, Mongol, African, and Hyperborean."[41]

It was equally difficult to describe with any degree of precision the characteristics of each one of these groups, although it was generally agreed that the white was the superior one, the prototype not only of physical perfection but also of an ingenious and civilized people. David Hume declared that never "was a civilized nation of any other complexion than white, nor even any individual eminent either in action or speculation," while Antillón noted that whites had always been dominant, never having been "subjugated by a foreign race."[42] Other races were also distinguished by physical traits beyond skin color, including size, physical structure, the cranium, eyes, and hair.[43] There were also variations in intellectual traits, ranging from those with some limitations on their speculative abilities to the complete lack of "aptitude for complex thought, sustained reflection, comparative discernment, and profound discourse" of the Africans or the Hyperborean likeness to animals.[44]

The preceding pages have demonstrated that Spaniards participated in the development of new theories of human diversity. But to understand the evolution of racialist ideologies in the Hispanic world, these theories must be contextualized in the complex ethnographic realities of the colonies. Because of their presence in the Americas, Spaniards were at the heart of eighteenth-century racialist speculations, and this was especially evident when it came to passing judgment on native inhabitants. For Enlightened Spaniards, especially those who abandoned Christian epistemology for the interpretation of social and biological reality, human beings—their historical evolution and different manifestations—could now be studied scientifically and not only theologically. Moreover, for many of these authors, the New World, of the Americas or the Indies, best illustrated precisely the need for new concepts and theories of human diversity.

The impulse was not new, but the approach was different in the 1700s. In previous centuries there was still something of a sense of wonderment at the New World, a celebration of the immensity of God and His creation. In the eighteenth century new attitudes were emerging, and the New World was seen as something akin to a laboratory to demonstrate, among other things, that God had not intended to create all men equal. Joseph de Gumilla alluded to this when he observed that the "New World" deserved its name not only for being the last to be discovered but also because "compared with this old World, that one is new in every sense, and diverse in everything." Everything was new there—the animals, the plants, the trees, the rivers, and, above all, the human beings: "new men," although it seems this "novelty wears off once their lack of rational capacity becomes apparent." There was "also a need for new ideas" to interpret and understand them fully.[45]

Nothing substantially changed, however, in the legal status of indigenous populations. From the monarchy's point of view, the "defense of the Indian" was still the central element in the justification of Spanish dominion over the Americas. In the eighteenth century, institutions and officials who administered the overseas possessions continued to insist that the progressive civilization of the indigenous nations and their total integration into the civilized world were the key measures of their policy's success. Still treated as "minors," the natives continued to be under the protection of the crown as a separate Republic of Indians.

Many of these authors, as well as the official propaganda, argued that the Spanish empire and its officials were the only Europeans who had never resorted to the racial denigration of the Indians and who, to the contrary, had demonstrated to the rest of the world that it was possible to construct a colonial society in which all were equal. "If you should have been governed by these nations [England, France or the Netherlands]," wrote the Catalan Jesuit Juan Nuix, in the most cited contemporary defense of Spain's record and actions in the Americas, you "Mexicans, Peruvians, Chileans, Chiquitos, or Californians, whom the Spanish consider to be [like] Europeans, the best you would have hoped for would have been to still occupy that low station reserved for the Hurons, the Iroquois, and the Eskimos. Like them, you would thus be submitted to the world at large as models of stupidity and barbarism."[46] For these authors, and, more importantly, for the governing organs of the monarchy, the Indians were members of the great Spanish family, although not fully integrated.

At the same time, views of the Indians developed in previous centuries persisted. Since at least the mid-1600s, those who insisted that the Native Americans were essentially similar to the Spaniards, physically and mentally, had dominated the discussion on the nature of the Americans. Perhaps they were at a different stage of cultural or intellectual development than the Europeans, but it was generally accepted that, in Feijóo's words, "those natives are of the same species as [the Spaniards], and sons of the same father (Adam)."[47] The famous and influential Mexican Jesuit Francisco Saverio Clavijero, for example, recognized that despite certain physical traits that Europeans tended to perceive unfavorably—"their disagreeable color, the narrowness of their brow, the sparseness of their beard, and the thickness of their hair"—the Mexican Indians might be placed at some point midway between "ugliness and beauty," with skin color that was closer to white than black. They also had the same intellectual capacities as Europeans, albeit perhaps somewhat more impassioned and a little more torpid.[48] Clavijero and others, recalling the theories of Las Casas, highlighted the fact that before that Spanish arrival there had been indigenous nations—above all the Mexica and the Inka—who were politically and culturally highly developed. This demonstrated that the Natives were fully equipped to reach the level of civilization of the Spaniards.

Those who advanced these ideas also clearly explained Indians' lack of cultural or religious progress or their passivity, disengagement, and refusal to play a constructive role in the future of colonial societies. These limitations were not a reflection of the Indians' nature but the fruit of Spanish colonial policies. The first problem, as with the Moriscos in the Iberian Peninsula, was that Spaniards had not done enough to Christianize and civilize the Indians, to turn them into "useful vassals." To the contrary, "due to idleness, indolence and lack of good [educational] measures," the Spaniards had transformed them into and had come to treat them as "virtually irrational and useless."[49] Viceroy Agustín de Jáuregui, the author of these words, and many of his contemporaries were convinced that there was only one viable policy, which was to integrate and hispanize the natives by promoting "frequent interaction with Spaniards" but also suppressing "their native tongue," proceeding with their Christianization, regulating their labor, and prohibiting their exploitation by colonists.[50] The Abate Gándara claimed that Spaniards needed to persuade Indians to alter all of their customs and become hispanized to turn them into industrious, "useful vassals." The monarchy would derive profit, loyalty, and productive labor from a vast number of individuals with this policy.[51]

These dominant perceptions of the indigenous people were increasingly challenged from the mid-eighteenth century on by two groups of authors, each composed of highly influential figures in contemporary Spain. One group included those who, without casting doubt over the existence of a single human race, still saw Indians as clearly inferior in ability to Europeans. Some of the most famous proponents of this view of the indigenous peoples were the Count of Buffon, authors of the essay on America that appeared in the Spanish edition of the *Encyclopédie Méthodique*, and especially the authors of the two histories most popular with the Spanish Enlightened public, the Scotsman William Robertson and the Spaniard Juan Bautista Muñoz. In each case, these authors intended to demonstrate that although some of these nations—the Aztecs and the Inka—had reached a higher level of civilization than the rest, it was not comparable to the level attained by the Europeans in antiquity, in marked contrast to the opinions of Las Casas in the sixteenth century and Clavijero in the eighteenth. As proof these authors argued that Indians, without exception, had changed little since the arrival of the Spanish. This was a sign either of neglect by the Spanish authorities or, more unsettling, of an inherent character that impeded Indians' progress and condemned them to a permanent, childlike state.[52]

Beginning in the 1760s another group of authors began to question the dominant view of the Indians. Few passages are as illustrative of the changes afoot as those written by two Enlightened explorers, Antonio de Ulloa and his companion Jorge Juan, in one of the most influential works of the century, *Relación histórica del viaje a la América meridional* (*Historical Relation of the Voyage to South America*, 1748). In this work some Indian peoples are described as clear examples of humans incapable of improvement or change. "If considered as part of the human species," wrote Ulloa and Juan, "the narrow limits of their understanding seem to clash with the dignity of the soul"; they are indifferent to everything, the temporal and the eternal, nothing disturbs or makes an impression on them, nothing is of any interest, and neither fear, respect, nor punishment can compel or stimulate them. They are of a singular nature, unresponsive to external influences, seemingly incapable of abandoning ignorance or moving "a single step away from their natural indolence."[53]

Nevertheless, it was Ulloa who instigated an epistemological shift in approaches to the Indian, with the 1772 publication of his *Noticias americanas: entretenimientos físicos-históricos sobre la América meridional y la septentrional oriental.*[54] In many respects Ulloa was ideally equipped to provide this new reading of the American Indian, as someone who possessed all the qualities that made him the paragon of an Enlightened individual in a period of imperialist resurgence. To begin with, Ulloa was a practical man with an interest in the sciences and considerable military and administrative experience. But he was also a scholar of natural and human diversity. Between 1736 and 1744 Ulloa and Juan had served as members of the French Geodesic Mission, which culminated in an essential book for understanding Spanish views on America and its inhabitants: the *Historical Relation.*[55] Ulloa occupied two important posts in the Americas, as governor of Huancavelica (Peru, 1758–1764) and of Louisiana (1766–1768) after the French had ceded the latter to the Spanish monarchy in return for territories lost during the Seven Years' War. Following his departure from Louisiana after a rebellion by the French colonists, Ulloa retained his post in the Spanish navy and published works on natural history as a member of the Royal Society of London and the Royal Swedish Academy of Sciences.

Ulloa was interested in two questions of crucial importance. He wanted to determine, first, whether the Indians were all part of one clearly differentiated race and, second, if the Indians had failed to improve their level of civilization because of Spanish colonial conditions or their physical and mental constitution. The starting point for the first question was obvious to Ulloa. There were at least three human groups identifiable by skin color—whites, blacks, and reds. Clearly each one of these races or groups included various nations differentiated by their "regions, states and provinces" of residence and sometimes mutually distinguishable by the tone of their complexion. According to Ulloa, Indians themselves instinctively developed the idea that they were members of the same red race ("those who live in the Northern regions [of America] refer to themselves as colored men to set them apart from the other species") although some Europeans had also designated the Indians generally as members of a "red race."[56]

In studying the Indians, Ulloa was uninterested in why some were redder than others. The main objective was to demonstrate that skin color was unrelated to climate and that Indians, regardless of place of origin, were all red. Perhaps climate was responsible for the variety of tones or shades, but none of these peoples diverged significantly from the basic color. They were all identical: "Having seen one Indian of any region," he claimed, "one has assuredly seen them all," at least in terms of color and physique. Ulloa was struck that all of them, regardless of skin tone, "preserved the semblance of the race, and cannot be confused with the mulattos, who are closest to them in color." All Indians shared certain external, physical traits—skin color, hair, lack of a beard—and other physical attributes that identified them as members of the same race. Their craniums were "thicker than the norm," and their skin was also thicker, as Ulloa himself had been able to verify from his "surgical operations, and the skeletons taken from graves." These characteristics led him to conclude that "their system [is] rougher and more resistant, and therefore less sensible."

Ulloa's verdict on Indians' mental capabilities was even more important. The starting point once again was the purported similarity between all Indians with regard to "their uses and customs, their character, disposition, inclinations and traits, wherein such similarities are observed as if distant territories were one and the same." All Indians were thus given to "leisure and indolence," whether they lived in Peru, Louisiana, or Canada and whether they were "civilized or savage." They were all cowards, traitors, deceivers, and drunkards. From this "rusticity and barbarism . . . follows their shortage or lack of sense," a profound and immutable limitation on their intellect: "Among the race of Indians one must distinguish the actions and operations of the mind from those that are nothing but manipulation or industry . . . ; in the first they are completely lacking, extremely dim-witted and without discernment or comprehension . . . they are occupied with nothing but appearances and external actions, and while they show artifice in certain things, this is unremarkable, and bodes no strong light of understanding."

Many of the texts published by Spanish authors from this point on, including the most widely read ones, judged the Indians to be a race from which one should not expect too much intellectually. The Indians should remain protected, they still required help in comprehending religious doctrine, and while their labor and economic burdens should be lightened, there was apparently no reason to doubt that the Americas should not belong to their first inhabitants, the Indians, but to their Spanish conquerors. The future of America essentially depended on this—on Spaniards remaining there as proprietors of the land and as sovereign rulers, not merely Indians' administrators and tutors.[57]

New and old theories contrast with new realities. In the eighteenth century, numerous Indian peoples still remained outside Spanish control, although the colonial authorities attempted to integrate these "barbarian Indians," especially in the second half of the century, through a combination of negotiation and selective repression.[58] More important, this was a time of demographic recovery following centuries of decline. The available data for the years around 1800 show not only that the native population was recovering but that in certain regions the indigenous population was still in the majority. Out of a total population of 11,200,000 in the territories under Spanish control in 1800, 5,200,000 were indigenous (nearly 46 percent), while the number of mestizos (of mixed Indian-white ancestry) was approximately 1,140,000 (10 percent of the total). The percentage of indigenous or mestizo population was especially high in Mexico (72 percent of the total), Peru (83 percent), and Ecuador (67 percent), three regions in which Creoles were extremely powerful in spite of being a minority: 18 percent of the total in Mexico, 37 percent in Peru, and 25 percent in Ecuador.[59]

More important than the demographic recovery, and perhaps one of its consequences, was the growing activism of the natives under Spanish rule.[60] In New Spain, disturbances in the eighteenth century were limited to a few local revolts. It seemed that old divisions between indigenous nations persisted, as did strategies developed earlier, which meant that the only form of resistance against Spanish colonialism was to insist on the maintenance of the legal separation between the Republic of Indians and the Republic of Spaniards. The situation was radically different in the viceroyalty of Peru. Between 1740 and 1780 there were at least three major indigenous revolts, which at their height threatened the entire regional colonial system. The first of these, and one of the most serious rebellions of the entire colonial period, lasted from 1742 to 1750 and unified natives, mestizos, and mulattos under the leadership of a Spanish-educated Indian of the middling class who took the name Tupac Amaru II. Another revolt around the same time was led by an Aymara Indian, Julián Apaza—or Tupac Katari—who threatened the city La Paz (in modern-day Bolivia) as the head of an indigenous army. The ideology of these rebel indigenous communities was explicitly anti-imperialist, and they demanded independence from Spanish rule. Their grievances and demands were very similar to those expressed by Guaman Poma de Ayala in the early seventeenth century—the ceding of power and jurisdiction over the American territories to native inhabitants—except that the threat to Spanish power was now real. "I will send all the Europeans on their way, back to their own lands," Tupac Katari proclaimed, while his wife added: "We will be left as the ultimate owners of this place and of its wealth. We alone will rule." For these indigenous liberators, Spanish dominion over the Americas was a usurpation, and there was only one way to shake off the yoke of European colonialism—military victory.[61]

The defeat of these revolts was significant for a number of reasons—first, for the number of deaths that resulted from the rebellions and the subsequent repression. It is estimated that some 100,000 Indians and 10,000 Spaniards were killed in these uprisings.

For Creole elites in the viceroyalty, these rebellions quickened distrust of the indigenous population and the fear that any future revolt against royal authorities by any demographic group would be seen by the Indians as an opportunity to dismantle the entire colonial system.[62] The defeat, however, had the gravest and most enduring consequences for the indigenous communities because in many ways it vindicated their fatalism about the struggle against Spanish colonialism and convinced them that the best form of resistance to exploitation was to isolate themselves from the colonial system, and from Spaniards, as much as possible.

With regard to Africans, there was an emerging general agreement among Europeans in the last decades of the 1700s about the existence of a "black race" that, like the Indian, was distinguished by common physical and intellectual characteristics. One thing that had not changed, however, was that Africa and its inhabitants were still great unknowns for Europeans. The authors of the *Encyclopédie Méthodique* confessed as much when they observed that many African territories were still unexplored, that even knowledge of those with some European presence was "very imperfect and flawed," and that this was unlikely to change soon.[63] The situation was no different in Spain, where very few works about Africa and Africans were published, with the exception once again of missionaries' writings—but these continued to rely on old Spanish sources whose trustworthiness had already been questioned.[64]

Many eighteenth-century peninsular Spaniards continued to insist that Africans' black color was the effect of extreme heat and that in theory it could change with habitat and no substantial alterations in the body or mental capacity.[65] Moreover, Spaniards also still believed that Africa had been occupied by a variety of people with different physical and mental characteristics and that throughout history these peoples had continuously mingled. It is interesting, for instance, that Spaniards still saw Africa as a continent whose northern half was dominated by "Muslim Arabs" and its center and southern half by a combination of different people with a variety of black skin tones. It was therefore impossible to claim that the various African nations were all members of the same race.[66]

Things started to change in the late 1700s, when Europeans gradually accepted the existence of a black race with intrinsic and permanent characteristics.[67] These new theories also left their mark on the Hispanic world, where, as in the case of Indians, by the closing years of the eighteenth century "blacks" or "African *castas*" were looked upon as members of a single race regardless of skin tone, with certain essential traits in common, regardless of region. African peoples' initial exposure to different climatic conditions had resulted in biological differences from the white race, similar to the view of America's indigenous populations. Many Spanish Americans and peninsular Spaniards shared this opinion. According to the author of the famous *The Blind Wayfarers' Guide (Lazarillo de ciegos caminantes)*, the most civilized blacks "are infinitely coarser than the Indians," while the Mexican Francisco Javier Clavijero held that the blacks "are the furthest removed from the general notion we have of beauty and of the perfection of the human body." They were marked "by the darkness of their color, or by some greater irregularity, or some more remarkable defect" that distinguished them from Indians, who were themselves inferior to Europeans.[68]

In Spain these new theories were best summarized by the liberal geographer Isidoro Antillón, who followed naturalists such as Samuel Stanhope and the Comte de Lacépède when he noted that blacks differed from whites not only in skin color but also, and essentially, in their bone and cranial structures. "Nature," he wrote, "has stamped the head of the negro with the unmistakable marks that set him apart from other lineages of men, and especially Europeans." For instance, the Africans had a smaller facial angle (70 degrees, in contrast to the Europeans who measured 80 degrees and the ancient Greeks at 90). Many drew the conclusion that blacks generally were "incapable of reason or virtue [and] could never have the qualities of a citizen."[69]

In the Spanish imperial context, however, representations of the African were still mediated by the persistence of a slave regime and not primarily by contemporary racialist theories. Or, put another way, the racialist discourse used in Spain to describe Africans adopted the grammar of slavery. There is no indication that any significant changes occurred in the justification of slavery, and officially slavery continued to be a civil institution. Slaves were captives taken in just war or the children of enslaved women, all treated as "things," completely under the will of their owners, who were required, although rarely compelled, to treat them humanely.[70]

Justifications of slavery did not change, but the number of slaves coming to Spanish American territories did. Following a period of decline, the number of slaves recovered dramatically beginning in the 1720s and 1730s. In some regions—Mexico, Chile, Central America, and Bolivia—there seems to be plenty of evidence that slavery was lightly rooted, and in others it began to disappear entirely by the mid-1600s, a process that continued into the 1700s. However, in other regions, the number of slaves rose rapidly. Although figures are incomplete, historians calculate that between 300,000 and 400,000 slaves ended up in Spanish colonies between 1700 and 1820.[71] Cuba was the prime example of this revival of large-scale slavery. Between 1700 and 1810 some 250,000 slaves arrived in Cuba to work in the burgeoning sugar economy, and it has been estimated that by 1800, some 200,000 lived on the island, or almost 35 percent of the total population.[72] Although not quite reaching those levels, significant numbers of slaves lived in Venezuela (some 115,000 in 1800), Colombia, and Argentina (between 60,000 and 70,000 in each one).[73] In no region of the Americas was the proportion of Africans, slave and free, as high as it was in Saint Domingue (Haiti) on the eve of the 1791 revolution, when slaves alone comprised 80 percent of the total population.

Eighteenth-century Spanish authorities were even more firmly convinced than their predecessors that they needed to limit the power of masters over slaves and to use their "paternal" vigilance to improve slaves' living conditions.[74] No one questioned that first and foremost, slaves had to be useful to their masters, but these legitimate private interests had to be balanced by the maintenance of peace in the colonies. Reducing feelings of discontent among slaves would in turn reduce their desire for rebellion and would also allow slaves to participate more actively in the defense of colonies against attacks by other imperial powers.[75] With these objectives in mind the Caroline Black Code of Santo Domingo (1784) and the Royal

Order on Slaves (1789) ordered masters to educate their slaves in matters of Christian faith to avoid extreme or unnecessary violence, to respect slaves' right to marry and keep their family together, and to not force them to work during religious holidays and on Sundays. Masters were also required to ensure that their slaves received a basic education in "good habits" that would kindle appreciation for the respect owed to their masters and to civil and ecclesiastical authorities.[76]

The defense of these "rights," remnants of older laws, was undercut by monarchial efforts to impress upon the slaves a well-defined racial hierarchy. Until the appearance of the Code of Santo Domingo, the sons of "whites of all [social] classes" mixed with "pardos and free blacks" in primary schools, but this "confusion and mingling" gave the children "sinister impressions of equality and familiarity with one another." To avoid this, schools after the Code were closed to "all blacks and first-generation pardos, who should all be directed towards agriculture" and who were prohibited from "mingling with the whites, the *tercerones*, *cuarterones* and the rest, who should be placed in separate classrooms, to be instructed by white persons of probity and learning, who from an early age would impress upon their heart the feelings of respect and affinity for the whites, whose equals they must be one day." Prohibitions against blacks and intermediate *castas* of blacks challenging, contradicting, or entering into disputes with whites further reinforced the racial hierarchy. Likewise, all freedmen were threatened with the loss of their liberty if they committed crimes against their old masters or other whites. The code also restricted freedmen's social mobility by stipulating that blacks or black *castas* could not exercise the offices of whites because "the white and intermediate colored population would be defrauded." It was further decreed that pardos, *tercerones*, *cuarterones*, and their sons could not leave the profession of their fathers at least until the fifth generation and the "sixth grade of color."[77]

Based on the language of this code, it seems evident that while ideas about slavery had not changed, they started to get "racialized" to an unprecedented extent. The purpose was to associate the black color with social inferiority and dependency, not only in those who were enslaved but in all who shared the same origins and physical characteristics. The Spanish friar Benito Jerónimo Feijóo had already drawn attention to this association when he noted that as a consequence of slavery the Africans "see the black color debased in the wretchedness of their state; and, conversely, whiteness covered in the splendor of domination."[78] Even worse, the stigma applied to all, slaves as well as their descendants and even to freedmen. It was carried in the blood and was virtually impossible to eradicate. In the imperial context, "the black color . . . seems to be the characteristic sign of servitude," and being black—the "most dishonorable human color in the world"—could only signify that one was a slave or descended from slaves.[79]

Nevertheless, the reality of Africans was more complex and irreducible to the stigma of slavery or to the racial uniformity postulated by these theories. If one aspect of the American reality stands out, it is the sheer number of freedmen, Africans, and mixed-bloods who were active members of the colonial society, unlike the Indians. Although already present in earlier centuries, the number of freedmen grew quickly in the eighteenth.[80] The explorer Félix de Azara, for example, claimed that there were 174 freedmen for every ten slaves in Paraguay, and this proportion appears to have characterized many other areas as well.[81] Recent studies have confirmed these impressions, to the extent that in 1800, freedmen outnumbered slaves almost everywhere. In Mexico, there were 300,000 free persons of African descent and some 10,000 slaves; in Venezuela, 198,000 were free and 80,000 enslaved; and in the viceroyalty of New Granada (Colombia and Ecuador), the ratio was 420,000 freedmen to 80,000 slaves. The numbers were more balanced in Peru (41,000 and 40,000), Santo Domingo (80,000/15,000), Puerto Rico (35,000/7,000), and Paraguay (7,000/4,000). In Cuba the situation was radically different, with some 114,000 freedmen and 250,000 slaves.[82]

It was claimed in the 1700s that these great numbers of freedmen owed to the more liberal slave system of the Spanish empire in contrast to those of other Europeans. The Mexican bishops invoked this perceived difference when they compared the English and Spanish systems: "The English have them [i.e. slaves] in their colonies, but without releasing them from their condition of slavery, and so they have risen in violent revolts, while we, guided by the piety of our faith, give them liberty afterwards, either [granted by] the one who purchased the slave in his testament, or the son or heir, and our cities are inundated with free Blacks."[83] In reality the reasons for the large freedmen population were somewhat more complicated. The structure of slave labor in the Spanish colonies must be taken into account, as it was dedicated primarily to services rather than plantation work, which made it relatively easier to obtain one's liberty. It has been demonstrated that in the wake of the eighteenth-century revival of slavery, the number of slaves was lower, certainly lower than that of freedmen, and even more important in places where the number of slaves increased in the eighteenth century, a majority of them were born in Africa and not in the Americas.[84]

The pressure exerted by slaves themselves, who saw manumission as a right guaranteed by colonial authorities and courts, should also be flagged as one reason for the growing number of freedmen. The few studies of manumission in the Spanish and Portuguese territories show that, while old slaves were occasionally manumitted, in the majority of cases slaves purchased their own freedom. Twice as many female slaves than male slaves were manumitted; many of the manumitted were children; and a majority of all those who attained freedom came from cities and towns, were born in the Americas, and were most likely to be mixed-blood individuals, usually mulattos.[85] Perhaps more significant is that the seventeenth-century slavery crisis reduced the number of slaves and even caused slavery's disappearance in some regions, which meant that the progeny of older slaves, and especially their mixed-blood descendants, were more likely to be born free.

A vast population of Africans lived in Spanish American cities and towns, and many performed important social functions. Africans were prominent in urban militias throughout the Americas, and on numerous occasions—such as the foiled English attacks on Cuba and Buenos Aires in the second half of the century—they played a decisive role in fighting and sometimes defeating the Spanish empire's enemies. African freedmen were soldiers but also officers, up to the rank of captain, and were found in a widening range of occupations—as artisans, surgeons, and other professionals. Hence, they were becoming a cornerstone of local societies.[86] Very few would hold public offices, and, legally, none of them could become full citizens in Spanish cities, but they never doubted that they formed an important and active community in many cities.

Among those who challenged the racial hierarchy in the Americas was a mestizo from Venezuela, Don Juan Germán Roscio. A lawyer by profession, Roscio was a man with impeccable social credentials, a tenured professor, and a member of the guild and faculty of the Royal and Pontifical University of Caracas and of the Royal Academy of Spanish Law.[87] However, Roscio was accused of having "black blood" through his mother, and it was also claimed that his brothers had married pardos. He rebutted these charges by proving that his mother was a mestiza (daughter of an Indian woman and a Spaniard) and that he had not even a drop of black or pardo blood. Of greater interest here is Roscio's critique to all and every racialist practices during his times. In his statement, Roscio first set out to show that Indians were not members of a "red race" but were in fact a white race akin to the European, since they were the descendants of Shem, son of Noah. More importantly, he maintained that Spanish laws differentiated between "Indians" and "Spaniards," not between "Indians and Whites." The term *Indian* was not a signifier of color but of birth in the Indies. *Mestizo*, on the other hand, was not meant to indicate any particular color or race but only that one was the descendant of "a man and a woman of two different nations."

Roscio was critical of the racialization of the Indians and the use of racial criteria for social hierarchies. When it came to determining the worth of any individual, he noted, "men were all born free . . . and are equally noble, as they are formed of the same matter, and nurtured in the image and semblance of God." From time immemorial, when men first came together to form societies and create republics and monarchies, those chosen to govern were not "the fairest, the most handsome, the darkest, or the ruddiest, but those with the greatest talent and virtue," and virtue, as it was written in the *Siete Partidas*, was not linked "to birth and color." To be sure, humans had introduced social distinctions based on skin color, but it was important to remind everyone that this was "an accidental alteration, or variation between individuals of the human species." Some had come to deny that Ethiopians were descended from Adam, but "in truth only the ignorance of natural laws . . . could make anybody to exclude the Negroes from the human species." It should never be forgotten that an individual was worthy when he possessed the virtues necessary for helping to administer the communities, but these aptitudes came in all different colors.

A growing number of studies have shown that, from at least the close of the seventeenth century, those who were by and large genuinely integrated into Spanish society, and in many cases able to secure public offices, were mestizos, mulattos, and other mixed-blood individuals, not Indians or Africans. This provokes three questions profoundly relevant to social relations in Spanish America but that also shaped debates on the evolution of different population groups: to what extent did biological mixing affect different human species? Which American inhabitants had the potential to become members of the Spanish family? And what were the implications of new opportunities for social mobility created by biological mixing for African descendants? These were not easy questions, but it is clear that the answers, and the policies they were meant to inform, had an enormous influence at this time and in the early nineteenth-century constitutional debates.

Biological mixing in the Spanish world has attracted enormous attention from modern scholars. In recent years, nothing seems more fascinating than the study of the so-called "casta paintings," a genre that emerged primarily in New Spain during the eighteenth century. These paintings generally depict a series of marital combinations of individuals of different *castes*, a term that especially in the eighteenth century came to refer "to the children of unions between members of the three main 'trunks' of colonial society: Spaniards, Native Americans and Africans."[88] These *casta* paintings were commissioned by peninsular Spanish elites who wanted to collect exotic materials from the Americas to display in the very fashionable private cabinets of curiosities. But the paintings were also clear evidence of the growing interest in the reality of biological mixing in Spain and the Americas.[89] Contemporaries were not primarily concerned about so-called "racial passing," a phenomenon whereby reported racial identity changes, whether through administrative error or self-reporting by the individuals concerned. We know that many individuals tried to present themselves as members of other *castas;* for instance, many mulattos tried to pass for mestizos (Spanish-Indian mix), and many others tried to pass for white. But this passing was primarily to evade restrictions imposed by fairly inflexible legislation on the rights and obligations of each one of the primary groups. Instead, what is being analyzed here are the opinions of Spaniards and Americans on the subject of racial mixing, the phenomenon of "whitening," and how these processes affected the collective self-image of Spanish American society.

Undoubtedly, as in previous centuries, biological mixing provoked anxiety among Spaniards on both sides of the Atlantic. The Spanish antiquarian of Irish origin Pedro Alonso O'Crouley, referring to the *casta* paintings, observed that one of the distinctive features of New Spain was "the confusion, mixing of blood, and the multiplication of lineages."[90] This bewildering variety of racial mixes transformed many colonial cities into veritable "Babylons of confusion," according to the historian and geographer Pedro Murillo Velarde.[91] Many American observers viewed biological mixing as the cause of myriad social and racial ills. As on many other issues, Antonio de Ulloa was perhaps one of the most critical voices on the social effects of miscegenation. The proliferation of racial mixes since the Spanish arrival had yielded a vast number of mixed individuals, and eventually this would mean that all American territories "would be populated entirely by a mixed race that would partake of all, without being perfectly of either one of the primitive [races]."[92] Jorge Juan and Antonio Ulloa even believed that mestizo women had a clear strategy to whiten the entire American population. They were prepared and willing to cohabitate with men from the highest social ranks and to conceive individuals who were ever whiter in appearance, versed in white customs, and in turn able to marry or cohabitate with recently arrived Spaniards in the Indies or with Creoles of the middling classes.[93]

Given these negative perceptions of biological mixing, it is very revealing to consider Spanish authorities' efforts, and those of many contemporary writers, to underscore the positive aspects of miscegenation. The issue was addressed by Juan Bautista Muñoz in his history of America. He included among the Spanish contributions to the continent the great number of Europeans who had settled there, the introduction of the Africans, and, above all, the multitude of mixed races, who "if not in number then at least in quality, have compensated abundantly for the lose of pure Americans."[94] Many others saw these mixed-race individuals as necessary for colonial stability. Murillo Valverde, for instance, advocated the proliferation of mulattos, the offspring of Spaniards and black women, because they were generally "brave, intrepid, daring, resolute, very skillful horsemen, and extremely fond of the Spaniards" with whom they tended to ally against the Indians or against foreign attackers.[95] Curiously, in the majority of cases, such mixes, especially with Africans, were seen not as proof of the racial degeneration of the Spaniards but as an avenue for the improvement of other races. If white was the color of racial perfection, the argument held, then race mixing and the gradual whitening of the offspring of interracial unions were the only way to restore the pristine uniformity of human color.[96] The "mixing of races improves" non-European peoples, wrote Félix de Azara, because it whitens them, which in the long term should lead to the total racial domination of Europeans over the rest.[97]

These ideas and processes have attracted the attention of many scholars, but until now it has been difficult to explain why such a significant number of Spaniards, and certainly the royal authorities, saw this race mixing as a positive development at a time when racialist ideology was becoming predominant. In a thought-provoking article, Max S. Hering Torres observed that "as a result of Enlightened projects, *mestizaje* ceased to be a fount of impurity and instead became a mechanism of cultural assimilation, with the objective of civilizing and domesticating the brutishness, the torpor, and the indolence that were inscribed in the body and character of the Native." "Whitening" through biological mixing was encouraged, he argues, as a way of eliminating "the impurity of color or lineage." For this reason some authors and colonial and peninsular authorities no longer saw miscegenation as the racial corruption of the white man. Instead they saw it as key to the "civilizing [process] in which the goal was to homogenize the population under a single ensign, the ensign of whiteness."[98]

Certainly, it is possible to find opinions at the time that appear to support this analysis. But it seems highly unlikely that these individuals, and especially colonial authorities, believed that the future of humanity was racial amalgamation. In the Spanish world, beyond a few isolated cases, as we have seen, there was no clear program to implement what William Nelson has called the "Enlightenment ideas of racial engineering."[99] We know that the monarchy and the colonial state never put forward a conscious strategy to create equality among its subjects through miscegenation. We also know that central authorities never discussed the possibility of opening access to public offices in the Indies to all free subjects, regardless of ancestry, until the early nineteenth century.[100]

More than supporting a program of racial amalgamation, Spanish authorities seemed to be interested in ensuring political and social stability. Conscious of the growing number of intermediate *castas*, of the upward mobility of many of these groups and their thirst for rewards, colonial authorities understood that the only way to avoid social and perhaps even political upheaval was through co-optation of the most prominent among them, albeit without compromising the dominant racial logic. There is no better example of this than the military reforms that began in the 1770s. All the armed forces created from this date onward allowed entry, along with a certain measure of equality, to individuals of all the different *castas* as well as Creoles, Spaniards, and Indians—although each *casta* had its own separate unit.[101]

Colonial authorities' desire for stability meshed with the *casta* elite's aspiration for social mobility. We should analyze the laws and policies of whitening within this context. There is clear evidence that even in the 1600s, free Africans, and especially free mulattos, started petitioning for access to public offices in addition to trying to form defensive militias.[102] In the eighteenth century, however, the initiative came mainly from colonial authorities. In the Code of Santo Domingo, as in other legal edicts, the monarchy promoted so-called racial and legal "whitening" *(blanqueamiento)*, which illustrates the new approach to mulattos' integration. The policy gave the opportunity to some black *castas*, those with a greater admixture of white blood, to improve their standing to the point of being legally regarded as white. The code, for instance, stipulated that for an individual to be considered white and to enjoy the privileges associated with whiteness, one had to be descended from six generations of mixed marriages. The first generation would be a mix of black and white, engendering a mulatto, whose marriage to a white would produce pardo offspring, followed by a *tercerón*, *cuarterón*, mestizo, and, finally, white.[103]

Perhaps more interesting is that royal authorities also introduced in the 1770s the so-called "régimen de las gracias al sacar." This made it possible, in exchange for a fixed payment, to obtain a writ or certificate of whiteness or, put another way, the legal right to seek offices and honors reserved for Spaniards, including access to public offices.[104] Modern scholars have also drawn attention to the phenomenon whereby many pardos, *morenos*, and mulattos began to petition for racial dispensations to practice certain professions—surgeons, scribes, and notaries. In some cases, mulattos and blacks could purchase "dispensations of casta," which allowed them to be considered legally white, regardless of their physical features.

The two arguments most frequently used by those who tried to purchase these privileges were, first, that for all intents and purposes they already possessed the physical attributes of whites; or, as one petitioner put it, "neither his father nor his grandfathers were of the color and name of Negroes or pardos." This supplicant, named Bernardo Ramírez, noted in his petition that successive mixtures of blacks and whites produced "quarterones" in whom "all the note of color" disappeared, and in the next "generation and family passes in the class of Spaniards."[105] The same logic was applied by members of a pardo battalion who petitioned against the admission of a certain Juan Bautista Arias into their ranks because his complexion was closer to "a Negro or Indian" and thus he had no place among those who "are drawing ever closer to the whites . . . fairness of color being of no little import in this matter, according to señor Jorge Juan [and Antonio de Ulloa] in their account of the journey to Cartagena."[106] The second and more frequently used argument, however, was that petitioners or their ancestors had rendered great services to the crown and society, clear proof that they were beginning to claim a place in society, whatever their racial features.

American Creoles offered the strongest opposition to any integration of the different *castas* or laws that would encourage their whitening. The reason was straightforward—namely, their desire to maintain the dominant racial hierarchy but also the fear among eighteenth-century Creoles that peninsular Spaniards were beginning to see them as biologically contaminated. To recall, Spaniards felt pressured to become fully European, and in the imperial context this resulted in a hardening of the lines that separated those included and excluded from the nation. In the case of the Creoles, the movement toward the whitening of peninsular Spaniards meant the simultaneous "darkening" of the Creoles.

The reasoning behind such perceptions seems clear. According to dominant colonial ideology, an African was thought of as improved if she or he was a pardo. Mixing with Indians or Africans, however, degraded a white man or woman. Peninsular Spaniards saw this precisely as one of the problems with Creoles. There is no doubt that Europeans saw Creoles as strange and paradoxical individuals, so similar and yet so very different—but this in itself was nothing new in the Hispanic world.[107] In the seventeenth century many peninsulars had tended to regard Creoles as degenerate beings, which was often attributed to the influence of the climate and the American natural environment. Eighteenth-century peninsulars inherited many of these theories, although now Creoles were also to be treated as colonial subjects and racialized to an unprecedented degree. Murillo Valverde called them "White Indians" because "they are Indians in substance, and Spaniards only in accident."[108] Meanwhile, for the author of the entry on America in the *Encyclopédie Méthodique*, Spaniards born on the American continent were brutish imbeciles, resembling Indians. The belief was beginning to take hold that they had also suffered biological alterations due to climate. The eccentric Canarian aristocrat Cristóbal del Hoyo Solórzano y Sotomayor, Marquis of San Andrés, referred to Creoles as "biformed Centaurs" precisely because of the mixed blood in their veins, in which the Spanish element was getting eclipsed with each generation by the blood of "Negroes or Indians."[109]

This was only part of the story, however. Some peninsulars had a negative view of Creoles, but others defended them unstintingly.[110] For them, Creoles not only had retained their physical and mental attributes but were clearly still Spanish and therefore active participants in the monarchial government. The point was not only to vouch for their good qualities but to urge the crown to do everything in its power to ensure that Creoles were not marginalized. Many of the era's most important reformers considered it crucial to involve Creoles in new reformist projects and to allow them to take advantage of new avenues for economic and intellectual progress. This was the attitude of the two state attorneys Pedro Rodríguez de Campomanes and José Moñino. In a meeting of the Council of Castile, convened to discuss the situation in the Indies, they called attention to the growing discontent among Creoles over being treated as mere colonial subjects and noted that "for the vassals of Your Majesty in the Indies to love the matrix which is Spain, there must be a community of interest, and, because at such a great distance one cannot rely on bonds of affection, the only way to promote this beneficial aim is to allow them to apprehend the sweetness and partaking in the rewards, honors, and favors."[111]

Creoles also defended themselves. First, based on the logic of the law of nature, Creoles tirelessly insisted that they were the principal part of the kingdoms of the Indies and as such had the right to exercise offices in their own land or at least a significant number of them. The Creole elite collectively observed in a memorandum addressed to Carlos III in 1770 that despite the fact that they were natives of these kingdoms, they were compelled to demand the creation of a community of equals—of Creoles and peninsulars, sharing offices, wealth, honors, and a common future.[112] In asserting their right to a share of political power in the Indies, Creoles found support in arguments such as the one used by the governor of the Council of the Indies, Antonio Porlier. In his reflections on the "love of the patria" he maintained that "Spanish Americans" were the descendants of "our European populations" and that "the Dominions where they or their descendants have settled," together with Spain in Europe, "form a single Nation, the same Body politic, which binds and links all of us closely."[113] In response to these petitions, it appears that the crown made great efforts to integrate a larger number of Creoles, to introduce laws favorable to them, and especially to incorporate them into the new colonial defensive forces created after 1770. There is also evidence that in some regions, especially Cuba and Peru, these measures succeeded, creating a colonial political elite that remained remarkably loyal to the Spanish monarchy during political crises in the turbulent first decade of the nineteenth century.[114]

The Creoles' main intent, however, was to deny that they were a racially mixed nation. Like other social groups, Creoles heeded the racial hierarchy constructed in the eighteenth century and placed themselves at its apex. Montesquieu had observed this at the beginning of the century, and Humboldt confirmed it 100 years later: "In a country governed by whites, the families reputed to have the least mixture of negro or mulatto blood are also naturally the most honored. . . . Color establishes even a certain equality among men [who] . . . take a particular pleasure in dwelling on the prerogatives of race and origin."[115] This was indeed a view that Creoles were ready to defend and justify. In a 1771 memorandum to Carlos III, for instance, even though they acknowledged that their first ancestors had mixed with natives in the immediate aftermath of the conquest, "those unions had been with the royal families of the [indigenous] nation," and they had not introduced "any vileness into the spirits of their descendants." Many generations had passed since then, and there could be no question of mingling because "whosoever in their sixteen great-great-grandparents only has one Indian, he is naturally, and is considered from all intents and purposes a pure and clean Spaniard, without admixture of any other blood." These had been virtually the only instances of race mixing because from that moment onward it had simply been shunned, since Indian women are "of disagreeable appearance, most unpleasant color, coarse features, slovenly, if not naked then lacking cleanliness, uncultured and irrational in their manner, have great aversion to Spaniards, and are even reluctant to converse with them." Any Spaniard who had mixed with them "would find his children deprived of the honors due to Spaniards; and even excluded from enjoying the privileges granted to Indians. The same could be said, and with greater cause, of those cases when the mixing was with blacks, mulattos, or other *castas* proceeding from these; and so these [mixes] are unusual, and far less common than malicious [voices] would have it."[116]

Such notions largely explain Creole attitudes about policies that could affect their social standing. They were in favor of Carlos III's decision to extend the royal pragmatic on marriages *(Real Pragmática Sanción sobre Matrimonios)* to the Indies, prohibiting young sons and daughters of the elite from marrying without parental permission, in order to avoid unions that could damage family honor and their descendants' opportunities for social mobility. Significantly, this measure had its origins in the Spanish nobility's desire to ensure that their offspring did not marry members of inferior social classes, while in the Americas, the objective was to prevent heirs of Creole houses from marrying individuals of ambiguous or impure racial stock.[117] It is no accident that in the eighteenth century there was renewed emphasis on the use of blood purity statutes in America, no longer as a means to discriminate against those with some Jewish or Moorish blood but against all those who could not demonstrate their purity of white or Spanish blood.[118]

Even more vehement was Creole opposition to the policy of "whitening," and indeed Creole pressure led to the abolition of the system that allowed candidates to purchase certificates of whiteness and blocked the implementation of the Black Code of Santo Domingo. The arguments against "whitening" were invariably the same. The Creole-dominated municipal government of Caracas, for example, was opposed to a petition by the pardos of the city for the right to marry lower-class white women because everyone should remain "within their own [racial] sphere." If such marital unions were permitted, it would become impossible to distinguish between families that were mixed and those that were not. This in turn would be an obstacle to many marriages because whites would not marry "except other whites."[119] The faculty of the University of Caracas, also dominated by Creoles, opposed a petition by the mulatto Diego Mexías for his heirs and other mulattos to be allowed to attend the university.[120] Although these academics declared support for the idea that skin color should not influence the measure of individual merits, they were no less convinced that it was necessary to prevent pardos from "profaning by introducing their impure hands in the sanctuary of Literature." Even if many of these Africans and their descendants were now free, they had nevertheless arrived from Africa marked "with all the ignominy of barbarism, and all the infamy of slavery." The mulattos, they argued, would never be rid of these stigmas because "this race betwixt and between whites and blacks" was nothing more than the product of "ungainly (biological) exchanges, proscribed by all laws."

The Venezuelan Creoles, the most directly affected by the crown's policies promoting free pardos and mulattos, also claimed that the social promotion of the pardo, his elevation to a status heretofore reserved exclusively for whites, would have serious consequences for the political stability of the colonies and ultimately for the preponderance of whites in the Americas. If the ethnic homogeneity of peninsular Spain made it possible to implement policies designed to stimulate social mobility, they claimed, the same was not true of the Indies. There, clear hierarchies had to be maintained, and these could only be based on racial criteria. It was common knowledge, they maintained, that the mulattos "aid one another to attain higher status," and they ceaselessly reminded colonial authorities of the Haiti example. The crisis in Haiti, they claimed, began when the French colonial authorities sought to elevate the free pardos, just as the Spanish authorities were trying to do in their colonies. Once they had obtained positions of privilege, these pardos wanted more rights and power, and to achieve this they unhesitatingly aligned themselves with slaves against whites. This racial alliance culminated in the revolution of 1791 in Haiti (Saint-Domingue), which resulted in "demolished haciendas" and the destruction "in a fleeting moment, of the great labors of more than a century." Even more horrendously, they "did not leave a drop of European blood unspilled." Spanish America's stability, they declared, owed to the fact that pardos and other inferior classes of men were kept in "submission" while peninsular and American Spaniards acted as equal partners.

It is far from certain that Spanish America at the end of the eighteenth century was really on the threshold of a race war, as the Venezuelan Creoles predicted. Throughout the eighteenth century there were major indigenous revolts and rebellions as well as slave uprisings in various parts of the Americas, but these either were violently suppressed or had limited and localized effect. Historians have also shown that the Haitian Revolution of 1791 provoked enormous anxiety among colonial elites and raised equally great expectations among slaves and free blacks in Spanish America, but in fact there were very few, if any, conflicts that could rival the violence and radicalism of the Saint Domingue revolt, at least in the 1700s.[121] The Creoles were not so much fearful of slave revolts, however, as they wanted instead to manipulate these fears to convince the colonial authorities to respect Creoles' rights and preeminence in colonial society.

It also seemed scarcely possible, and hard even to imagine, that a conflict between Spanish Americans and the imperial authorities could result in a rupture. True, since the 1760s there had been many obvious signs of Creole discontent. Between 1765 and 1781, middle-class Creoles were on the vanguard of several major revolts, such as the Quito riots of 1765 and most notably the so-called Revolt of the Comuneros of New Granada in 1781. Yet nothing in these revolts, generally directed against Bourbon reforms, indicated a strong desire for independence.[122]

In the last decades of the eighteenth century, however, among Spaniards and Europeans generally, there was a belief that European colonies in the Americas were entering an advanced stage of maturity. They were societies that could, as demonstrated by the struggle for independence of the Thirteen Colonies, in the near future seek their separation from the metropolis.[123] The confluence of these ideas and the independence of the Thirteen Colonies led various Spanish ministers to propose schemes for the peaceful and orderly separation of the colonies from the metropolis and the creation of a series of autonomous states that would remain dynastically linked to Spain.[124]

Yet something rather more dangerous was going on in the Americas. If the peninsular Spaniards increasingly saw themselves as "Spaniards, whites, and Europeans," more and more disconnected and distinct from their American "brothers," then something similar was occurring among Creoles, who began to see themselves as American whites, politically and ethnically closer to the English colonists in the north who had taken up arms against the oppression of the British metropolis. These ideas were especially prevalent among the many exiled Latin Americans scattered across Europe, who were beginning to articulate a kind of Creole patriotism, one that was no longer merely cultural but now also political.

From London, the heart of that rival metropolis, an exiled Creole, the Peruvian Jesuit Juan Pablo Viscardo, equipped his compatriots with an ideology that could transform their cultural and racial anxiety into political discontent. In his *Letter to the Spanish Americans*, written shortly before his death in 1798 and published in 1799, Viscardo reminded his "brothers and compatriots" that "our patria" is the New World, "its history is our history, and in this light we must examine our present situation, in order to determine the necessary steps for the conservation of our rights, and those of our descendants." From the Spanish authorities the American Creoles had come to expect only "ingratitude, injustice, servitude and desolation" in spite of which, since the conquest and until the present time, the Spanish Americans had "respected, preserved, and cherished the devotion of our fathers to their first patria," Spain. Perhaps the time had come to break the ties that bound them to "a country that is foreign to us, to which we owe nothing, on which we do not depend, and from which we can expect nothing." It was time to break the chains of Spanish tyranny because there was only one alternative to independence: "ignominious slavery."[125] Whatever influence Viscardo's ideas had when this letter was first published, there is no doubt that the piece presaged some of the key arguments in a political and military confrontation between peninsular Spaniards and Creoles that would soon commence, and with great vigor after 1808, when Spain itself would be invaded by the powerful armies of Napoleon Bonaparte.

7

From Empire to Nation

By 1800 spain was widely perceived as a moribund empire and nation. The image of the country in the minds of most observers was that of a poor, backward, uncivilized country with a corrupt government and a king, Carlos IV, who was weak and incompetent.[1] The Anglo-Irish conservative Edmund Burke claimed that Spain lacked the nerve and leadership to confront its momentous problems and was incapable of discarding its political and ideological dependence on France. "The spirit of melioration which has been going on in that part of Europe, more or less during this century," he continued, "and the various schemes very lately on foot for further advancement, are all put a stop at once."[2] At about the same time, the Mexican Creole Servando Teresa de Mier designated Spain as the land of "despotism," inhabited by people who were uncultured, plagued by underdevelopment, and without hope for the future.[3]

American Creoles and foreigners were not the only ones who felt that Spain was in the throes of a deep crisis. The Spanish liberal Isidoro de Antillón declared that he was living in an age of repression, contempt for reason, and governmental despotism.[4] There appeared to be neither the desire nor an ideology that would enable Spain to undergo the revolutionary changes experienced by France or the British colonies in America. In Spain, neither the people nor the elites understood the "science of politics," according to a contemporary witness.[5]

There were admittedly objective reasons for Spaniards' fatalism. Since 1793 Spain had been embroiled in international conflicts that had cost many lives, much suffering, and great material losses. It sided initially with Great Britain against Revolutionary France (1793–1795) and then against the former in alliance with Napoleonic France (1796–1802, 1806–1807). The country also experienced a series of crises provoked by power struggles within the royal family, the political corruption attributed to Manuel Godoy (the king and queen's favorite) and other ministers, and the inability of any of these figures to provide a clear direction for the country. Alcalá Galiano compared the situation in Spain during this period not to George IV's Great Britain but rather to France before the Revolution: George IV, he wrote, was also despised by a significant part of the population, but the monarchy had never been in danger because of its constitutional nature. In pre-revolutionary France the situation had been quite different. Resentment of a corrupt royal family had shaken to its core a monarchy without constitutional support and whose eventual fall was spectacular and bloody.[6]

The constitutionalization of the monarchical state with the Constitution of Cádiz (1812), the first and perhaps the most influential charter in Spanish history, followed after the Napoleonic invasion of Spain, the resistance of a large number of the Spanish people to the invasion. Many in the nineteenth century, like today, claimed that a nation was based, in more or less equal part, on remembrance and forgetting, collective memory and selective oblivion. Remembrance was necessary to appreciate the common achievements and ideologies that fostered national unity and brotherhood, oblivion to forget or reinterpret everything that had once been nationally divisive—civil wars, invasions, conquests, victories and defeats, and ideologies of racial differentiation such as purity-of-blood statutes or the expulsion of Moriscos and Jews. The Constitution of Cádiz was the product but also the instrument of endeavors to retain the memory of all that had brought Spaniards together and to forget or remember selectively all that had divided them. It was an attempt to imagine or invent—to use a more fashionable term—a new nation.

Whether the attempt succeeded is not the issue here, but the Constitution of Cádiz provides the perfect conclusion to a study of discourses about nation and race elaborated by Spaniards over the course of several centuries. Above all the debates around each of the articles of the constitution reveal which concepts were privileged and which ideologies were obviated, used explicitly, or not. Perhaps wrongly, many Spaniards firmly believed that with the constitution they were creating for the first time a nation that would be blind to the territorial, ethnic, or cultural diversity of its inhabitants and in which the only thing that mattered would be their shared identity as Spaniards. The story that emerges from the scripting of the constitution is a combination of older terms with new ones and the product of revolutionary and modernizing processes that had been taking place since the late eighteenth century. Clearly, however, the political elites who participated in the constitutional process were convinced that they were drafting nothing less than the blueprint for a nation called Spain, one that would incorporate all the territories that constituted the Spanish empire and encompass all of its inhabitants regardless of ethnic origin. The goal was also to fashion a new state, not an imperial one, composed of various kingdoms but a national state. It would still be a monarchy but one founded on the political consent of its inhabitants.

If these were important issues of debate, even more crucial was the determination of who were Spaniards, who should have active political rights, and who should be citizens of the new nation. The debate centered on the question whether all those born in Spain—this new Spain, which would thenceforth include all the far-flung parts of the empire in Europe, America, and Asia—should have the same political rights in the new constitutional state, or was it necessary to maintain the ethnic distinctions already described? Was it legitimate to invoke the difference between new and old Christians to decide who could have full membership in the new society? Would the new political order be based on a patriarchal conception of the nation, or would there be room in it for women? How did deputies at Cádiz resolve the issues of race and citizenship, and how did their solutions differ from or resemble those adopted by other national communities? What were the effects of the continued vitality of the slave system on the new nation, and how did it confront the ideological and cultural heritage of slavery?

The Cádiz deputies debated many of the issues that had preoccupied previous generations and resorted to familiar concepts to try to explain new realities. If the goal was to create a new nation and state—as Cádiz deputies argued—was it also necessary to forge new concepts, or would the old ones suffice? Any response to these questions, which in turn became the focus of parliamentary and extra-parliamentary discussion, requires apprehending the uses of concepts and ideologies inherited from the past. In her study of the Anglo-American world, the historian Barbara Fields has observed that, in general, ideas and ideologies "offer a ready-made interpretation of the world . . . , but their prime function is to make coherent . . . sense of the social world." It is why "new experience constantly impinges on them, changing them in ways that are diabolically difficult for the detached observer, let alone the engaged participant, to detect." This is precisely what happened in the first years of the nineteenth century in the Spanish world. Here, too, it would be a far simpler task to analyze the new realities if the ideas behind them were also new. It would be much easier if "when things changed, the vocabulary died away as well. But far the more common situation in the history of ideologies is that instead of dying, the same vocabulary attaches itself, unnoticed, to new things."[7]

It should be emphasized that the debates of the early nineteenth century hold interest for us not because they represent the endpoint of a simple arc, the final unraveling of ideological threads first woven in the late fifteenth century. The Constitution of Cádiz was also a beginning—the inception of a new national metanarrative and ideology that would subsequently become dominant. Within it one may find vestiges of older concepts, histories, and attitudes but now with new meanings attached to them and put to new uses. This period, and the Constitution of Cádiz in particular, is a clear example of what the German scholar Reinhart Koselleck called "Sattelzeit" (saddle or threshold period), a time of rapid change in which older concepts begin to signify new political and social realities.[8] The Cádiz deputies tried to put an end to the Ancien Régime and create a new state. The political circumstances after 1814 would not prove favorable to the constitutionalists in this respect. But they were rather more successful in creating a new vision of Spain and the Spanish—constructs that still exert powerful influence in twenty-first-century Spain.

There would be no revolution in Spain, unlike in France or the Thirteen Colonies. What transpired in the first years of the nineteenth century was a political crisis, kindled by a crisis of government, stoked by feuds between members of the royal family (the Bourbon king Carlos IV and his allies on one side and Ferdinand, the prince and heir, and his supporters on the other), sparked by pressure exerted on Spain by Napoleon and Napoleonic expansionism. In 1806, Carlos IV had agreed to renew the war against Great Britain in alliance with France. As part of this new coalition Spain signed the treaty of Fontainebleau in 1807, which included an agreement for a joint invasion of Portugal. The treaty allowed Napoleon to send a force of at least 50,000 soldiers across Spanish territory, ostensibly to conquer Portugal. Facing an assault from the north by Spanish troops and with the French advancing on Lisbon, the Portuguese royal family fled the country on November 29, 1807, and relocated to Brazil. Portugal, however, turned out to be only a secondary objective for Napoleon. The bulk of the French troops ended up occupying some of the major urban centers of northern, eastern, and central Spain itself—including Burgos, Salamanca, Pamplona, San Sebastián, Barcelona, and Madrid.

The Spanish crisis became even more acute because of a parallel dynastic crisis. Bowing to pressure from Napoleon, Carlos IV, the queen, their son Ferdinand, and other members of the royal family were enticed to Bayonne, a French town close to the Spanish border, in early May 1808. There, the Emperor compelled both Carlos and Ferdinand to renounce their rights to the Spanish throne in his favor, and in turn he ceded the throne to his brother Joseph Bonaparte, who became the new Spanish monarch, as Joseph I. From the Spanish perspective, not only the king but now the country itself was in the tyrannical clutches of the eternal enemy, the French. Spaniards frequently said in those days that the nation was now enslaved.

The political, military, and dynastic crisis provoked by the forced exile of the Spanish royal family unleashed a wave of popular protests across Spain. The most important and consequential was the popular uprising of May 2, 1808, in Madrid, for all intents and purposes the true beginning of the war against Napoleon. At the start the protests were nothing more than an attempt to prevent the French forces from carrying off the last remaining members of the royal family to France and may be interpreted as uprisings in defense of royal legitimacy. The presence of French troops in Madrid, however, and the decision to violently crack down on the popular movement transformed the May 2 rising into the first of many movements of national liberation. The city's neighborhoods became scenes of confrontation between hundreds of poorly armed Madrileños and a well-equipped and battle-hardened French army. The violence and the French repression on the day of and day after the revolt were extreme: hundreds of rebels died in the capital's streets, and a significant number of those taken prisoner were executed without trial by French firing squads.[9]

The popular uprisings, the heroic resistance of a number of cities against the French, and some early victories by the Spanish and English regular armies raised many Spaniards' hopes that their country would prove to be the downfall of Napoleonic tyranny. Many claimed it would not be the first time that Spaniards' heroism and sacrifice had brought them victory and liberation from the nation's foreign oppressors. In these early days of the resistance, many observers were convinced that they were witnessing the beginning of a popular revolution. An unbridled people in arms would fill the vacuum left by the absence of central authority. Alcalá Galiano aptly summed up the situation and the feelings of the time, claiming that "never, in Spain or in any other nation, at any other time, has there been a more perfect democracy than our patria in those first days of the uprising against the French. The people governed then, the people such as it was," with its many virtues and just as many vices, righteous at times yet with a propensity for senseless violence on many other occasions.[10]

The moment was fleeting and the popular revolution short-lived. Once it had recovered from the initial shock of unexpected resistance, the French army reconquered most of the Spanish cities, including Madrid and, by the end of 1808, controlled nearly the whole peninsula. Only a few pockets remained beyond its reach, including Cádiz, where the national parliament would be convened. By late summer of 1808, Bonaparte's hold on Spain was taking on an air of permanence. Joseph I's government was coming to grips with the administration of the country, his armies seemed invincible, and under his rule, Spain received its first constitution, the so-called Statute of Bayonne. This constitutional document was written by a Frenchman, Jean-Baptiste Esménard, revised by the emperor himself, discussed and ratified by an assembly of Spanish representatives led by the Duke of Santa Fe, a Spaniard who collaborated with the French, and supported by a number of political and intellectual luminaries. These included some liberals: José Marchena, better known as Abate Marchena, a supporter of the French Revolution from its beginning (he lived in France from 1793 to 1796) and one of the most interesting personalities of his age; the Franco-Spaniard Francisco Cabarrus (Count of Cabarrús), who became minister of finance under Joseph I; Pedro Estala, translator of Buffon into Spanish; and Juan Meléndez Valdés, an important literary figure of the period.[11]

The statute, promulgated with unusual celerity, given that its implementation was decreed on July 6, 1808, did not introduce many novelties into the political-institutional structure of Spain. But it did contain enough elements to make it attractive to liberals, conservatives, and, most importantly, the American elites. Spanish conservatives applauded that the Bayonne constitution reaffirmed the monarchical nature of the government (a monarchy that was sovereign and unconstrained), established Catholicism as the official state religion, and allowed for parliamentary representation for the nobles and clergy. Some of the Spanish liberals saw the statute as the start of the creation of a representative parliament. For their part, American elites were won over by the proclamation of equality between the colonies and the metropolis. In fact, the former were not referred to as colonies but "kingdoms and provinces of America and Asia," which should "enjoy the same rights as the Metropolis," although the number of American representatives in the Parliament (only 22 of 172) was not proportionate to their share of the population.[12]

This was the context of popular uprisings against Napoleonic forces and the start of what would be known to Spaniards as the War of Independence, a long (1808–1813), brutal, and devastating conflict. During its course, much of the already decrepit national infrastructure was completely destroyed, hunger and plague epidemics besieged the whole country, and all sides engaged in the most extreme violence—not only between contending armies and irregular forces but also against civilians, prisoners, populations of cities that refused to surrender, children, and women.[13] It is no accident that in later decades, the Spanish War of Independence would be a prime example for those who argued for regulation of military conflicts in order to avoid a state of anarchy and the spilling of innocent blood by warring parties.[14] The demographic consequences were catastrophic for Spain, which in the first fourteen years of the nineteenth century lost between 600,000 and 900,000 inhabitants, or nearly 10 percent of its total population.[15]

Defeated militarily and politically, Spaniards realized that the war of national liberation was going to be "terrible" because it would bring death and destruction. For some, however, it could also be a "salutary" war if it could help regenerate Spaniards' national and patriotic spirit and reconstitute the nation.[16] The War of Independence exhibited many features of what Robert Palmer designated decades ago as the "age of democratic revolution."[17] The Hispanic world, like its Anglophone and Francophone counterparts, witnessed movements of national liberation, the development of new ideas of the nation and the state, the spread of the concept of citizenship, and the advent of national constitutions. The War of Independence encompassed or facilitated many of these developments, but it was also one of the most chaotic periods in the history of Spain, with Spaniards pitted against Spaniards, Spanish Americans against their peninsular brethren, and the nation deeply divided between those who wished to preserve the structures, outlooks, and ideologies of the Ancien Régime and others who wanted to establish a different type of state and nation.

It was widely claimed that the resistance against the French was a war of national unity in which everyone—nobles and paupers, men and women, and inhabitants from all regions—took part. They would perish or triumph together. Without a doubt, members of various social classes participated in the urban uprisings, defending their cities against invading French forces, but they also joined the guerrilla bands who bore the brunt of the Spanish military resistance to the Napoleonic army. If we believe the chronicles of the period, it seemed that everyone had caught the "patriotic fever." "The whole world," wrote José García de León y Pizarro, "even the women on the balconies, was anxiously inquiring after the state of the struggle."[18] The resistance to Napoleon created an opportunity for many women to play a more active role than before. They were among the protagonists of the first uprisings, certainly the one in Madrid, but they also organized resistance in many Spanish cities. A contemporary witness, Mor de Fuentes, present in Zaragoza during that city's struggle against the French army, described the women of the lower classes as having been "turned into infernal furies" when they volunteered to carry munitions to the frontline, "urging on, and sometimes putting to shame the men whom they served."[19]

In some cities besieged by the French, the role of women in their defense was so remarkable, and instrumental to the outcome, that it inspired the official creation of women's battalions, such as the Battalion of St. Barbara in Gerona, which at one point numbered more than 200. Its members took part in the defense of the city as combatants, not in a supporting role.[20] This unprecedented degree and new forms of women's engagement did not pass unnoticed and did not fail to inspire anxiety: "While it's true that women have played important parts in all political revolutions," they were nevertheless reminded that it was not their place to participate in armed struggle but to help "the men to be brave."[21]

Spaniards used the idea that all Spaniards, regardless of social class, region of birth, or even sex, were obliged to give their life in defense of the *patria* to summon their American brethren to fight alongside them. The peninsular Spaniards argued that the freedom and independence of the *patria* were an essential element of the national pact between themselves and the Spanish Americans.[22] "All Spaniards must know," a Catalan deputy, Felipe Aner de Esteve, told his American counterparts, "that with Bonaparte they will never have liberty, they will be slaves, and their property will be distributed to the barbarous conquerors." The Americans also had to know that this was their war, an "eternal war; a war of blood and death against perfidious France."[23] This sentiment was shared by American inhabitants, where initial responses to the news from Spain were to hastily assemble all manner of institutions, in both the Republic of Spaniards and the Republic of Indians, unanimously resist Napoleon, and call for the restoration of the Spanish king to the throne. The city council of Mexico set the tone in a statement signed August 5, 1808, and sent to the viceroy. The *Ayuntamiento* supported the popular uprisings in Spain "to redeem themselves from French slavery" and praised "the gallant national spirit that had always been able to overcome every obstacle, in the four corners of the world." The Mexicans also promised to fight shoulder to shoulder with the Spanish to "avenge the throne, save the king, defend the faith, their liberty, their homes, their inhabitants, and the sacred rights of the patria."[24]

These rallying cries and promises of Spanish unity were in many cases more illusory than real. On the peninsula itself, Spaniards of various ideological stripes from the beginning chose to support the Napoleonic regime. Some of them were conservatives who welcomed the government of Joseph Bonaparte as a bulwark of political stability. Others were liberals who accepted the Napoleonic regime as a guarantee that structures and ideologies of the Ancien Régime would be dismantled. The situation in the American territories was especially grave and complex because at least since 1808, there was every indication that the war would be primarily fought not in support of Spanish independence from French domination but for some kind of American independence from Spain. In virtually every region of the Americas, coalitions of Creoles, mestizos, mulattos, and other groups from 1808 onward wanted to establish parallel structures of power, and in some places this political activism rapidly transformed itself into open struggles for independence. This was the case in Buenos Aires, Mexico, Paraguay, and Venezuela. By the end of 1810, there was already talk in Spain of an "America in flames" and of the need to intervene quickly to avert its permanent loss.[25]

America was ablaze militarily but also constitutionally. Neither the Statute of Bayonne nor Napoleon made a deep impression on the American elites, but it quickly became obvious that the crisis unleashed by the Napoleonic invasion of the Iberian Peninsula had also awakened the yearning for freedom and independence in the American continent. Some of these first independence movements were unable to consolidate their early gains, but the trend was clear: the Spanish empire was falling apart from within and not due to attacks or any pressure exerted by foreign powers. The best example of this political dynamic was Venezuela, where initial stirrings had led to the creation of the Confederation of Venezuela, which declared independence from Spain on July 5, 1811. The declaration of independence undersigned by the Venezuelan leaders was in effect a denunciation of what they believed to be a long history of despotism at home that could only be resolved by breaking all ties that still bound them to Spain. Their thinking was similar that of the Thirteen Colonies. Perhaps the rebels' most significant act, however, was the approval of the Federal Constitution of Venezuela, ratified on December 21, 1811, several months before the Spanish, in which Venezuela was declared to be an independent nation, with a constitutional system similar to the North American one. Other American regions that did not choose the path of early independence nevertheless favored a federalist solution to the Spanish imperial crisis—for example, the Constitution of Cundinamarca (Santa Fe de Bogota, Colombia, April, 1811) or the Chilean *Reglamento*, a provisional constitution ratified in October, 1812—but whatever the case it was abundantly clear that the empire was being dismantled.[26]

There were also very pronounced ideological divisions within the anti-French camp in Spain. Some who fought against Napoleon wanted to reaffirm the power of the king and the Catholic faith and, most of all, to cleanse Spain of all foreign influence. In other words they sought military as well as ideological liberation from the French. Few summed this up better than the Catalan Antonio de Capmany in one of his earliest political pamphlets, *Sentinel against the French* (*Centinela contra franceses*, 1808). Here, he claimed that thanks to this war "we will go back to being old-fashioned Spaniards; . . . which is to say, we will go back to being brave, formal, and sober. We will have a patria"—a pure Spanish *patria*.[27] Conservative women advanced a similar discourse. The Patriotic Fraternity of the Ladies of Seville (*Hermandad Patriótica de Señoras de Sevilla*), founded in 1809, swore to defend the faith, the king, and the *patria*.[28] The guerrillas were mostly in the conservative camp, prepared to expel the invaders and to restore the old and traditional Spain.[29]

Nevertheless, many other men and women hoped that the war would lead to not only liberation from French oppression but the creation of a new Spain. They wished to do away with the absolute monarchy, establish freedom of the press, abolish the Inquisition, transform subjects into citizens, and even limit the power of the church.[30] English conservative Lord Holland described these individuals as people who "had imbibed their notions of freedom from the encyclopedists of France, rather than from the history of their ancient institutions, or from the immediate wants of their own country."[31] There were undoubtedly many moderate liberals, who desired changes but feared revolutions. For them it was not a question of completely dismantling the Ancien Regime but of moderating and reforming some of its most authoritarian aspects.[32]

In this context of ideological struggle, the peninsular elites quickly realized that the only hope of uniting Spaniards against the Napoleonic army and thwarting the independence movements gathering steam in the Americas was to create a new state and nation. This was not a universally endorsed objective, but from early 1809 it was widely believed that ideological consensus could only be achieved by a constitution, which would intersect all the disparate visions and political viewpoints in one document.[33] The need to identify elements to unify these divergent ideologies and groups explains the political elite's willingness in late 1808 to summon the national parliament, the Cortes, with the main purpose of devising a new constitution. With nearly all the provinces occupied by the French, the vast majority of the deputies in the Cortes of Cádiz were elected by a relatively small number of individuals, generally by the provincial authorities (Provincial Juntas) charged with organizing the defense against the French, or by already existing institutions, such as municipal councils.

Of the more or less 300 who took their place in the Cortes of Cádiz, it seems that the highest percentage were clergymen (89, or 29.57 percent); followed by civil servants of every kind (67, or 22.25 percent); lawyers (47, or 15.61 percent); military officers (42, or

13.95 percent); professors (16, or 5.32 percent); nobles (15, or 4.98 percent); merchants (9, or 2.99 percent); and a smaller number of landowners, industrialists, intellectuals, and members of other liberal professions.[34] Each one of these occupational groups included individuals of a variety of ideological persuasions, conservatives and liberals. Yet the general perception held that liberals were in the majority in the Cortes, although a minority in the country at large.

For the first time in the history of political representation in Spain, the Cortes of Cádiz also included deputies from the colonies, although the term *colonies* was proscribed from parliamentary proceedings at the outset. As with peninsular representatives, the vast majority of the American deputies were also co-opted from among the Americans living in Spain at the time of the French invasion. Over time, these "substitutes" were replaced by representatives elected by the municipal councils of the capital cities of American regions. The American deputies generally participated and voted as a bloc in all debates and issues affecting the Americas, although they also manifested the same political divisions (between liberals and conservatives) as their peninsular counterparts. When the new constitution was finally voted on in 1812, there were 127 representatives from Spain and 52 deputies representing the American territories. These numbers belied the reality that the population of Spanish America at this time was already greater than that of Spain.[35] All of the American representatives were Creoles, with the one exception of Dionisio Inca Yupanqui, a Peruvian who belonged to an aristocratic Inka family but who had lived in Spain since childhood.

Spain was a country without constitutional experience or experience in parliamentary debates, and from the very beginning a point of contention was which tradition—Spanish or foreign—would serve as a model for the Cádiz assembly proceedings.[36] Two of the great revolutionary upheavals of the late eighteenth century, the North American and the French, had a considerable impact on the political and constitutional processes in Spain, as did the English constitutional tradition. Chronologically, the first was the Declaration of Independence of the Thirteen Colonies and their Constitution of 1789–1791. Although there were no explicit references to this tradition in the Cortes of Cádiz debates, it was evident that some liberals, and especially Spanish American deputies, felt an attraction for what everyone knew was the first republican constitution.[37] Two elements of the United States Constitution were especially appealing, not only to American representatives but also to deputies of the old peninsular kingdoms: the federal character of the state and the Senate as a chamber of deputies of the constituent states.

The French influence was more pronounced and certainly more enduring. The works of eighteenth-century French philosophes and the French constitutions since the 1790s are known to have been a source of inspiration for the Hispanic political elites as they developed a language of political rights. Especially for liberals, French constitutionalism offered other important principles—the nation as the repository of sovereignty as well as centralism and unicameralism, or the idea of national representation rather than representation based on estates or orders, typical of the Old Regime. There were some problems with the French example; for instance, its anti-monarchism, the tendency to destroy institutions and ideologies before creating new ones, or the association of the French constitutional experience with radical expansionism under Napoleon.[38]

Given that one of the stated objectives of the Spanish War of Independence was the restoration of Ferdinand VII, many parliamentary representatives turned to the English constitutional tradition as a possible model. The English influence was already felt before the French Revolutionary crisis, and it remained strong immediately before and during the constitutional process in the early nineteenth century. In 1785, the Duke of Almodóvar, who had served as Spanish ambassador to Great Britain, published a "Constitution of England" as an appendix to his Spanish edition of Abbe Raynal's book on European empires, and the French edition of *The Constitution of England*, by the Swiss Jean-Louis Lolme, published in 1771, circulated in Spain and was later translated into Castilian and published in Madrid in 1812. It was widely known that several of the most prominent political leaders during the War of Independence were anglophiles, and some had lived in England, including Agustín de Arguelles, between 1806 and 1808. More immediately, while the Cortes was in session, various Spanish leaders were in contact with the English conservative group headed by Lord Holland, and one of

Holland's allies, John Allen, offered Spanish liberals a constitutional program, *Suggestions to the Cortes*, based on the English model of reforming old laws and institutions in lieu of revolution.[39] Many elements of the English constitutional tradition were extremely attractive for the Spanish parliamentarians, especially for the more conservatively minded liberals: the constitutional nature of the monarchy, the defense of collective and individual liberties, and the notion that colonies did not need to be represented in the national parliament as well as the bicameral parliament, which allowed for wider representation while also ensuring representation from the nobility and the church.[40]

These were the foreign traditions, then, that would inspire aspects of the Constitution of Cádiz, although the political and ideological conventions of the time dictated that parliamentary leaders would have to demonstrate that the Spanish constitution was based exclusively on Spanish traditions. At the start of the constitutional process, it was generally accepted that Spain already possessed an "ancient constitution," represented by Spanish legal codes. The historian Martínez Marina made this claim in his introduction to an edition of the *Siete Partidas*, commissioned by Carlos IV in 1794 and completed in 1806.[41] Some liberals, along with the vast majority of conservatives, were ready to acknowledge that in many ways the medieval Spanish legal codes reflected the culture and character of the Spaniards. From the modern constitutional perspective these codes were an "extravagant mix of liberty and slavery, of wisdom and ignorance, of good and bad," in the expressive words of José Canga Arguelles, the liberal deputy for Asturias.[42] Of greater concern was that these codes—originating from all the constituent kingdoms of the Spanish monarchy—preached the necessity of maintaining the state structure of a monarchy divided into kingdoms, with their own rights and prerogatives, and that the nation's representative body was designed to ensure the presence of the old estates—cities, the church, and nobility—that would divide and not unify the nation.[43]

The alternative to all these traditions, native and foreign, was a new constitutional framework altogether, albeit one that used language derived from Spanish legislative and constitutional heritage. The *Preliminary Discourse (Discurso Preliminar)* that accompanied the

Constitution, written by its true father, Agustín Arguelles, argued that the new constitution was nothing more than a reordering of the various codes and laws instituted in Spain since Visigothic times and that everything pertaining to liberties and rights, such as limitations on the power of kings and subjects' right to elect their rulers, was already present in these ancient codes. These were the venerable precedents by which Spaniards had been able to create an "admirable constitution," which had been hijacked and manipulated by a succession of incompetent and absolutist regimes over the centuries. The Constitution of Cádiz appeared therefore not as the product of a political revolution, a concept the liberals wanted to avoid, but simply as the restoration of a model of good government devised by successive generations of Spaniards. As Arguelles wrote, in the ancient Cortes of Castile and Aragon one could already find "the ideas of true political and civil liberty, maintained and upheld by our elders," which were now being reclaimed by the Cortes of Cádiz to create a new and modern nation.[44] This was the inaugural act of political myth-making in the history of the nation, a Spanish past now imagined as a democratic one, with a deeply rooted culture of citizens' rights and a monarchy that had been constitutional and limited since its inception.

Some of the parliamentary decisions, and certain parts of the Constitution of Cádiz, are not particularly relevant here. Many of these touched on questions of the moment: the form of government; Spaniards' rights; procedures for the election of members of parliament; the fiscal system for the new state; the abolition of the Inquisition, press censorship, and the private jurisdictions of the nobility; and the creation of a national army for the first time in the history of Spain.

Matters pertaining to the Spanish "nation," the creation of a nation-state, debates over who should be considered Spanish, and, above all, who was entitled to Spanish citizenship occupied center stage. In this regard, the Constitution of Cádiz was manifestly heir to the French Revolutionary tradition, not because it intended to completely dismantle the ideologies and structures of the Old Regime but rather because it tried to engender a new nation-state. Given the texture of debates and reflections on the Spanish nation, the characteristics of Spaniards in previous centuries, and the need for a unifying constitution, it is unsurprising that the first section of the Constitution was dedicated to "the Spanish Nation, and the Spaniards." It opened with an article that was, in effect, a declaration of first principles: "The Spanish Nation is the congregation of all Spaniards from both hemispheres." The term *Spaniards* was not meant by the constitution's writers to refer to individuals who were of Spanish origin, wherever they happened to live, but to all the inhabitants of Spain, the Americas, and the Philippines who, as free men and women, had been born in any of the "dominions of the Spains (las Españas)," were children of Spaniards, lived in any town or city under Spanish sovereignty, or had been naturalized if they were foreign-born. Leaving no doubt as to the inclusive aim, the article stipulated that "the free blacks, from the moment they secured their liberty in the Spains" (Art. 5) were also Spaniards, although on this point there was opposition from some representatives who wanted all descendants of Africans, slave or free, to be treated as foreigners.

This group of articles provides the clearest evidence that the Cádiz parliamentarians set out to symbolically transform an empire into a nation and thus to reverse the strategy followed in the previous century. An empire was a composite polity made up of a multitude of territories and individuals with different origins, cultures, languages, and rights, with the metropolis as the dominant part and only its natives—the peninsular Spaniards—enjoying full membership in the community. The constitution changed the terms, by implying the symbolic transformation of what had been an empire into a diverse nation, comprising individuals of different origins, races, cultures, and languages. To be sure, all had to be Catholics ("The religion of the Spanish Nation is and shall always be the Catholic" [Art. 12]), but all enjoyed the same rights and obligations, and all were now "Spaniards."

But the nation was no longer simply a community of subjects under the sovereignty of a royal dynasty. Article 2 defined the nation as "free and independent, which is not, and cannot be, the patrimony of any family or person." This definition provoked comparatively little debate. Article 3, on the locus of sovereignty, was a different issue altogether and inspired lengthy and impassioned debates because it was seen as crucial to the nation's future. For more conservative deputies, the only rightful holder of sovereignty, historically, was the king, and he should remain so. Centrist delegates suggested a kind of compromise solution, with sovereignty to be shared by the nation and king. The liberal response, clearly inspired by the North American and French experiences, was unambiguous: "Sovereignty resides essentially in the Nation, which retains the exclusive right to establish its [own] fundamental laws."[45]

It is true that the decision to declare all the inhabitants of the empire as Spaniards was at least partly driven by political interests, especially among those peninsulars who hoped to gain the support, financial backing, and political loyalty of the American populations, without whom they saw no chance of defeating Napoleon or preserving the empire. But there was more than this in the articles of the constitution. They offered new conceptions of the nation, the *patria*, and the love of both. Although these concepts had been modified in the course of the eighteenth century, both before and during the Cortes of Cádiz, the majority of Spaniards thought of love of the nation or the *patria* as a natural sentiment and, therefore, as one clear link to older visions of the nation, that "local particularism" that Feijóo so sharply criticized in the eighteenth century. This concept made it possible to speak of Spain as a political entity composed of various nations, each with its own idiosyncrasies.

Many of the Cortes deputies who represented the old non-Castilian kingdoms, but also the American representatives, insisted precisely on this: that Spain should be a state comprising various "nations" rather than only one. In other words, the proposal debated in the Cortes was the creation of a common state (the same king, central authorities, and laws) with a confirmation of the existence of various nations that had their own legislation, prerogatives, and government institutions. The Catalan representatives certainly imagined a post-Napoleonic Spain as a country where the legal existence of the old kingdoms would be recognized, entities that would conserve "not only . . . their existing privileges and laws, but also those enjoyed in the time when the Spanish Throne was occupied by the august House of Austria" (the Habsburgs). This was a reference to the political system created by the Catholic monarchs and in place until the early 1700s.[46]

Catalan and Valencian representatives opposed every attempt to legally abolish the old kingdoms to make way for a territorial and administrative structure that would divide the state into equal provinces with the same rights and characteristics. The Catalan Felipe Aner best articulated these concerns, arguing that what was being proposed as the new territorial subdivision of Spain was "to divide provinces whose boundaries are already drawn under a particular denomination, such as Catalonia, Aragon, etc., etc., appending to one what is dismembered from another, this I am opposed to." He wondered, "Is there any political justification for sundering [provinces] that share the same customs and language in order to augment others where these are different? Catalans cannot forget that they are Catalans" who unanimously desire "to preserve its name and integrity." His Valencian colleague Francisco Xavier Borrull y Vilanova foresaw strong opposition to the division of the "Spanish territory into departments, dispensing with the names of its various kingdoms, and incorporating the peoples of one into another . . . [This would be] most prejudicial; it cannot but be impeded by the intimate unity that mediates between the people of the same kingdom, and must encounter the greatest resistance among them."[47]

Many American representatives argued similarly, not in the spirit of defending old rights and privileges but in an attempt to respond to the growing inclination toward independence in the former colonies. José Miguel Guridi y Alcocer, deputy for Tlaxcala, believed that the crucial aim of the Cortes should not be to construct a unified Spanish nation—with all of its inhabitants declared to be "Spaniards"—but to construct a single and unified state under whose aegis would coexist different nations, communities, and territories. What he proposed was far from novel, he argued, since throughout history there had been states that had managed to reconcile "the diversity of religions, which may be seen in Germany, England, and other countries; of territories, as in our own, separated by an immense ocean; languages and colors, also evident among us, and even distinct nations, such as Spaniards, Indians, and Negroes." The unity of all these diverse territories, languages, colors, and nations could only be encompassed in a shared government or a common state without reducing all to membership of a single nation.[48]

Similarly, American deputies insisted that only the natives of each province or kingdom might be elected as its representatives in the Cortes. The greatest love for their "natural patria" comes from those who had been born there, claimed the Tlaxcalan deputy Guridi y Alcocer. His compatriot Morales Duárez also argued that "men distinguish from one another by their opinions more than their countenances, and my [opinion] on this matter is that, if patria is understood in its primary sense (as the love of the land of one's birth), the obligation to love her must be imprinted on each page of every dictionary . . . as a natural and divine duty."[49] The message was clear: the Americas could only be represented by Americans, those who were born there, and certainly not by peninsular Spaniards, as had earlier been the case.

For a majority of the liberal peninsular Spanish deputies, the future of Spain depended on the reconstruction of the nation as a unified entity and Spain as the common homeland, the only object of loyalties and obligations. The parliamentary representatives had not come to defend their *patrias chicas*, their home regions. They had come, or should have come, to represent and defend Spain and Spaniards. Antonio Panadero argued that the "Aragonese, the Valencian, the Catalan, along with the Galician, and the Castilian, are all Spaniards" and every attempt "to maintain the laws and particular charters of each province will spawn federalism, and, consequently, our ruin."[50] The Extremaduran Diego Muñoz Torrero, a member of the Constitutional Commission, offered the liberal alternative with the greatest clarity and force. After accusing the American and Catalan deputies of "speaking as if the Spanish Nation were not one, and was instead made up of different kingdoms and states," he continued that these divisions had to be erased, the laws of each had to be subsumed in one, and all had to be made equal "so that together they may form a single family, with the same laws and Government." The reality of the past, and of the present moment, was "the belief that in Spain there were six or seven nations . . . I would like us to remember [instead] that we constitute a single Nation, and not a composite of different nations."[51]

Liberal deputies ensured that these ideas were articulated in the Constitution of 1812, albeit provisionally. Having acknowledged that the territorial restructuring of the monarchy and overcoming the opposition of the non-Castilian kingdoms required time, the liberals were able to secure the inclusion of two articles that effectively deferred this thorny issue to future parliamentary meetings. The first of these, Article 10, enumerated the provinces that constituted peninsular and American Spain without ever mentioning the old kingdoms or viceroyalties. Article 11 simply postponed the issue of the territorial structure of the country: "A more convenient division of the Spanish territory will be enacted as a constitutional law, once the political circumstances of the Nation allow it." The Cortes that eventually approved this constitution was thus unable to create a blueprint for a vision of Spain composed of provinces, with the kingdoms legally and practically abolished, but it did issue a statement of intent in this direction. The territorial structure of Spain, of a nation that from 1820 onward would be limited to the Iberian Peninsula and a few islands in the Caribbean and the Pacific, was a complicated issue that took decades to resolve, but the predominant belief, already evident in the Cortes of Cádiz, was that the basic territorial unit should be the province, not the kingdom or principality.[52]

The binding force for the inhabitants of the Spanish monarchy would no longer be membership in the same lineage or the same race but a shared passion for one's nation and *patria*. This explains why immediately following the articles on the identity of Spaniards, deputies inserted clauses to proclaim the obligation to love and defend the *patria*: "The love of the patria is one of the principal obligations of every Spaniard" (Art. 6), and all had a duty "to defend the Patria with arms" (Art. 9). Liberals were instrumental in the adoption of these articles, the ones who supported the idea of modern love of the *patria*. Neither race nor lineage nor the region of one's birth but the love of and service to the *patria* "could render States happy and independent. When men are guided by [these precepts],

MAP 5. Spain in 1833: The new nation-state
After decades of debates, including during the Cortes de Cádiz, in 1833 the Spanish government divided Spain into 49 provinces, since then the foundation of the territorial organization of Spain.

they will sacrifice themselves in defense of their country," will die for it, all together as one.[53] With this in mind, Parliament approved the establishment of a national education system—to teach children to read and write, the principles of religion, and their civil obligations (Art. 366)—because "the State, as well as soldiers to defend it, also needs citizens to enlighten the nation and promote their [collective] happiness."[54]

The experiment under way in Cádiz, as had been the case in France and the Thirteen Colonies, among other nations, was essentially an attempt to transform the country's inhabitants from subjects into citizens.[55] This had proven to be a thorny issue elsewhere due to the belief that the rights of citizens should be reserved for men of

European descent (in the case of the Thirteen Colonies) or only those who resided in the imperial metropolis and not the colonies (in the British case). In all the constitutional countries, citizenship was also limited to men, and only men of sufficient means. Spaniards of the constitutional period, at least those involved in the political process, showed pronounced enthusiasm for this new concept of citizenship. Its implementation and regulation were perhaps the most conclusive proof that Spaniards were becoming active patriots rather than passive subjects. If anything suggested that tyranny, whether Napoleonic or that of the absolute monarchs, was being vanquished, it was precisely the fact that Spaniards now had the opportunity to participate as citizens in shaping their own destiny and their nation's.[56]

This was not unlike the political experience of other nations, but from the outset of the constitutional process one may discern certain features that appear unique to the Spanish case, and the reason is clear: the need to limit the political repercussions of the decision to convert the empire into a nation and all of its inhabitants into Spanish nationals. One of the most interesting elements of Spanish constitutionalism in this period is the distinction made between "Spaniards" and "Spanish citizens."[57] To be sure, other constitutions were marked by a degree of political inequality. The French constitution of 1791 and the American one of 1789 distinguished between active citizens and others, with only the former entitled to elect the nation's representatives and to stand for election themselves. But legally, there was no distinction between being "American," and being an "American citizen" or between being "French" and being a "French citizen." The Constitution of Cádiz was unique in this respect because it instituted a clear separation between these two. The rules for determining citizenship were included in Chapter IV of the Constitution, particularly in Articles 18 to 26. There were few novelties here with respect to other constitutions. As in other such documents, some articles stipulated who had the right to citizenship and under what circumstances citizenship rights could be lost or suspended. The Spanish case was interesting in its handling of citizenship, especially, because of the resurgence of the ethnic element that the constitution had dispensed with in its opening articles.

As in other contemporary constitutions, in the Cádiz the rights to vote and be elected to office were limited to men. Without a doubt, many women had played important political and military roles in the struggle against the French, and some of them were even true heroines of the nation, worthy of remembrance. Nevertheless, as elsewhere, these vital contributions by women in wartime did not seem to merit serious consideration of greater rights to women generally, and certainly not the same rights as men. It was evident that some women were capable of transcending the limits of their sex, becoming true patriots, and fighting and dying for the motherland. In the struggle against the French, however, these exceptional women were not fighting for the rights of women but for the liberty of Spain. This attitude explains why the Cortes of Cádiz did not spend any time discussing the role or rights of women in the new nation.[58]

In this sense the Spanish experience was far from unique. We might recall the words of John Adams, the future president of the United States, to the liberal lawyer James Sullivan. He observed that not all men should be granted citizenship rights because "very few Men, who have no Property, have any Judgment of their own." If they were granted such rights, Adams warned, all would demand the same, and even "Women will demand a Vote . . . an equal Voice with any other in all Acts of State." The only effect of this would be "to confound and destroy all Distinctions, and prostrate all Ranks, to one common Level," he concluded. Women were unfit to participate in political processes because "their Delicacy renders them unfit for Practice and Experience, in the great Business of Life, and the hardy Enterprises of War, as well as the arduous Cares of State. Besides, their attention is So much engaged with the necessary Nurture of their Children, that Nature has made them fittest for domestic Cares."[59]

Manuel Quintana, a liberal leader, similarly argued in 1805 that women had to restrict themselves to important "domestic duties, which they are destined for."[60] Echoing Adams, another liberal member of the Constitutional Commission, Diego Muñoz Torrero, justified the Cortes' decision not to extend full citizenship rights to all men regardless of racial origin because in that case "it would be incumbent upon us to concede civil and political rights to women, and to admit them to electoral boards, and even to the Cortes (parliament) itself."[61] The deputies in the Cádiz Cortes went even further, denying women the opportunity to take part, even passively, in the constitutional debates. The procedural regulations of the Cortes *(Reglamento para el gobierno interior de las Cortes)* stipulated, in what appears to be a decision without precedent in other countries, that "Women will not be permitted to enter any of the galleries of the assembly hall," while on the other hand "men of all classes may attend without distinction."[62]

Spanish men's qualifications for citizenship, in contrast, were beyond question. Solely by virtue of having been born in Spain and having parents of Spanish lineage, they earned the prerogative of being Spanish citizens; in other words, this was a kind of natural right, and at no point during the constitutional debates was this inherent right of Spanish peninsular men questioned. In neither the constitution nor its preceding debates was there any reference to the existence of distinct lineages in Spain or the fact that citizens had to be what in other times had been defined as "pure Spaniards," nothing therefore that would suggest the exclusion of those with Jewish, Moorish, or African blood, even though the purity-of-blood statutes were not formally rescinded until 1837. Even the gypsies, in spite of their "African origins," should be considered fully Spanish for all intents and purposes. As the Catalan representative José de Espiga y Gadea put it, "this small group of men, having arrived in Spain three centuries ago, have throughout this time intermarried with Spanish families, and have disappeared" as a separate nation.[63]

Creoles, or, as they increasingly preferred to be known, the American Spaniards or Spanish Americans, were the other group of Spanish men who were poised to enjoy unconditional citizenship rights. It seemed that nothing would stand in their way—certainly not their lineage, since, although born in America, they were descendants of Spaniards and therefore possessed the necessary virtues, qualities, and education to assume a leading role in their country. One possible impediment to their acquisition of citizenship might have been the fact that the Americas were to remain outside the constitutional system created by the Cortes of Cádiz, but this was not the case. The decision taken in Spain at the very beginning of the resistance against Napoleon was to consider all territories equal when it came to the allocation of rights and obligations. This was the official position from the outset of the conflict, when the central authorities declared "these [American] dominions an integral and essential part of the Spanish Monarchy. As such they are entitled to the same rights and prerogatives as the metropolis," while "the Spanish Americans" were asked "to see yourself elevated to the dignity of free men; you are no longer laid low under a yoke that was harsher the more distant you were from the center of power, looked upon with indifference, harassed by greed, and destroyed by ignorance." All were now part of "one and the same monarchy, the same nation, and one family."[64] With these declarations in mind, it is not surprising that in parliamentary debates, Spanish Americans were included without protest among those automatically recognized as citizens. They were natural-born Spaniards, and as such their right to citizenship was inherent. There was no discussion of the purity of their origins or whether their ancestors had mixed with the native inhabitants of the Americas or Africa.[65]

This formal recognition of equality between peninsular and American Spaniards, however, obscured a great deal of mutual distrust. From the first meeting of the Cortes, the American representatives openly stated their belief that, despite all official declarations, Spaniards in reality continued to treat Americans, including Spanish Americans, as colonial subjects. This was the legacy of centuries of colonial history, and especially of the discourses and political reforms of the eighteenth century. The American deputies as a group voiced this opinion in a declaration presented during a plenary session of the Cortes on August 1, 1811, in which it was attested that "men believe themselves degraded by a government that has tended to look upon them with disdain, as Colonials; this is to say, as upon a wretched class of humanity, or a subordinate species of men, who have never possessed the rights that are essential to all. This has been followed up with taunts, epithets, and sarcasms, with which they have been perpetually denigrated by those who, born on a different soil, believe themselves superior due to nothing more than this accident." In contrast, they had always felt themselves to be in conformity with peninsular Spaniards in every respect, in "language, inclinations, and customs . . . ; their habitual respect for the government of Spain, and the age-old obedience and submission which has become second nature, tied one to the other with knots tighter than the Gordian." There had been revolts, attacks on Spanish troops, and criticism of colonial authorities, American deputies conceded, but none of this indicated a desire for independence: "Their revolution is not rebellion, or sedition, or schism, or independence, in the political sense" but simply the continuation of resistance against centuries of Spanish colonial oppression and tyranny.[66] The Creoles, both in the Cortes of Cádiz and in America, essentially invented a narrative similar to the one contrived by the rebels in the Thirteen Colonies: they represented America and all Americans under Spanish sovereignty; they had suffered most from Spanish oppression; it was incumbent upon them to lead the struggle for liberty; and they should be the ones to govern lands that were, or should be, free.

For their part, Spaniards on the peninsula and in the Americas created their own narrative of relations between America and Spain, using some familiar tropes but adding new ones destined to endure in the peninsular Spanish consciousness. From the standpoint of peninsular deputies, the problems unfolding in America were not the product of Spanish tyranny and certainly not the result of the policies of the new authorities or the national parliament. All Spanish subjects had been victims of tyranny and despotism, Americans as well as peninsulars, and they were now all victims of Napoleon's expansionist and dictatorial ambitions. But the new central authorities, and the Cortes, were opposed to these old ideas and practices and from the very beginning had proclaimed equality between America and the Americans, on one hand, and Spain and the Spaniards, on the other. Spaniards found yet more absurd the Creole complaint that they had been, and continued to be, treated as colonial subjects. The Indians certainly had grounds for complaint, since they had been the victims of rapacious Spanish colonists and colonial authorities. But Creoles could have no such grievances because they had been the ones who exploited the Indians and who had appropriated the continent's riches. The Spanish Americans were "the grandchildren of the founders of the Spanish dominions in those quarters, of the first settlers, and of Spanish emigrants . . . What are the complaints that the Creoles, given their origins, had to raise against Pizarro, Dávila, and Cortés?"[67]

The "American problem," as far as Spaniards were concerned, was not the consequence of tyranny imposed by the new authorities but simply Creoles' desire to usher the Americas toward independence and thus continue to enjoy the land's riches. In newspapers and parliamentary debates, the first uprisings in the Americas were described as something more sinister than spontaneous and desperate acts of a people tired of oppression: "premeditated conspiracies; stores of weapons prepared in advance; thousands of men trooping in revolt; towns and cities inundated and agitated by violence; the sworn extermination of all Europeans." The objective of all these revolts and complaints was also clear: to become completely independent from the metropolis.[68] The Spanish deputies were convinced that Creoles were taking advantage of the French invasion of the peninsula for their own benefit, calculating that the independence of America in these circumstances, "rather than only possible and remote, was imminent and inevitable."[69]

The most polemical arguments against the Creoles, however, questioned their capacity to govern a new America. This line of argument was adopted on September 16, 1811, during the reading and subsequent debate over a representation from the *Real Consulado del Comercio de México* (Merchants' Corporation of Mexico), written by Francisco Arrámbari, a Spaniard who had served for several years in America.[70] The main objective of this appeal was to petition the Cortes to allow European-born Spaniards in the Americas to be represented "by persons of their own class and choosing" and not by Americans because they were unfit to assume this role. From the perspective of Spanish colonial history, there was nothing new in this petition of the Mexican Consulado. Over the course of three centuries of Spanish domination, the monarchy had consistently preferred to put peninsular Spaniards in charge of colonial government, at the expense of Creoles, with very few exceptions. Indeed, there was a good reason for this, according to Arrámbari, a defender of imperial practice, because neither the Indians nor those who called themselves "American Spaniards" possessed the civic virtues required to defend and govern the nation. "He who lacks the capacity and the will to vote sincerely," wrote Arrámbari, "he who offends [the patria] with evil customs, he who lacks full liberty, he who has neither goods nor fortune to protect; he who does not contribute directly to the State, he who is not a true citizen, an honorable *vecino*, a man of means, is excluded from all participation, from all direct and indirect influence over public order, even in purely Democratic republics." The Creoles also fell into this category of those temporarily unsuited for the rights of citizenship because their vices exceeded their virtues. They were indolent and scorned political and intellectual reflection. He concluded that Spain had committed a grave error in having given political rights to the Americans when they were unprepared for it. No other imperial power—the Romans, English, or Dutch—had granted "sovereignty or representation to colonists, in spite of the predicaments and the precarious circumstances in which they at times found themselves."

The public reading of this text caused a great commotion in the Cortes, and with it came an almost definitive split between American and Spanish deputies.[71] For the former, Arrámbari's text was proof that the imperialist ideology still prevailed in Spain, and among Spaniards. It also proved that European Spaniards still saw the Spanish Americans as inferior, making it abundantly clear that they were not trying to create a single nation based on the unity and equality of all territories. To demonstrate that Spaniards were genuinely prepared to treat Creoles as equals, the latter appealed to the Cortes to have this "subversive, slanderous and incendiary" text publicly burned and its authors prosecuted, judged, and punished. The peninsular deputies of all ideological stripes, however, were less concerned with a symbolic reconciliation. Most were prepared to acknowledge that the tone of the text was somewhat harsh and that perhaps it should not have been read in public. Nevertheless, they felt that the text contained some important truths about the situation in the Americas and even regarding the Spanish Americans' qualifications—or lack thereof—for being active in a new political system. Not everything contained in the text was erroneous or false, insisted the Catalan deputy Antonio Capmany, who considered the *Consulado*'s representation to be "a detailed and well-informed account." Another Catalan deputy, Felipe Aner de Esteve, justified Arrámbari's stance and that of his colleagues by noting that European Spaniards in the Americas were direct witnesses to "the disasters of America; they had suffered the harm resulting from the insurrection; they still see themselves in imminent danger; they share the misfortune of the many European victims of the disorder." Only a few "true Spaniards" sustained "the national cause in those parts, and without their assistance perhaps America would already be lost to us." To try to defuse the situation, the Cortes decreed that the text should be archived and was not to be read in public again. It was also resolved, however, that the authors should not be made to suffer any consequences and, even more importantly, that it was not necessary for the Cortes to officially censure or condemn the report's contents or its authors.

The debates between American and European Spaniards continued over the issue of the two other "nations" mentioned by the Mexican deputies in their description of the ethnic realities in the Americas, the "Indian" and the "African." It seems clear that both communities, or, more precisely, their potential roles in the new nation, were pawns in the great ideological debates and power struggles between Creoles and peninsulars. Both presented themselves publicly as sincere defenders of these populations while hurling accusations of political and electoral manipulation at one another. In the debates and resolutions of the Cortes on these and other issues, the Creoles saw clear evidence that European Spaniards wanted to minimize American representation in future assemblies and not recognize what America actually was: demographically, the principal part of the monarchy. Peninsulars, on the other hand, felt that Creoles were only defending Indians and Africans to increase the number of Creole representatives in the parliament and that their real goal was a political monopoly to add to the economic one they already enjoyed.

The political realities were obvious to everyone and less important than the ideologies and concepts used by both groups to discuss the role of indigenous peoples and Africans in the new constitutional nation. The constitutional debates in the Cortes of Cádiz were the first occasion in European history when an empire deliberated how to transform itself into a nation and the first time it was decided that the new nation would be based on ethnic diversity (Art. 1). Defining "citizenship" and determining who could be a citizen was much less straightforward because it involved not only the establishment of prerequisites, such as place of birth, level of education and training, and social status, but also the determination of whether all ethnic groups or *castas* (and *casta* was the term used, not *race*) had the necessary qualifications to become citizens. Agustín de Arguelles cited ethnic diversity as perhaps the single major obstacle when it came to transforming an empire into a nation. According to Arguelles, the population of Spanish territories in Europe was ethnically homogenous, while the inhabitants of Spanish America were divided into innumerable *castas*, each one forming a faction with its own interests and strategies.[72] The Cortes of Cádiz had to keep this reality in mind when they deliberated granting citizenship to American natives and Africans, which would give them the right to vote as well as the right to be elected as members of parliament in a nation politically dominated by whites.

The members of the convention that approved the Constitution of the United States of America in 1789 did not seem to think that the Indian question required much attention or that the Indian population settled in the territory of the new nation should be a constituent part of this nation in any sense, and certainly not as active citizens.[73] In Cádiz, on the contrary, the Spanish parliament dedicated many hours of debate to the Indian question, not in the least because since the 1500s Indians had been a constituent part of the Spanish monarchy, subject to her laws and interests. It was clear to all that to speak of the creation of a new community of citizens without including American natives would in many ways amount to the rejection of Spanish colonial history and, even worse, proof of the failure of the Spanish empire. There were many problems, however: if the empire had to be transformed into a nation, and if this nation had to be composed of active citizens, then were Indians qualified to go from being protected subjects to full-fledged citizens? Equally important, how would they be integrated into the new nation—as individuals or collectively, as the Republic of Indians?

One issue that seemed to be on everyone's mind from the opening debates in the Cortes was Indians' alleged passivity and their lack of interest in political processes that had been unfolding in the Americas since at least 1808. The German explorer Alexander von Humboldt made a reference to this when he highlighted the near complete absence of the "bronze race" in what he called revolts to defend the "national cause." He attributed this to their "timid mistrust and their mystifying impassiveness."[74] Others could not refrain from pointing out that, in spite of the fact that the Indian population was the majority in the continent as a whole, their parliamentary representation was minimal. They had only one deputy, Dionisio Inca Yupanqui, which reflected Indian indifference to the nation's political process or simply the conviction prevalent among Creoles that Indians could not represent all Americans in Cádiz.

The Creole discourse on American natives, before and after 1808, was profoundly negative and would be even more so after independence, but in Cádiz they unanimously defended the natives and their right to be an integral part of the new nation. As part of their denunciation of Spanish colonialism, American deputies argued that indigenous passivity and tendencies toward depression and ignorance were the consequence of 300 years of negligence, exploitation, and imperialism. Their "inferiority, simplicity, and abasement," said the substitute deputy for Buenos Aires, Francisco López Lisperguer, "in addition to not being as extreme as it is painted, is the effect of the oppression and tyranny of the authorities; it is not due to a lack of talent or [the right] attitude, but the injustice of their treatment. Nothing renders a man more dull and timorous than oppression and injustice; nothing ensures the triumph of despotism so much as keeping peoples in ignorance." The Indians, it was said, had always been treated as "minors," almost as slaves. More important, Indians were historically deprived of the communication with Spaniards that would have allowed them to imbibe their virtues, experience, and knowledge.[75]

Creole representatives, along with Dionisio Inca Yupanqui, always pointed out that by nature the natives possessed the same qualities as Europeans and compared the Inka and the Mexica to the Greeks, Egyptians, and Romans, their societies already "wise," their "governments based on liberal and paternal principles."[76] With these arguments, as well as the sense that Indians were the true native Americans, the only possible conclusion was that they should be granted citizenship rights commensurate with Spaniards and Creoles that should also extend to their mestizo descendants. This was the purpose of the petition presented by the American deputies on January 9, 1811: "that the national representation of the provinces, cities, towns, and villages of the American *tierra firme* and its islands, and of the Philippines, in relation to their natives, and the natives of both hemispheres, Spaniards and Indians, and the children of both classes, should and will be the same in order and form . . . as that currently and henceforth enjoyed by the legitimate natives of the provinces, cities, towns, and villages of the Peninsula and islands of European Spain."[77]

The peninsular representatives did not form a monolithic bloc in discussions of the Indian question. Some strongly disagreed with the Creole explanation for Indians' alleged passivity, arguing that, rather than being the result of imperial legislation, it was a reflection of the natural (racial) qualities of American natives. "Such is the narrowness of their spirit," claimed the deputy for Seville, Juan Pablo Valiente, in a full session of the Cortes, "their lack of ingenuity, their inclination to leisure, and to obscurity and seclusion, always avoiding interaction with the other classes, that after three centuries of advantageous and determined measures to acquaint them with common sense and norms, they appear no different than at the time of the discovery of the Indies."[78] Still more critical was Arrámbari, author of the Mexican merchants' *Representación*, who claimed that neither the Incas nor the Mexica had progressed from the savage state and that the present population was still inferior to other Americans despite three centuries of paternal Spanish colonization.[79] Those who saw the Indians as naturally inferior, or at best as people who would struggle to comprehend the European, national political culture they would join, requested careful and serious consideration of whether at present or even the near future they could be granted citizenship rights. They could be given rights that pertained to all other inhabitants, but to elevate them "to the sublime position of legislator," to partake in "ideas that are beyond their reach, that contradict the fact of their legal minority, and the continuation of their privileges" would be an injustice toward them, and the rest of the nation. Indians had no "patriotic sentiment or social outlook," and they were not the least bit interested in changes of government, regime, or nation. The critics also noted that transforming the Indians into individuals, and thus dismantling the Republic of Indians, would be to deprive them of the protection they enjoyed, possibly making way for their extermination, as had happened in the North American states.[80]

Yet other Spaniards were inclined to recognize that the Indians' ignorance was the result not of their racial inferiority but of the colonial regime imposed on them by Spain.[81] Spanish culpability, however, could not be undone simply by granting rights that the Indians were wholly unprepared to exercise. This was the position taken by Arguelles—who maintained that it was impossible to extend citizenship rights to Indians until they had a better grasp of their present state—or the even more radical political commentator José Blanco White. Writing in the influential journal *El Español*, he argued that to grant rights to Indians simply because they were the original inhabitants of the continent did not make sense; the Indians had neither the virtue nor the education to assume such a responsibility: "to give them authority over the other *castas* because their grandparents had been the original proprietors of that land," even if "it should be possible, would be more pernicious than anything contemplated by religious or revolutionary fanaticism."[82] Blanco suggested a potential solution to this conundrum: analyze the situation, determine the reasons for Indians' backwardness, and identify those among them who were prepared to assume the rights of citizens and the measures to be adopted to convert the rest into potential citizens.

The final resolutions of the Cortes of Cádiz on these issues combined the proposals of American and Spanish deputies. The most important, which contributed to the subsequent mythification of the Constitution of Cádiz as the most advanced of its time, was the inclusion of Indians and their descendants (including mestizos) in Article 18 as Spanish "citizens." But the Cortes also decreed that questionnaires should be sent to religious and secular authorities to find out their views on the Indians, their progress, and the best ways to integrate them into the new society. Some of the responses have survived, and once again they reveal the coexistence of the two ideological tendencies discussed above: the Indians' backwardness as the consequence of racial traits or the Spanish colonial system. They nevertheless convinced many parliamentarians in Cádiz that the best course of action was the gradual, rather than immediate, integration of Indians into the new nation.[83] But the Cortes of Cádiz also adopted measures to dismantle the colonial system: they abolished indigenous tribute, along with the *mita* and other personal labor services; outlawed corporal punishment; and gave them access to the land. More important, the Republic of Indians was abolished and legal equality instituted for all inhabitants of the Americas. All the same, modern scholars believe that despite these measures, neither Creoles nor Spaniards showed genuine concern for the Indians, and in many ways this community would have the most to lose, first with the introduction of the liberal regime conceived in Cádiz and second with the independence of the American territories.[84]

In the same text in which he described natives' passivity during the 1808 crisis, Alexander von Humboldt also made reference to how the free coloreds (blacks, mulattos, and mestizos) had "enthusiastically embraced the national cause."[85] Scholarly research has confirmed Humboldt's assessment, that members of the "African caste," free blacks and slaves, indeed played an important role in the Americas' political and military conflicts beginning in 1808. Moreover, they did so on both sides of the divide, supporting the Spanish authorities in certain regions while favoring independence in others.[86] Their numbers, and their political and social engagement, made them the focus of attention for both factions, and during the Wars of Independence both sides were generous in their promises. They tantalized with the abolition of the slave trade, the manumission of all slaves, and especially the promise everything would be done to integrate the African caste in the community of citizens of the new nations.

This was an exclusively American social reality, however. Regardless of what it had been in previous times, the number of Africans in the peninsula was negligible by this point, and Africans as a distinct nation were simply nonexistent or invisible for the majority of the population and their parliamentary representatives. The Spanish population was homogenous, which is to say, white, as Arguelles had argued, and this view was shared by American deputies.[87] The Cortes nevertheless became embroiled in debates over matters related to the condition and the future of what was referred to as the African caste: the issue of slavery and the right to citizenship of Spanish Africans. These were among the most intense and longest debates of the parliamentary session.

As had long been the case, when it came to appraising Africans or the African caste, foremost in Spaniards' minds was the issue of slavery, and this was indeed the first topic of discussion in the Cortes before the question of their citizenship could be broached. The Hispanic world was certainly not the only sphere where slavery was debated. Revolutionary France had decreed the abolition of slavery in 1791, a decision revoked following the revolution in Haiti. In Great Britain the question was not so much the abolition of slavery as the slave trade, which was approved by Parliament in 1807 following years of debate and pressure from the Committee for the Abolition of the Slave Trade, founded in 1787.[88]

More pertinent was the debate on slavery, and on the status of free blacks, in the United States of America. The Thirteen Colonies had based their resistance against Great Britain on an uncompromising defense of "liberty" as a natural and civil right. Certainly the struggle against the English enabled the emergence of a large number of freedmen—between 25,000 and 100,000—although in the first years of the existence of the new nation there were no attempts to challenge the basics of the system of slavery. The opening of the Constitutional Convention and the approval of the constitution in 1789 (ratified by the states in 1791) brought both problems to the fore: the slave trade and the future of slavery as a legal institution. The convention where these issues were debated was split into two opposing factions, divided on the issue of slavery. One side argued that the existence of slavery on American soil was a stain on the young nation and to a certain extent invalidated a political system based on individual liberty; the other argued that slavery was simply another aspect of the dominant economic system in some states and that the abolition of slavery would be extremely prejudicial to private property rights, one of the fundamental rights recognized by the constitution, and that it had no impact whatsoever on the character of the new nation or its political system. The resulting constitution was the fruit of compromise between two ideological camps. It granted powers to the federal government over the regulation of the slave trade (which would eventually be prohibited in 1808), it recognized that each state had the right to regulate slavery within its borders and even to abolish it, it allowed the number of slaves to be taken into account in the allocation of the number of state representatives in the Congress (the famous 3/5 clause), and it protected property rights by decreeing that any slave who escaped to a state where slavery had been abolished had to be returned to his or her legitimate master.[89]

The debates on these issues in the Hispanic context were in many ways shaped by tendencies and ideas in the United States. As in North America, in Spain the struggle against Napoleon, and more generally against authoritarian government, was justified as a struggle for national and individual liberty, an ideological viewpoint that was at first blush incompatible with slavery. This was plainly yet poignantly articulated by the representative from Lima, Dionisio Inca Yupanqui, who observed that "a people that oppresses another cannot be free."[90] There were also practical considerations that made it convenient for Spanish members of parliament to discuss if not the outright abolition of slavery then at least the implementation of reforms that would put an end to the slave trade, with a view to the eventual dismantling of the system: they needed to reinforce the alliance with Great Britain, which had proclaimed the abolition of the slave trade in 1807, and win the support of the many slaves and freedmen in the Americas.

However, other factors made the abolition of slavery unlikely. The first was constitutional and common to all liberal movements of the late eighteenth and early nineteenth centuries: the declaration of property rights as one of the fundamental and inviolable rights of new nations. This was a principle enshrined in the American and French constitutions, and the Spanish one would follow suit.[91] The second factor was the need to secure the financial backing of the wealthiest Spanish American provinces in order to sustain the fight against Napoleon. More specifically, the Spanish parliamentary leaders wished to secure the support of the Cuban elites, more firmly committed to the protection of slavery than any of their peers in the American territories and who made great efforts to ensure that slavery would not become a topic of discussion in the Cortes. The Cuban elites and their representatives argued that slavery should be an internal issue for the provinces and states to resolve, echoing the argument in the United States, although they were open to the abolition of the slave trade, a matter they considered to be under the jurisdiction of the central government. They also made repeated requests to the Cortes that all debates on slavery should be conducted in secret sessions so as not to kindle speculation among slaves and perhaps even riots and rebellions, as had happened in Haiti.[92]

Another issue that seemed of crucial importance to everyone involved, both liberals and conservatives, Americans and peninsulars: if the abolition of slavery were contemplated, it should be enacted gradually in stages. A hasty and abrupt freeing of all slaves could provoke revolts like those in Haiti, but it would also be advantageous to avoid certain social and political consequences that such a precipitous change could have in the new societies. The ultraliberal José Blanco White, in expressing his opposition to immediate manumission of all slaves, invoked the Haitian crisis and observed that the sudden liberation "of the Negro population in various American provinces could have extremely disastrous consequences" because "there are varying degrees of social liberty, and it requires a certain disposition in those who are to enjoy it." Although Europeans must shoulder the blame for the fact that the Africans live in ignorance and brutality, still "due to the slaves' moral deficiencies [they cannot be granted] liberty all at once and so suddenly."[93]

This ideological framework explains the proposals and resolutions in the Cortes. The first and the most comprehensive came from the Mexican deputy Guridi y Alcocer, presented to the Cortes on March 26, 1811, and which undoubtedly constituted a threat to the survival of the slave system. Guridi demanded the total abolition of the slave trade, freedom for the children of slaves, treatment of slaves as free servants (although with the proviso that unlike the latter slaves could not leave their masters) who would be paid a salary commensurate with their work and attitude, greater opportunities for manumission, and requirements that owners care for and maintain slaves who were no longer able to work due to illness or old age. The liberal leader Agustín de Arguelles presented on April 2, 1811, another more limited proposal. It requested only the abolition of the slave trade.[94]

The debates on both proposals—and it was obvious that a majority in the Cortes preferred to discuss Arguelles's more limited resolution—revealed the deep influence of Cuban slave owners but also demonstrated the limited impact of abolitionism in the Hispanic world. Abolitionist ideas had circulated among the Hispanic political elites, but a great deal of evidence suggests that moral justifications of slavery (a system required to "save" Africans from their own barbarism), theories about Africans' natural inferiority, and the weight of property rights were much more compelling and persuasive ideological factors. The Cortes of Cádiz did not in fact institute a single measure related to the slave trade or of the improvement of slaves' living conditions or even the future of slavery as a system—a clear indication that the majority of the representatives in the Cortes of Cádiz, and thus also the constitution itself, were implicitly or explicitly pro-slavery or at the very least privileged the interests of slave owners, as peninsular elites would continue to be for the rest of the nineteenth century.[95]

Discussion of the rights and role of Africans in new liberal nations was also not confined to the Hispanic world. As elsewhere, including the newly independent Thirteen Colonies, Spaniards and Spanish Americans had to confront what Thomas Holt has called "the problem of liberty": how societies with a dominant white population dealt with the presence of large numbers of freedmen who, at the time of independence, lacked political rights. This process revealed the difficulties and limitations in any attempt to integrate a group that the vast majority of the white population viewed not only as foreigners, and thus unable to grasp the political culture of the new nation, but as incapable of becoming active citizens.[96] In each one of the countries that had to engage in these debates, there were specific, local circumstances that have to be taken into account, but they all shared similar attitudes. In the North American case, for instance, the gradual increase in the "free black population" did not open new political opportunities but did exactly the opposite. Confronted with an increasing number of free blacks, white majorities "began to restrict blacks' access to civil liberties . . . and by the early nineteenth century . . . free blacks were not considered to be part of the sovereign people by a large portion of the citizenry," a vision opposed by the black community.[97]

These attitudes and tendencies were even more evident in the Hispanic world. Around 1800, in nearly all regions of Spanish America, with the exception of Cuba and Santo Domingo, free blacks outnumbered slaves. Many of them were descended from families that had been free for generations, and many were active members of their urban communities. Equally important was the fact that from 1808 on, free blacks and pardos were involved in the debates and struggles over the future of the Americas as part of the Spanish empire.[98] In spite of their numbers and their political and social engagement, the Cortes of Cádiz, or at least its peninsular majority, never came to accept the so-called African caste as one of the communities that should be part of the citizenry of the new nation. The free members of the African caste would be considered Spaniards but not Spanish citizens. This decision was enshrined in Article 22, perhaps one of the most famous clauses of the Constitution of Cádiz, famous because of what it definitively precluded, in many ways permanently. The text of the clause is unambiguous:

> For those Spaniards who are through any lineage taken for and reputed to be natives of Africa, the doors of virtue and worthiness of becoming citizens are open: in their eminence, the Cortes will grant a letter of citizenship to those who render a genuine service to the Patria, or to those who distinguish themselves by their talent, application, and conduct, on the condition that they should be sons of legitimately married and honest parents; that they should be married to an honest woman, and be established residents *(avecindados)* in the dominions of the Spains (Las Españas), and that they exercise some useful profession, office, or skill, having an independent source of wealth.

The key words in this clause are undoubtedly "through any lineage taken for and reputed to be natives of Africa," which implied that neither the degree of mixture nor the amount of time a family had been living in the Americas nor whether they had been free for only a generation or several mattered.

If anyone found this insufficiently clear, the deputy for Orense in Galicia, José Calatrava, noted that the purpose of the article was precisely to establish that the "quality [of being African] cannot dissipate over time so long as the castas endure. The blacks will always remain natives of Africa even after fifty generations, and at the end of as many yet again, their descendants through any line, will always be said to have the same origin through that line, and will therefore be encompassed by the said article, and deprived of the rights of citizens, although with the chance to obtain these through merits and virtues." He foresaw a day when there would no longer be slaves. But there would, and should, continue to be individuals identified by their African origins.[99]

It has been hard for historians to explain why at such a critical moment, when it was imperative to secure the support of such a significant part of the population as those of African descent, the same concessions granted to Indians were not extended to Africans. And on this point both American and peninsular Spaniards shared similar attitudes. The former generally tended to demand that free blacks should receive only partial citizenship rights: the right to vote but not to be elected as representatives in the national parliament. The logic behind this proposal was divulged by the deputy for Guatemala, Antonio Larrazábal y Arrivillaga. He explained that no one, anywhere, in the past or at the present time, intended to elevate the Africans who resided in the Spanish territories "to the offices appertaining to the nobility" because there was no legal stipulation that all citizens must have the same rights.[100] The peninsular representatives were even more forthright in denying them the right both to vote and to be elected.

No one in the course of the debates in the Cortes indicated that a distinctly racialist viewpoint was behind this denial of rights to free Africans. This should not be taken to mean that Spaniards, in contrast to the North Americans, for instance, had not embraced racialist discourses. In fact, contemporary Spaniards and Spanish Americans indeed possessed a racialist language and, like other Europeans, also speculated during this period about the existence of various human races arrayed in a clear hierarchy. We should not forget that these were precisely the ideas promoted by one of the liberal leaders in the Cortes, Isidoro de Antillón, in his *Disertación sobre el origen de la esclavitud de los negros (Thesis on the Origins of the Slavery of the Blacks)*, first published in 1811, and his *Lecciones de geografía* (1804–1806). Even in the debates of the North American Constitutional

Convention, racialist discourses were not used overtly to justify the denial of rights of citizenship to free blacks. In both cases, and certainly in the Spanish, denial of rights to the African caste was justified by reference to the "stigma of slavery."[101] If the Africans were uniquely destined to be slaves, if slavery was compatible with natural law, which proclaimed the existence of natural social inequalities among humans, and if all those who had been enslaved, as well as their descendants, were marked by this, then slavery could be used as a rationale to discriminate against an entire population, denying them rights of citizenship. In other words, as long as slavery existed, slaves as well as their free descendants were marked by the taint of racial inferiority.

This was perhaps the key difference between the general attitude toward the Africans and the ideological stance toward American natives. They too had been racialized in the eighteenth century, but they were collectively recognized as citizens, while the Africans were not. The reasons for the difference once again seem to derive from the need to legitimate Spanish imperialism, which before and during this period had always been justified on the basis of the "protection and integration of the Indian." If Indians were not integrated into the new nation, it would mean that Spain had failed in their defense, protection, and civilization. This was not the case with Africans. They had been brought to the Americas as slaves and were essentially foreigners and not part of the community of Native Americans. The only responsibility assumed by the Spanish authorities, and Spaniards in general, toward the Africans was to treat them humanely, not to integrate them into society. This was made clear by the Mexican deputy Morales y Duárez, who indicated that previous kings had already demonstrated "their wish to always maintain this foreign caste originating from various parts of Africa, whether Mahometans or pagans *(gentilicio)*, apart from the other classes of Americans, and without any access to jobs or civil honors." It was a clear strategy applied to "foreigners" who were subject to "the restrictions or constraints that are deemed conducive to their good order and security, the same that a father of the family may impose to keep the lodger within the limits set by the honesty and tranquility of his daughters and dependents."[102]

It fell to Arguelles once again to provide the political justification for this decision. In his speech in the Cortes in September 1811, he acknowledged that the Africans were not responsible for their backwardness. They had been taken against their will from Africa and forced to live in the Americas, where they became part of a system of slavery that was "equally flawed, [and that] far from improving their fortune and alleviating their condition, had aggravated both." Their enslavement had made the Africans seem vile, and all Americans considered them "barbarians," which, combined with the lack of education, explains why they could not be citizens. Spaniards, yes, if they were free, because it would be inhumane to abandon them to their fate or force them to return to Africa. But they could not be made citizens because this would give them the right of access to all public offices, to elect and to be elected as members of parliament, to be viceroys or captains general, and to attend Congress "to represent themselves, their fellow citizens, the entire nation, to deliberate as her (the nation's) worthy defenders . . . The quality of [being a] citizen entitles each Spaniard to be anything in his country." All this meant that the deputies had to be cautious in deciding who could be a citizen: "If one multitudinous class was not currently prepared to assume all the rights of the citizen, would it not be more prudent and just to supply the means by which, progressively and gradually, it could obtain [these rights]?"[103] There were moreover numerous examples in other countries of such marginalization of Africans—Jamaica, for instance, whose inhabitants "are not English, and do not enjoy any rights of citizenship," and yet the island was prosperous; or Carolina and Virginia, where some of the landowners were African but none of them were citizens, and "they are all excluded from civil and military posts" and yet perfectly happy living "under the sage laws of the United States."[104]

Various American deputies and all the American free blacks who participated in these debates openly declared that arguments used by Article 22's supporters were nothing but a cloak for the idea of African inferiority. This was the central argument of the "pardo Spaniards of Lima," who claimed that over many decades they had demonstrated virtues necessary for becoming part of the body of citizens: They were free; had served as loyal and committed citizens, constantly working and defending their communities, in which they were socially and economically integrated; were prepared to defend the land and the monarchy with their lives—and paid taxes. Yet in spite of their contributions they were shunned simply for their African origins.[105]

The discrimination against those "of African ancestry" was in fact one of the most widely criticized aspects of the constitution, even among some of its greatest defenders. Among these was Ramón Salas, professor of public law, who in 1820 claimed that Article 22 had been a mistake. He asked, "Why should Spaniards who through any lineage are taken and reputed to be of African ancestry be treated less favorably than those of Asian, American, and European origin?" Political leaders should struggle against popular prejudices, not reinforce them, which is precisely what this article had done. "The Spaniard reputed to be of African ancestry who has rendered noteworthy services to the patria, or has distinguished himself by his talent, application, and conduct, will obtain from the Cortes a letter of citizenship as a favor," and this would have grave social repercussions because "he would always be marked in the public opinion as a man to whom it had been necessary to grant a dispensation, or to pardon something in order to elevate him to the status of a citizen." Salas criticized another aspect of the article, its failure to stipulate any temporal limit on African ancestry, just as the purity-of-blood statutes had failed to do. But if this was applicable to men of African ancestry, then why not also to Spaniards of the peninsula, for, given the ethnic history of Spain, "if one goes far enough, many Spaniards will find that they have African origins, and yet they are not as a result worth less than Europeans, Americans, and Asians."[106]

Salas analyzed the Constitution of Cádiz from the standpoint of his profession, as a jurist, but he was also invoking his countrymen's ambivalence in the formation of their nation and in their specification of the criteria that would grant someone the indisputable right to be considered truly and genuinely Spanish. Those who were involved in constitutional debates, and, one might venture to say, the majority of Spaniards, believed that as far as peninsular inhabitants were concerned, the situation was clear: they were all full members of the nation and pure Spaniards, and there was no longer any trace of difference among them. The tensions formerly caused by the presence of large and visible ethnic-religious minorities (above all, Jews and Arabs) had disappeared. In the 1810s and beyond, Spain was completely homogenous. As a Cortes deputy claimed, it was a place where everyone shared the same characteristics, and there were no more Africans or Gypsies or Arabs or Jews—only Spaniards.

From the perspective of the great Spanish-Atlantic family, the situation was more complex. It is here that the concept of the nation, of belonging to the Spanish nation, came under greatest pressure due to many Spaniards' ideas about race. Their attitudes toward Creoles and Native Americans suggested the potential for but also the impediments to a nation that would be multicultural as well as multiethnic. During the constitutional process, peninsular Spaniards claimed that the problem with the Creoles was not the influence of climate on their intellect but the probability of their being contaminated with Indian or African blood, which was their true reason for seeking independence. They were recognized as brothers, and there was a desire for them to be part of the political nation, but at the same time it was unclear whether Spaniards truly believed that Creoles were their equals in every sense. These suspicions about Creoles' racial purity would be an enduring factor in relations between peninsular Spaniards and Spanish Americans.

The situation of the Native Americans, racialized in the eighteenth century, was less problematic. The constitutional debates on their citizenship status avoided any reference to Indians as racially inferior. This had less to do with a favorable image of the Native Americans and more to do with the desire to demonstrate that for three centuries Spain had been a model colonial ruler. The exclusion of Africans, on the other hand, was far more easily justified, for in their case the stigma of slavery was compounded with racial stigma. They were the most clearly distinct, the least equal, and the ones who would require generations, perhaps centuries, to be integrated as Spaniards.

Lauded at the time and in later periods as a seminal document of constitutional history, for many Spaniards, the Constitution of Cádiz was a product of circumstances and the fruit of compromise between opposing ideological forces in contemporary Spain. It was neither radically revolutionary—in order to preserve the political unity that was key to victory over Napoleon—nor too conservative or traditionalist, which would have alienated many liberals who were opposed to the French occupation but also hoped to reform the political and constitutional structure of the monarchy.[107] The most reactionary elements scorned and rejected a constitution they saw as an attempt to destroy the monarchy, to question Spain's Catholic identity, and to eliminate all uniquely Spanish traditions. This attitude explains why the practical influence of the Constitution of Cádiz as a foundational charter was very limited. Approved by a majority of members of parliament on March 19, 1812, following several months of intense debates, the Constitution of Cádiz remained in force for less than two years, between late 1812 and early 1814, and its practical impact was minimal in a country gripped by war and essentially paralyzed. The absolutist-minded Ferdinand VII abolished it in 1814 and ordered the arrest of all the liberal ringleaders on charges of treason. The Constitution of Cádiz came into force again, also in tenuous circumstances, during the so-called Trienio Liberal ("Liberal Triennium," 1820–1823) and again between 1836 and 1837, and although it served as an inspiration for subsequent constitutional processes, it was for all intents and purposes stillborn.

The Constitution of Cádiz has nevertheless survived in the collective memory of Spaniards as one of their historical landmarks. Generations of Spaniards, including the present one, tend to recall the War of Independence as a time of national unity, when rich and poor, nobles and artisans, men and women of all regions of Spain, peninsular and American Spaniards, fought together to defeat Napoleon and liberate the country. This widespread admiration for the heroism of their ancestors also extends to the Constitution of Cádiz, which all observers, regardless of ideology, point to as proof that Spain was already a modern and democratic nation at the start of the nineteenth century. Of particular interest, from the perspective of this study, is the fact that the Constitution of Cádiz is seen by many as a singular document in yet another respect: as the first, and perhaps the only, great charter that was meant to apply within the territory not of a nation but an empire. In other words, the Constitution of Cádiz was the clearest attempt to transform, at least symbolically, an empire—the Spanish—into a nation—Spain.

Conclusion

BEFORE THE 1990s, many Spaniards believed that the national problem was definitively solved, and in a way that protected the interests and identities of the historical nations and upheld a shared Spanish identity. Catalans could feel like Catalans and Spaniards without apparent contradiction or conflict. Thanks to the constitution of 1978 and regional statutes, Catalonia and other historical regions were recognized as autonomous communities within a quasi-federal state.[1] The constitution declares Spain to be a multinational state, in which the rights of the "nationalities and regions" are recognized. It underlines the "indissoluble unity of the Spanish Nation, the common and indivisible homeland of all Spaniards." This milestone development contrasted starkly with the repression of national identities and cultures during the Franco dictatorship from 1939 to 1975. For example, the laws regulating Catalonia's autonomy (Estatuto de Autonomía de Cataluña, approved in 1979, and reformed in 2006) define it as a "nationality" constituted as an autonomous community within the constitutional frame, with recognized prerogatives (including the declaration of Catalan as co-official language in the region) and rights of self-government.[2] Many Spaniards viewed this arrangement as a democratic solution and the perfect conclusion to a shared, if conflictive, history.[3]

But before long debates about the existence of various nations within Spain resurged and intensified. In the 1990s, a growing number of people in several of these nations, especially Catalonia, defended their right to self-determination. Spain was living through what seemed a great paradox: a resurgent nationalism during a time of intense globalization. This was not only a Spanish but also a European phenomenon. Tony Judt characterized this period as "a bizarre resurrection of the ghosts of particularism"—clear evidence that nationalism as a mobilizing ideology never dies, whatever the circumstances or political accomplishments to the contrary.[4]

The resurgence of Catalan aspirations to independence came as a surprise to many Spaniards, who viewed it primarily as an expression of Catalonia's material interest. For the Catalanists, however, their desire for independence had profound historical roots. They believed that Catalonia had been a political nation since its inception as a kingdom in medieval times. And since the nineteenth century, Catalanists have believed that Catalonia was an ethnic nation, with a people distinct in origin and character from other peninsular inhabitants.[5]

The most dramatic argument of the pro-independence Catalans holds that they are still part of Spain only because the construction of the Spanish nation was predicated on the repression, if not the elimination, of their identity, rights, and nationhood. The Catalanist literature identified two historical phases in this process, both studied in this book. During the first phase, in the sixteenth and seventeenth centuries, one of the kingdoms—Castile—transformed itself into the aggressor and attempted to politically control the Spanish monarchy. During the second phase, from the eighteenth century onward, monarchs, governments, and in general the elites coming from the non-Catalan regions tried to neutralize and eliminate the rights and identity of Catalonia to impose a Spanish identity upon the entire population of the peninsula. Symbolically, this politics of resentment was evident in the early twentieth century, when the Catalanists decided that the *Día Nacional de Cataluña o Diada* should be September 11, commemorating the date in 1714 when Philip V's troops conquered the rebel city of Barcelona and the monarchy eliminated the privileges and rights of the Principality of Catalonia. To further substantiate this argument and the validity of their political interpretation of the Spanish past, in 2013 pro-independence Catalans organized a symposium of historians, with the support of the regional government, emphatically titled "Spain against Catalonia, 1714–2014."[6]

Opponents contest this historical interpretation. They argue that Catalonia entered voluntarily into the entity called Spain as part of the matrimonial agreements between Ferdinand and Isabel, and that all the constituent kingdoms participated in the transformation of the Spanish monarchy into a Spanish nation. In addition, archaeologists and demographers have sought to demonstrate that all of the inhabitants of the peninsula have common ethnic origins. There has always existed a "Spanish race or people" to which all peninsular communities belonged. They insist that Spain was a nation on civic terms, forged by the political will of a majority of the inhabitants of the Spanish kingdoms and provinces, but also a nation on ethnic terms, forged by this genetic commonality.

All sides in these debates utilized more than political and ideological arguments to make their point and legitimize their positions. Without exception, they referenced history as well. They drew largely on the early modern period, where evidence could be found to support all sides in the debates: that Spain was a unified nation, or that Spain was not a nation but a state composed of multiple nations.

This book emerged out of these social and political debates in the 1990s, which insistently pointed back to the evolution of the national question in the early modern period, and the process of national construction over many centuries. Fundamentally, this inquiry has revealed that not only was the Spanish identity and nation invented, but so too were the peninsula's other identities or nations: the Catalan, the Castilian, the Basque, and the Portuguese. A national identity, the Spanish one in this case, was built on the foundation of others. Castilianization, for instance, was a process, and one tied to monarchial repression. But the construction of a Spanish nation and national identity was also the product of collaboration between the elites and peoples of the various kingdoms and provinces, a shared quest for those elements that unified rather than differentiated. This conception of the nation animated the Constitution of Cádiz (1812). The fundamental idea behind it was very simple: from distinct and occasionally opposed regional and provincial identities, a great nation could be created that did not eliminate these differences but subsumed them within an all-encompassing Spanish identity and nation.

Today, this conception has been called into question. Apace with the resurgence of regional identities in the 1990s, xenophobic attacks increased against immigrants, especially of Arab and Latin American origin, and this provoked a debate about whether Spaniards' political behavior was motivated by racism. Although racial tensions are not as high in Spain as in other countries, there have been clear demonstrations of profound xenophobia, including violent attacks against communities of foreigners, especially Arabs, in several cities throughout the country, particularly in Andalusia and Catalonia. There is other evidence that many Spaniards still reject several ethnic groups. In the 1990s, when Spanish young adults were asked with which ethnic group they were least likely to marry, the answers constituted a virtual radiography of the racial history of Spain: 50 percent insisted they would never marry Gypsies or Arabs/Moors; 33 percent refused to marry Jews, 30 percent African blacks, 26 percent Asians, 26 percent black Latin Americans, 25 percent Native Americans from the former Spanish colonies, 19 percent mestizos from Latin America, 18 percent mulattos from Latin America, 15 percent Portuguese, 12 percent Latin Americans, and 9 percent Americans from the United States. In the case of Jews, 43 percent of those Spanish young adults surveyed who identified themselves as belonging to the upper classes rejected potential marriages, and so did 51 percent of those who identified themselves with far right ideology and 43 percent who defined themselves as Basque or Catalan nationalists.[7]

Central and local authorities, and a significant number of intellectuals and scholars, have held that these attacks and conflicts have social and economic origins rather than ethnic or racial ones. They point to high levels of unemployment, for example, or to the growth in the number of migrants. Until the 1980s Spain was more an exporter than a recipient of immigrants. But thereafter the number rose uninterruptedly, from 923,879 in 1998 to 5.75 million in 2010, or approximately 13 percent of the total population. By 2015, that number had fallen by almost a million, but even with this drop, the number of foreigners in Spain is comparable to that in France, Italy, or the United Kingdom—all countries with larger overall populations.

The Spanish case is interesting because recent racial conflicts notwithstanding, a majority of Spanish intellectuals offer assurances that Spaniards were and are not racist. They explain that in contrast to other countries, Spain did not have a political culture marked by explicitly racist ideologies and political parties. It is argued that very few Spaniards have embraced racism, as proven by the comparatively small number of racist and xenophobic attacks and the fact that the extreme-right and xenophobic parties in Spain, unlike in other European countries, have not achieved any significant political influence.

As in the debates over national identity and Catalan independence, most scholars and journalists summon the history of Spain and the Spanish empire—and especially the absence of racialist theories during the early modern period—as their main refutation to charges of racism in contemporary Spain. Since the early nineteenth century Spanish scholars and intellectuals have claimed that medieval Spain was characterized by the *Convivencia* of Jews, Christians, and Muslims, and that converted Jews were finally assimilated in the early modern period. Purity-of-blood statutes and the drastic decision to expel the Moriscos are interpreted as the product of a profound fear of religious contamination, rather than anti-Semitism or Islamophobia. According to these interpretations of their history, an important number of Spaniards believe that Spain was always a racial paradise, a racial democracy avant la lettre. To prove that Spaniards have learned from past mistakes, the Spanish government has done everything possible to repudiate the edict of expulsion of the Jews in 1492, has recognized those expelled as Spaniards, and has allowed their descendants to apply for their rights as Spanish citizens. Although the government has not proposed that descendants of the Moriscos also be able to request citizenship rights, Spaniards have come to accept theories crediting the Arabs, those who resided in Spain for centuries, for their contributions to Spanish culture and character.[8]

Scholars—nationals and foreigners—have collaborated in the reinvention of Spain as a racial paradise for Jews and Muslims, but also for Native Americans and Africans. Since the late eighteenth century, and especially during the nineteenth and twentieth centuries, Spaniards construed themselves as religiously and racially universalist. They searched always for that which united rather than separated peoples. No one articulated this position more clearly than Angel Rosenblat, a historian descended from Polish Jews who emigrated to Argentina in 1908 when he was six years old. He claimed that early modern Spaniards completely lacked racial prejudices as resulting from the very "formation of the Iberian man, a result of the most diverse mixtures," from the Phoenicians to the peoples of North Africa.[9]

Coincident with some of the most violent attacks against Muslim immigrants in late 1999, although its publication had nothing to do with these events, an op-ed made essentially the same claim. It appeared in *El País*, the most important Spanish newspaper, and was written by one of the most influential Mexican historians, Enrique Krauze. In it, Krauze insisted that while racism represented "the burning stake of Europe and continues to tear the North American social fabric, [the] problem of Mexico [and of the Spanish colonial system] is not primarily racial, but social, political, and economic."[10]

Many of the articles published following each of these conflicts explained that they had erupted not from Spanish racism but from the more radical attitude of a new generation of Muslims in Spain, resistant to assimilation. These Arab youths wanted to reaffirm their "identity" as Muslims in opposition to what they perceived as the excessive Hispanicization or Europeanization of their parents. Such a position inevitably led to conflict. As long as the internal others, it was argued, accepted Spanish culture, habits, and behaviors and definitively assimilated into Spanish society, there would be no problems or attacks because nothing—not skin color, accent, origins, or social status—determined or delimited the sensibilities of the Spanish people, historically characterized by the accommodation of other cultures and peoples.

This book has shown that such interpretations, although they draw on history, go against the weight of historical evidence. Spaniards of the early modern period most assuredly did not believe in the equality of distinct peoples, and no one defended the necessity of uniting all of these peoples through racial mixture. The oft-idealized *Convivencia* between Christians, Jews, and Moriscos did not exist in medieval Spain, or during the early modern period. Spanish authorities discriminated against Jews, Muslims, conversos, and Moriscos, not only for their religion but for their distinct ethnic origins and the consequent fear of biological contamination. Native Americans were treated as inferior and incapable of becoming Spaniards. Africans were discriminated against not only because they had descended from slaves but also for having African origins.

The Spaniards of the early modern period classified the monarch's subjects using biological or racial criteria, and as early as the eighteenth century, they also contributed to the beginning of the development of scientific racism.[11] Racial mixture, justified *a posteriori* as a mechanism of assimilation, was in reality a product of the exploitation of colonial subjects and of their subjugation. The only process that allowed distinct peoples to integrate and to enjoy full political rights was their absolute assimilation into the Spanish cultural and physical mold, which meant abandoning their distinct identities.

In the years to come, Spaniards will continue to confront the national question and the existence of peoples of varied ethnicity in their midst. They will have to decide if they can continue speaking of the Spanish nation and identity, or if this nation will end up splintering, with the separation of Catalonia and/or the Basque Country. The point of departure in confronting these challenges should not be to deny the existence of a history profoundly marked by discriminatory behaviors toward others who did not consider themselves Spaniards. Spain will have to rethink its historic relations with those described here as "others within and without"—Hispanic peoples of Jewish, Arab, Native American, or African origin—in order to understand their relations with new immigrants. The history of the evolution of race and nation in this book proves that real union comes not from the imposition of uniformity but from recognizing and accepting ethnic and cultural differences and the right of the various nations to decide their own future.

NOTES

ACKNOWLEDGMENTS

INDEX

NOTES

Introduction

1. A good analytical synthesis of the various theories on nation and nationalism is Jonathan Hearn, *Rethinking Nationalism: A Critical Introduction* (New York: Palgrave, 2006).

2. Eric Hobsbawm, *Nations and Nationalism since 1789* (Cambridge: Cambridge University Press, 1992), 9–10; on the modernists' theories, Hearn, *Rethinking Nationalism*, chap. 4, 5.

3. Hearn, *Rethinking Nationalism*, chap. 1, 2.

4. Anthony D. Smith, *Myth and Memories of the Nation* (Oxford: Oxford University Press, 1999), 10.

5. Race, n.6." OED Online. Oxford University Press, September 2016. Web. 19 August 2016.

6. Edward Said, *Orientalism* (1977) (London: Penguin, 2003), 3.

7. Charles Mills, *The Racial Contract* (Ithaca, NY: Cornell University Press, 1997).

1
Spains

1. Pablo Fernández Albaladejo, *Materia de España: cultura política e identidad en la España moderna* (Madrid: Marcial Pons, 2007); Tamar Herzog, *Defining Nations: Immigrants and Citizens in Early Modern Spain and Spanish America* (New Haven: Yale University Press, 2003); and, Mateo Ballesteros Rodríguez, *La identidad española en la edad moderna (1556–1665): discursos, símbolos y mitos* (Madrid: Tecnos, 2010).

2. J. G. A. Pocock, "The Third Kingdom in Its History," in J. G. A. Pocock, *The Discovery of Islands* (Cambridge: Cambridge University Press, 2005), 94–95.

3. Richard Kagan, *Clio and the Crown* (Baltimore: The Johns Hopkins University Press, 2009).

4. Archivo General de Simancas, Estado, leg. 840, fol. 25: "Tercera respuesta de los diputados de su majestad a los de la reina de Inglaterra," 6 June 1600.

5. Antonio de Nebrija, *Gramática castellana* (Salamanca: Juan de Porras, 1492), Dedicatory to Isabel of Castile, n.p. On the Spanish monarchy from 1500

till 1700 see now, Xavier Gil Pujol, *La fábrica de la monarquía. Traza y conservación de la monarquía de España de los Reyes Católicos y los Austrias* (Madrid: Real Academia de la Historia, 2016).

6. Francisco Tomás y Valiente, "El gobierno de la monarquía y la administración de los reinos de España," in *Historia de España, vol. 25, La España de Felipe IV*, ed. Francisco Tomás y Valiente (Madrid: Espasa Calpe, 1982), 48.

7. Pablo Fernández Albaladejo, *Fragmentos de monarquía* (Madrid: Alianza Editorial, 1992); Xavier Gil, "Spain and Portugal," in *European Political Thought, 1450–1700*, ed. H. A. Lloyd, G. Burgess, and S. Hodson (New Haven: Yale University Press, 2007), 416–457.

8. Fernández Albaladejo, *Materia de España*, 205.

9. Pedro Cardim, "De la nación a la lealtad al rey," in *Extranjeros y enemigos en Iberoamérica*, ed. D. González Cruz (Madrid: Silex, 2010), 57–88.

10. Bartolomé Filipe, *Tractado del Consejo y de los Consejeros de los Príncipes* (Turin: Gio Vincenzo del Pernetto, 1589), 151v; Pablo Fernández Albaladejo, "España desde España," in *Idea de España en la edad moderna* (Valencia: Universidad de Valencia, 1998), 70. Phillip Soergel, "Religious Patriotism in Early Modern Catholicism," *Patria und Patrioten vor dem Patriotismus* (Wiesbaden: Harrassowitz, 2005), 91–104.

11. Diego Saavedra Fajardo, *Corónica góthica, castellana y austriaca* (1646), in *Obras completas*, ed. Angel González Palencia (Madrid: Aguilar, 1946), 880.

12. Bernardo de Aldrete, *Del origen y principio de la lengua o romance que hoy se usa en España* (Rome: Carlo Vullieto, 1606), 33; Saavedra Fajardo, *Corona góthica*, 727; Juan de Mariana, *Historia general de España* (1601) (Madrid: Andrés García de la Iglesia, 1678), vol. 1, bk. 1, chap. 6, 8.

13 Norman Housley, "*Pro deo et patria mori:* sanctified patriotism in Europe, 1400–1600," in *War and Competition between States*, ed. P. Contamine (Oxford: Oxford University Press, 2000), 221–248.

14. Cécile Vincent-Cassy, *Les saintes vierges et martyres dans l'Espagne du XVIIe siècle* (Madrid: Casa Velázquez, 2011); Erin Rowe, *Saint and Nation* (University Park: Penn State University Press, 2011).

15. One of the best examples of this official policy was the voyage undertaken on Philip II's orders by Ambrosio de Morales. The goal was to identify the remains of martyrs, traces of the presence of saints and their relics, as well as the burial places of the king's ancestors. Ambrosio de Morales, *Relación del viaje de Ambrosio de Morales a los reynos de León, Galicia y Pricipado de Asturias* (Madrid: Ediciones Guillermo Blázquez, 1985). Philip II decided to construct the palace of El Escorial a few kilometers from the new capital, Madrid, as, among other uses, a reliquary to house the remains of saints, but especially Spanish saints.

16. Oscar Recio Morales, "La gente de naciones en los ejércitos de los Austrias hispanos," in *Guerra y sociedad en la Monarquía Hispánica*, ed. E. García and D. Maffi (Madrid: CSIC, 2006), vol. 1, 651–680; I. A. A. Thompson, "El soldado del Imperio," *Manuscripts* 21 (2003): 28; Luis Ribot, "Las naciones en el ejército de los Austrias," in *La monarquía de las naciones*, 653–677.

17. Raffaele Puddu, *Soldado gentiluomo* (Bologna: Il Mulino, 1982); David García Hernán, *La cultura de la guerra y el teatro del Siglo de Oro* (Madrid: Silex, 2006), 242–247.

18. In Manuel de Montoliu, *El alma de España* (Barcelona: Editorial Cervantes, 1942), 117.

19. Carlos García, *Oposición y conjunción de los dos grandes luminares de la Tierra, o la antipatía de franceses y españoles* (1617), ed. Michel Bareau (Alberta: Alta Press, 1979); José Pellicer de Ossau, *Defensa de España contra las calumnias de Francia* (Venice: n.p., 1635); Juan de Palafox y Mendoza, *Sitio y socorro de Fuenterrabía* (1638), ed. J. M. Usunáriz (Pamplona: Asociación de Amigos del Monasterio de Fitero, 2003); Bertrand Haan, "L'affirmation d'un sentiment national espagnol face à la France du début des guerres de Religion," in *Le sentiment national dans l'Europe méridionale aux XVIe et XVIIe siècles (France, Espagne, Italie)*, ed. Alain Tallon (Madrid: Casa Velazquez, 2007), 75–90; José M. Jover, *1635: Historia de una polémica y semblanza de una generación* (Madrid: CSIC, 1949); Linda Colley, *Britons: Forging the Nation, 1707–1837* (New Haven: Yale University Press, 1994).

20. García, *Oposición y conjunción de los dos grandes luminares*, 248.

21. Benito de Peñalosa, *Libro de las cinco excelencias del español que despueblan a España* (Pamplona: Carlos de Labayen, 1629), fol. 159v.

22. Miguel de Cervantes, *Don Quijote de la Mancha* (1605–1615), ed. Francisco Rico (Barcelona: Crítica, 1998), Part. 2, chap. 27, 859–860.

23. Aristotle, *Ocho libros de la republica*, trans. Simon Abril (Zaragoza: Lorenzo y Diego de Robles, 1584), bk. 1; Jean Bodin, *Los seis libros de la republica*, trans. Gaspar de Anastro Isunza (Turin: Herederos de Bevilaqua, 1590), bk. 1. The best summary of these ideas is Anthony Pagden, "Heeding Heraclides: Empire and Its Discontents 1619–1812," in *Spain, Europe, and the Atlantic World: Essays in Honour of John. H. Elliott*, ed. Richard Kagan and Geoffrey Parker (Cambridge: Cambridge University Press, 1995), 316–333.

24. John H. Elliott, "A Europe of Composite Monarchies," *Past and Present* 137 (1992): 52–53.

25. António M. Hespanha, "As façes de una 'revolução,'" *Penélope* 9/10 (1993): 9–10; and James Amelang, "The Peculiarities of the Spaniards: Historical Approaches to the Early Modern State," in *Public Power in Europe*, ed. J. Amelang and S. Beer (Pisa: Pisa University Press, 2006), 39–56.

26. Martín de Viciana, *Alabanzas de las lenguas hebrea, griega, latina, castellana y valenciana* (1574) (Valencia: Salvador Faulí, 1765), n.p.

27. Pedro de Valencia, "Consideración de Pedro de Valencia, su cronista, acerca de enfermedades y salud del reino," in Pedro de Valencia, *Obras completas*, ed. Rafael González Cañal (León: Universidad de León, 1999), vol. 4, part 2, 524.

28. Nuria Sales, "Naturalizações catalãs. Séculos XV a XVIII." *Ler Historia* 9 (1986): 41–63; Nuria Sales, "Naturals i alienígenes," in Nuria Sales, *De Tuïr a Catarroja* (Barcelona: Afers, 2002), 95–125; José María Pérez Collados, *Una aproximación histórica al concepto jurídico de nacionalidad* (Zaragoza: Instituto Fernando el Católico, 1993); and Herzog, *Defining Nations*, specially chaps. 4 and 5.

29. Bodin, *Los seis libros de la República*, bk. 1, chap. 6, 40.

30. Guido Zernatto, "Nation: The History of a Word," *The Review of Politics* 6 (1944): 352. Also Yves Durand, "Nation, Nations," *Dictionnaire de L'Ancien Régime. Royaume de France XVie–XVIIIe siècle*, ed. Lucien Bély (Paris: Presses Universitaires de France, 1996), 882–883.

31. Nebrija, *Gramática castellana*, bk. 3, chap. 4, n.p.

32. Sebastian de Covarrubias, *Tesoro de la lengua castellana o española* (1611), ed. I. Arellano y R. Zafra (Madrid: Universidad de Navarra/Iberoamericana, 2006), "Patria," 1349.

33. Porfirio Sanz, "Algunas reflexiones sobre las condiciones de natural y extranjero en el Aragón de finales del siglo XVI," in *Actas de la V reunión científica de la Asociación Española de Historia Moderna*, ed. J. L. Pereira (Cádiz: Universidad de Cádiz, 1999), vol. 1, 350.

34. Cicero, *Libro de Marco Tulio Cicerón en que trata de los Oficios, de la Amicicia, de la Senectud*, trans. Francisco de Támara (1542) (Salamanca: Pedro Lasso, 1582), 22v–23r.

35. The subject of the histories of the kingdoms that made up the monarchy is becoming one of the most popular in the field. Some of the best works on the topic include Fernando Bouza, "Dar Galicia y el gallego a la imprenta," *Obradoiro de Historia Moderna* 18 (2009): 9–44; Jesús Villanueva, *Política y discurso histórico en la España del siglo XVII* (San Vicente del Raspeig: Universidad de Alicante, 2004); and Xavier Baró, *La historiografia catalana en el segle del Barroc (1585–1709)* (Barcelona: Publicacions de l'Abadia de Montserrat, 2009).

36. Núria Sales, "Estat, monarquia i llengua," *Afers* 23/24 (1996): 357–365.

37. Ricardo García Cárcel, *Historia de Cataluña: siglos XVI y XVII* (Barcelona: Ariel, 1985), vol. 1, 135.

38. Miguel Herrero, *Ideas de los españoles del siglo XVII* (Madrid: Gredos, 1928), 132–170; Pedro Cardim, "Los portugueses frente a la Monarquía Hispánica," *Monarquía de las naciones: patria, nación y naturaleza en la monarquía de España*, ed. B. J. García and A. Álvarez-Ossorio (Madrid: Fundación Carlos de Amberes, 2004), 355–83.

39. Pedro Cardim, *Portugal unido y separado* (Valladolid: Universidad de Valladolid, 2014), 138, 131–218.

40. I. A. A. Thompson, "Castile, Spain, and the Monarchy: The Political Community from *patria natural* to *patria nacional*." In *Spain, Europe, and the Atlantic World*, 125–159.

41. Javier Barrientos Grandon, *El gobierno de las Indias* (Madrid: Fundación Rafael del Pino, 2004), 39.

42. Pedro Cardim, "The Representatives of Asian and American Cities at the Cortes of Portugal," in *Polycentric Monarchies: How Did Early Modern Spain and Portugal Achieved and Maintained a Global Hegemony?*, ed. Pedro Cardim et al (Eastbourne: Sussex Academic Press, 2012) , 43–53.

43. Carlos Garriga, "Patrias criollas, plazas militares: sobre la América de Carlos IV," in *La América de Carlos IV*, ed. Eduardo Martiré (Buenos Aires: Instituto de Investigaciones de Historia del Derecho, 2006), 35-130; Oscar Mazín, "Architect of the New World: Juan de Solórzano Pereyra and the Status of the Americas," in *Polycentric Monarchies*, 27–42; *Las Indias Occidentales: procesos de integración territorial (siglos XVI–XIX)*, ed. Oscar Mazín and Javier J. Ruiz (México: El Colegio de México, 2013).

44. Javier Barrientos Grandon, *Guía prosopográfica de la judicatura letrada indiana (1503–1898)* (Madrid: Fundación Histórica Tavera, 2000).

45. Gonzalo Fernández de Oviedo, *Historia general y natural de las Indias* (1535), ed. J. Amador de los Ríos (Madrid: Real Academia de la Historia, 1852), vol. 2, 4. The second and third part of his history were written by Fernández de Oviedo before his death in 1557, but they were not published until the nineteenth century. The first part, published in 1535, appears to have been one of the most widely read works on the Spanish conquests in the sixteenth and seventeenth centuries.

46. Anthony Pagden, "Identity Formation in Spanish America," in *Colonial Identity in the Atlantic World, 1500–1800*, ed. N. Canny and A. Pagden (Princeton: Princeton University Press, 1989), 53.

47. Tamar Herzog, "Los americanos frente a la monarquía. El criollismo y la naturaleza española," in *La monarquía de las naciones*, 84–88; Garriga, "Patrias criollas, plazas militares"; Pagden, "Identity Formation in Spanish America," 51–93; Herzog, *Defining Nations*, 60 and 65.

48. Valencia, "Consideración de Pedro de Valencia," 515.

49. Christian Desplat, "Louis XIII and the Union of Béarn in France," in *Conquest and Coalescence*, ed. Mark Greengrass (London: Edward Arnold, 1991), 68–83. On the consolidation of the royal domain in Renaissance France, Arlette Jouanna, *La France du XVIe siècle, 1483–1598* (Paris: PUF, 1996), Introduction, chap. 8–14.

50. Baltasar Gracián, *El político don Fernando el Católico* (1640), in *Obras* (Antwerp: Geronymo y Juan Bautista Verdussen, 1669), vol. 1, 497.

51. James VI and I, "Speech to Parliament of 19 March 1604," in *Journal of the House of Commons: Volume 1, 1547–1629* (London: His Majesty's Stationery Office, 1802), 143.

52. For an excellent study of the proposals and debates on the union of England and Scotland in the first years of James's reign, see Bruce Galloway and Brian Levack, "Introduction," in *The Jacobean Union. Six Tracts of 1604*, ed. Bruce Galloway and Briasn Levack (Edinburg: Scottish Society, 1985), ix–lxxx.

53. See in general Krishan Kumar, *The Making of English National Identity* (Cambridge: Cambridge University Press, 2003).

54. Valencia, "Consideración de Pedro de Valencia," 526.

55. Tommaso Campanella, *La Monarquía Hispánica* (c.1600), ed. P. Mariño (Madrid: Centro de Estudios Constitucionales, 1982), 149.

56. Álamos de Barrientos, *Discurso político*, 106–107.

57. Valencia, "Consideración de Pedro de Valencia," 513.

58. On the post of royal chronicler of Castile, frequently translated by modern historians as the royal chronicler of *Spain*, but also more generally on the writing of history in sixteenth- and seventeenth-century Spain, Kagan, *Clio and the Crown*.

59. Fernando Bouza, *El libro y el cetro: la biblioteca de Felipe IV en la Torre Alta del Alcázar de Madrid* (Salamanca: Instituto de Historia del Libro y de la Lectura, 2005), chap. 2.

60. On the Spanish language from the perspective of other European countries, *Post tenebras spero lucem. Los estudios gramaticales en la España medieval y renacentista*, ed. A. M. González (Granada: Universidad de Granada, 2010), 321–351, 379–403, 405–429, 431–455. On the evolution of Castilian and its relation

to other languages, Xavier Gil Pujol, "Las lenguas en la España de los siglos XVI y XVII: imperio, algarabía y lengua común," en *Comunidad e identidad en el mundo ibérico,* ed. F. Chacón Jiménez and S. Evangelisti (Valencia: Universidad de Valencia, 2013), 81–119.

61. On the different languages in the Iberian Peninsula and their evolution, relationships, and influences, see María Teresa Echenique and Juan Sánchez, *Las lenguas de un reino* (Madrid: Gredos, 2005).

62. Juan de Valdés, *Diálogo de la lengua* (1535) (Madrid: J. Martín Alegría, 1860), 30.

63. Viciana, *Alabanzas de las lenguas,* 3; Aldrete, *Del origen y principio de la lengua,* 56–57.

64. Nebrija, *Gramática de la lengua castellana,* n.p.

65. Valencia, "Consideración de Pedro de Valencia," 526–527.

66. "Autosemblanza de Felipe IV" (1633), in *Cartas de Sor María de Jesús de Agreda y de Felipe IV,* ed. Carlos Seco Serrano (Madrid: BAE, 1958), 232.

67. Aldrete, *Del origen y principio de la lengua,* 100; Bernardo de Aldrete, *Varias antiguedades de España, Africa y otras provincias* (Antwerp: Jean Hasrey, 1614), 73. See also Mariana, *Historia general de España,* bk. 1, chap. 5, 7–8.

68. Peter Burke, *Languages and Communities in Early Modern Europe* (Cambridge: Cambridge University Press, 2004), 7.

69. Ibid., 71, 83.

70. Marinela García-Sempere and Alexander S. Wilkinson, "Catalán and the Book Industry in the Crown of Aragón, 1475–1601," *Bulletin of Spanish Studies* 89 (2012): 557–574.

71. García Cárcel, *Historia de Cataluña,* vol. 1, 81–90; James S. Amelang. *Honored Citizens of Barcelona* (Princeton: Princeton University Press, 1986), chap. 8; Nuria Sales. "Estat, monarquia i llengua"; Manuel Peña Díaz, "El castellano en la Cataluña de los siglos XVI y XVII," *Manuscrits* 15 (1997): 149–155; Joan-Lluís Marfany, "Fue, en una palabra, una lengua nacional," in *La llengua maltractada. El castellà i el català a Catalunya del segle XVI al segle XIX* (Barcelona: Editorial Empúries, 2001), 107–190; and "La història de la diglòssia a Catalunya," in *Llengua, nació i diglòsia* (Barcelona: L'Avenç, 2008), 85–106.

72. Ana Isabel Buescu, "Aspectos do bilinguismo portugués-castelhano na época moderna." *Hispania* 64 (2004): 13–38.

73. Campanella, *La Monarquía Hispánica,* 150–151.

74. "Copia de papeles que ha dado Su Majestad el Conde Duque, gran canciller, sobre diferentes materias de gobierno de España," in *Memoriales y cartas del conde duque de Olivares,* ed. John Elliott and Francisco de la Peña (Madrid: Alfaguara, 1978), vol. 1, 94–95.

75. Jesús Gascón Pérez, *La rebelión aragonesa de 1591* (Unpublished Ph.D., University of Zaragoza, 2000).

76. Antonio Feros, *Kingship and Favoritism in the Spain of Philip III, 1598–1621* (Cambridge: Cambridge University Press, 2000), 160.

77. Cit Xavier Gil Pujol, "Un rey, una fe, muchas naciones," in *La monarquía de las naciones,* 63.

78. "Copia de papeles que ha dado a Su Majestad el Conde Duque, gran canciller, sobre diferentes materias de gobierno de España," vol. 1, 97.

79. Ibid. On Olivares' initiatives, John H. Elliott, *The Count Duke of Olivares: The Statesman in an Age of Decline* (New Haven: Yale University Press, 1986), 169–202.

80. Elliott, *The Count Duke of Olivares*, 244–277.

81. James Casey, "Patriotism in Early Modern Valencia," in *Spain, Europe, and the Atlantic*, 188–210; Xavier Gil, "Aragonese Constitutionalism and Habsburg rule," in *Spain, Europe, and the Atlantic*, 160–187.

82. Pedro de Valencia, *Tratado acerca de los moriscos de España* (1605), in Valencia, *Obras completas*, vol. 4, part 1, 130.

83. John H. Elliott, *The Revolt of the Catalans* (Cambridge: Cambridge University Press, 1963), 452–588; Xavier Torres Sans, *Naciones sin nacionalismo. Cataluña en la Monarquía Hispánica (siglos XVI–XVII)* (Valencia: Universitat de València, 2008), 123–343; Antonio Simón i Tarrés, *Els origens ideològics de la revolució catalana de 1640* (Barcelona: Publicacions de l'Abadia de Montserrat, 1999). For a general summary of events in 1640, see Elliott, *The Count Duke of Olivares*, 553–599.

84. Torres Sans, *Naciones sin nacionalismo*, 248–256; María Soledad Arredondo, "Armas de papel. Quevedo y sus contemporáneos ante la guerra de Cataluña," *La Perinola* 2 (1998): 117–151.

85. *Discurso del duque de Alba* (1645), cit. Pedro Cardim, "História, política e reputação no discurso del Duque de Alba al Católico Felipe IV sobre el consejo, que se le diò en abril passado, para la recuperación de portugal . . . (1645), de Braz da França," in *Repensar a Identidade. O mundo ibérico nas margens da crise da consciência europeia*, ed. Pedro Cardim et al. (Lisbon: Universidade Nova de Lisboa, 2015), 106.

86. Cardim, *Portugal unido y separado*, 223.

87. Jacqueline Hermann, *No reino do desejado* (Sao Paulo: Copanhia das Letras, 1998); Fernando Bouza, *Portugal no tempo dos Filipes* (Lisbon: Edições Cosmos, 2000); Cardim, *Portugal unido y separado*, 171–264.

88. Eva Serra, "Catalunya després del 1652: recompenses, censura i repressió," *Pedralbes* 17 (1997): 191–216; *Los bombardeos de Cataluña*, ed. J. Sisinio et al (Madrid: Catarata, 2014), chaps. 1–2; Manuel Peña Díaz, "La Inquisición y la memoria histórica de la revuelta catalana de 1640," *Bulletin of Spanish Studies* 92 (2015): 747–769.

89. Oscar Jané Checa, *Catalunya i França al segle XVII* (Catarroja: Editorial Afers, 2006).

90. Gracián, *El político don Fernando el Católico*, vol. 1, 522.

91. Juan de Palafox y Mendoza, "Juicio interior y secreto de la monarquía para mi solo," in J. M. Jover Zamora, "Sobre los conceptos de monarquía y nación en el pensamiento político español del siglo XVII." *Cuadernos de Historia de España* 13 (1950): 145–146. Palafox occupied several highly influential posts, serving as bishop of Puebla in Mexico, viceroy of Mexico in 1642, and bishop of Osma in the province of Soria, Spain, where he died.

2
Spaniards

1. Gonzalo Fernández de Oviedo, *Historia general y natural de las Indias* [1535], ed. J. Amador de los Ríos (Madrid: Real Academia de la Historia, 1851), vol. 1, bk. 2, chap. 13, 54.

2. Giovanni Botero, *Relaciones universales del mundo*, trans. Diego de Aguiar (Valladolid: Herederos de Diego de Córdoba, 1603), vol. 2, 96.

3. Sebastián de Covarrubias, *Tesoro de la lengua castellana o española* (1611), ed. I. Arellano y R. Zafra (Madrid: Universidad de Navarra/Iberoamericana, 2006), 830–831.

4. Girolamo Vittori, *Tesoro de las tres lenguas francesa, italiana y española. Thresor des trois langues françoise, italienne et espagnolle* (Ginebra: Philippe Albert & Alexandre Pernet, 1609), "Raça."

5. Covarrubias, *Tesoro de la lengua castellana o española*, 1395. The etimological evolution of the term *raza* in Joan Corominas, *Diccionario crítico etimológico de la Lengua Castellana* (Berna: Editorial Francke, 1954), vol. 3, 1019–1021.

6. Ricardo García Cárcel, *La leyenda negra* (Madrid: Alianza Editorial, 1998); J. N. Hillgarth, *The Mirror of Spain, 1500–1700* (Ann Arbor: University of Michigan Press, 2000); Santiago López Moreda, *Hispania en los humanistas europeos. Detractores y defensores* (Madrid: Ediciones Clásicas, 2013).

7. Joannes Boemus, *El libro de las costumbres de todas las gentes del mundo y de las Indias*, trans. Francisco Támara (Antwerp: Martin Nucio, 1556). Also Giacomo Bergamo, *Suma de todas las crónicas del mundo*, trans. Mosén Narcís (S.L., 1510). On Boemus, Diego Pirillo, "Relativismo culturale e 'armonia del mondo': l'enciclopedia etnográfica di Johannes Boemus," in *L'Europa divisa e i nuovi mondi*, ed. M. Donattini et al. (Edizioni della Normale, 2011), vol. 2, 67–77.

8. Boemus, *El libro de las costumbres*, fol. 4v.

9. Francisco López de Gómara, *Primera y segunda parte de la historia general de las Indias* (Medina del Campo: Guillermo de Millis, 1553), fol. 118r–v.

10. Ibn Khaldun, *The Muqaddimah*, ed. N. J. Dawood (Princeton: Princeton University Press, 1969), 58–59.

11. Jean Bodin, *Los seis libros de la República*, trans. Gaspar de Añastro Isunza (Turin: Herederos de Bevilaqua, 1590), bk. 5, chap. 1, 395–418. Marian J. Tooley, "Bodin and the Medieval Theory of Climate," *Speculum* 28 (1953): 64–83; Luis Urteaga. "La teoría de los climas y los orígenes del ambientalismo," *Geo Crítica* 99 (1992): 5–55; Noga Arikha, *Passions and Tempers: A History of the Humours* (New York: Ecco, 2007).

12. Baltasar Álamos de Barrientos, *Aforismos al Tácito español* (1614), ed. J. A. Fernández-Santamaría (Madrid: Centro de Estudios Constitucionales, 1987), vol. 1, 55.

13. Oliva Sabuco de Nantes, *Nueva filosofía de la naturaleza del hombre* (Madrid: Pedro Madrigal, 1588), fol. 59v.

14. Francisco de Quevedo, *España defendida y los tiempos de ahora* (1609), ed. R. Selden Rose (Madrid: n.p., 1916), 84. See also López de Reta's introduction to his translation of Ogier Gislenio Busbeq, *Embajada y viajes de Constantinopla*, trans. Esteban López de Reta (Pamplona: Carlos de Labayen, 1610).

15. Miguel Herrero García, *Ideas de los españoles del siglo XVII* (Madrid: Gredos, 1966), 94–314; Fernando Bouza, "La visión de Cataluña en el pensamiento castellano," *Manuscrits* 15 (1997): 135–147; Pablo Fernández Albaladejo, *Materia de España: cultura política e identidad en la España moderna* (Madrid: Marcial Pons, 2007), 287–321. For a curious example of these debates between the kingdoms, see, Pedro Fernández de Castro, *El buho gallego* (1620s), ed. J. A. Álvarez Blázquez (Vigo: Ediciones Monterrey, 1951).

16. Juan Gutiérrez Godoy, *Tres discursos para probar que están obligadas a criar sus hijos a sus pechos todas las madres* (Jaén: Pedro de la Cuesta, 1629), fol. 97r; Joyce Chaplin, "Natural Philosophy and an Early Racial Idiom in North America: Comparing English and Indian Bodies," *The William and Mary Quarterly* 54 (1997): 235. On desirable qualities in wet nurses, Luis Lobera de Ávila, *El libro del régimen de la salud* (1551), ed. Baltasar Hernández (Madrid: Imprenta de Cosano, 1923), 266–268.

17. Pedro de Mexía, *Silva de varia lección* (Lyons: Herederos de Iacobo Iunta, 1556), bk. 1, chap. 42, "Que sea la causa de parecer los hijos a los padres o madres, como se causa la diversidad en los gestos de los hombres y los hijos, de los sabios no salir ellos de tales y otras cosas al propósito," fols. 172–176. See also Juan Benítez Quintero, *Questión moral pertinente al estado eclesiastico, la cual ha resuelto y decidido* (Granada, 1688), fol. 9v.

18. Maurice Olender, *Race and Erudition*, trans. J. M. Todd (Cambridge: Harvard University Press, 2009), x.

19. Arlette Jouanna, *L'Idee de Race en France au XVIème Siecle t au debut di XVIIème Siecle (1498–1614)* (Lille: Université de Lille III, 1976), 3 vols.; Jouanna, *Ordre social. Mythes et hiérarchies dans la France du XVIe siècle* (Paris: Hachette, 1977), 13–83; Jouanna, "Race," *Dictionnaire de L'Ancien Régime. Royaume de France XVIe–XVIIIe siècle*, ed. Lucien Bély (Paris: Presses Universitaires de France, 1996), 1045–1047. Also André Devyver, *Le sang épuré. Les préjugés de race chez les gentilshommes français de l'Acien Régime (1560–1720)* (Bruxelles: Editions de L'Universitie de Bruxelles, 1973); Pierre H. Boulle, "La construction du concept de race dans la France d'ancien regime," *Outre-Mers* 89 (2002): 155–175; Gillaume Aubert, "'The Blood of France": Race and Purity of Blood in the French Atlantic World," *The William and Mary Quarterly* 61 (2004): 439–478, cit. 443–444.

20. Alfonso Martínez de Toledo, Arcipreste de Talavera, *O Corbacho*, ed. J. González Muela (Madrid: Castalia, 1985), 85. The notion that nobility of the blood was something "natural" and inherent in a particular group retained force throughout the early modern period, despite theories that proclaimed an individual's "nobility" as determined by moral qualities and the desire to serve his homeland and the king rather than blood. Antonio Domínguez Ortiz, *Las clases privilegiadas en el Antiguo Régimen* (Madrid: Istmo, 1973), 29–31, 186–188; José Antonio Guillén, *La idea de nobleza en Castilla durante el reinado de Felipe II* (Valladolid: Universidad de Valladolid, 2007).

21. Álamos de Barrientos, *Aforismos al Tácito español*, vol. 1, 21–22. Essential reading on this subject is Fernando Wulff, *Las esencias patrias* (Barcelona: Crítica, 2002).

22. See also Benito Arias Montano, *Libro de la generación y regeneración del hombre o Historia del género humano*, ed. Fernando Navarro (Huelva: Universidad de Huelva, 1999), bk. 3, chaps. 3–5, 222–236.

23. Mexía, *Silva de varia lección* bk. 1, chap. 26, 100. Spaniards also claimed some mythical origins, like having been settled by some of the Trojans exiled from their ruined city by victorious Athenians, and some commentators routinely insisted that mythical heroes, including Geryon and Hercules, had been present on Spanish soil. This was indeed colorful but rather less important than the belief that Tubal and his descendants were the original settlers of Hispania. On European parallels to these theories, Colin Kidd, *British Identities before Nationalism* (Cambridge: Cambridge University Press, 1999), 287–289.

24. Pedro de Medina, *Grandezas y cosas notables de España* (Alcalá de Henares: Juan Gracián, 1595), 9r.

25. Benito Peñalosa y Mondragón, *Libro de las cinco excelencias del español que despueblan a España para su mejor potencia y dilación* (Pamplona: Carlos de Labayen, 1629), fol. 5r.

26. Covarrubias, *Tesoro de la lengua castellana o española*, 1279.

27. Ambrosio de Morales, *La Corónica general de España* (Alcalá de Henares: Juan Iñiguez de Lequerica, 1574–1577), vol. 1: 98v.

28. Florián de Ocampo, *Los cinco libros de la Crónica general de España* (Medina del Campo: Guillermo de Millis, 1553), fol. 2r; Wulff, *Esencias patrias*, 23–35.

29. On the Goths in Spain, Morales, *La Corónica general de España*, bk. 10; Gregorio López Madera, *Excelencias de la Monarchia y Reyno de España* (Valladolid: Diego Fernández de Córdoba, 1597), chap. 2; Juan de Mariana, *Historia de España* ((1601) (Madrid: Andrés García de la Iglesia, 1678), vol. 1, bk. 5; Diego Saavedra Fajardo, *Corona góthica, castellana y austriaca* (1646), in Obras completas, ed. Angel González Palencia (Madrid: Aguilar, 1946).

30. Mariana, *Historia general de España*, vol. 1, bk. 6, chap. 1, 233–235.

31. Peñalosa, *Libro de las cinco excelencias*, fos. 75r–76r. See also Saavedra Fajardo, *Corona góthica*, 1051–52; Esteban de Garibay, *Los cuarenta libros del compendio historial de las crónicas y universal historia de todos los reynos de España* (Barcelona, Sebastián de Cormellas: 1628), vol. 2, 325.

32. "Relación de las calidades de los españoles," sec. 15

33. The implications of these theories on how descendants of Jews and Muslims were perceived will be discussed in the next chapter along with how some Spaniards contested these ideas and laws.

34. On these theories in France, Arlette Jouanna, *L'idée de race en France au XVIe siècle et au debut du XVIIe; (1498–1614)*, 3 vols. (Ph.D. diss, Université de Paris-IV, 1976); Andre Devyver, *Sang épuré, les préjugés de race chez les gentilshommes français de l'Ancien Régime, 1560–1720* (Brussels: Editions de l'Université de Bruxelles, 1973).

35. Elena Postigo Castellanos, *Honor y privilegio en la corona de Castilla: el Consejo de las Ordenes y los caballeros de hábito en el siglo XVII* (Valladolid: Junta de Castilla y León, 1987), 140.

36. The quotation comes from a document generated by the Military Order of Santiago, AHN, Consejo de las Ordenes Militares, Pruebas de Caballeros de la Orden de Santiago, exp. 5374, 1701. One of the best studies of the legal process is Juan Hernández Franco, *Cultura y limpieza de sangre en la España moderna. Puritate sanguinis.* (Murcia: Universidad de Murcia, 1996).

37. On the Toledo statute, and the statutes in general, Albert Sicroff, *Los estatutos de limpieza de sangre. Controversias entre los siglos XV y XVII*, trans. Mauro Armiño (Madrid: Taurus, 1985), on the Toledo statute, 141–169; Max S. Hering Torres, "Limpieza de sangre ¿Racismo en la edad moderna?," *Tiempos Modernos: Revista Electrónica de Historia Moderna* 9 (2003). These studies insist on the importance of analyzing the creation of this discourse of social and genealogical distinction, but few have analyzed how effective these statutes were as well as Enrique Soria Mesa, *La realidad tras el espejo. Ascenso social y limpieza de sangre en la España de Felipe II* (Valladolid: Universidad de Valladolid, 2016), and "Los estatutos municipales de limpieza de sangre en la Castilla moderna. Una revisión crítica," *Mediterranea*, 27(2013): 9-36.

38. Medina, *Grandezas y cosas notables*, 8r.

39. Cif. Ricardo García Cárcel, *Historia de Cataluña: siglos XVI y XVII* (Barcelona: Ariel, 1985), vol. 1, 67. Morales, *La Corónica general de España*, also referred to the extreme whiteness of the first Gothic arrivals, resembling that of the Germans and other northern Europeans (1: 2v).

40. Carlos García, *Oposición y conjunción de los dos grandes luminares de la tierra, o la antipatía de franceses y españoles* (1617), ed. Michel Bareau (Alberta: Alta Press, 1979), 232.

41. "Relación de las calidades de los españoles," section 21.

42. Nicolás Antonio, *Bibliotcca Hispana Nuevu* (1672), ed. and trans. Francisco Pérez (1788), fac. ed. 2 vols. (Madrid: FUE, 1999).

43. Spanish emigration to the Indies during the colonial period has been relatively well studied; María del Carmen Martínez, "El cambio demográfico," in *La formación de las sociedades iberoamericanas (1568–1700)*, ed. Demetrio Ramos (Madrid: Espasa Calpe, 1999), 63–86; Carlos Martínez Shaw, *La emigración española a América (1494–1824)* (Oviedo: Archivo de Indianos, 1994); Carlos Martínez Shaw, "La procedencia geográfica de la emigración española a América (1492–1824)," *Españoles de ambas orillas: emigración y concordia social*, ed. José Antonio Escudero López (Madrid: Sociedad Estatal Lisboa 98, 1998), 25–40. Still useful is Nicolás Sánchez Albornoz, "The Population of Colonial America," in *Cambridge History of Latin America*, ed. L. Bethell (Cambridge: Cambridge University Press, 1984), vol. 2, 3–35.

44. The requirements for emigration may be found in Lib. 1, cap. 29, of Joseph de Veitia Linage, *Norte de la contratación de las Indias occidentales* (Sevilla: Juan Francisco de Blas, 1672), 218–231; Rocío Sánchez Rubio and Isabel Testón Núñez, "Fingiendo llamarse . . . para no ser conocido: Cambios nominales y emigración a Indias (siglos XV–XVIII)," *Norba. Revista de Historia* 21 (2008): 213–239.

45. Although all passengers to the Indies were required to prove they did not descend from Jews or Arabs, it is believed that many lied and forged the necessary documents while many others simply chose to emigrate illegally. Modern scholars have estimated that around 1600, only in the viceroyalty of Mexico there may have been roughly 10,000 converted Jews or their descendants. Nathan Watchel, "Una América subterránea. Redes y religiosidades marranas," in *Para una historia de América II. Los nudos I*, ed. M. Carmagnani, A. Hernández, and R. Romano (México: FCE, 1999), 21. The number of Moriscos who emigrated to the Indies is also unknown, but see Hernán Taboada, *La sombra del Islam en la conquista de América* (México: FCE, 2004).

46. On the increasingly frequent use of the term *white* (*blanco*) in place of *brown* or *dark* (*moreno*) to describe Spanish emigrants to the Indies, Joanne Rappaport, "Así lo parece por su aspecto: Physiognomy and the Construction of Difference in Colonial Bogotá," *Hispanic American Historical Review* 91 (2011): 620–622.

47. Stuart Schwartz, "La nobleza del Nuevo Mundo," *Revista de* Historia, 8 (1979): 10.

48. Juan López de Velasco, *Geografía y descripción universal de las Indias*, ed. Justo Zaragoza (Madrid: Sociedad Geográfica de Madrid, 1894), 36.

49. Ibid., 2.

50. Martínez, "El cambio demográfico," 68; Sánchez Albornoz, "The Population of Colonial America," 18; José Luis Martínez, *Pasajeros de Indias. Viajes trasatlánticos en el siglo XVI* (México: Fondo de Cultura Económica, 1999), 206–212.

51. Juan de Solórzano Pereira, *Política indiana* (Madrid: Diego Díaz de la Carrera, 1647), bk. 2, chap. 28, 233.

52. Solange Alberro, *Del gachupín al criollo: o de cómo los españoles de México dejaron de serlo* (México: Colegio de México, 1992).

53. Oscar Mazín, "Architect of the New World: Juan de Solórzano Pereyra and the Status of the Americas," in *Polycentric Monarchies: How Did Early Modern Spain and Portugal Achieved and Maintained a Global Hegemony?*, ed. Pedro Cardim et al (Eastbourne: Sussex Academic Press, 2012), 28–30; Magdalena Chocano Mena, *La América colonial (1492–1763)* (Madrid: Síntesis, 2000).

54. Serge Gruzinski, *Les quatre parties du monde. Histoire d'une mondialisation* (Paris: Éditions de la Martinière, 2004); Ida Altman, *Emigrants and Society: Extremadura and Spanish America in the Sixteenth Century* (Los Angeles: University of California Press, 1989); Ida Altman, *Transatlantic Ties in the Spanish Empire Brihuega, Spain, and Puebla, Mexico, 1560–1620* (Stanford: Stanford University Press, 2000); Solange Alberro, "La aculturación de los españoles en la América colonial," in *Descubrimiento, conquista y colonización de Amèrica a quinientos años*, ed. Carmen Bernard (Madrid: Fondo de Cultura Económica, 1994), 249–265.

55. Tamar Herzog, *Defining Nations: Immigrants and Citizens in Early Modern Spain and Spanish America* (New Haven: Yale University Press, 2003), 60.

56. Bernardo Aldrete, *Varias antiguedades de España, África y otras provincias* (Amberes: Iuan Hasrey, 1614), 73.

57. Baltasar Álamos de Barrientos, *Discurso político al rey Felipe III al comienzo de su reinado* (1599), ed. M. Santos (Barcelona: Anthropos, 1990), 15.

58. This topic has been widely studied, but see above all Jorge Cañizares Esguerra, "New World, New Stars: Patriotic Astrology and the Invention of Indian and Creole Bodies in Colonial Spanish America, 1600–1650," *The American Historical Review* 104 (1999): 33–68.

59. López de Velasco, *Geografía y descripción universal de las Indias*, 37–38.

60. Buenaventura de Salinas y Córdoba, *Memorial de las historias del nueuo mundo:Peru* (Lima: Gerónimo de Contreras, 1631), especially Discurso II, De los méritos y excelencias de la ciudad de Lima; Buenaventura de Salinas y Córdoba, *Memorial, informe y manifiesto* (c. 1646)), fos. 20–24v; Cañizares Esguerra, "New World, New Stars," 49–52. On the Creoles, see Bernard Lavallé, *Las*

promesas ambiguas. Ensayos sobre el criollismo colonial en los Andes (Lima: Pontificia Universidad Católica del Perú, 1993); and Brioso Santos, *América en la prosa literaria de los siglos XVI y XVII*, 105–167.

61. Peñalosa y Mondragón, *La cinco excelencias del español*, fol. 6v.

62. Solórzano Pereira, *Política Indiana*, bk. 2, chap. 30, 244.

63. "Lope García de Castro al Consejo de Indias," 1567, cit. Carmen Bernand, *Negros esclavos y libres en las ciudades hispanoamericana* (Madrid: Fundación Histórica Tavera, 2000), 19; López de Velasco, *Geografía y descripción universal de las Indias*, 43; "Carta del jesuita José de Teruel, rector del Colegio de Cuzco, 1 febrero 1585," cit. Berta Ares Queija, "Mestizos, mulatos y zambaigos (Virreinato del Perú, siglo XVI)," in *Negros, mulatos, zambaigos. Derroteros africanos en los mundos ibéricos*, ed. B. Ares and A. Stella (Sevilla: CSIC, 2000), 85.

64. Martínez, "El cambio demográfico," 68.

65. Alexander O. Exquemelin, *The history of the buccaneers of America* (1678) (Boston: B.B. Mussey & Co., 1853), 28.

66. "Relación del Virrey de Nueva España, Juan de Mendoza y Luna, Marqués de Montesclaros, 2 de agosto de 1607," 282.

67. Gregorio García, *Origen de los Indios del Nuevo Mundo* (1607) (México: FCE, 1981), bk. 4, chap. 25, 306.

68. María Elena Martínez, "The Black Blood of New Spain: Limpieza de Sangre, Racial Violence, and Gendered Power in Early Colonial Mexico," *The William and Mary Quarterly* 61 (2004): 479–520; María Elena Martínez, *Genealogical fictions: limpieza de sangre, religion, and gender in colonial Mexico* (Stanford: Stanford University Press, 2008).

69. Martínez, *Genealogical Fictions*. Also the important works collected in, *El peso de la sangre. Limpios, mestizos y nobles en el mundo hispánico*, ed. N. Böttcher, N. Hausberge, and M. S. Hering (México: Colegio de México, 2011).

70. Javier Sanchiz, "La limpieza de sangre en Nueva España, entre la rutina y la formalidad," in *El peso de la sangre*, 113–135.

71. The situation was different in Portugal, where there was a larger proportion of blacks in comparison with Spain, which explains why, starting in the seventeenth century, many of the blood purity statutes excluded candidates with black and mulatto ancestry. Didier Lahon, "Black African Slaves and Freedmen in Portugal during the Renaissance: Creating a New Pattern of Reality," in *Black Africans in Renaissance Europe*, 278–279.

72. Thomas C. Holt, "Of Blood and Power: An Introduction," *William and Mary Quarterly* 61 (2004): 436.

73. Olender, *Race and Erudition*, xiv.

3
The Others Within

1. J. G. A. Pocock, "The Politics of History. The Subaltern and the Subversive," *The Journal of Political Philosophy* 6 (1998): 221.

2. Eduardo Manzano Moreno, *Historia de España: Épocas medievales* (Barcelona: Crítica/Marcial Pons, 2011), 89–90.

3. Jane S. Gerber, *The Jews of Spain* (New York: The Free Press, 1992); Jonathan Ray, *The Sephardic Frontier. The Reconquista and the Jewish Community in Medieval Iberia* (Ithaca: Cornell University Press, 2006); and *Remembering Sepharad: Jewish Culture in Medieval Spain* (Madrid: Seacex, 2003).

4. On the Jewish population in Spain, see *Judíos, sefarditas, conversos. La expulsión de 1492 y sus consecuencias,* ed. Angel Alcalá (Valladolid: Ambito, 1992).

5. The everyday life of medieval Jews, was regulated by several laws, especially by the *Siete Partidas,* a code of law compiled during the reign of Alfonso X of Castile (1252–1284). Although Castilian in origin, the *Siete Partidas* also influenced the law in other Christian kingdoms. With the marriage of Isabel and Ferdinand, the *Siete Partidas* became one of the national law codes, influencing legal thinking and codification until the nineteenth century. The sections related to these communities (both Jews and Muslims or Moors) are included in the seventh part, which contains the laws pertaining to other minorities or communities enjoying special juridical status. *Las Siete Partidas del sabio rey Don Alonso el IX, con las variantes de más interés y con la glosa del Lic Gregorio López,* ed. I. Sanponts y Barba, R. Martí de Eixala, and J. Ferrer y Subirana (Barcelona: Imprenta de Antonio Bergnes, 1844), vol. 4. The English translations are drawn from *Las Siete Partidas,* trans. S. Parsons Scott; ed. Robert Burns, S. J. (Philadelphia: University of Pennsylvania Press, 2001), vol. 5. In quotations from the *Siete Partidas,* the first number corresponds to the Spanish edition, the second to the English. Robert Burns, "Jews and Moors in the *Siete Partidas* of Alfonso X the Learned: A Background Perspective," in *Medieval Spain: Culture, Conflict and Coexistence. Studies in Honour of Angus MacKay,* ed. R. Collins and A. Goodman (Houndmills: Palgrave Macmillan, 2002), 46–62.

6. On the regulation of sexual relations between Jews and Christians, see David Nirenberg, *Communities of Violence* (Princeton: Princeton University Press, 1996), chap. 5; and "Conversion, Sex, and Segregation: Jews and Christians in Medieval Spain," *The American Historical Review* 107 (2002): 1065–1093.

7. *Siete Partidas,* part 7, law 1, 670/1433; law 8, 673/1436; law 9, 674/1436; law 11, 675/1437.

8. There are not many studies of the ritual crime and its significance in Spain. The best, and more recent, is José María Monsalvo Antón, "Los mitos cristianos sobre *crueldades judías* y su huella en el antisemitismo medieval europeo," in *Exclusión, racismo y xenofobia en Europa y América,* ed. Ernesto García Fernández (Bilbao: Universidad del País Vasco, 2002), 13–87. In general, see Miri Rubin, *Gentile Tales: The Narrative Assault on Late Medieval Jews* (New Haven: Yale University Press, 1999).

9. The best study of these riots and pogroms is José María Monsalvo Antón, *Teoría y evolución de un conflicto social* (Madrid: Siglo XXI, 1985).

10. David Nirenberg, "Enmity and Assimilation: Jews, Christians, and Converts in Medieval Spain," *Common Knowledge* 9 (2003): 137–155.

11. On these conflicts see Eloy Benito Ruano, *Los orígenes del problema converso* (Barcelona: Ediciones El Albir, 1976), 41–92. The first of two key texts was the so-called "Sentence-Statute of Pero Sarmiento," implemented in Toledo on June 5, 1449. The other document of interest was the memorandum sent by Marcos García de Mora in support of the Sentence-Statute to the royal and

ecclesiastical authorities, also in 1449; see Eloy Benito Ruano, "El memorial contra los conversos del bachiller Marcos García de Mora," *Sefarad* 17 (1957): 314–351. See also *De la Sentencia Estatuto de Pero Sarmiento a la Instrucción del Relator*, ed. T. González Rolán and P. Suárez-Somonte (Madrid: Aben Ezra Ediciones, 2012).

12. Teófanes Egido, "La defensa de los conversos," in *Dogmatismo e intolerancia*, ed. E. Martínez Ruiz and M. de Pazzis (Madrid: Actas, 1997), 194, 195.

13. Cullen Murphy, *God's Jury. The Inquisition and the Making of the Modern World* (Boston: Houghton Mifflin Harcourt, 2012).

14. There were two decrees of expulsion: the one to be implemented in the crown of Castile was signed by Isabel and Ferdinand; the other, to be implemented in the crown of Aragon, was signed only by Ferdinand. Although there were some variations, both decrees contained the same final decisions. There are hundreds of copies of both decrees available in printed materials and on the web.

15. Ladero Quesada, "El número de judíos en la España de 1492: los que se fueron," in *Judíos, sefarditas, conversos*, 174.

16. David Nirenberg, "Was There Race before Modernity?" in *The Origins of Racism in the West*, ed. Miriam Eliav-Feldon, Benjamin Isaac, and Joseph Ziegler (Cambridge: Cambridge University Press, 2009), 242.

17. Alonso de Cartagena, *Defensorium unitatis christianae*, ed. and trans. G. Verdán Díaz (Oviedo: Universidad de Oviedo, 1992); Juan de Torquemada, *Tratado contra los madianitas e ismaelitas*, ed. C. del Valle (Madrid: Aben Ezra, 2002); Alonso de Oropesa, *Lumen ad revelationen gentium et gloriam plebis Dei Israel, de unitate fidei et concordi et pacífica aequalitate fidelium (Luz para conocimiento de los gentiles)* (1465), ed. L. A. Díaz y Díaz (Madrid: Universidad Pontificia de Salamanca, 1979); Hernando de Talavera, *Católica impugnación*, ed. F. Martín Fernández (Barcelona: Juan Flor Editor, 1961); Fernando del Pulgar, "Letra XIII: para un su amigo de Toledo," in *Los claros varones de España, y las Treinta y dos cartas* (Bruselas, 1632), fols. 61v, 62r, 63v. Pulgar published his *Letras* between 1485 and 1494. On these and other authors, see María Laura Giordano, "La ciudad de nuestra conciencia: Los conversos y la construcción de la identidad judeocristiana (1449–1556)," *Hispania Sacra* 62/125 (2010): 43–91. Elaine Wertheimer, "Converso 'Voices' in Fifteenth- and Sixteenth-Century Spanish Literature," *The Conversos and Moriscos in Late Medieval Spain and Beyond*, ed. K. Ingram (Leiden: Brill, 2009), 97–119. On the profound "royalism" of many converso writers of the period, José M. Nieto Soria, "Las concepciones monárquicas de los intelectuales conversos en la Castilla del siglo XV," *Espacio, Tiempo y Forma, serie III, Historia Medieval* 6 (1993): 229–248.

18. Cartagena, *Defensorium*, 107.

19. Pulgar, "Letra XIII: para un su amigo de Toledo."

20. Cartagena, *Defensorium*, 189.

21. Cartagena, *Defensorium*, 135.

22. Torquemada, *Tratado contra los medianitas*, 260.

23. Juan de Lucena, *Libro de vida beata. Diálogo moral entre don Alonso de Cartagena, obispo de Burgos; don Iñigo López de Mendoza, marqués de Santillana, y Juán de Mena, cordobés*, (1463), in *Opúsculos literarios de los siglos XIV a XVI*, ed. A. Paz y Meliá (Madrid: Sociedad de Bibliófilos Españoles, 1892), 182.

24. María del Pilar Rábade Obradó, "La invención como necesidad: genealogía y judeoconversos," *En la España medieval* 29 (2006): 183–202; Miguel Angel Ladero Quesada, "Coronel, 1492: de la aristocracia judía a la nobleza cristiana en la España de los Reyes Católicos," *Boletín de la Real Academia de la Historia* 201 (2003): 11–24; Marie-Claude Gerbet, *Las noblezas españolas en la edad media: siglos XI–XV* (Madrid: Alianza Editorial, 1997), 327.

25. Fernán Pérez de Guzmán, *Generaciones y semblanzas* (1450?), in *Crónicas de los Reyes de Castilla desde Alfonso el Sabio hasta los católicos don Fernando y Doña Isabel*, ed. C. Rosell (Madrid: Ribadeneyra Editor, 1875–1878), vol. 2, 709.

26. The best study of the period 1540–1700 is Jaime Contreras and Gustav Henningsen, "Forty-four Thousand Cases of the Spanish Inquisition (1540–1700): Analysis of a Historical Data Bank," in *The Inquisition in Early Modern Europe: Studies on Sources and Methods*, ed. Gustav Henningsen (Dekalb: Northern Illinois University Press, 1986), 101–129. On the Toledo case, Jean-Pierre Dedieu, "¿Pecado original o pecado social? Reflexiones en torno a la constitución y a la definición del grupo judeo-converso en Castilla," *Manuscrits* 10 (1992): 67.

27. Antonio Domínguez Ortiz, *La clase social de los conversos en la edad moderna* (Granada: Universidad de Granada, 1991).

28. Linda Martz, "Relations between Conversos and Old Christians in Early Modern Toledo: Some Different Perspectives," in *Christians, Muslims, and Jews in Medieval and Early Modern Spain*, ed. M. Meyerson and E. D. English (Notre Dame: University of Notre Dame Press, 1999), 220–240; and Linda Martz, *A Network of Converso Families in Early Modern Toledo: Assimilating a Minority* (Ann Arbor: University of Michigan Press, 2003).

29. Martín González de Cellorigo, "Alegación en que se funda la justicia y merced que algunos particulares de los reynos de Portugal, que esan dentro y fuera de los confines de España, piden y suplican a la Católica y real Magestad del Rey don Felipe Tercero nuestro señor, les haga y conceda" (1619), published by I. S. Révah in *Revue de Etudes Juives* 122 (1963): 345.

30. Albert Sicroff, *Los estatutos de limpieza de sangre. Controversias entre los siglos XV y XVII*, trans. Mauro Armiño (Madrid: Taurus, 1985); and Juan Hernández Franco, *Sangre limpia, sangre española. El debate sobre los estatutos de limpieza (siglos XV–XVII)* (Madrid: Cátedra, 2011).

31. Michelle Olivari, "Tensiones religiosas hispano-romanas durante el reinado de Felipe III," *Historia, Antropología y Fuentes Orales* 46 (2011), 91-110.

32. Luis de León, *De los nombres de Cristo* (Salamanca: Juan Fernández, 1595), fols. 112r–v. See also Pedro de Ribadeneira, "Al Padre Claudio Aquaviva, Madrid 1597," and "Las razones que se me ofrecen para no hacer novedad en admitir gente en la compañía, Madrid 1593," in Patris Petri de Ribadeneira, *Confessiones, epistolae, aliaque scripta inedita* (Madrid: La Editorial Ibérica, 1923), vol. 2, 189–192, 374–381. Juan de Mariana refers to these issues in the chapter on honors and rewards of his *De regia et regis institutione* and the bad conversos in his *Historia de España* in the chapter on the expulsion of the Jews, which he appears to disapprove. Juan de Mariana, *Historia general de España* (1601) (Madrid: Andrés García de la Iglesia, 1678), vol. 2, bk. 26, 180–182. The debate on the statutes among Jesuits, including the opinions of Ribadeniera, Mariana,

and many others, has been analyzed in Robert A. Maryks, *The Jesuit Order as a Synagogue of Jews* (Leiden: Brill, 2010).

33. Benito de Peñalosa, *Libro de las cinco excelencias del español* (Pamplona: Carlos de Labàyen, 1629), chaps. 14–15, fols. 101r–106v; González de Cellorigo, "Alegación en que se funda la justicia y merced," 325–398; Pedro Fernández de Navarrete, *Conservación de monarquías y discursos políticos* (1626), ed. Michael D. Gordon (Madrid: Instituto de Estudios Fiscales, 1982), 68, 69–70. On Olivares's policies designed to limit the effect of purity of blood statutes, see *Memoriales y cartas del Conde duque de Olivares*, ed. J. H. Elliot y J. F. de la Peña (Madrid: Alfaguara, 1978–1980), vol. 1, 72–74, 85; vol. 2, 97, 148, 260. Above all, see J. I. Gutiérrez Nieto, "El reformismo social de Olivares: el problema de la limpieza de sangre y la creación de una nobleza de mérito," in *La España del Conde Duque de Olivares*, ed. J. H. Elliott y A. García Sanz (Valladolid: Universidad de Valladolid, 1990), 417–441.

34. Fray Agustín Salucio, *Discurso sobre los estatutos de limpieza de sangre* (1599), ed A. Pérez Gómez (Murcia: Cieza, 1975), fos. 9v, 3r-v, and 4v. Salucio's text, or at least some of its aspects, has been analyzed on many occasions. One recent study is Vincent Parello, "Entre honra y deshonra: El *Discurso* de Fray Agustín Salucio acerca de los estatutos de limpieza de sangre (1599)," *Criticón* 80 (2000): 139–153.

35. Pedro de Valencia, "Tratado acerca de los moriscos de España" (1605), in Pedro de Valencia, *Obras completas, IV: Escritos sociales, escritos políticos*, ed. R. González and H. B. Riesco (León: Universidad de León, 1994), 124, 126.

36. According to an email from Yosef Kaplan, by 1675 there were aproximately 15,000 former Iberian conversos living in several European cities.

37. It is obviously very difficult to know how many conversos lived in the Iberian Peninsula in this period; Juan Hernández Franco and Raimundo A. Rodríguez Pérez ("La limpieza de sangre en las ciudades hispánicas durante la Edad Moderna," *Revista de historiografía* 16 (2012): 75) believe there were 300,000 at the beginning of the sixteenth century.

38. Martín González de Cellorigo, "Memorial sobre los moriscos," in *Memorial de la política necesaria y útil restauración a la república de España, y estados de ella, y del desempeño universal de estos reynos* (Valladolid: Juan de Bostillo, 1600), 6r.

39. There were dozens even hundreds of conversos who gained access to public offices by forging their genealogical histories. Enrique Soria Mesa in *La realidad tras el espejo. Ascenso social y limpieza de sangre en la España de Felipe II* (Valladolid: Universidad de Valladolid, 2016), and "Los estatutos municipales de limpieza de sangre en la Castilla moderna. Una revisión crítica," *Mediterranea*, 27 (2013): 9-36.

40. On this point one is tempted to invoke the words of Eric Hobsbawm, who wrote in reference to modern North America that it was "pointless to look for consciously Jewish elements in the songs of Irving Berlin or the Hollywood movies of the era of the great studios, all of which were run by immigrant Jews: their object, in which they succeeded, was precisely to make songs or films which found a specific expression for 100 per cent Americanness." Eric Hobsbawm, *Interesting Times: A Twentieth-Century Life* (London: Abacus, 2003), 110–11.

41. Nicolás Antonio, *Biblioteca Hispana Nueva* (1672), ed. and Spanish trans. F. Pérez Bayer (1788), fac. ed. (Madrid: Fundación Universitaria Española, 1999), vol. 1, iii.

42. Studies on this topic have proliferated in the past few years. See the contributions in *Las dos grandes minorías étnico-religiosas en la literatura española del siglo de oro: los judeoconversos y los moriscos,* ed. Irene Andrés-Suarez (Paris: Annales littéraires de l'Université de Besançon, 1995); and *Judíos en la literatura española,* ed. I. M. Hassán and R. Izquierdo Benito (Cuenca: Ediciones de la Universidad de Castilla-La Mancha, 1999); and Paloma Díaz-Mas, "La visión del otro en la literatura oral: judíos y musulmanes en el romancero hispánico," *Studi Ispanici* 32 (2007): 9–36.

43. Antonio López de Vega, *Paradojas racionales. En forma de diálogo entre un filósofo y un cortesano* (1654), ed. Máximo Higuera (Madrid: Trifaldi, 2005); Juan de Zabaleta, "El linajudo," in *Obras históricas, políticas, filosóficas y morales de Don Juan de Zabaleta* (Madrid, 1728), 264. Zabaleta's work containing this chapter, *El día de fiesta por la mañana,* appeared in 1654 and was, along with the second part titled *Día de fiesta por la tarde,* one of the genuine best sellers of the seventeenth and eighteenth centuries.

44. Prudencio de Sandoval, *Historia de la vida y hechos del Emperador Carlos V* (Pamplona: Bartolomé París, 1614), Second Part, bk. 29 fol. 635, cit. Hering Torres, "La limpieza de sangre. Problemas de interpretación," *Tiempos Modernos,* 9 (2003-2004): 43.

45. Francisco de Quevedo, *Execración contra los judíos,* ed. F. Cabo and S. Fernández (Barcelona: Crítica, 1996), 23, 14. The best modern biography of the author is Pablo Jauralde Pou, *Francisco de Quevedo (1580–1645)* (Madrid: Castalia, 1998).

46. Fray Francisco de Torrejoncillo, *Centinela contra judíos puesta en la torre de la Iglesia de Dios* (Madrid, 1673). In this chapter I refer to the Pamplona edition of 1691, Francisco de Torrejoncillo, *Centinela contra judíos puesta en la torre de la Iglesia de Dios* (Pamplona: Juan Mico, 1691), although I have consulted other editions. The book was originally published in Madrid in 1673, and it proved to be very popular, with at least twelve editions between 1673 and 1745 (Madrid 1673, 1674, 1676, 1679, 1728, 1736; Pamplona 1691, 1718, 1720; Barcelona 1731; Lisbon 1684; Porto 1745). On this book, François Soyer, *Popularizing Anti-Semitism in Early Modern Spain and Its Empire* (Leiden: Brill, 2014).

47. A good summary in English of the history of Muslims Spain is Hugh Kennedy, *Muslim Spain and Portugal* (London: Longman, 1996). However, the best studies are Eduardo Manzano Moreno, *Conquistadores, emires y califas: los Omeyas y la formación de al-Andalus* (Barcelona: Crítica, 2006); and Moreno, *Historia de España,* chaps. 3–5.

48. The best study of Muslim Granada is still Rachel Arié, *El reino Nasrí de Granada* (Madrid: Mapfre, 1992) (original French edition 1973).

49. José Ramón Hinojosa Montalvo, *Los mudéjares: la voz del Islam en la España cristiana* (Teruel: Centro de Estudios Mudéjares, 2002), vol. 1; David Nirenberg, "Varieties of Mudejar Experience: Muslims in Christian Iberia, 100–1526," in *The Medieval World,* ed. P. Linehan and J. Nelson (London: Routledge, 2011), 60–76.

50. The great Arab historian Ibn Khaldun (1332–1406) had already called attention to the integration and cultural "Christianization" of the Castilian Mudéjares. Khaldun, *The Muqaddimah*, trans. Franz Rosenthal; ed. N. J. Dawood (Princeton: Princeton University Press, 1969), 116.

51. Brian Catlos, *The Victors and the Vanquished: Christians and Muslims of Catalonia and Aragon, 1050–1300* (Cambridge: Cambridge University Press, 2004).

52. Mark D. Meyerson, *The Muslims of Valencia in the Age of Fernando and Isabel: Between Coexistence and Crusade* (Berkeley: University of California Press, 1991).

53. There are many studies on the relations between Christians, Muslims, and Jews in medieval Spain, sometimes drawing contrasting conclusions. Two examples of this scholarship are Jerrilyn D. Dodds, María Rosa Menocal, and Abigail Krasner Balbale, *The Arts of Intimacy: Christians, Jews, and Muslims in the Making of Castilian Culture* (New Haven: Yale University Press, 2008); and Nirenberg, *Communities of Violence*.

54. *Siete Partidas*, 675/1438.

55. On the question of sex, violence, and relations between Christians, Muslims, and Jews in medieval Spain, see Nirenberg, *Communities of Violence*, chap. 5.

56. Ana Echevarría, *The Fortress of Faith* ((Leiden: Brill, 1999), 103.

57. Juan de Mariana, *Historia general de España* (1601), vol. 2, bk. 25, chap. 18, 177–179.

58. Miguel Garrido Atienza, *Capitulaciones para la entrega de Granada* (Granada. Paulino Ventura, 1910), 257–295.

59. Francisco J. Simonet, *Glosario de voces ibéricas y latinas usadas entre los mozárabes* (Madrid: Real Academia de la Historia, 1888), 353.

60. Bernard Vincent, "Ser morisco en España en el siglo XVI," *El saber en Al-Andalus*, ed. J. Ma Carabaza Bravo and Al. Tawfik Mohamed Essawy (Sevilla: Universidad de Sevilla, 1999), vol. 2, 301–307.

61. Serafín de Tapia Sánchez, "Los moriscos de Castilla la Vieja, ¿Una identidad en proceso de disolución?" *Sharq al-Andalus* 12 (1995): 179–195; Serafín de Tapia Sánchez, *La comunidad morisca de Avila* (Salamanca: Universidad de Salamanca, 1991); James B. Tueller, *Good and Faithful Christians: Moriscos and Catholicism in Early Modern Spain* (New Orleans: University Press of the South, 2002); Trevor Dadson, *Los moriscos de Villarrubia de los Ojos (siglos XV–XVII)* (Madrid: Iberoamericana-Vervuet, 2007).

62. On the Moriscos of Valencia, Tulio Halpherin Donghi, *Un conflicto nacional: moriscos y cristianos viejos en Valencia* (Valencia: Institución Alfonso el Magnánimo, 1980); Rafael Benítez Sánchez-Blanco, *Heroicas decisiones: la monarquía católica y los moriscos valencianos* (Valencia: Institució Alfons el Magnánim, 2001). A typical depiction of the Valencian Moriscos is given in Miguel de Cervantes, *Los trabajos de Persiles y Sigismunda*, ed. J. B. Avalle-Arce (Madrid: Castalia, 2005), bk. 3, chaps. 10–13.

63. The Moriscos have also been the subject of lively and important historiographical debates. Three examples of these debates should suffice: Alvaro Galmés de Fuentes, *Los moriscos (desde su misma orilla)* (Madrid: Publicaciones

del Instituto Egipcio de Estudios Islámicos, 1993); Bernard Vincent, *El río morisco* (Valencia: Universidades de Valencia, Granada y Zaragoza, 2006); and Francisco Márquez Villanueva, *El problema morisco (desde las otras laderas)* (Madrid: Ediciones Libertarias, 1998). Mercedes García-Arenal has produced undoubtedly the most subtle and cogent analyses of the Morisco minority and minorities in early modern Spain in general. From among her numerous works one might select "De judíos y moros a 'cristianos nuevos,'" prologue to James Amelang, *Historias paralelas. Judeoconversos y moriscos en la España moderna* (Madrid: Akal, 2012), 5–21; and "Religious Dissent and Minorities: The Morisco Age," *Journal of Modern History* 81 (2009): 888–920. Mercedes García-Arenal and Fernando Rodríguez Mediano, *Un Oriente español. Los moriscos y el Sacromonte en tiempos de Contrarreforma* (Madrid: Marcial Pons Historia, 2010), published in English edition in 2013, is one of the best works on the history of Spain published in the past several years. The best general survey is still Antonio Domínguez Ortíz and Bernard Vincent, *Historia de los moriscos: vida y tragedia de una minoría* (Madrid: Revista de Occidente, 1978). As in the case of the Judeo-conversos, the best historiographical study of the Moriscos is Amelang, *Historias paralelas*, 35–85.

64. Valencia, "Tratado acerca de los moriscos de España," 80. Also Marcos de Guadalajara y Javier, *Memorable expulsión y justísimo destierro de los moriscos de España* (Pamplona: Nicolas de Assiayn, 1613), second part, chap. 27, fol. 154v, where he also claims that Hagar was a "gypsy," that is to say Egyptian.

65. Julián del Castillo, *Historia de los reyes godos que vinieron de Scythia de Europa contra el imperio romano y a España. Con sucesión de ellos hasta los católicos reyes don Fernando y doña Isabel* (1582) (Madrid: Luis Sánchez, 1624), 4.

66. Valencia, "Tratado acerca de los moriscos de España," 81.

67. Cit. Luce López-Baralt, "La estética del cuerpo entre los moriscos del siglo XVI o de cómo la minoría perseguida pierde su rostro," in *Le corps dans la société espagnole des XVIe et XVIIe siècles*, ed. A. Redondo (Paris: Publications de la Sorbonne, 1990), 336.

68. Jerónimo Cortés, *Phisionomía y varios secretos de naturaleza* (1587) (Tarragona: Felipe Roberto, 1609), fol. 1r. The 1680 edition introduces an interesting variation, although it is probably nothing more than a typographical error: "The good color, or tan, indicates a good complexion" ("El color bueno, o moreno, dize buena complexión" (Madrid: Marcos del Ribero, 1680), fol. 1r. Cortés's book is in fact a Spanish translation of Michael Scot, *Liber physiognomie*, originally published in Venice, 1477. Martin Porter, *Windows of the Soul: Physiognomy in European Culture, 1470–1780* (Oxford: Clarendon Press, 2005), 97.

69. Bernard Vincent, "Cuál era el aspecto físico de los moriscos?" in Bernard Vincent, *Andalucía en la Edad Moderna, Economía y Sociedad* (Granada: Diputación de Granada, 1985), 303–313.

70. The real author of Diego de Haedo's *Topografía e historia general de Argel*, was in reality Antonio de Sosa, *Topographia e historia general de Argel: repartida en cinco tratados do se veran casos estraños* (Valladolid: Diego Fernández de Córdoba, 1612), 9. There is now an English edition of this important work, *An Early Modern Dialogue with Islam: Antonio de Sosa's Topography of Algiers* (1612), ed. María Antonia Garcés, trans. Diana de Armas Wilson (Notre Dame, IN:

University of Notre Dame Press, 2011). Other Europeans were in the habit of describing the Moors and Moriscos as "blacks." Cesar Oudin, *Tresor des deux langues Françoise et Espagnole* (Paris, 1607), "Moro—more, negre; Morisco—more fait Chretien." John Minsheu, *A Dictionarie in Spanish and English* (London, 1599), "Morisco—a black Moor become or turned Christian; Negro—black, also a black Moor of Ethiopia."

71. Antonio Domínguez Ortiz, "Profesiones y niveles de vida de los moriscos," in *La esclavitud en Castilla en la edad moderna y otros estudios de marginados* (Granada: Editorial Comares, 2003), 65–86; Luis F. Bernabé Pons, "On Morisco Networks and Collectives," in *The Conversos and Moriscos in Late Medieval Spain and Beyond,* 121–134; William Childers, "An Extensive Network of Morisco Merchants Active circa 1590," in *The Conversos and Moriscos in Late Medieval Spain and Beyond,* 135–160.

72. Valeriano Sánchez Ramos, "Un rey para los moriscos: el infante don Juan de Granada," *Sharq al-Andalus* 14–15 (1997–1998): 285–315.

73. M. C. Álvarez Márquez y J. A. García Luján, "Las lecturas de don Pedro de Granada Venegas, I marqués de Campotéjar (1559–1643)," *Historia, Instituciones y Documentos* 35 (2008): 149–189.

74. Enrique Soria Mesa, *La nobleza en la España moderna. Cambio y continuidad* (Madrid: Marcial Pons Historia, 2007), 97. On the Morisco elite, see Enrique Soria Mesa, "Una gran familia: las élites moriscas del reino de Granada," *Estudis* 35 (2009): 13–22; Enrique Soria Mesa, "Una versión genealógica del ansia integradora de la élite morisca: el origen de la casa de Granada," *Sharq Al-Andalus* 12 (1995): 213–221. See also Antonio Agustín, *Diálogos de las armas y linajes de la nobleza de España,* ed. G. Mayans y Siscar (Madrid: Juan de Zúñiga, 1734), Dialogue 6, 91–92, on the existence of a noble class among the Moriscos.

75. "Parecer de Francisco Suárez, Valladolid 28 August 1603," included in J. A. de Aldana, "Un parecer de Suárez sobre un estatuto de la Orden Militar de Alcántara," *Archivo Teológico Granadino,* 11 (1948): 271–285; Suárez's written opinion on 276–285.

76. Sebastian de Covarrubias, *Tesoro de la lengua castellana o española* (1611), ed. I. Arellano y R. Zafra (Madrid: Universidad de Navarra/Iberoamericana, 2006), 1140.

77. Youssef El Aloui, *Jésuites, morisques et indiens. Etude comparative des méthodes d'évangélisation de la Compagnie de Jésus d'après les traités de José de Acosta (1588) et d'Ignacio de las Casas (1605–1607)* (Paris: Honoré Champion Editeur, 2006). Many of the most prominent Moriscos have been analyzed in García-Arenal and Rodríguez Mediano, *Un Oriente español.*

78. Salucio, *Discurso sobre los estatutos de limpieza de sangre,* fol. 22v. Miguel de Cervantes, *Coloquio de los perros,* in Miguel de Cervantes, *Novelas exemplares* (Sevilla: Francisco de Liria, 1641), 325r–326r.

79. Javier Castillo Fernandez, "La asimilación de los moriscos granadinos: un modelo de análisis," in *Disidencias y exilios en la España moderna,* ed. A. Mestre Sanchís et al. (Alicante: Universidad de Alicante, 1997), 359.

80. Rafael Carrasco and Bernard Vincent, "Amor y matrimonio entre los moriscos," in Bernard Vincent, *Minorías y marginados en la España del siglo XVI* (Granada: Diputación Provincial de Granada, 1967), 63–65.

81. Salucio, *Discurso sobre los estatutos de limpieza de sangre,* fol. 25r; Valencia, "Tratado acerca de los moriscos," 84–86.

82. Chapters 10–13 in the third book of Miguel de Cervantes, *Los trabajos de Persiles y Sigismunda,* describe the Moriscos as accomplices of North African pirates. On the Moriscos and pirate attacks along the Spanish coastline, and the broader subject of Spanish captives in North Africa, there is a growing number of works. Two of the best are also two of the most recent: José Martínez Torres, *Prisioneros de los infieles: vida y rescate de los cautivos cristianos en el Mediterráneo musulmán (siglos XVI–XVII)* (Barcelona: Ediciones Bellatera, 2004); and Daniel B. Herhsenzon, *Early Modern Spain and the Creation of the Mediterranean: Captivity, Commerce, and Knowledge* (Ph.D. dissertation, University of Michigan, 2011).

83. Valencia, "Tratado acerca de los moriscos," 81. Baltasar Álamos de Barrientos, *Discurso político al rey Felipe III al comienzo de su reinado* (1599), ed. M. Santos (Barcelona: Anthropos, 1990), 50.

84. George M. Fredickson, *Racism: A Short History* (Princeton: Princeton University Press, 2002), 33–34.

85. Renée Levine Melammed, "Judeo-conversas and Moriscas in Sixteenth-Century Spain: A Study of parallels," *Jewish History* 24 (2010): 155–168.

86. Mercedes García-Arenal, *Inquisición y moriscos: los procesos del Tribunal de Cuenca* (Madrid: Siglo XXI, 1978), 84.

87. Luis Mármol de Carvajal, *Historia de la rebelión y castigo de los moriscos del reino de Granada* (Málaga: Juan Rene, 1600), bk. 2, chap. 7, fol. 37r.

88. "Memorial de Francisco Núñez Muley," ed. R. Foulche-Delbosc, *Revue Hispanique* 6 (1899): 205–239. There is an English edition, Francisco Núñez Muley, *A Memorandum for the President of the Royal Audiencia and Chancery Court of the City and Kingdom of Granada,* ed. V. Barletta (Chicago: University of Chicago Press, 2007).

89. Manuel Barrios Aguilera, *Granada morisca, la convivencia negada,* (Albolote: Comares, 2002), chaps. 12–14; Domínguez Ortiz and Vincent, *Historia de los moriscos,* chap. 3; Valeriano Sánchez Ramos, "La Guerra de las Alpujarras (1568–1570)," in *Historia de Granada* (Granada: Universidad de Granada, 2000), ed. Manuel Barrios Aguilera and Rafael Gerardo Peinado, vol. 2, 507–542.

90. Aurelia Martín Casares, *La esclavitud en la Granada del siglo XVI: género, raza y religión* (Granada: Universidad de Granada, 2000), 91–97; Santiago Otero Mondéjar, "Moro herrado, moro esclavo. Nuevas perspectivas de la esclavitud morisca en el reino de Córdoba (1570–1609)," *Ámbitos* 22 (2009): 65–75.

91. Valeriano Sánchez Ramos, "Los moriscos que ganaron la guerra," in *Melanges Louis Cardaillac,* ed. A. Temimi (Zaghouan: FTERSI, 1995), vol. 2, 613–627; Sánchez Ramos, "La Guerra de las Alpujarras (1568–1570)"; Tapia Sánchez, "Los moriscos de Castilla la Vieja, ¿Una identidad en proceso de disolución?"; Tapia Sánchez, *La comunidad morisca de Ávila;* Dadson, *Los moriscos de Villarrubia de los Ojos (siglos XV–XVII);* Trevor Dadson, "Inquisitorial Activity and the Moriscos of Villarubia de los Ojos during the Sixteenth Century," in *The Conversos and Moriscos in Late Medieval Spain and Beyond. Volume Two: The Morisco Issue,* ed. Kevin Ingram (Leiden: Brill, 2010), 51-74.

92. "Memorial de Torrijos al rey sobre los inconvenientes de recompensar a los moriscos que fueron leales en la rebelión de Granada," January 31, 1580, in Javier Castillo Fernández, "El sacerdote morisco Francisco de Torrijos: un testigo de excepción en la Rebelión de las Alpujarras," *Chronica Nova* 23 (1996): 491.

93. In the words of the historians García-Arenal and Rodríguez Mediano, what the Moriscos who were behind these falsifications intended was to "construct an alternative history of the society in which they lived—a history traced from its sacred, Christian origins—that would allow for the inclusion of groups destined to remain on the margins: the Christians of Islamic and Jewish origin." García-Arenal and Rodríguez Mediano, *Un Oriente español,* 191–192.

94. *Los plomos del Sacromonte: invención y tesoro*, ed. M. Barrios Aguilera and M. García-Arenal (Valencia: Universitat de València, 2006).

95. Valencia, "Discurso sobre el pergamino y laminas de Granada," in Valencia, *Obras completas*, vol. 4, 427–455; García-Arenal and Rodríguez Mediano, *Un Oriente español,* 32, 39–40; Rafael Benítez Sánchez-Blanco, "El Discurso del licenciado Gonzalo de Valcárcel sobre las reliquias del Sacromonte," *Estudis* 28 (2002): 137–165. On Castillo and Luna, García-Arenal and Rodríguez Mediano, *Un Oriente español,* chaps. 4, 6.

96. Katie Harris, *From Muslim to Christian Granada: Inventing City's Past in Early Modern Spain* (Baltimore: The Johns Hopkins University Press, 2007).

97. Gregorio López Madera, *Excelencias de la Monarquía y Reino de España* (1597), ed J. L. Bermejo Cabrero (Madrid: Centro de Estudios Políticos y Constitucionales, 1999), 165. On the debates related to Castilian in this context, Kathryn A. Woolard, "Bernardo de Aldrete and the Morisco Problem: A Study in Early Modern Spanish Language Ideology," *Comparative Studies in Society and History* 44 (2002): 446–480.

98. On Román de la Higuera, García-Arenal and Rodríguez Mediano, *Un Oriente español,* chap. 7.; and Katrina Olds, *Forging the Past: Invented Histories in Counter-Reformation Spain* (New Haven: Yale University Press, 2015).

99. Miguel de Luna, *La verdadera historia del rey Don Rodrigo*, ed. L. F. Bernabé Pons (Granada: Universidad de Granada, 2001). The work was published in two parts, the first in 1592 and the second in 1600. From this point on the two parts were published in a single volume, which appeared in numerous Spanish editions and was translated into many languages. The work was published in Castilian in Granada: 1600; Zaragoza: 1603, 1606; Valencia: 1606, 1646; Madrid: 1654, 1676. In French: 1671, 1680, 1687, 1699, 1702, 1708, 1721. In English: 1627, 187, 1693. Luna presented this work not as an original study but as a translation of a thirteenth-century chronicle that he had rediscovered—although once again we know this to have been an invention.

100. This reunification was Luna's ultimate aim but also that of the authors of the numerous prophecies that circulated among Moriscos that foretold the "reconquest" of Al-Andalus or Spain by the followers of Mohammad. Luce López-Baralt, "Las profecías moriscas: entre la combatividad política y las lágrimas," en ibid. *La literatura secreta de los últimos musulmanes de España* (Madrid: Editorial Trotta, 2009), 181-235; Reem F. Iversen, *Prophecy and Politics: Moriscos and Christians in Sixteenth- and Seventeenth-Century Spain* (Ph.D. dissertation,

Princeton University, 2002; Marya T. Green-Mercado, *Morisco Apocalypticism: Politics of Prophecy in the Early Modern Mediterranean*) Ph.D. dissertation, University of Chicago, 2012.

101. Luna, *La verdadera historia del rey Don Rodrigo*, 71.

102. Salucio, *Discurso sobre los estatutos*, fols. 4–5. Other authors, probably in response to histories such as Luna's, claimed that this biological mixing had been forced rather than voluntary, part of the suffering inflicted on the native population by the invaders; Castillo, *Historia de los reyes godos*, fol. 122.

103. Valencia, "Tratado acerca de los moriscos de España."

104. On the political context that precipitated the expulsion of the Moriscos, Antonio Feros, *Kingship and Favoritism in the Spain of Philip III, 1598–1621* (Cambridge: Cambridge University Press, 2000), chap. 9; Antonio Feros, "Rhetoric of Expulsion," in *Expulsion of the Moriscos from Spain: A Mediterranean Diaspora*, ed. Mercedes García-Arenal and Gerard Wiegers (Leiden: Brill, 2014), 60–101; and Carlos Garriga, "Enemigos domésticos. La expulsión católica de los moriscos (1609–1614)," *Quaderni Fiorentini* 38 (2009): 225–287.

105. "Orden de Juan de Mendoza, marqués de San Germán," Sevilla 12 de enero de 1610; this is a printed copy found at Biblioteca Nacional de España Ms. 11773, fols. 623r–v.

106. Dadson, *Los moriscos de Villarubia de los ojos*, 777–798; Enrique Soria Mesa, *Los últimos moriscos. Pervivencias de la población de origen islámico en el reino de Granada (siglos XVII-XVIII)* (Valencia: Universitat de Valéncia, 2014); James B. Tueller, "Los moriscos que se quedaron o que regresaron," *Los Moriscos. La expulsión y después*, ed. M. García-Arenal and G. Wiegers (Valencia: Universidad de Valencia, 2012), 191–209.

107. See, for example, Pedro Fernández de Castro, *El buho gallego con las demás aves de España haciendo Cortes* (1620s), ed. J. M. Álvarez Blázquez (Vigo: Ediciones Monterrey, 1951), where Andalusia is represented by an Arab "turkey" and the land described as still marked by the Arab presence and the deficient Catholicism of the natives who may well be descended from Arabs.

108. A search through the *Combined Catalogue of Spanish Bibliographic Patrimony* (Catálogo Colectivo del Patrimonio Bibliográfico Español) revealed that the number of publications specifically on the Moriscos was fairly significant between 1571 and 1620 (111 titles), only to dwindle to virtually nothing after this date, with only twenty-three titles between 1621 and 1700. The relative absence of Moriscos from fictional literature has already been pointed out by Miguel Herrero García, *Ideas de los españoles del siglo XVII* (Madrid: Editora Voluntad, 1928), 575. There were nevertheless scholars in Spain who still believed it was essential to learn Arabic and to become familiar with Arab culture as one of the most ancient. Daniel Hershenzon, "Traveling Libraries: The Arabic Manuscripts of Muley Zidan and the Escorial Library," *Journal of Early Modern History* 18 (2014): 535–558.

4
The Others Without

1. Serge Gruzinski, *The Mestizo Mind*, trans. D. Dusinberre (New York: Routledge, 2002), 63.

2. This definition of *subaltern* is taken from the *Diccionario de la lengua castellana*, also known as *Diccionario de Autoridades* (Madrid: Imprenta de la Real Academia Española, 1739), vol. 6, 166. This meaning of the term *subaltern* was known from the early seventeenth century through bilingual dictionaries.

3. George M. Fredickson, *Racism: A Short History* (Princeton: Princeton University Press, 2002), 39.

4. Gary B. Nash, "The Hidden History of Mestizo America," in *Sex, Love, Race: Crossing Boundaries in North American History*, ed. Martha Hodes (New York: New York University Press, 1999), 17.

5. James Sweet, "The Iberian Roots of American Racist Thought," *The William and Mary Quarterly* 54 (1997): 143–166; and Jorge Cañizares-Esguerra, "New World, New Stars: Patriotic Astrology and the Invention of Indian and Creole Bodies in Colonial Spanish America, 1600–1650," *The American Historical Review* 104 (1999): 33–68.

6. Cañizares-Esguerra, "New World, New Stars," 35.

7. Anthony Pagden, *The Burdens of Empire: 1539 to the Present* (Cambridge: Cambridge University Press, 2015), 98.

8. Francisco López de Gómara, *Primera y segunda parte de la historia general de las Indias* (Medina del Campo: Guillermo de Millis, 1553), n.p. The first edition appeared in 1552. This Medina del Campo edition features the emperor's shield on its frontispiece, surmounted by a motto indicative of the book's contents: *Hispania Victrix* ("Spain victorous").

9. *Os Lusiadas*, first published in 1572. Published in Castilian many times, for example, in 1639 as *Luisadas escritas*, as the cover indicates, by Luis de Camoens, "the Prince of Spanish Poets." Luis de Camoens, *Lusiadas* (Madrid, 1639), 2 vols.

10. Juan de Mariana, *Historia general de España* (1601) (Madrid: Andrés García de la Iglesia, 1678), vol. 2, bk. 26, chap. 3, 183.

11. Serge Gruzinski, *Les quatre parties du monde: histoire d'une mondialisation* (Paris: Martinière, 2004).

12. Louis Le Roy, *De la vicissitude ou variété des choses en l'universe* (1577), cit. Klauss A. Vogel and Alisha Rankin, "Cosmography," in *Cambridge History of Early Modern Science*, ed. K. Park and L. Daston (Cambridge: Cambridge University Press, 2003), 495.

13. Paulo Ferrer a Juan de Mariana, 1599?, cit. Enrique García Hernán, "Construcción de las historias de España en los siglos XVI y XVII," *La construcción de las historias de España*, ed. R. García Cárcel (Madrid: Marcial Pons Historia, 2004), 139; Bernardo de Vargas Machuca, *Milicia y descripción de las Indias* (1599), ed. M. Cuesta and F. López-Rios (Valladolid: Universidad de Valladolid, 2003), 67.

14. An English translation of *Inter caetera* in *European Treaties Bearing on the History of the United States and Its Dependencies to 1648*, ed. F. G. Davenport (Washington, DC: Carnegie Institution of Washington, 1917), 75–78.

15. Columbus to Santángel, February 15, 1493, in Francisco Morales Padrón, *Primeras cartas sobre América (1493–1503)* (Sevilla: Universidad de Sevilla, 1990), 78–79; David Abulafia, *The Discovery of Mankind. Atlantic Encounters in the Age of Columbus* (New Haven: Yale University Press, 2009). Columbus's conflictive relations with the island natives and other colonists have been analyzed in Isabel Aguirre and Consuelo Varela, *La caída de Cristóbal Colón: el juicio de Bobadilla* (Madrid: Marcial Pons Historia, 2006).

16. The first sentence comes from the Benedictine friar Benito de Peñalosa y Mondragón, summarizing in the 1620s the debates about the Americans, *Libro de las cinco excelencias del español que despueblan a España para su mejor potencia y dilación* (Pamplona: Carlos de Labayen, 1629), fol. 35r. Aristotle, *La philosophía moral de Aristóteles, éthicas, políticas y económicas* (Zaragoza: George Coci Aleman, 1509), bk. 1, chap. 3, n.p.; this is a translation of the Tuscan edition by Pedro Aretino, by a translator whose name is not given. Aristotle, *Los ocho libros de república del Filósofo Aristóteles*, trans. P. Simón Abril (Zaragoza: Lorenzo y Diego de Robles, 1584), bk. 1, chap. 3, 13v

17. López de Gómara, *Primera y segunda parte de la historia general de las Indias*, fol. 118v. The wholesale enslavement of the American natives remained legal from 1493 to 1542. After that date, the crown only permitted the enslavement of the so-called "indios rebeldes" (rebellious Indians), at least until 1679, when this exception was rescinded, and the so-called "indios barbaros" (barbarian Indians) until the end of the colonial period, in the early nineteenth century. Manuel Lucena Salmoral, *Leyes para esclavos. El ordenamiento jurídico sobre la condición, tratamiento, defensa y represión de los esclavos en las colonias de la América española* (Madrid: Fundación Histórica Tavera, 2000), 46–129.

18. These debates, their many protagonists, the various phases, and the variety or arguments used have been analyzed in countless works, and the passages dedicated to these debates here have been inspired by this substantial body of scholarship. Anthony Pagden, *The Fall of Natural Man* (Cambridge: Cambridge University Press, 1982); Rolena Adorno, *The Polemics of Possession in Spanish American Narrative* (New Haven: Yale University Press, 2007); and David Brading, *The First America* (Cambridge: Cambridge University Press, 1993), chaps. 2–4.

19. Noble D. Cook, *Born to Die: Disease and New World Conquest, 1492–1650* (Cambridge: Cambridge University Press, 1998). It has never been demonstrated that the Spanish conquerors and explorers planned or implemented deliberate campaigns of extermination, but their combined actions still mean that the Spanish conquest of the Americas was one of the most violent and cruel in the history of humanity, a veritable genocide, even though it may have been "unpremeditated": Gruzinski, *The Mestizo Mind*, 43. See also Tzvetan Todorov, *The Conquest of America* (New York: Harper and Row, 1984). There are innumerable testimonies of the horrors of the conquest, from a wide variety of sources, but it was the Dominican friar Bartolomé de las Casas who provided the first systematic account, albeit probably replete with inaccuracies and overestimations, of the many outrageous crimes committed by Spaniards in each of the hitherto conquered regions. Bartolomé de las Casas, *Brevísima relación de la destrucción de las Indias* (n.p., 1552).

20. Pagden, *The Fall of Natural Man*, 9.

21. Francisco de Vitoria, "On the American Indians" (1537–39), in Francisco de Vitoria, *Political Writings*, ed. A. Pagden and J. Lawrance (Cambridge: Cambridge University Press, 1991), 250–251.

22. Three of the so-called letters of relation sent by Cortés to Charles I were published in his lifetime—the second and the third in Seville (1522 and 1523), the fourth in Toledo (1525). The second letter was translated into Latin and published in Nuremberg in 1524. Cortés's letters of relation, or at least much of the information and many of the personal judgments they contained, were incorporated into and shaped later histories published in Spain and other European countries. Hernán Cortés, *Cartas de relación*, ed. A. Delgado (Madrid: Castalia, 1993); Hernán Cortés, *Letters from Mexico*, ed. A. Pagden (New Haven: Yale University Press, 1986).

23. "Instrucciones a Hernán Cortés, 26 junio 1523," in Jesús Bustamante García, "El conocimiento como necesidad de estado: las encuestas oficiales sobre Nueva España durante el reinado de Carlos V," *Revista de Indias* 60 (2000): 35.

24. Pagden, *The Fall of Natural Man*, chaps. 5 and 6; Brading, *The First America* , chap. 4.

25. Philip II's royal order, signed in 1573, was included in its entirety in the *Recopilación de las Leyes de Indias*, bk. 4. For a summary of these ordinances, see Marta Milagros del Vas Mingo, "Las Ordenanzas de 1573, sus antecedentes y consecuencias," *Quinto Centenario* 8 (1985): 83–101.

26. *Los Indios y las ciudades en Nueva España*, ed. Felipe Castro Gutiérrez (México: UAM, 2010).

27. Juan de Solórzano Pereira, *Política Indiana* (Madrid: Diego Díaz de la Carrera, 1647), bk. 2, chap. 1, 66. R. Jovita Baber, "Categories, Self-Representation and the Construction of the *Indios*," *Journal of Spanish Cultural Studies* 10 (2009): 27–41.

28. Jesús Bustamante García, "Nueva Roma: el señorío indígena novohispano y su asimilación política," in *Carlos V y la quiebra del humanism politico en Europa*, ed. J. Martínez (Madrid: Sociedad Estatal para las Conmemoraciones, 2001), vol. 4, 15–28; Sonia Fernández Rueda, "Educación y evangelización: el colegio franciscano de caciques San Andrés (siglo XVI)," in *Passeurs, mediadores culturales y agentes de la primera globalización en el Mundo Ibérico, siglos XVI–XIX*, ed. S. O'Phelan and C. Salazar (Lima: Pontificia Universidad Católica del Perú, 2005), 129–144.

29. Juan Zapata y Sandoval, *De iustitia distributiva et acceptione personarum ei opposita disceptatio* (1609), ed. C. Baciero et al (Madrid: CSIC, 2004), 261–263.

30. Serge Gruzinski and Nathan Wachtel, "Cultural Interbreedings: Constituting the Majority as a Minority," *Comparative Studies in Society and History* 39 (1997): 234. See Real Cédula, March 26, 1697, in Richard Konetzke, *Colección de documentos para la historia de la formación social de Hispanoamérica, 1493–1810* (Madrid: Consejo Superior de Investigaciones Científicas, 1962), vol. 3, 65–66.

31. This generalized opposition to being ruled by natives was common in the Spanish and Portuguese empires. Charles Boxer, *The Portuguese Seaborne Empire, 1415–1825* (New York: A. A. Knopf, 1969), chap. 11, 249–272.

32. Tamar Herzog, *Defining Nations: Immigrants and Citizens in Early Modern Spain and Spanish America* (New Haven: Yale University Press, 2003), 54.

33. Juan Ginés de Sepúlveda, *Demócrates segundo, o Tratado sobre las justas causas de la guerra contra los indios*, ed. M. Menéndez y Pelayo (México: FCE, 1941), 101. The comparison of Indians to monkeys appeared only in one of the many manuscript versions of *Demócrates Segundo.* Sepulveda was unable to publish his *Demócrates segundo* but was able to publish a Latin version of his argument under the title *Apologia pro libro de iustis belli causis* in Rome in 1550. On the various versions of *Demócrates* and the *Apología*, see Juan Ginés de Sepúlveda, *Obras completas*, ed. A. Coroleu Lletget and A. Moreno Hernández, vol. 3 (Salamanca: Ayuntamiento de Pozoblanco, 1997). It is important to underline that Ginés de Sepúlveda was a respected intellectual authority at the Spanish court, as demonstrated by the fact that Charles I appointed Sepúlveda as royal chronicler in 1535, and one of the tutors of Charles's son and heir, Prince Philip. As royal chronicler he wrote a history of Charles' military victories, although it was not published during his lifetime, and a history of the New World or, better still, a history of Spanish conquests in the New World. For similar views to those expressed by Sepúlveda, see Tomás López Medel, *Colonización de América: informes y testimonios, 1549–1572*, ed. L. Pereña, C. Baciero, and F. Maseda (Madrid: CSIC, 1990), 36; Juan López de Velasco, *Geografía y descripción universal de las Indias*, ed. Justo Zaragoza (Madrid: Sociedad Geográfica de Madrid, 1894), 26–34; "Relación del virrey Juan Mendoza y Luna, marqués de Montesclaros," 2 August 1607, in *Los Virreyes españoles en América durante el gobierno de la casa de Austria: México*, ed. L. Hanke (Madrid: Atlas, 1977), vol. 2, 276.

34. For the intelectual impact of the New World on the Old, see John H. Elliott, *The New World and the Old, 1492–1650* (Cambridge: Cambridge University Press, 1970); and Anthony Grafton, *New Worlds, Ancient Texts: The Power of Tradition and the Shock of Discovery* (Cambridge, MA: Harvard University Press, 1992).

35. Anthony Pagden, *European Encounters with the New World: From Renaissance to Romanticism* (New Haven: Yale University Press, 1993), 17–49. This and his *The Fall of Natural Man*, are the best general intellectual histories of European perceptions of the Amerindians.

36. López de Gómara, *Primera y segunda parte de la historia general de las Indias*, Dedicatory to Charles I, n.p.

37. Alessandro Geraldini, *Itinerario por las regiones sub-equinocciales* (1631), ed. E. Rodríguez (Santo Domingo: Editora del Caribe, 1977), 47 and 49.

38. Cañizares Esguerra, "New World, New Stars," 35.

39. Antonello Gerbi, *Nature in the New World*, trans. J. Moyle (Pittsburgh: University of Pittsburgh Press, 1985); Jesús Bustamante García, "De la naturaleza y los naturales americanos en el siglo XVI: algunas cuestiones críticas sobre la obra de Francisco Hernández," *Revista de Indias*, 52 (1992), 297–328; José Pardo Tomás, *El tesoro natural de América* (Tres Cantos: Nivola, 2002).

40. López de Gómara, *Primera y segunda parte de la historia general de las Indias*, fol. 118r–v.

41. Franklin Pease, "Estudio preliminar," to Gregorio García, *Origen de los indios del Nuevo Mundo* (1607), ed. (México: FCE, 1981), ix–xli; Jesús M. García

Añoveros, "Opiniones y reflexiones de tres clásicos hispanos acerca de la procedencia de los indios del Nuevo Mundo," in Gregorio García, *Origen de los indios del Nuevo Mundo e Indias Occidentales* (1607), ed. C. Baciero et al (Madrid: CSIC, 2005), 19–34; Eduardo Matos Moctezuma, *Ideas acerca del hombre americano (1570–1916)* (México: SEP, 1987).

42. José de Acosta, *Historia natural y moral de las Indias* (Sevilla: Iuan de León, 1590), bk. 1, chap. 24, 81–82. The first book is dedicated to a discussion of the treatment of the New World by ancient writers, and the diverse theories on the origins of the Indians.

43. Joannes Boemus, *El libro de las costumbres de todas las gentes del mundo y de las Indias*, trans. Francisco de Támara (Antwerp: Martin Nucio, 1556), 7r–v.

44. These paragraphs on the classifications of humans come from José de Acosta, *De procuranda indorum salute* (1588), ed. L. Pereña et al. (Madrid: CSIC, 1984), vol. 1, 61–69.

45. Acosta, *De procuranda*, bk. 1, chap. 8, 149–151. On these interpretations of human differences as the product of education, and therefore surmountable, Jesús Bustamante García, "¿Degradación universal o identidad particular? El problema de la diversidad cultural y linguística en la Europa y América del siglo XVI," in *Historia y Universidad. Homenaje a Lorenzo Mario Luna*, ed. E. González (México: UNAM, 1996), 75–104.

46. López de Velasco, *Geografía y descripción universal de las Indias*, 27–29. The royal official Tomás López Medel, for example, claimed that the Indians were in general brown skinned, but that there were among them "peoples and nations [who were] fairly white" and would be even more so if protected from the heat of the sun; Tomás López Medel, *Meditacion sobre las Indias*, in *Colonización de América: informes y testimonios, 1549–1572*, ed. L. Pereña, et al (Madrid: Consejo Superior de Investigaciones Científicas, 1990), 307.

47. The subject of the conversion of the Indians is crucial to understanding how the Spaniards viewed the indigenous population. One of the best analyses of this issue, Juan Carlos Estenssoro Fuchs, *Del paganismo a la santidad. La incorporación de los Indios del Perú al catolicismo, 1532–1750* (Lima: IFEA, 2003).

48. Solórzano Pereira, *Política indiana*, bk. 2, chap. 28, 230.

49. Acosta, *De procuranda*, bk. 2, chap. 15, 355.

50. Peñalosa y Mondragón, *Cinco excelencias*, 40r–v.

51. Bernabé Cobo, *Historia del Nuevo Mundo*, 4 vols (Sevilla: E. Rasco, 1890–1893).

52. Cobo, *Historia del Nuevo Mundo*, vol. 3, bk. 11, chap. 2, 13–16; he insists on these ideas in vol. 3, bk. 11, chap. 9, 48

53. Douglas Cope, *The Limits of Racial Domination: Plebeian Society in Colonial Mexico City, 1660–1720* (Madison: University of Wisconsin Press, 1994), 3.

54. *Rebeliones indígenas de la época colonial*, ed. M. T. Huerta and P. Palacios (México: Instituto Nacional de Antropología e Historia, 1976). A relevant essay on seventeenth-century revolts in the Americas, Anthony McFarlane, "Challenges from the Periphery: Rebellion in Colonial Spanish America," in *Rebelión y Resistencia en el Mundo Hispánico del siglo XVII*, ed. W. Thomas (Leuven: Leuven University Press, 1992), 250–269. On the violent 1692 revolt in Mexico City, which greatly preoccupied the authorities, Cope, *Limits of Racial Domination*, 125–160.

55. On the use of legal mechanisms and Spanish tribunals by the natives in defense of their rights, Lauren Benton, *Law and colonial cultures. Legal regimes in world history, 1400–1900* (Cambridge: Cambridge University Press, 2002), 80–126. For a specific case of this, Thomas Abercrombie, *Pathways of Memory and Power: Ethnography and History among an Andean People* (Madison: University of Wisconsin Press, 1998).

56. Susan Kellog, "Hegemony Out of Conquest: The First Two Centuries of Spanish Rule in Central Mexico," *Radical History Review* 53 (1992): 27–46. Elizabeth Anne Kuznesof, "Ethnic and Gender Influences on 'Spanish' Creole Society in Colonial Spanish America," *Colonial Latin American Review* 4 (1995): 154–155.

57. Serge Gruzinski, "Mutilated Memory: Reconstruction of the Past and the Mechanisms of Memory among 17th Century Otomis," *History and Anthropology* 2 (1986): 337–353; Sabine MacCormack, *On the Wings of Time: Rome, the Incas, Spain and Peru* (Princeton: Princeton University Press, 2007), chap. 2: "Writing and the Pursuit of Origins." A summary of the historical visions of indigenous authors, Francisco Esteve Barba, *Historiografía Indiana,* 2nd ed. (Madrid: Gredos, 1992), 246–277, 330–338, 513–559; and Sonia V. Rose, "El Barroco," in *Los amerindios en la narrativa occidental,* ed. Alicia Mayer and Pedro Perez Herrero (Madrid: Marcial Pons, 2010),

58. Felipe Guaman Poma de Ayala, *El primer nueva corónica y buen gobierno* (1615/1616) (København, Det Kongelige Bibliotek, GKS 2232 4°). A facsimile of the original manuscript, annotated transcription, documents, and other digital resources. Ed. Rolena Adorno: http://www.kb.dk/permalink/2006/poma/titlepage/es/text/?open=id3083608. Rolena Adorno is the foremost expert on Guaman Poma de Ayala but also the author of the best available analysis of indigenous historiography and its implications. Rolena Adorno, *Guaman Poma: Writing and Resistance in Colonial Peru* (Austin: University of Texas Press, 1986).

59. Bernardo de Aldrete, *Varias antiguedades de España, Africa y otras provincias* (Amberes: Iuan Hasrey, 1614), bk. 3, chap. 2, 330. For an assessment of the extent and nature of knowledge of Africa in early modern Spain, Antoine Bouba Kidakou, *África negra en los libros de viajes españoles del Siglo de Oro* (Madrid: Editorial Académica de España, 2012). Robert Launay, "Africa´s Shifting Place in Early Modern European Conceptions of the World," *Cahiers D´Études Africaines* 50 (2010): 455–470.

60. Alonso de Sandoval, *Naturaleza, policía sagrada y profana, costumbres, ritos, disciplina y catecismo evengélico de todos etíopes* (Sevilla: Francisco de Lira, 1627), fol. 14v.

61. Ibn Khaldun, *The Muqaddimah*, ed. N. J. Dawood (Princeton: Princeton University Press, 1969), 59–61.

62. López de Gómara, *Primera y segunda parte de la historia general de las Indias,* fol. 118r–v.

63. Juan Huarte de San Juan, *Examen de ingenios para las ciencias* (Valencia: Pedro de Huete, 1580), 251–252. This work was censored by the Inquisition and republished in 1594, although the words cited here remained unchanged in all later editions.

64. Antonio de San Román, *Historia general de la India oriental* (Valladolid: Luis Sánchez, 1603), 3, 75. See also Joseph Pellicer de Tovar, *Misión evangélica al reyno del Congo por la seráfica religión de los Capuchinos* (Madrid: Domingo Garcia y Morràs 1649), fols. 57v, 57v–58r. On the similar views on the Black Africans in Renaissance England, see Anu Korhonen, "Washing the Ethiopian White: Conceptualizing Black Skin in Renaissance England," in *Black Africans in Renaissance Europe*, ed. Thomas Earle and Kate Lowe (Cambridge: Cambridge University Press, 2005), 94–112.

65. Thomas Browne, *Pseudodoxia Epidemica, or, Enquiries into Very Many Received Tenets, and Commonly Presumed Truths* (1646) (London: Edward Dod, 1658), 6th ed., bk. 6, chaps. 10–12.

66. "Nouvelle Division de la Terre, par les differentes Especes ou Race d'hommes qui l'habite, envoyee par un fameux Voyageur a M. l'Abbe de la Chambre," *Journal des Scavants*, 24 April 1684, 133–140; "A New Division of the Earth," English trans. Janet L. Nelson, *History Workshop Journal* 51 (2001): 247–250. On Bernier's theories, Siep Stuurman, "François Bernier and the Invention of Racial Classification" *History Workshop Journal* 50 (2000): 1– 21; Pierre H. Boulle, "François Bernier and the Origins of the Modern Concept of Race," in *The Color of Liberty: Histories of Race in France*, ed. Sue Peabody and Tyler Stovall (Durham: Duke University Press, 2003), 11–27. Pagden, *The Burdens of Empire*, 98–99.

67. Pagden, *The Burdens of Empire*, 99; Boulle, "François Bernier and the Origins of the Modern Concept of Race," 20.

68. Aurelia Martín Casares, "Free and Freed Black Africans in Granada in the Time of the Spanish Renaissance," *Black Africans in Renaissance Europe*, 248–249.

69. Acosta, *De procuranda indorum salute*, vol. 1, bk. 1, chap. 1, 77. The complementarity of these two positions is also present in the work of Alonso de Sandoval, *Naturaleza, policía sagrada y profana, costumbres, ritos, disciplina y catecismo evengélico de todos etíopes.*

70. Nicolás Antonio, *Biblioteca Hispana Nueva* (1672), ed. and trans. Francisco Pérez (1788), fac. ed. 2 vols. (Madrid: FUE, 1999)., vol. 1, 668–669.

71. Barbara Fields, "Slavery, Race and Ideology in the United States of America," *New Left Review* 181 (1990): 106.

72. There are countless works on the subject of slavery, its ideological justifications, and the development of the various slave systems in the Americas. The intention here is not to provide a major reassessment of these studies but to highlight the importance of slavery and of reflections on the theory and reality of slavery to understanding the views of the Africans within the Spanish world. David Brion Davis, *The Problem of Slavery in Western Culture* (New York: Oxford University Press, 1966), is still an indispensable work for understanding the development of a slaveholding ideology in the Western world. In recent years there has been an explosion of works on slavery in the Iberian world, in the peninsula as well as the colonies. For a limited sample of these studies, see Lucena Salmoral, *Leyes para esclavos*; William Phillips, *Slavery in Medieval and Early Modern Iberia* (Philadelphia: University of Pennsylvania Press, 2013);

Alessandro Stella, *Histoire d'esclaves dans la péninsule* ibérique (Paris: EHESS, 2000); José Andrés-Gallego, *La esclavitud en la América española* (Madrid: Ediciones Encuentro, 2005); José Ramos Tinhorão, *Os negros em Portugal: uma presença silenciosa* (Lisboa: Caminho, 1988); Stuart Schwartz, *Sugar Plantations in the Formation of Brazilian Society: Bahia, 1550–1835* (Cambridge: Cambridge University Press, 1985).

73. Aurelia Martín Casares, "Evolution of the Origin of Slaves Sold in Spain from the Late Middle Ages till the 18th Century," *Serfdom and Slavery in the European Economy 11th–18th Centuries* (Florence: Firenze University Press, 2014), vol. 2, 409–430; Lucena Salmoral, *Leyes para esclavos*; Tatiana Seijas, *Asian Slaves in Colonial Mexico: From Chinos to Indians* (Cambridge: Cambridge University Press, 2014).

74. James Muldoon, "Spiritual Freedom, Physical Slavery: The Medieval Church and Slavery," *Ave Maria Law Review* 3 (2005): 69–93.

75. *Siete Partidas*, part 4, title. 21, law 1.

76. Andrés-Gallego, *La esclavitud en la América española*, 36–57.

77. On this topic, see Andrés-Gallego, *La esclavitud en la América española*, section 2, "La consideración de la esclavitud en el mundo hispano."

78. We now have an excellent analysis of the slave trade to Spanish America from 1501 to 1867: Alex Borucki, David Eltis, and David Wheat, "Atlantic History and the Slave Trade to Spanish America," *American Historical Review* 120 (2015): 433–461.

79. The Spanish American territories were still very profitable in the late seventeenth century, especially due to bullion production, but had fallen behind dramatically in export staple production. Borucki, Eltis, and Wheat, "Atlantic History and the Slave Trade," 436.

80. María del Carmen Martínez, "El cambio demográfico," in *La formación de las sociedades Iberoamericanas (1568–1700)*, ed. Demetrio Ramos (Madrid: Espasa Calpe, 1999), 68.

81. Borucki, Eltis, and Wheat, "Atlantic History and the Slave Trade," 458. Jean-Paul Zúñiga, "Visible Signs of Belonging: The Spanish Empire and the Rise of Racial Logics in the Early Modern Period," in *Polycentric Monarchies: How Did Early Modern Spain and Portugal Achieve and Maintain a Global Hegemony?*, ed. P. Cardim, T. Herzog, J. J. Ruiz, and G. Sabatini (Eastbourne: Sussex Academic Press, 2012), 127

82. A good summary of the different bodies of laws on slavery is Sue Peabody, "Slavery, Freedom, and the Law in the Atlantic World," *Cambridge History of Slavery*, ed. David Eltis and Stanley Engerman (Cambridge: Cambridge University Press, 2011), vol. 3, 594–630.

83. This and the following paragraphs follow Lucena Salmoral, *Leyes para esclavos*. See also Michelle A. McKinley, *Fractional Freedoms. Slavery, Intimacy, and Legal Mobilization in Colonial Lima, 1600-1700* (Cambridge: Cambridge University Press, 2016), and "Fractional Freedoms: Slavery, Legal Activism, and Ecclesiastical Courts in Colonial Lima, 1593-1689," *Law and History Review*, 28 (2010), 750-761; José Ramón Jouve Martín, *Esclavos de la ciudad letrada. Esclavitud, escritura y colonialismo en Lima (1650-1700)* (Lima: Instituto de Estudios Peruanos, 2005). Herman Bennett, *Colonial Blackness. A History of Afro-Mexico* (Bloomington: Indiana University Press, 2009).

84. The possibilities and methods for obtaining liberty in Lucena Salmoral, *Leyes para esclavos*, 150–152; and Jean-Pierre Tardieu, *Relaciones interétnicas en las Américas* (Madrid: Fundación Tavera, 2000), 74–88.

85. Nicole von Germeten, "Black Brotherhoods in Mexico City," in *The Black Urban Atlantic in the Age of the Slave Trade*, ed. Jorge Cañizares-Esguerra, Matt D. Childs, and James Sidbury (Philadelphia: University of Pennsylvania Press, 2013), 249.

86. There are many copies of the French Code Noir; see an English translation by John Garrigus at https://directory.vancouver.wsu.edu/sites/directory.vancouver.wsu.edu/files/inserted_files/webintern02/code%20noir.pdf. Best study, Louis Sala-Molins, *Le Code Noir, ou Le calvaire de Canaan* (Paris: Presses Universitaires de France, 2002).

87. April 1691-ACT XVI. An act for suppressing outlying slaves http://www.virtualjamestown.org/laws1.html#36

88. Seijas, *Asian Slaves in Colonial Mexico.*

89. Antonio Mira de Amescua, *El negro del major amo* (n.p., 1624?); Baltasar Fra Molinero, *La imagen de los negros en el teatro del Siglo de Oro* (Madrid: Siglo XXI, 1995); Antonio Santos Morillo, "Caracterización del negro en la literatura española del siglo XVI," *Lemir* 15 (2011): 23–46.

90. Francisco de Quevedo, *Obras de Francisco de Quevedo Villegas* (Amberes: Cornelis and Henri Verdussen, 1699), vol. 1, 270.

91. Juan Meléndez, *Tesoros verdaderos de las Indias* (Roma: Nicolas Angel Tinassio, 1681), vol. 1, bk. 4, chap. 4, 347–359, cit. 354.

92. Martín Casares, *La esclavitud en la Granada del siglo XVI*, 435–438; Jesús Bravo Lozano, "Mulos y esclavos. Madrid, 1670," *Cuadernos de Historia Moderna y Contemporánea* 1 (1980): 11–30.

93. Cristóbal Suárez de Figueroa, *Plaza universal de todas las ciencias y artes* (Madrid: Luis Sánchez, 1615), fol. 307v; Jean Bodin, *Los seis libros de la República*, trans. Gaspar de Añastro Isunza (Turin: Herederos de Bevilaqua, 1590), bk. 1, chap. 6, 41.

94. Mauricio Valiente Ots, "Negros, zambos y mulatos en la estructura político-administrativa indiana," *Anuario de Historia del Derecho Español* 78–79 (2008–2009): 399–421.

95. Celia Cussen, *Black Saint of the Americas. The Life and Afterlife of Martín de Porres* (Cambridge: Cambridge University Press, 2014).

96. Jean-Pierre Tardieu, "Las vistas de un arbitrista sobre la aparición de un hombre nuevo en las Indias occidentales (mitad del siglo XVII)," *Anuario de Estudios Americanos* 50 (1993): 239.

97. *Recopilación de Leyes de los Reynos de Indias*, bk. 7, tit. v, "De los mulatos, negros, berberiscos e hijos de indios," law 15. All the laws under this heading are intended to limit the freedom of movement but also to protect and ensure the independence of blacks, both slaves and freedmen. On rebellions of the blacks in colonial cities, albeit rare, see Tardieu, *Relaciones interétnicas*, 92–101.

98. *Recopilación de las leyes de los Reinos de Indias*, bk. 7, tit. V, law 3 (1577).

99. Phillips, "Slavery in the Atlantic Islands and the Early Modern Spanish World," in *Cambridge History of Slavery*, vol. 3, 344–345; Manolo Florentino and Márcia Amantino, "Runaways and *Quilombos* in the Americas," in *Cambridge History of Slavery*, vol. 3, 708–739; Jean-Pierre Tardieu, *Cimarrones de Panamá: la*

forja de una identidad afroamericana en el siglo XVI (Madrid: Iberoamericana, 2009); Tardieu, *Relaciones interétnicas*, 92–97.

100. Tardieu, "Las vistas de un arbitrista sobre la aparición de un hombre nuevo en las Indias occidentales (mitad del siglo XVII)," 244–246; Tardieu, *Relaciones interétnicas*, 103–118; Berta Ares Queija, "Mestizos, mulatos y zambaigos," in *Negros, mulatos, zambaigos. Derroteros africanos en los mundos ibericos*, ed. Berta Ares Queija and Alessandro Stella (Sevilla: Escuela de Estudios Hispano-Americanos, 2000), 76.

101. A summary of this phenomenon in Tardieu, *Relaciones interétnicas*, 22–28; Ben Vinson, *Bearing Arms for His Majesty: The Free-Colored Militia in Colonial Mexico* (Palo Alto: Stanford University Press, 2001).

102. Meléndez, *Tesoros verdaderos de las Indias*, vol. 1, bk. 4, chap. 4, 347–359.

103. Herzog, *Defining Nations*, chap. 3.

104. Joanne Rappaport, *The Disappearing Mestizo: Configuring Difference in the Colonial New Kingdom of Granada* (Durham: Duke University Press, 2014), 7–13.

105. Juan Felipe Hoyos and Joanne Rappaport, "El mestizaje en la epoca colonial: un experiment documental a traves de los documentos de Diego de Torres y Alonso de Silva, caciques mestizos del siglo XVI," *Boletín de Historia y Antiguedades* 94 (2007): 301–315.

106. Stuart Schwartz, "Spaniards, Pardos, and the Missing Mestizos: Identities and Racial Categories in the Early Hispanic Caribbean," *New West Indian Guide/Nieuwe West-Indische Gids* 71 (1997): 10.

107. Kuznesof, "Ethnic and Gender Influences on 'Spanish' Creole Society in Colonial Spanish America," 160–161.

108. Inca Garcilaso de la Vega, *Comentarios reales de los Incas* (Lisbon, 1609), bk. 9, chap. 31, 255r. Garcilaso de la Vega (El Inca) lived in Spain from a young age, served in the army that defeated the rebellious Moriscos of Granada, and wrote his works during his stay there. In the prologue, the Inca dedicated the second part of his history of Peru, a narrative of the conquest of Peru by the Spaniards, to "the Indians, Mestizos, and Creoles of the Kingdoms and Provinces of the great and prosperous Empire of Peru, el Inca Garcilaso de la Vega their brother, compatriot and countryman, health and felicity." Inca Garcilaso de la Vega, *Historia general del Perú* (Córdoba: Viuda de Andrés Barrera, 1617), n.p. His father was indeed a hidalgo and recognized his son, but he never married the mother, Palla Chimpu Ocllo, an Inca princess, baptized with the name Isabel Suárez Chimpu Ocllo, who would later be forced to marry a man of inferior social rank, Juan de Pedroche, with whom she had two daughters.

109. Guillaume Aubert, "The Blood of France: Race and Purity of Blood in the French Atlantic World," *William and Mary Quarterly* 61 (2004): 452, 453–457. This policy of assimilation not only failed but was in fact opposed by the French authorities in Europe and the colonies and above all by the French colonists who were meant to marry Indian women.

110. Studies of the *encomenderos* of the Quito region have shown that, with one or two exceptions in the early stages of colonization, after 1500 not a single one of them married an Indian, black, mestizo, or mulatto woman. Javier Ortiz de la Tabla Ducasse, *Los encomenderos de Quito, 1534–1660* (Sevilla: CSIC, 1993),

70–75. This was not an attitude unique to the Spaniards in the Indies. The elites in the peninsula also did everything possible to avoid marrying their social inferiors, although the consequence was once again the large number of illegitimate children. Ignacio Atienza Hernández and Mina Simón López, "Aunque fuese con una negra si S.M. así lo desea: Sobre la autoridad real, el amor y los hábitos matrimoniales de la nobleza hispana," *Familia y Sociedad* 1 (1989): 36. McKinley, "Fractional Freedoms: Slavery, Legal Activism, and Ecclesiastical Courts in Colonial Lima, 1593-1689," 751-752.

111. "Carta del jesuita José de Teruel, rector del Colegio de Cuzco, 1 febrero 1585," 84. In Spanish towns, about 50 percent of those baptized were born out of wedlock, while in surrounding Indian towns the rate of illegitimacy rose as high as 90 to 95 percent. See Alberto Filippi, "Laberintos del etnocentrismo jurídico-político. De la limpieza de sangre a la destrucción étnica," in *Para una historia de América II. Los nudos I*, ed. Marcello Carmagnani, Alicia Hernández Chávez and Ruggiero Romano (Mexico DF: Colegio de México, 1999), 330.

112. Solórzano Pereira, *Política Indiana*, bk. 2, chap. 30, 246. *Las mujeres en la construcción de las sociedades Iberoamericanas*, ed. P. Gonzalbo and B. Ares (México: Colegio de México/CSIC, 2004); *Women of the Iberian Atlantic*, ed. S. E. Owens and J. E. Mangan (Baton Rouge: Louisiana State University Press, 2012).

113. Stuart B. Schwartz and Frank Salomon, "New Peoples and New Kinds of People: Adaptation, Readjustment, and Ethnogenesis in South American Indigenous Societies (Colonial Era)," in *The Cambridge History of the Native Peoples of the Americas*, ed. Frank Salomon and Stuart B. Schwartz (Cambridge: Cambridge University Press, 1999), 444, 478. This is the process that had led Joanne Rappaport to speak of the disappearing mestizo because depending on the "circumstances people classified as mestizos dropped out of the mestizo slot and into other categories," Rappaport, *The Disappearing Mestizo*, 10. For a more nuanced analysis, Kuznesof, "Ethnic and Gender Influences on 'Spanish' Creole Society in Colonial Spanish America,," 153–170; and Stuart Schwartz, "Colonial Identities and the Sociedad de Castas," *Colonial Latin American Review* 4 (1995): 185–194.

114. Juan Melendez, *Tesoros verdaderos de las Indias* (Rome: Nicolas Angel Tinassio, 1681), vol. 1, bk. 4, chap. 4, 347–359, cit. 354.

115. María Elena Martínez, *Genealogical Fictions. Limpieza de Sangre, Religion, and Gender in Colonial Mexico* (Stanford: Stanford University Press, 2008); *El peso de la sangre. Limpios, mestizos y nobles en el mundo hispánico*, ed. N. Böttcher, N. Hausberge and M. S. Hering (México: Colegio de México, 2011).

116. Cope, *Limits of Racial Domination*, 55.

117. These cases in Berta Ares Queija, "Las categorías del mestizaje: desafíos a los constreñimientos de un modelo social en el Perú colonial temprano," *Histórica* 28 (2004): 196–198.

118. Cope, *Limits of Racial Domination*, chaps. 3 and 4.

119. Ibid., 68–85; Jean Paul Zúñiga, "Ir a valer mas a Indias: las peregrinaciones de un granadino en Indias en el siglo XVII," in *La movilidad social en la España del Antiguo Régimes*, ed. I. Gómez and M. L. López-Guadalupe (Granada: Comares, 2007), 153–172. Magnus Morner, *Race Mixture in the History of Latin America* (Boston: Little, Brown and Co., 1967), 27.

120. Letter of the viceroy Toledo, 1574, cit. Berta Ares Queija, "Mancebas de españoles, madres de mestizos. Imágenes de la mujer indígena en el Perú colonial temprano," in *Las mujeres en la construcción de las sociedades iberoamericanas*, ed. P. Gonzalbo and B. Ares (Sevilla and México: CSIC and Colegio de México, 2004), 37.

121. Cope, *Limits of Racial Domination*, 83–84; Rappaport, *The Disappearing Mestizo*, chap. 2.

122. María Elena Martínez, "The Black Blood of New Spain: Limpieza de Sangre, Racial Violence, and Gendered Power in Early Colonial Mexico," *The William and Mary Quarterly* 61 (2004): 484.

123. Solórzano Pereira, *Política Indiana*, bk. 2, chap. 30, 246; Covarrubias Horozco, *Tesoro de la lengua castellana o española*, 1302; Baltasar Fra Molinero, "Ser mulato en Espana y America: discursos legales y otros discursos literarios," in *Negros, mulatos, zambaigos. Derroteros africanos en los mundos ibericos*, 123–147.

124. Tardieu, "Las vistas de un arbitrista sobre la aparición de un hombre nuevo en las Indias occidentales (mitad del siglo XVII)," 248.

125. Cope, *Limits of Racial Domination*, 83.

126. Ben Vinson, "Race and Badge: Free-Colored Soldiers in the Colonial Mexican Militia," *The Americas* 56 (2000): 471–496; Ben Vinson, "Articulating Space: The Free-Colored Military Establishment in Colonial Mexico from the Conquest to Independence," *Callaloo* 27 (2004): 150–171.

5
A New Spain, a New Spaniard

1. Linda Colley, *Britons: Forging the Nation* (New Haven: Yale University Press, 1992), 17.

2. Ibid., 6.

3. José Coroleu and José Pella y Forgas, *Los Fueros de Cataluña* (Barcelona: Imprenta de Luis Tasso Hijo, 1878), 869. On the so-called "austracismo" in general, see Javier Fernández Sebastián, "España, monarquía y nación. Cuatro concepciones de la comunidad política española entre el Antiguo Régimen y la Revolución liberal," *Studia Histórica-Historia Contemporánea* 12 (1994): 48–53.

4. Agustín López de Mendoza, Conde de Robres, *Historia de las guerras civiles de España* (1708–1709), ed. B. Mediano y Ruiz (Zaragoza: Diputación Provincial de Zaragoza, 1882), 1. Although not published until the nineteenth century, Robres wrote these memoirs immediately after the Philipist occupation of the Valencian and Aragonese kingdoms. Another contemporary historian, Nicolás de Jesús Belando, referred to these events as "the civil war that Spain experienced in her dominions," *Historia civil de España, sucesos de la guerras y tratados de paz* (Madrid: Manuel Fernández, 1740), vol. 1, Prólogo, n.p.

5. Melchor de Macanaz, *Regalías de los señores reyes de Aragón*, ed. J. Maldonado Macanaz (Madrid: Revista de la Legislación, 1879), 8; Pedro Molas i Ribalta, "Vida cotidiana en la Guerra de Sucesión," *Cuadernos de Historia Moderna. Anejos* 8 (2009): 229–239.

6. Macanaz, *Regalías de los señores reyes de Aragón*, 28.

7. Joaquim Albareda Salvadó, *La Guerra de Sucesión de España (1700-1714)* (Barcelona: Crítica, 2010), 420; Virginia León Sanz, "Represión borbónica y exilio austracista al finalizar la Guerra de Sucesión española," in *La pérdida de Europa: La guerra de Sucesión por la monarquía de España*, ed. A. Álvarez-Ossorio, B. J. García García, and V. Léon (Madrid: Fundación Carlos de Amberes, 2006), 567–589.

8. Marqués de Castelrodrigo a Manuel Vadillo, Barcelona, 7 September 1715, cit. Enrique Giménez López, "Contener con más autoridad y fuerza: la represión del austracismo en los territorios de la Corona de Aragón," *Cuadernos Dieciochescos* 1 (2000): 138.

9. There are hundreds of works on this subject, but see above all *Génesis territorial de España*, ed. J. A. Escudero (Zaragoza: El Justicia de Aragón, 2007).

10. *Novísima Recopilación de las Leyes de España*, bk. 3, title 3, law 1.

11. On the Union of 1707, see above all *A Union for Empire: Political Thought and the British Union of 1707*, ed. John Robertson (Cambridge: Cambridge University Press, 1995); and Allan I. Macinnes, *Union and Empire. The Making of the United Kingdom in 1707* (Cambridge: Cambridge University Press, 2007).

12. Robres, *Historia de las guerras civiles de España*, 384.

13. J. G. A. Pocock, "Empire, State and Confederation: The American Independence in Multiple Monarchy," in *A Union for Empire*, 331.

14. Robres, *Historia de las guerras civiles de España*, 367. It seems possible to say that the Spanish road to nationhood was rather more similar to the French case than to the British. On the development of a nation-state in France beginning in the eighteenth century, David Bell, *The Cult of the Nation in France: Inventing Nationalism, 1680–1800* (Cambridge: Harvard University Press, 2001); and Anne-Marie Thiesse, *La création des identités nationales: Europe XVIIIe–XXe siècle* (Paris: Éditions du Seuil, 1999), and *Ils apprenaient la France: l'exaltation des régions dans le discours patriotique* (Paris: Editions de la Maison des sciences de l'homme, 1997).

15. *La transición del siglo XVII al XVIII (transición del siglo XVII al XVIII) entre la decadencia y la reconstrucción*, ed. P. Molas i Ribalta (Madrid: Espasa Calpe, 2000). The writer José Cadalso, author of a work that was very influential in late eighteenth-century Spain, observed that the wealth produced by Catalonia was greater than that generated by the American colonies and suggested that Catalans should be placed in charge of the ministries of economy and finance; José Cadalso, *Cartas Marruecas* (Madrid: Imprenta de Sancha, 1793), letter 45, 114.

16. Juan Antonio de la Gándara, *Apuntes para el bien y el mal de España* (1759) (Madrid: Viuda de López, 1820), 2: 72–73. Written in 1759, the *Apuntes* was not published until 1804, but even in manuscript form it was one of the most well-known and most widely imitated works in the second half of the eighteenth century.

17. *Novísima Recopilación*, title 3, law 1, vol. 2: 13.

18. Ramón Lázaro de Dou y de Bassóls, *Instituciones del derecho público general de España con noticia del particular de Cataluña y de las principales reglas de gobierno en qualquier Estado*, 9 vols. (Madrid: Benito García y Compañía, 1801), vol. 4, bk. 1, tit. VII, "De naturales y extranjeros," 176–177.

19. Pere Molas i Ribalta, "Aragón en el Consejo de Castilla," *Cuadernos Dieciochescos* 2 (2001): 13–35.

20. Gregorio Mayans i Siscar, "Orígenes de la lengua española," in *Orígenes de la lengua española compuestos por varios autores* (Madrid: Juan de Zúñiga, 1737), 1–198; also "Discurso proemial sobre el origen de la lengua Castellana," *Diccionario de la Lengua Castellana,* vol. 1, xlii–xlvii. Felix San Vicente Santiago, "Filología," in *Historia literaria de España en el siglo XVIII,* ed. F. Aguilar Piñal (Madrid: Editorial Trotta, 1996), 593–669.

21. Order of Philip V, October 3, 1714, *Novísima Recopilación,* bk. 8, title 20; "Real cédula de Su Majestad a consulta de los señores del Consejo . . . para que se actúe y enseñe en lengua castellana," reproduced by Gabriel Lompart, "La real Cédula de 1768 sobre la difusión del castellano y su repercusión en la diócesis de Mallorca," *Boletín de la Sociedad Arqueológica Luliana* 33 (1965): 365.

22. Pere Molas i Ribalta, "Las Cortes nacionales en el siglo XVIII," in *Cortes y Constitución de Cádiz,* ed. J. A. Escudero (Madrid: Espasa Calpe, 2011), vol. 1, 156–172; Felipe Lorenzana de la Puente, *La representación política en el Antiguo Régimen. Las Cortes de Castilla, 1655–1834* (Madrid: Congreso de los Diputados, 2014).

23. Pere Molas Ribalta, "Los comienzos del centralismo en España. Una perspectiva catalana," in *Posibilidades y límites de una historiografía nacional* (Madrid: CSIC, 1984), 219; on Catalan views of the Nueva Planta decrees, see James Amelang, "Memoria histórica y tradición cívica: algunas reflexiones sobre el caso de Barcelona en la edad moderna," in *Los Borbones. Dinastía y memoria de nación en la España del siglo XVIII,* ed. P. Fernández Albaladejo (Madrid: Marcial Pons Historia, 2001), 533–548.

24. José Rodrigo, Fiscal del Consejo de Castilla, 1716. Cit. Carlos Garriga, "Los derechos propios de los Reinos Hispánicos," in *Manual de Historia del Derecho,* ed. Marta Lorente and Jesús Vallejo (Valencia: Tirant lo Blanch, 2012), 219.

25. "Memorial de greuges de 1760" (Spanish and Catalan edition, although the memorial was written in Castilian), *Textos Jurídics Catalans* (Barcelona: Generalitat de Catalunya, 1990), 1–19. On the persistence of Catalanism in the eighteenth century, see Ernest Lluch, *Las Españas vencidas del siglo XVIII: claroscuros de la ilustración* (Barcelona: Crítica, 1999); Rosa María Alabrús Iglesias, *Felip V i l'opinió dels catalans* (Barcelona: Pagès Editors, 2001). On the Valencian case, J. M. Palop Ramos, "Centralismo borbónico y reivindicaciones políticas en la Valencia del setecientos. El caso de 1760," *Homenaje al Dr. D. Juan Reglá Campistol* (Valencia: Universidad de Valencia, 1975), 2: 65–77; J. M. Palop Ramos, "Centralismo borbónico y reivindicaciones económicas en la Valencia del setecientos," *Estudis* 4 (1975): 191–212.

26. José M. Portillo, *Crisis atlántica* (Madrid: Fundación Carolina y Marcial Pons Historia, 2006), 40–46. Also his *Monarquía y gobierno provincial: poder y constitución en las provincias vascas (1760–1808)* (Madrid: Centro de Estudios Constitucionales, 1991); and Garriga, "Los derechos propios de los Reinos Hispánicos," 221.

27. Gándara, *Apuntes sobre el bien y el mal de España,* 1: 17.

28. Antonio de Capmany, *Centinela contra franceses* (Madrid: Gómez Fuentenegro y Compañía, 1808), 73–74.

29. *Diccionario de la lengua castellana*, vol. 4 (1734), "Nación" and "Patria."

30. Benito Jerónimo Feijóo, "Amor a la patria y pasión nacional," in *Teatro crítico universal* (Madrid: Imprenta de Francisco del Hierro, 1729), vol. 3, disc. 10, 226.

31. Ibid., 244.

32. *Informe de la Imperial Ciudad de Toledo al Real y Supremo Consejo de Castilla sobre igualación de pesos y medidas en todos los reynos y señoríos de S. Maj. según las leyes* (Madrid: Joachin Ibarra, 1758), iv–v. The report was prepared by the jurist Andrés Marcos Burriel.

33. Antonio Capmany, Discurso en la Real Academia de la Historia. RAH, Discursos Manuscritos, ms 11/8234, July 6, 1804.

34. On writing history in eighteenth-century Spain, Jorge Cañizares-Esguerra, *How to Write the History of the New World: Histories, Epistemologies, and Identities in the Eighteenth-Century Atlantic Wworld* (Stanford: Stanford University Press, 2001); José Antonio Maravall, "Mentalidad burguesa e idea de la historia en el siglo XVIII," in José A. Maravall, *Estudios de la historia del pensamiento español (siglo xviii)* (Madrid: D.L., 1991), 113–38; José Álvarez Junco and Gregorio de la Fuente Monge, "Las historias de España. Visiones del pasado y construcción de identidad," in *Las Historias de España*, ed. J. Álvarez Junco (Barcelona: Crítica/Marcial Pons, 2013), 3-437.

35. "Breve noticia del principio y progresos de la Real Academia Española de la Historia," in *Fastos de la Real Academia Española de la Historia*, Año 1 (Madrid: Real Academia de la Historia, 1739), 12.

36. A good summary in Álvarez Junco and Fuente Monge, "Las historias de España. Visiones del pasado y construcción de identidad," 197–206. On the Catalan case specifically, Javier Antón Pelayo, "La historiografía catalana del siglo XVIII. Luces y sombras de un proyecto ilustrado y nacional," *Revista de Historia Moderna* 18 (2000): 289–310; and Javier Antón Pelayo, "Antoni de Capmany (1742–1813): Análisis del pasado catalán para un proyecto español," *Obradorio de Historia Moderna* 12 (2003): 11–45.

37. Tomás de Iriarte, *Lecciones instructivas sobre la historia y la geografía dirigidas a la enseñanza de los niños* (Madrid: Imprenta Real, 1794), "Parte histórica, Lecciones de historia de España," 45.

38. Three of the most popular compilations were Jean Baptiste Duchesne, *Compendio de la historia de España* (1741), trans. José Francisco de Isla (Madrid: Joachin Ibarra, 1758) (although it was first published in 1754 in Antwerp), 2 vols.; Louis Pierre Anquetil, *Compendio de la historia de España*, trans. Francisco Vázquez, 2 vols. (Madrid: Gómez Fuentenebro y Compañía, 1806); Tomás de Iriarte, *Lecciones instructivas sobre la historia y la geografía dirigidas a la enseñanza de los niños* (Madrid: Imprenta Real, 1794), 45–328. Many authors included summaries of the history of Spain, in its general outlines, in their essays or reform proposals. Gándara makes numerous references to Spanish history in his *Apuntes sobre el bien y el mal de España*, but the most famous example is Feijóo, "Glorias de España, partes 1 y 2," *Teatro crítico*, vol. 4, disc. 13 and 14; and Cadalso in the third letter of his *Cartas Marruecas*. On history in theatrical works, see Emilio Palacios Fernández, "Teatro," in *Historia literaria de españa en el siglo XVIII*, 145–148, 193–200.

39. Gándara, *Apuntes sobre el bien y el mal de España,* 1: 9. The prologue, which is the source of this quotation, is addressed "To the Spanish Nation."

40. Juan Pablo Forner, *Amor de la patria. Discurso en la Junta General de la Real Sociedad Económica de Sevilla* (Sevilla: Hijos de Hidalgo y González de la Bonilla, 1794), xii, xv–xvi, xviii. From an opposing ideological perspective, similar expressions of Spanish patriotism are found in Pedro León de Arroyal, *Pan y toros* (Madrid: Espinosa, 1820 [1790s]), 29.

41. Juan Nuix, *Reflexiones imparciales sobre la humanidad de los españoles en las Indias, contra los pretendidos filósofos y políticos. Para ilustrar las historias de MM. Raynal y Robertson,* trans. Pedro Varela y Ulloa (Madrid: Joaquín Ibarra, 1782), prólogo del autor, xxxiii–xxxiv. Nuix wrote these "Reflections" in Italian while living in exile in Italy following the expulsion of the Jesuits from Spain.

42. The term, and the sentiment, appeared earlier in English (1726) and French (1750) than in Castilian (1760). Pedro Álvarez Miranda, *Palabras e ideas: el léxico de la Ilustración temprana en España (1680-1760)* (Madrid: Real Academia Española, 1992), 245–246.

43. Joseph López de la Huerta, *Examen de la posibilidad de fijar la significación de los sinónimos de la lengua castellana* (Madrid: Imprenta Real, 1799), 94–96. The first edition of this text appeared in Vienna in 1789.

44. Antonio Porlier, *Amor a la patria* (1803), in *Discursos al Consejo de Indias,* ed. M. S. Campos (Madrid: Centro de Estudios Pollíticos y Constitucionales, 2002), 149–152.

45. López de la Huerta, *Examen de la posibilidad,* 46–48.

46. Cadalso, *Cartas Marruecas,* letter 2: 5–6; letter 26: 73; see also letter 67: 154–155.

47. Gándara, *Apuntes sobre el bien y el mal de España,* 2: 1–2, 7.

48. Varela, "Nación, patria y patriotismo," 34. The Jovellanos quote is from *Elogio de Carlos III* (1788). On these societies, see Inmaculada Arias de Saavedra, "Las Sociedades Económicas de Amigos del País: Proyecto y realidad en la España de la Ilustración," *Obradoiro de Historia Moderna* 21 (2012): 219–245; and Luis Miguel Enciso Recio, *Las Sociedades Económicas en el Siglo de las Luces* (Madrid: Real Academia de la Historia, 2010).

49. Cadalso, *Cartas Marruecas,* letter 26: 73.

50. Colin Kidd, *British Identities before Nationalism: Ethnicity and Nationhood in the Atlantic World, 1600–1800* (Cambridge: Cambridge University Press, 1999); Roxann Wheeler, *The Complexion of Race: Categories of Difference in Eighteen-Century British Culture* (Philadelphia: University of Pennsylvania Press, 2000); Pauline Kra, "The Concept of National Character in 18th Century France," *Cromohs* 7 (2002): 1–6, http://www.cromohs.unifi.it/7_2002/kra.html; Paul Stock. "Almost a Separate Race: Racial Thought and the Idea of Europe in British Encyclopedias and Histories, 1771–1830," *Modern Intellectual History* 8 (2011): 3–29.

51. Nicolle de la Croix, *Geografía moderna, escrita en francés por el Abad Nicollé de la Croix, traducida y aumentada con una Geografía nueva de España por Josef Jordán y Frago,* 8 vols. (Madrid: Joachin Ibarra, 1779), 1: 143.

52. Francisco Fernández de Navarrete, "Disertación sobre el carácter de los españoles," in *Fastos de la Real Academia de la Historia* (Madrid: Antonio Sanz, 1739), 137, 142, 154, 156–157. Fernández de Navarrete was a member of the Royal Academy of History but also a member of the medical faculty of the University of Granada, the king's personal physician, and a member of the Medical Academy of Madrid.

53. Lorenzo Hervás y Panduro, *Catálogo de las lenguas de las naciones conocidas*, 6 vols. (Madrid: Imprenta de la Administración del Real Arbitrio de Beneficencia, 1800–1805), 1: 10.

54. On the idea of decline in eighteenth-century Europe, J. G. A. Pocock, *Barbarism and Religion*. 5 vols. (Cambridge: Cambridge University Press, 2001–2011).

55. I am using the English edition published in 1782: *A Philosophical and Political History of the Settlements and Trade of the Europeans in the East and West Indies. By the Abbé Raynal* (Edinburgh: W. Gordon, 1782), 6 vols. Citations from vol. 2, VI, 252-253, and vol. 3, VIII, 147.

56. Nicolas Masson de Morvilliers, "Espagne," *Encyclopédie Méthodique: Géographie Moderne* (Paris: Panckoucke, 1782), vol. 1, 565. Although Masson's critical vision was generally known in Spain, the Spanish edition of this essay omitted the passages in which the author denied that Spain had made any contribution to Europe's intellectual or scientific development. The Spanish editors of the work did, however, include an "Addition to the Article on Spain," a rebuttal of Morvilliers' negative assessments. *Encyclopedia metódica: Geografía moderna*, trans. J. Arribas y Soria, and J. De Velasco (Madrid: Antonio de Sancha, 1792), vol. 2, 79–105.

57. Cornelius de Pauw, *Recherches philosophiques sur les Américains, ou Mémoires intéressants pour servir a l'Histoir de l'Espéce humaine* (Berlin: George Jacques Decker, 1768), vol. 1, Discourse Préliminaire; Pablo Fernández Albaladejo, "Entre la 'gravedad' y la 'religión': Montesquieu y la 'tutela' de la monarquía católica en el primer seteciento," in *Constitución en España: orígenes y destinos*, ed. J. M. Iñurritegui and J. M. Portillo (Madrid: Centro de Estudios Políticos y Constitucionales, 1998), 27.

58. Conde de Buffon, *Historia natural del hombre*, trans. Alonso Ruíz de Piña (Madrid: Andrés Ortega, 1775), 2: 205; Jean-François Dubroca, *Conversaciones de un padre con sus hijos sobre la historia natural* (1802), trans. M. de Ascorgorta y Ramírez (Madrid: Imprenta Fuentenebro, 1826), 2: 301.

59. Buffon, *Historia natural del hombre*, 2: 336.

60. José Servando Teresa de Mier Noriega y Guerra, *Memorias* (Madrid: Editorial-América, 1917), 396; Giuseppe Baretti, *A Journey from London to Genoa through England, Portugal, Spain, and France* (London: T. Davies and L. Davis, 1770), 4 vols. "Letter XXXI, Lisbon, September 15, 1760," 1: 273–275. There are no references to mixing of whites and blacks in his letters from Spain but many allusions to the presence, in the past and present, of "Moors" and "Jews" among the Spaniards. A reference, tinged with something between sympathy and irony, to the color of many Spaniards, similar to the descendants of blacks and whites in the American South, in "William Short to Thomas Jefferson,

27 February 1798," in http://founders.archives.gov/documents/Jefferson/01-30-02-0098, accessed August 30, 2015.

61. Jean-Frédéric Schaub, *La France espagnole: les racines hispaniques de l'absolutisme français* (Paris: Seuil, 2003); David Howarth, *The Invention of Spain: Cultural Relations between Britain and Spain, 1770–1870* (Manchester: Manchester University Press, 2007); Gabriel Paquette, "The Image of Imperial Spain in British Political Thought, 1750–1800," *Bulletin of Spanish Studies* 81 (2004): 187–214.

62. Werner Krauss, "Sobre el concepto de decadencia en el siglo ilustrado," *Cuadernos Hispanoamericanos* 215 (1967): 297–312; Jorge Cañizares-Esguerra, "Eighteenth-Century Spanish Political Economy: Epistemologies of Decline," *Eighteenth-Century Thought* 1 (2003): 295–314.

63. Antonio Elorza, *La ideología liberal en la ilustración española* (Madrid: Tecnos, 1970); Ignacio Fernández Sarasola, *Proyectos constitucionales en España (1786–1824)* (Madrid: Centro de Estudios Políticos y Constitucionales, 2004), 5–72.

64. Anonymous, "Idea del siglo XVIII," *Memorial Literario*, 1 (1801), 44; Pascual Ramón Gutiérrez de la Hacera, *Descripción general de la Europa y particular de sus estados y cortes especialmente de las ciudades, villas y pueblos más notables de España* (Madrid: Josef Doblado, 1782), vol. 1, 1–22; *Encyclopedia metódica* "Europa," 2: 117–121.

65. Gloria Mora, *La arqueología clásica espanola en el siglo XVIII: historias de mármol* (Madrid: Polifemo, 1998); Gloria Mora, "Literatura anticuaria," in *Historia literaria de españa en el siglo XVIII*, 883–914; also Manuel Álvarez Martín-Aguilar, *La antigüedad en la historiografía española del siglo XVIII: el Marqués de Valdeflores* (Málaga: Universidad de Málaga, 1996).

66. Hervás y Panduro, *Catálogo de las lenguas conocidas*, vol. 4, 6.

67. Hervás y Panduro advanced these theories in many of his writings, but especially in *Catálogo de las lenguas conocidas*, especially vols. 4, 5, and 6.

68. Juan López, in his translation of Strabo's work, appends a long explanatory note on the theories, both ancient and modern, regarding the expansion of the Celts and their presence in Spain. Strabo, *Libro tercero de la geografía de Estrabón*, trans. Juan López (Madrid: Viuda de Ibarra e Hijo, 1787), 28–30.

69. Real Academia Española, *Diccionario de la lengua castellana* (Madrid: Francisco Hierro, 1726), vol. 1, 616.

70. Fernández de Navarrete, "Disertación sobre el carácter de los españoles," 163–164, 214–215, 166–168.

71. Juan Francisco de Masdeu, "Discurso histórico filosófico sobre el clima de España, el genio y el ingenio de los españoles para la industria y literatura, y su carácter político y moral," in vol. 1 of his *Historia crítica de España y de la cultura española* (Madrid: Antonio de Sancha, 1783).

72. De la Croix, *Geografía moderna, escrita en francés por el Abad Nicollé de la Croix*, 1: 174.

73. Inmaculada Tamarit Vallés, *Representaciones de la mujer española en el imaginario francés del siglo XVIII* (Valencia: Universitat de València, 2004).

74. Dorinda Outram, *The Enlightenment*, 3rd ed. (Cambridge: Cambridge University Press, 2013), 85; Silvia Sebastiani, "'Race,' Women, and Progress in

the Scottish Enlightenment," in *Women, Gender and Enlightenment*, ed. Sarah Knott and Barbara Taylor (New York: Palgrave, 2005), 75–96.

75. Mónica Bolufer Peruga, "Neither Male, nor Female: Rational Equality in the Early Spanish Enlightenment," in *Women, Gender and Enlightenment*, 389–409.

76. Benito Jerónimo Feijóo, *Teatro crítico universal*, vol. 1 (1726), disc. 16, "Defensa de las mujeres,," 313–378. For a discussion of women in the Spanish Enlightenment, see Mónica Bolufer Peruga, *Mujeres e Ilustración. La construcción de la feminidad en la Ilustración española* (Valencia: Institució Alfons el Magnànim, 1998).

77. Fernández de Navarrete, "Disertación sobre el carácter de los españoles," 166–168.

78. Inés Joyes y Blake, *El príncipe de Abisinia. Novela traducida del ingles por . . . Va inserta a continuación una apología de las mujeres en carta original de la traductora a sus hijas* (Madrid: Imprenta de Sancha, 1798). The "Apology" begins on p. 173. Cit. 175, 181, 195, 204.

79. Ignacio Jordán de Asso y del Río and Miguel de Manuel Rodríguez, *Instituciones del Derecho Civil de Castilla* (Madrid: Imprenta Ramón Ruíz, 1792), bk. 1, tit. 1, chap. 2 and 3, 3.

80. Lorenzo Hervás y Panduro, *Historia de la vida del hombre* (Madrid: Imprenta de la Administración de la Rifa del Real Estudio de Medicina Práctica, 1798), 5: 155, 220–221.

81. Arturo Morgado García, "La esclavitud en el Cádiz de la modernidad. Una primera aproximación," in *Homenaje a Don Antonio Domínguez Ortíz*, ed J. L. Castellano and M. L. López-Guadalupe (Granada: Universidad de Granada, 2008), 2: 633–650.

82. Tamar Herzog, "How Did Early-Modern Slaves in Spain Disappear? The Antecedents." *Republics of Letters* 3, no. 1 (September 15, 2012): http://rofl.stanford.edu/node/106; Isidoro Moreno, *La Antigua hermandad de los negros de Sevilla* (Sevilla: Universidad de Sevilla, 1997); Mercedes Vidal Tibbits, "El hombre negro en el teatro peninsular del siglo XIX," *Hispania* 89 (2006): 1–12.

83. Hervás y Panduro, *Historia de la vida del hombre*, 5: 220–221.

84. On the belief that only Spaniards from the lower classes were anti-Semitic, see Benito Jerónimo Feijóo, "Reconvenciones caritativas a los Profesores de la Ley de Moisés. En respuesta a un Judío de Bayona de Francia" (1750), in *Cartas eruditas y curiosas*, vol. 3 , letter VIII, 86; Feijóo, "Observaciones comunes," *Teatro crítico universal*, vol. 5 (1730), disc. 5, 110–111; and Antonio Alcalá Galiano, *Recuerdos de un anciano* (1878) (Madrid: Librería de la Viuda de Hernando, 1890), 112. On the persistence of anti-Semitism among the elites, Leandro Fernández de Moratín, *Apuntaciones sueltas de Inglaterra*, ed. A. Rodríguez Fischer (Madrid: Cátedra, 2005), 191–192.

85. Juan de Ferreras, *Synopsis histórica y cronológica de las cosas de España* (Madrid: Imprenta de Francisco del Hierro, 1716), fourth part, 17; Enrique Flórez, *Clave historial con que se abre la puerta a la historia eclesiástica* (Madrid: Manuel Fernández, 1743), 135.

86. Martín F. Ríos Saloma, *La Reconquista. Una construcción historiográfica (siglos XVI–XIX)* (Madrid: Marcial Pons Historia, 2011), 118–152.

87. Feijóo, "Reconvenciones caritativas a los Profesores de la Ley de Moisés," 86; "Observaciones comunes," 110–111; "Suplemento al Tomo Quinto del Teatro crítico universal," in *Teatro crítico universal*, vol. 9 (Madrid: Herederos de Francisco de el Hierro, 1740), num. 27 and 30, 177–178.

88. *Compendio de la Historia Natural de Buffon, clasificado según el sistema de Lineo por Renato Ricardo Castel*, trans. Pedro Estala (Madrid: Imprenta de Villapando, 1802), vols. 3 and 4, De la naturaleza del hombre; cit. 4: 21.

89. Feijóo, "Reconvenciones caritativas a los Profesores de la Ley de Moisés." On this text and other debates related to the Jews in Spain, see Paul J. Hauben, "The Enlightenment and Minorities: Two Spanish Discussions," *The Catholic Historical Review* 65 (1979): 1–19.

90. *Real Cédula de Su Majestad . . . sobre los individuos del Barrio llamado de la Calle de la Ciudad de Palma*, January 3, 1782, in Antonio Cortijo Ocaña, "De la Sentencia-Estatuto de Pero Sarmiento a la problemática chueta (Real Cédula de Carlos III, 1782)," *eHumanista* 21 (2012): 521. The royal *cédula* or order also prohibited insults against these individuals for being Jews, Hebrews, or Chuetas or the use of any other offensive term that would single them out as different from other Spaniards (522). The recommendations of the Council of Castile for putting an end to the discrimination against the descendants of Jews, *Reflexiones del Consejo de Castilla sobre los judíos (chuetas) de la isla de Mallorca* (1767) (Madrid: Imprenta la Neotipia, 1942). The purity-of-blood statutes were in force until 1837, when all particular rights were abolished and labor laws standardized so that access to all offices was declared to be the right of every Spaniard regardless of origins.

91. This is also the argumentation used in the eighteenth century in defense of the descendants of conversos as well as other minorities; see Miguel de Lardizábal y Uribe, *Apología de los agotes de Navarra y los chuetas de Mallorca, con una breve digresión a los vaqueros de Asturias* (Madrid: Viuda de Ibarra, Hijos y Cia, 1786).

92. For reflections on Jews and Jewishness in the eighteenth century, Joaquín Álvarez Barrientos, "Los judíos y su cultura en la producción literaria española del siglo XVIII: la construcción del tópico 'judeo-masón-liberal' durante la Ilustración y el Romanticismo," in *Judíos en la literatura española*, ed. J. M. Hassán, and R. Izquierdo Benito (Cuenca: Universidad de Castilla-La Mancha, 1999), 267–300.

93. For the complex and sometimes contradictory approach to Arabs and Islam in eighteenth-century Europe, Alistair Hamilton, "Western Attitudes to Islam in the Enlightenment," *Middle Eastern Lectures* 3 (1999): 69–85.

94. Masdeu, *Historia crítica de España y de la cultura española*, vol. 13, 171, 170. Masdeu dedicated four volumes of his massive *Historia crítica* to Arab Spain.

95. Concha Varela-Orol, "Sarmiento y los estudios orientales: La edición de la *Biblioteca Arabigo-Hispana* de Casiri," *Revista General de Información y Documentación* 22 (2012): 9–33; Juan Bautista Muñoz, *Discurso en la Academia de la Historia sobre las dificultades que se ofrecen para ilustrar la historia nacional y algunos medios para vencerlos*, 6 January 1792, RAH, Discursos Manuscritos, Ms 11/8235; Gaspar Melchor de Jovellanos, "Informe que dio siendo individuo de la Academia de San Fernando sobre arreglar la publicación de los monumentos de Granada y Córdoba" and "Informe sobre la materia anterior" (1786), in *Obras del*

Excelentísimo Señor D. Gaspar Melchor de Jovellanos (Madrid: Imprenta de Francisco Oliva, 1840), vol. 7, 6–20.

96. Diego Clemencín, "Ensayo sobre la geografía de España en tiempo de los moros," 12 September 1800. RAH, Discursos Manuscritos, Ms 11/8234. The Royal Academy of History published a part of this discourse, *Examen y descripción geográfica de España atribuída a Rasis, leido en la Academia de la Historia por Don Diego Clemencín* (Madrid: Real Academia de la Historia, 1800).

97. Clemencín discussed the subject of the Moriscos and their expulsion in notes 31–46, pp. 306–317, in vol. 7 of his edition of *Don Quixote*, by then already seen as the quintessential Spanish novel. Miguel de Cervantes, *Don Quijote de la Mancha* (1833–1839), ed. Diego Clemencín (Madrid: Librería de Perlado y Páez, 1917), 7: 312, n. 34.

6
Race and Empire

1. José Servando Teresa de Mier Noriega y Guerra, *Memorias* (Madrid: Editorial América, 1917?), 282; José Servando Teresa de Mier, "Sobre las castas de Américas," in *Escritos inéditos*, ed. J. M. Miquel i Vergés and H. Díaz-Thomé (Mexico: Colegio de México, 1944), 342.

2. Benedict Anderson, *Imagined Communities. Reflections on the Origin and Spread of Nationalism* (London: Verso, 2006, rev. ed.), chap. 4, 49–68.

3. For the most interesting responses to Benedict Anderson's arguments, see *Imaginar la nación*, ed. Francois-Xavier Guerra and Mónica Quijadas (Münster: AHILA, 1994); Claudio Lomnitz, "Nationalism as a Practical System. Benedict Anderson's Theory of Nationalism from the Vantage Point of Spanish America," in *The Other Mirror. Grand Theory through the Lens of Latin America*, ed. Miguel Angel Centeno and Fernando López-Alves (Princeton: Princeton University Press, 2000), 329–359; and *Beyond Imagined Communities*, ed. Sara Castro-Klarén and John Charles Chasteen (Baltimore: The Johns Hopkins University Press, 2003).

4. *Economía y economistas españoles. Vol. 3: La Ilustración*, ed. E. Fuentes Quintana (Madrid: Galaxia Gutenberg/Círculo de Lectores, 1999); Enrique Llopis, "Expansión, reformismo y obstáculos al crecimiento (1715–1789)," in *Historia económica de España, siglos X–XX*, ed. F. Comín, M. Hernández, and E. Llopis (Barcelona: Crítica, 2002), 121–164; Regina Grafe, *Distant Tyranny: Markets, Power, and Backwardness in Spain, 1650–1800* (Princeton: Princeton University Press, 2012).

5. Charles-Louis de Secondat, Baron de Montesquieu, *The Spirit of the Laws* (1748), eds. A. Cohler, B. Miller and H. Stone (Cambridge: Cambridge University Press, 1989), 22; Silvio Zavala, *América en el espíritu francés del siglo XVIII* (México: El Colegio Nacional, 1998). See also, Heinz Kluppelholtz, "La presentation de la conquete du Pérou dans l'*Histoire des deux Indies*," and Manfred Tietz, "La vision correlative de l'Espagne et du Portugal dans les trois versions de *l'Histoire des deux Indes* (1770, 1774, 1780)," in *L'Histoire des deux Indes: réécriture et polygraphie*, ed. Hans-Jurgen Lusebrink and Anthony Strugnell (Oxford: Voltaire Foundation, 1995), 189–204, 263–277.

6. Jorge Juan and Antonio de Ulloa, *Noticias secretas de América sobre el estado naval, militar y politico de los Reynos del Peru y provincias de Quito, Costas de Nueva Granada y Chile* (1747), ed. David Barry (London: R. Taylor, 1826), second part, chap. 6, 423, 437–438, 443–444.

7. Juan Antonio de la Gándara, *Apuntes para el bien y el mal de España* (1759) (Madrid: Viuda de López, 1820), 69, 151, 216, 218–219. Ramon Ezquerra, "La crítica española sobre América en el siglo XVIII," *Revista de Indias* 22 (1962): 159–283; Miguel Artola, "América en el pensamiento español del siglo XVIII," *Revista de Indias* 29 (1969): 51–78.

8. Bernardo Ward, *Proyecto económico* (1761) (Madrid: Viuda de Ibarra, 1787), part 2, chap. 2, 226.

9. José M. Portillo Valdés, *Crisis atlántica. Autonomía e independencia en al crisis de la monarquía hispánica* (Madrid: Marcial Pons Historia, 2006), 20.

10. Ward, *Proyecto económico*, part 2, chap. 2, 239. Also Victoriano de Villava, *Apuntes para una reforma de* España (1797) (Buenos Aires: Imprenta de Álvarez, 1822), 39.

11. There are many works on this topic, but one might draw attention especially to Fidel Tavárez, *The Commercial Machine: Reforming Imperial Commerce in the Spanish Atlantic, ca. 1740–1800* (Ph.D. dissertation, Princeton University, 2016).

12. Gabriel Paquette, *Enlightenment, Governance, and Reform in Spain and Its Empire 1759–1808* (New York: Plagrave Macmillan, 2008).

13. Mónica Ricketts, "The Rise of the Bourbon Military in Peru, 1768–1820," *Colonial Latin American Review* 21 (2012): 413–439.

14. Nancy Farriss, *Maya Society under Colonial Rule: The Collective Enterprise of Survival* (Princeton: Princeton University Press, 1984)

15. David Weber, *Bárbaros: Spaniards and Their Savages in the Age of Enlightenment* (New Haven: Yale University Press, 2005).

16. For a summary of the expeditions, *Science in the Spanish and Portuguese Empires, 1500–1800*, ed. Daniela Bleichmar et al. (Stanford: Stanford University Press, 2009); Juan Pimentel, *La física de la monarquía. Ciencia y política en el pensamiento colonial de Alejandro Malaspina (1754–1810)* (Madrid: Ediciones Doce Calles, 1999); Jorge Cañizares-Esguerra, *Nature, Empire, and Nation* (Stanford: Stanford University Press, 2006); Neil Safier, *Measuring the New World: Enlightenment Science and South America* (Chicago: Chicago University Press, 2008); and Marta Portuondo, *Secret Science: Spanish Cosmography and the New World* (Chicago: Chicago University Press, 2009).

17. José Antonio Ferrer Benimeli, *Expulsión y extinción de los jesuitas (1759–1773)* (Bilbao: Mensajero, D.L. 2013).

18. Thomas Chavez, *Spain and the Independence of the United States* (Albuquerque: University of New Mexico Press, 2002); Angel Antonio Pozuelo Reina, *Las fronteras en América del Sur, 1750–1900* (Saarbrücken: Editorial Académica Española, 2011).

19. Mark Burkholder and D. S. Chandler, *From Impotence to Authority: The Spanish Crown and the American Audiencias, 1687–1808* (Columbia: University of Missouri Press, 1977); Mark Burkholder, *Spaniards in the Colonial Empire: Creoles vs. Peninsulars?* (Chichester: Wiley-Blackwell, 2013). On Spanish emigration to

the Americas in the eighteenth century, Carlos Martínez Shaw, *La emigración española a América, 1492–1824* (Colombres: Archivo de Indianos, 1994), chap. 5, 163–246.

20. The debates on what kind of history of the Americas should be promoted and encouraged were intense in the eighteenth century. From the point of view of the government and the crown, the histories that were considered official were those by Solís and Muñoz, although there were other members of the cultural elite who favored the work of the Italian collector and historian Lorenzo Boturini, while yet others preferred Robertson, who was thought to be superior to all others from the historiographical point of view. The debates on what sort of history of America should be written and encouraged in Spain have been analyzed on a multitude of occasions, but the best study is Jorge Cañizares-Esguerra, *How to Write the History of the New World* (Stanford: Stanford University Press, 2002).

21. The most important study of the French philosophers is still Michele Duchet, *Anthropologie et Histoire au siècle des Lumières* (Paris: Maspero, 1971). More general studies are Richard H. Popkin, "The Philosophical Basis of Eighteenth-Century Racism," *Studies in Eighteenth-Century Culture* 3 (1973): 245–262; Nicholas Hudson, "From 'Nation' to 'Race': The Origin of Racial Classification in Eighteenth-Century Thought," *Eighteenth-Century Studies* 29 (1996): 247–264; Colin Kidd, "Ethnicity in the British Atlantic World, 1688–1830," in *A New Imperial History. Culture, Identity, and Modernity in Britain and the Empire, 1660–1840*, ed. K. Wilson (Cambridge: Cambridge University Press, 2004), 260–277; Roxanna Wheeler, *The Complexion of Race: Categories of Difference in Eighteen-Century British Culture* (Philadelphia: University of Pennsylvania Press, 2000); Aaron Garrett, "Anthropology: The 'Original' of Human Nature," in *The Cambridge Companion to the Scottish Enlightenment*, ed. Alexander Broadie (Cambridge: Cambridge University Press, 2003), 79–93; Silvia Sebastiani, "L'orang-outang, l'esclave et l'humain: une querelle des corps en régime colonial," Bo Stråth (dir.), *L'Atelier du CRH* 11 (2013); Silvia Sebastiani, "Race as a Construction of the 'Other': 'Native Americans' and 'Negroes' in the Eighteenth-Century Editions of the Encyclopædia Britannica," in *Europe and the Other and Europe as the Other*, ed. Bo Stråth (Brussels: P.I.E.-Peter Lang, 2000), 195–228; Silvia Sebastiani, "Nations, Nationalism, and National Characters," in *The Routledge Companion to Eighteenth Century Philosophy*, ed. Aaron Garrett (London: Routledge, 2014), 593–617.

22. For dictionaries published by the Spanish Royal Academy, see http://www.rae.es/, and follow the link "Diccionarios académicos," where it is possible to search individual words in one edition at a time or all of the dictionaries published by the Royal Academy to 1992.

23. For the evolution of these terms in other languages, Hudson, "From 'Nation' to Race,'" 247–248.

24. Benito Jerónimo Feijóo , "Solución del gran problema histórico sobre la población de la América," *Teatro crítico universal* (Madrid: Imprenta de Francisco del Hierro, 1733), vol. 5, disc. 15, 321.

25. Conde de Buffon, *Historia natural del hombre*, trans. Alonso Ruíz de Piña (Madrid: Andrés Ortega, 1775), 2: 100.

26. Anonymous, "Idea del siglo XVIII," *Memorial Literario* 1 (1801): 28

27. Review of *Idea del sistema craniognómico de Gall, médico alemán*, in *Diario de Física, Química e Historia Natural de Francia, Memorial Literario* 4 (1804): 153.

28. *Anales de Historia Natural*, vol. 1,(1800), 196.

29. Lorenzo Hervás y Panduro, *Historia de la vida del hombre* (Madrid: Imprenta de la Administración de la Rifa del Real Estudio de Medicina Práctica, 1798), vol. 1, 22–39.

30. For some examples of Spanish authors who agreed with Buffon and Blumenbach, Feijóo, "Color etiópico," *Teatro crítico universal*, vol. 7 (1736), disc. 3, 86–89; Dubroca, *Conversaciones de un padre con sus hijos sobre la historia natural*, vol. 2, 228–230; *Memorial Literario* 3 (1802): 190–192; *Memorial Literario* 4 (1803): 228.

31. *Memorial Literario* 1 (1801): 153; 4 (1803): 58. Hervás y Panduro, *Historia de la vida del hombre*, vol. 5, 223; Panduro extensively discusses these topics on pp. 205–223. Feijóo, *Teatro Critico universal*, vol. 2 (1728), "Mapa intelectual y cotejo de naciones," disc. 15, 269–271.

32. Joseph Gumilla, *El Orinoco ilustrado y defendido* (Madrid: Manuel Fernández, 1745), vol. 1: 99–100; Isidoro de Antillón, *Lecciones de geografía astronómica, natural y política, escritas de orden de S.M. para uso principalmente del Real Seminario de Nobles de Madrid* (Madrid: Imprenta Real, 1804–1806), 2 vols. All the quotations are from vol. 2, lección 14, 2–22.

33. *Memorial Literario* 3 (1802): 190, quoting Buffon, *Historia natural del hombre.*

34. Joseph Gumilla, *El Orinoco ilustrado y defendido* (Madrid: Manuel Fernández, 1745), vol. 1, 99–100.

35. Buffon, *Historia natural del hombre*, 2: 343, 344.

36. Ibid., 2: 264; Gumilla, *El Orinoco ilustrado y defendido*, 93, 96.

37. On these difficulties and inconsistencies, Londa Schiebinger, *Nature's Body: Gender in the Making of Modern Science* (Boston: Beacon Press, 1993), 117–135, 142–152.

38. Dorinda Outram, *The Enlightenment*, 3rd ed. (Cambridge: Cambridge University Press, 2013), 62.

39. David Hume, "Of National Characters," in *Essays and Treatises on Several Subjects* (London: A. Millar, 1758), 125. Hume's essays were not translated into Castilian until the nineteenth century, but copies of English and French editions were available in many eighteenth-century Spanish public and private libraries.

40. Nicolle de la Croix, *Geografía moderna, escrita en francés por el Abad Nicollé de la Croix, traducida y aumentada con una Geografía nueva de España por Josef Jordán y Frago*, 8 vols. (Madrid: Joachin Ibarra, 1779), vol. 1, chap. 4, article 4, "De la figura y diversos colores de los habitantes de la tierra," 102–105.

41. Isidoro de Antillón, *Lecciones de geografía astronómica, natural y política, escritas de orden de S.M. para uso principalmente del Real Seminario de Nobles de Madrid* (Madrid: Imprenta Real, 1804–1806), 2 vols., lección XIV, 2: 9–12.

42. Hume, "Of National Characters," 125; Buffon, *Historia natural del hombre*, 2: 339–340; Antillón, *Lecciones de geografía*, 2: 9–12.

43. De la Croix, *Geografía moderna*, "De la figura y diversos colores de los habitantes de la tierra," 102–105.

44. Antillón, *Lecciones de geografía*, 2: 9–12.

45. Gumilla, *El Orinoco ilustrado y defendido*, prólogo, n.p.

46. Juan Nuix, *Reflexiones imparciales sobre la humanidad de los españoles en las Indias, contra los pretendidos filósofos y políticos. Para ilustrar las historias de MM. Raynal y Robertson*, trans. Pedro Varela y Ulloa (Madrid: Joaquín Ibarra, 1782), 65, 293–294.

47. Feijóo, *Teatro critico universal*, disc. 15, "Mapa intelectual, y cotejo de Naciones," vol. 2 (1728), 278–279.

48. Francisco Javier Clavijero, *Historia antigua de México* (1780), 2 vols. Spanish trans. J. J. de Mora (London: R. Ackerman, 1826), vol. 1, 72–76; vol. 2, 316.

49. Gándara, *Apuntes para el bien y el mal de España*, 204.

50. Agustín de Jáuregui, *Relación de gobierno. Perú (1780–1784)*, ed. R. Contreras (Madrid: CSIC, 1982), 168–196.

51. Gándara, *Apuntes para el bien y el mal de España*, 199–200.

52. Buffon, *Historia natural del hombre*, 2: 277–297, 307–309; *Encyclopedia Metódica: Geografía Moderna*, trans. Juan de Arribas y Soria and Julián de Velasco (Madrid: Imprenta de Sancha, 1792), 1: 95–121; William Robertson, *Historia de la América*, trans. Bernardino de Amati, 4 vols (Burdeos: Imprenta de Pedro Beaume, 1827), 2: bk. 4. Robertson's work was not published in Spain until the early nineteenth century, but the Royal Academy of History had prepared a translation at the end of the eighteenth century to be adopted as "the official history." Juan Bautista Muñoz, *Historia del Nuevo Mundo* (Madrid: Viuda de Ibarra, 1793), 10–24. A good summary of some eighteenth-century views of the Indians is Ilona Katzew, "That This Should Be Published and Again in the Age of the Elightenment? Eighteenth-Century Debates about the Indian Body in Colonial Mexico," in *Race and Classification: The Case of Mexican America*, ed. Ilona Katzew and Susan Deans-Smith (Stanford: Stanford University Press, 2009), 73–118.

53. Jorge Juan and Antonio de Ulloa, *Relación histórica del viaje a la América meridional* (Madrid: Antonio Marín, 1748), 4 vols. Citations from vol. 2, bk. 6, chap. 6, 506–507, 541, 542.

54. Antonio de Ulloa, *Noticias americanas: entretenimientos físicos-históricos sobre la América meridional y la septentrional oriental* (Madrid: Francisco Manuel de Mena, 1772). This work was reprinted in 1792 by the royal publishing house (Imprenta Real) without significant changes. The quotations are from the 1772 edition.

55. On the French Geodesic Mission (1735–1744) led by the French astronomer Charles Marie de la Condamine, see Safier, *Measuring the New World*.

56. As mentioned above, the Swedish naturalist Carolus Linnaeus was the first to suggest that all Indians belonged to a distinct human group characterized by its reddish complexion, although it's also true that around the same time the northern Indians, especially the nations occupying the territories of the modern United States, began describing themselves as red in order to differentiate themselves from other groups, especially all those of European origin. On this topic, Alden T. Vaughan, "From White Man to Redskin: Changing

Anglo-American Perceptions of the American Indian," *American Historical Review* 87 (1982): 917–953; and Nancy Shoemaker, "How Indians Got to Be Red," *American Historical Review* 102 (1997): 625–644. It should be pointed out that Antonio de Ulloa traveled extensively in Europe, visiting a number of countries including Sweden, Linnaeus's homeland.

57. See, for example, *Compendio de la Historia Natural de Buffon, clasificado según el sistema de Lineo por Renato Ricardo Castel,* trans. Pedro Estala (Madrid: Imprenta de Villalpando, 1802), vols. 3 and 4, "De la naturaleza del hombre"; but especially the work of Félix de Azara, *Voyage dans l'Amerique meridionale depuis 1781 jusqu'en 1801.* Although published in French in 1809 and not translated into Spanish until several years later, Azara's work was well known in Hispanic circles in Spanish America and in Spain. On the Indians, see Felix de Azara, *Viajes por la América del Sur desde 1789 a 1801* (1809) (Montevideo, 1850), 173–241.

58. Weber, *Bárbaros.*

59. George Reid Andrews, *Afro-Latin America, 1800–2000* (Oxford: Oxford University Press, 2003), 41.

60. Felipe Castro, *La rebellion de los indios y la paz española* (Tlalpan: CIESAS, 1996); Gustavo Faverón Patriau, *Rebeldes. Sublevaciones indígenas y naciones emergentes en Hispanoamérica en el siglo XVIII* (Madrid: Tecnos, 2006); Sergio Serulnikov, *Revolution in the Andes* (Durham: Duke University Press, 2013); Charles Walker, *The Tupac Amaru Rebellion* (Cambridge: Harvard University Press, 2014); Manuel Andrés García, *De peruanos a indios: la figura del indígena en la intelectualidad y política criollas (Perú: Siglos XVIII–XIX)* (Huelva: Universidad Internacional de Andalucía, 2007), 52–85.

61. Walker, *The Tupac Amaru Rebellion;* Serulnikov, *Revolution in the Andes.*

62. Sinclair Thomson, "Sovereignty Disavowed: The Tupac Amaru Revolution in the Atlantic World," *Atlantic Studies* 13 (2016): 407–431.

63. *Encyclopedia metódica. Geografía moderna.* The essay on Africa is on pp. 23–25 of the first volume. On Africa and Africans and Enlightenment, see T. Carlos Jacques, "From Savages and Barbarians to Primitives: Africa, Social Typologies, and History in Eighteenth-Century Philosophy." *History and Theory* 36 (1997): 190–215, which shows that French knowledge of the continent in the eighteenth century was virtually nonexistent; see also Hédia Khadhar, "La description de l'Afrique dans l'*Histoire des deux Indes,*" in *L'Histoire des deux Indes: réécriture et polygraphie,* 149–155.

64. See, for instance, Pedro Murillo Velarde, *Geografía histórica* (Madrid: Gabriel Ramírez, 1752), vol. 8: "Filipinas y África."

65. Feijóo, "Color etiópico," *Teatro crítico universal,* vol. 7, disc. 3, 86–94; and "Mapa intelectual y cotejo de naciones," *Teatro crítico universal,* vol. 2, disc. 15, 278.

66. Buffon, *Historia natural del hombre,* 2: 214–264.

67. Andrew S. Curran, *The Anatomy of Blackness. Science and Slavery in an Age of Enlightenment* (Baltimore: Johns Hopkins University Press, 2011).

68. Alonso Carrió de la Vandera (Concolorcorvo), *El Lazarillo de ciegos caminantes* (1775), ed. E. Carrilla (Barcelona: Editorial Labor, 1973), second part, chap. 20, 383; Clavijero, *Historia antigua de México,* vol. 2, 316–317. Rather than

defending the Indians, both, along with many other Creoles, were standing up for Americans, and everything American, against profoundly disparaging views emanating from Europe; on this debate, see Antonello Gerbi, *The Dispute of the New World: The History of a Polemic, 1750–1900* (Pittsburgh: University of Pittsburgh Press, 1973).

69. Isidoro de Antillón, *Disertación sobre el origen de la esclavitud de los negros* (Valencia: Domingo y Mompié, 1820), cit. 89, 121–122, 90. Antillón wrote this text in the opening years of the nineteenth century, and it was originally presented as a lecture in Madrid in 1802. It was published for the first time in 1810 and again in 1820. We will encounter Antillón again in the next chapter as one of the leaders of the liberal revolution in reaction to Napoleon's invasion of Spain.

70. For an understanding of official views on slaves and slavery in the Spanish world, see Ramón Lázaro de Dou y de Bassóls, *Instituciones del derecho público general de España con noticia del particular de Cataluña y de las principales reglas de gobierno en qualquier Estado*, 9 vols. (Madrid: Oficina de Benito García y Compañía, 1800–1803), 1: 113–120. Juan Francisco de Castro, *Dios y la naturaleza. Compendio histórico, natural y político del universo en que demuestra la existencia de Dios, y se refiere la historia natural y civil, la religión, leyes y costumbres de las naciones antiguas y modernas más conocidas del orbe*, 10 vols. (Madrid, 1780–1791), vol. 4, art. 6: "Disgresión sobre la esclavitud o servidumbre," 268–69.

71. Alex Borucki, David Eltis, and David Wheat, "Atlantic History and the Slave Trade to Spanish America," *American Historical Review* 120 (2014): 433–461.

72. María del Carmen Barcia Zequeira, "La esclavitud en Cuba. Caracterización de su desarrollo," in *La ilusión de un imperio: las relaciones económicas hispano-cubanas en el último siglo de dominación colonial*, ed. Salvador Palazón and María Candelaira Saiz (Alicante: Universidad de Alicante, 1998), 25–48.

73. Andrews, *Afro-Latin America*; Peter Blanchard, "The Language of Liberation: Slave Voices in the Wars of Independence," *Hispanic American Historical Review* 82 (2002): 504; Alex Borucki, "The Slave Trade to the Rio de la Plata, 1777–1812: Trans-imperial Networks and Atlantic Warfare," *Colonial Latin American Review* 20 (2011): 81–107.

74. *Código de Santo Domingo*, 1784, in Manuel Lucena Salmoral, *Los códigos negros de la América española* (Alcalá: Universidad de Alcalá, 1996), 197–248. Although this important code was never implemented due to opposition from slave owners, it is nevertheless representative of official policy on slavery. The contents of the text were very well known by not only the colonial authorities but also slaves, who saw it as a kind of code of rights and showed discontent over its nonimplementation. Andrews, *Afro-Latin America*, 34; Wilfredo Kapsoli Escudero, *Sublevaciones de esclavos en el Perú, siglo XVIII* (Lima: Universidad Ricardo Palma, 1975); Blanchard, "The Language of Liberation," 505.

75. *Código de Santo Domingo*, prologue, chap. 16; chap. 20, law 1, in Lucena Salmoral, *Los códigos negros de la América española*, 199, 219, 223.

76. On the contents, goals, and implementation of the slave codes, Thomas N. Ingersoll, "Slave Codes and Judicial Practice in New Orleans, 1718–1807," *Law and History Review* 13 (1995): 23–62.

77. *Código de Santo Domingo*, chap. 3, law 1; Lucena Salmoral, *Los códigos negros de la América española*, 202.

78. Feijóo, "Color etiópico," *Teatro crítico universal*, vol. 7 (1736), disc. 3, 84.

79. Castro, *Dios y la naturaleza*, 4: 264–265, 255. See also Jáuregui, *Relación de gobierno. Perú (1780–1784)*, 146. Carmen Bernard, "El color de los criollos: de las naciones a las castas, de las castas a la nación," in *Huellas de Africa en América: Perspectivas para Chile*, ed. Celia L. Cussen (Santiago de Chile: Editorial Universitaria, 2009), 18–19.

80. Herbert S. Klein and Ben Vinson, *African Slavery in Latin America and the Caribbean*, 196.

81. Azara, *Viajes por la América del Sur*, 269.

82. Klein and Vinson, *African Slavery*, 196–197; Andrews, *Afro-Latin America*, 41.

83. Alberto de la Hera Pérez-Cuesta, "Jucio de los obispos asistentes al IV Concilio mexicano sobre el estado del virreinato de Nueva España," *Anuario de Historia del Derecho Español* 31 (1961): 318; Juan Ignacio Molina, *Compendio de la historia geográfica, natural y civil del Reyno de Chile, Primera parte*, trans. Don Domingo Joseph de Arquellada Mendoza (Madrid: Don Antonio de Sancha, 1788), part 2, bk. 4, chap. 11, 324–326.

84. Borucki, Eltis, and Wheat, "Atlantic History and the Slave Trade," 447.

85. Stuart Schwartz, "The Manumission of Slaves in Colonial Brazil: Bahia, 1684–1745," *Hispanic American Historical Review* 54 (1974): 603–635; Lyman Johnson, "Manumission in Colonial Buenos Aires, 1776–1810," *Hispanic American Historical Review* 59 (1979): 258–279; Klein and Vinson, *African Slavery*, 200–205.

86. A good summary of the laws and social attitudes toward free individuals of African descent, and the social and institutional spaces they were increasingly occupying, in Ann Twinam, *Purchasing Whiteness: Pardos, Mulattos, and the Quest for Social Mobility in the Spanish Indies* (Stanford: Stanford University Press, 2015), 81–122. Andrews, *Afro-Latin America*, 41–52; Jane Landers, *Atlantic Creoles in the Age of Revolutions* (Cambridge: Harvard University Press, 2010); *Against the Odds: Free Blacks in the Slave Societies of the Americas*, ed. Jane Landers (London: Routledge, 1996); Klein and Vinson, *African Slavery*, 206–224; José R. Jouve Martin, *The Black Doctors of Colonial Lima. Science, Race, and Writing in Colonial and Early Republican Peru* (Montreal : McGill-Queen's University Press, 2014).

87. "Don Juan Germán Roscio a los señores decanos y oficiales del Ilustre Colegio de Abogados de Caracas sobre su limpieza de sangre para ser incorporado en ese cuerpo," Caracas, September 11, 1798, in Santos Rodulfo Cortés, *El régimen de las gracias al sacar en Venezuela durante el periodo hispánico* (Caracas: Academia Nacional de Historia, 1978), vol. 2, 129–150. The case instigated by Roscio in order to gain admittance to the Caracas bar association was not concluded until 1805. In 1808 Roscio became one of the leaders of the Venezuelan independence movement and occupied important administrative positions until his death in 1821; his seminal work, *El triunfo de la libertad sobre el despotismo* (ed. Domingo Miliani. Caracas: Biblioteca Ayacucho, 1996), was originally published in Philadelphia in 1817.

88. María Elena Martínez, "The Language, Genealogy, and Classification of 'Race` in Colonial Mexico," in *Race and Classification: The Case of Mexican America*, 29.

89. Numerous works on the *casta* paintings have appeared in the past twenty years, but see above all, Ilona Katzew, *Casta Painting: Images of Race in Eighteenth-Century Mexico* (New Haven: Yale University Press, 2004); Efraín Castro Morales, "Los cuadros de castas de la Nueva España," *Jahrbuch für Geschichte Lateinamerikas* 20 (1983): 671–690; Susan Deans-Smith, "Creating the Colonial Subject: Casta Paitings, Collectos, and Critics in Eighteenth-Century Mexico and Spain," *Colonial Latin America Review* 14 (2005): 169–204; Deans-Smith, "Dishonor in the Hands of Indians, Spaniards, and Blacks. The (Racial) Politics of Painting in Early Modern Mexico," in *Race and Classification: The Case of Mexican America*, 43–72.

90. A numismatist and art collector (with a penchant for casta paintings, among other things), O'Crouley included this idea in his *Idea compendiosa del Reino de la Nueva España* (1770s); cit. Castro Morales, "Los cuadros de castas," 676.

91. Pedro Murillo Velarde, *Historia de la Provincia de Philipinas de la Compañía de Jesús. Segunda Parte* (Manila: Imprenta de la Compañía de Jesús, 1749), 5r.

92. Ulloa, *Noticias americanas*, chap. 19, 346–348.

93. Juan and Ulloa, *Noticias secretas*, 173, 504–506, 527.

94. Muñoz, *Historia del nuevo mundo*, 18–19. See also Nuix, *Reflexiones imparciales*, 239–240; Gumilla, *El Orinoco ilustrado y defendido*, 90; Carrió de la Vandera, *El Lazarillo de ciegos caminantes*, first part, chap. 4, 168–169.

95. Murillo Velarde, *Geografía histórica*, vol. 9, 52.

96. Ibid.

97. Azara, *Viajes por la América del Sur*, 244, 267.

98. Max S. Hering Torres, "La limpieza de sangre. Problemas de interpretación: acercamientos históricos y metodológicos," *Historia Crítica* 45 (2011): 47.

99. William Max Nelson, "Making Men: Enlightenment Ideas of Racial Engineering," *American Historical Review* 115 (2010): 1364–1394

100. This discussion in Spanish government circles began when the Council of the Indies received an order from Secretary of State Joseph Antonio Caballero to discuss a letter from the Franciscan José Antonio Goicochea in 1802, in which he petitioned for better treatment of mulattos and zambos and for their social uplift. The letter in Laura Matthew, "Por que el color decide aqui en la mayor parte la nobleza": una carta de Fr. José Antonio Goicorchea, Guatemala, siglo XIX," *Mesoamérica* 34 (2013): 153–167; the debate in Twinam, *Purchasing Whiteness*, 414–415.

101. Ricketts, "The Rise of the Bourbon Military in Peru."

102. For the example of Panama, see Silvia Espelt-Bombín, "Notaries of Color in Colonial Panama: Limpieza de Sangre, Legislation, and Imperial Practices in the Administration of the Spanish Empire," *The Americas* 71 (2014): 37–69.

103. *Código de Santo Domingo,* Lucena Salmoral, *Los códigos negros en la América española,* 202.

104. There is still an insufficient number of studies of the relevant documents. Nevertheless at least two should be highlighted: Rodulfo Cortés, *El régimen de las gracias al sacar en Venezuela durante el periodo hispánico;* and Twinam, *Purchasing Whiteness.*

105. Twinam, "Racial Passing: Informal and Official 'Whiteness' in Colonial Spanish America," in *New World Orders: Violence, Sanction, and Authority in the Colonial Americas,* ed. John Smolenski and Thomas J. Humphrey (Philadelphia: University of Pennsylvania Press, 2005), 262–269.

106. "Petición de los representantes del batallón de Pardos pidiendo se excluya de el a Juan Bautista Arias," 1774, in Rodulfo Cortés, *El régimen de las gracias al sacar en Venezuela,* vol. 2, 19–20.

107. Linda Colley described the feelings of the British toward the American colonists in these terms in *Britons: Forging the Nation, 1707–1837* (New Haven: Yale University Press, 1992), 134. See, in general, Gerbi, *The Dispute of the New World.*

108. Murillo Velarde, *Geografía histórica,* vol. 9: "América," 46; the reference to the fact that all Creoles were the product of racial mixing in Juan and Ulloa, *Noticias secretas de América* (1748), part two, chap. 6, 415. On criticism directed at the Creoles, see Virginia Gil Amate, "¿Confiar en los Criollos? Apreciaciones sobre la condición de los españoles Americanos en el siglo XVIII," *Olivar* 14 (2010): 13–31; and Iñaki Iriarte López, "América-España," in *Diccionario político y social del mundo iberomaericano. La era de las revoluciones , 1750–1850,* ed. Javier Fernández Sebastián (Madrid: Centro de Estudios Políticos y Constitucionales, 2009), 119–121.

109. The quote from the Marquis of San Andrés in José Martín Félix de Arrate, *Llave del Nuevo Mundo, antemural de las Indias Occidentales* (1761), in *Los tres primeros historiadores de la Isla de Cuba,* ed. R. Cowley and D. A. Pego (Habana: Andrés Pego, 1876), vol. 1, 176; the other in Juan and Ulloa, *Noticias secretas de América,* 417–418.

110. Feijóo, *Teatro crítico universal,* vol. 4, disc. 6, 109–110; *Encyclopedia metodica. Geografía moderna,* trans. Juan Arribas y Soria and Julian de Velasco (Madrid: Imprenta de Sancha, 1792), vol. 1, "América o Nuevo Mundo o Indias Occidentales," 116.

111. "Consulta del Consejo Extraordinario, 5 marzo 1768." This *consulta* has been published in, Luis Navarro Garcia, "El Consejo de Castilla y su critica de la política indiana en 1768," *Homenaje al profesor Alfonso García-Gallo* (Madrid: Universidad Complutense, 1996), vol. 5, 187–208, cit. 204. Fidel Tavárez was kind enough to share with me his notes on the original consulta in the Archivo General de Indias.

112. "Representación que hizo la Ciudad de México al rey don Carlos III en 1771 sobre que los criollos deben ser preferidos a los europeos en la distribución de empleos y beneficios de estos reinos," in *Colección de Documentos para la Historia de la Guerra de Independencia de México,* ed. J. E. Hernández y Dávalos. Reimp. ed. V. Guedea and A. Ávila (México: Universidad Autónoma de México, 2007), 13, 23. See also Joseph Joaquín Granados y Gálvez, *Tardes americanas:*

gobierno gentil y católico, breve y particular noticia de toda la historia indiana . . . trabajadas por un indio y un español (México: Felipe de Zúñiga y Ontiveros, 1778), 395–441. Juan Ignacio Molina, *Compendio de la historia geográfica, natural y civil del Reyno de Chile, escrito en italiano por el Abate Don Juan Ignacio Molina, Primera parte*, trans. Don Domingo Joseph de Arquellada Mendoza (Madrid: Don Antonio de Sancha, 1788), part 2, bk. 4, chap. xi, 315–317. On the critiques and defense of the Creoles, Amate, "¿Confiar en los Criollos?" 13–31.

113. Antonio Porlier, *Amor a la Patria* (1803), in *Discursos al Consejo de Indias*, ed. M. S. Campos (Madrid: Centro de Estudios Pollíticos y Constitucionales, 2002), 156.

114. This incorporation of the Creoles into the colonial state machinery was especially thorough and enduring in Cuba, New Granada, and Peru. See Richard Konetzke, "La condición legal de los criollos y las causas de la independencia," *Estudios Americanos* 2 (1950): 44–54; Josep Maria Fradera, *Colonias para después de un imperio* (Barcelona: Bellaterra, 2005); Moreno Fraginals, *Cuba/España, España/Cuba* (Barcelona: Crítica, 2002); Sherry Johnson, *The Social Transformation of Eighteenth-Century Cuba* (Gainesville: University Press of Florida, 2001); Allan Kuethe, *Military Reform and Society in New Granada, 1773–1808* (Gainesville: University Presses of Florida, 1978); Ricketts, "The Rise of the Bourbon Military in Peru."

115. Alexander von Humboldt, *Ensayo político de la Nueva España*, trans. V. González Arnao (Paris: Casa de Rosa, 1822), vol. 1, bk. 2, chap. 7, 262.

116. "Representación que hizo la Ciudad de México al rey don Carlos III," 32, 31.

117. A study of this legislation, of the changes and amendments it underwent, and the obstacles to implementation created by the opposition of various individuals but also the royal authorities is in Verena Martínez-Alier, *Marriage, Class, and Color in Nineteenth-Century Cuba* (Cambridge: Cambridge University Press, 1974), chap. 1.

118. Maria Elena Martínez, *Genealogical fictions: limpieza de sangre, religion, and gender in colonial Mexico* (Stanford, Cal: Stanford University Press, 2008), chap. 8.

119. "Representación del Cabildo de Caracas," October 13, 1788, in Rodulfo Cortés, *El régimen de las gracias al sacar en Venezuela*, 2: 32–35.

120. "Informe de la Universidad de Caracas sobre los perjuicios que pueden seguirse de permitir que los hijos de Diego Mexías y otros se reciban en los estudios generales de ella, dispensándole para el efecto la calidad de pardo, Caracas 6 octubre 1803," in Rodulfo Cortés, *El régimen de las gracias al sacar en Venezuela*, 2: 189–196.

121. There are numerous works on the influence of the Haitian Revolution in the territories under Spanish sovereignty in the Indies, but the best one is without doubt Ada Ferrer, *Freedom's Mirror: Cuba and Haiti in the Age of Revolution* (Cambridge: Cambridge University Press, 2014).

122. Anthony McFarlane, "Civil Disorder and Popular Protests in Late Colonial New Granada," *Hispanic American Historical Review* 64 (1984): 17–54; John L. Phelan, *The People and the King: The Comunero Revolution in Colombia, 1781* (Madison: University of Wisconsin Press, 1978); and Anthony McFarlane,

"Identity, Enlightenment, and Political Dissent in Late Colonial Spanish America," *Transactions of the Royal Historical Society (Sixth Series)* 8 (1998): 309–335.

123. Donald Winch, *Classical Political Economy and Colonies* (Cambridge: Cambridge University Press, 1962); Sankar Muthu, *Enlightenment against Empire* (Prionceton: Princeton University Press, 2003); J. G. A. Pocock, *Barbarism and Religion. Vol. 3: The First Decline and Fall* (Cambridge: Cambridge University Press, 2005), "Part V. Republic and Empire: The Enlightened Narrative"; Francisco Ortega, "Ni nación ni parte integral. 'Colonia', de vocablo a concepto en el siglo XVIII iberoamericano," *Prismas* 15 (2011): 11–29.

124. Conde de Aranda, "Dictamen reservado . . . al Rey Carlos III, sobre la independencia de las colonias inglesas," in *Premoniciones de la Independencia de Iberoamérica*, ed. Manuel Lucena (Madrid: Ediciones Doce Calles, 2003), 81.

125. Juan Pablo Viscardo, "Carta dirigida a los españoles americanos," in Antonio Gutiérrez Escudero, "Juan Pablo Viscardo y su Carta dirigida a los españoles americanos," *Araucaria* 17 (2007): 329–343; quotes from 329–330, 342. Written shortly before his death in 1798, the "Carta" was published in 1799 in French and in 1801 in Spanish, translated by another Creole patriot, Francisco Miranda.

7
From Empire to Nation

1. Charles IV and his reign has recently been the subject of historiographical revisionism, but it seems that he was as weak a ruler as many of his contemporaries believed. Emilio La Parra, "La defensa de la monarquía," in *La época de Carlos IV*, ed. E. de Lorenzo (Oviedo: Instituto Feijóo, 2009), 41–53.

2. Edmund Burke, *Thoughts on French Affairs* (1791), in *The Works of the Right Honourable Edmund Burke* (London: F. and C. Rivington, 1802), vol. 4, 33.

3. José Servando Teresa de Mier, *Memorias* (Madrid: Editorial-América, 1917?), 332.

4. Isidoro de Antillón, *Disertación sobre el origen de la esclavitud de los negros* (1811) (Valencia: Domingo y Mompié, 1820), 3–4.

5. Antonio Alcalá Galiano, *Recuerdos de un anciano* (1878) (Madrid: Viuda de Hernando, 1890), 61. Alcalá Galiano was born in 1789 and died in 1865. His memoirs, and especially his *Recuerdos*, are among the most interesting sources from the period.

6. Ibid.

7. Barbara J. Fields, "Ideology and Race in American History," in *Region, Race, and Reconstruction: Essays in Honor of C. Vann Woodward*, ed. J. Morgan Kousser and James McPherson (New York: Oxford University Press, 1982), 152–153.

8. Reinhart Koselleck, "Introduction and Prefaces to the *Geschichtliche Grundbegriffe*," *Contributions to the History of Concepts* 6 (2011): 9–10.

9. The Madrid uprising and the subsequent repression were depicted by Goya in two of his best-known works, "May 2 in Madrid" and "May 3 in

Madrid," also known as "Los fusilamientos" ("The Firing Squad"). For an interesting and vivid description of the uprisings of May 2, see Arturo Pérez-Reverte, *Un día de cólera* (Madrid: Alfaguara, 2007). For a critical look at the visions of the revolt and the War of Independence, Ricardo García Cárcel, *El sueño de la nación indomable: los mitos de la Guerra de la Independencia* (Madrid: Temas de Hoy, 2007).

10. Alcalá Galiano, *Recuerdos de un anciano*, 108–109. See also Ramón Salas, *Lecciones de derecho público constitucional para las escuelas de España* (Madrid: Imprenta del Censor, 1821), vol. 1, v, viii–x; Antonio Calvo, "Dios nos libre de más revoluciones: el Motín de Aranjuez y el Dos de Mayo vistos por la condesa viuda de Fernán Núñez," *Pasado y Memoria* 10 (2011): 163–193.

11. María Reyes Domínguez, *El Estatuto de Bayona* (Ph.D. dissertation, Universidad Complutense, Madrid, 2004); Ignacio Fernández Sarasola, "La primera constitución española: El Estatuto de Bayona," *Revista de Derecho* 26 (2006): 89–109.

12. *Estatuto de Bayona*, Tit. X, art. 87. For the text of the article, and the debates about how to name the Spanish territories in the Americas, Reyes Domínguez, *El Estatuto de Bayona*, 222-228. A manuscript copy of the original statute in Archivo del Congreso de los Diputados, Sección Papeles reservados de Fernando VII. Sign. T.3,F.69-89, "Constitución original firmada de los que concurrieron a la Junta de Bayona (Estatuto de Bayona)," http://www.congreso.es/docu/constituciones/1812/Bayona_ed.pdf, accessed July 25, 2016

13. Few depicted the chaos and the violence unleashed by the war better than the contemporary Spanish painter Goya in his famous series "The Disasters of War." Goya, whose liberal and pro-French leanings were well-known, remained in Spain for the duration of the war and the opening years of Ferdinand VII's reign, but he left for a self-imposed exile in 1824, residing in the French city of Bordeaux until his death in 1828.

14. Charles Esdaile, *The Peninsular War: A New History* (New York: Palgrave McMillan, 2003); Esdaile, *Napoleon's Wars: An International History* (New York: Viking, 2003); David Bell, *The First Total War: Napopelon's Europe and the Birth of Warfare as We Know It* (Boston: Houghton Mifflin, 2007).

15. Ronald Fraser, *Napoleon's Cursed War: Spanish Popular Resistance in the Peninsular War* (London: Verso, 2008), 514. For an analysis of the war in each Spanish region, *La Guerra de la Independencia en el mosaico peninsular (1808–1814)*, ed. C. Borreguero (Burgos: Universidad de Burgos, 2010).

16. Antonio Capmany, *Centinela contra franceses* (Madrid: Gómez Fuentenebro y Cia., 1808), 16.

17. Robert Palmer, *The Age of Democratic Revolution: A Political History of Europe and America, 1760–1800* (1969) (Princeton: Princeton University Press, 2014).

18. José García de León y Pizarro, *Memorias de la vida del Excmo. Señor D. José García de León y Pizarro, escritas por él mismo* (1833) (Madrid: Sucesores de Rivadeneyra, 1894), vol. 1, 237, 251, 252. See also José Mor de Fuentes, *Bosquejillo de la vida y escritos de José Mor de Fuentes, delineado por él mismo* (1836), ed. M. Alvar (Zaragoza: Guara Editorial, 1981), 62–65.

19. Mor de Fuentes, *Bosquejillo*, 68.

20. Elena Fernández, "Las mujeres en los sitios de Girona: la 'Compañía de Santa Bárbara,'" in *Heroínas y patriotas. Mujeres de 1808*, ed. I. Castells et al. (Madrid: Cátedra, 2009), 105–128.

21. J. M., "Por qué en la insurrección española las mujeres han mostrado tanto interés, y aún excedido a los hombres en el empeño de sostenerla?" *Gaceta de Madrid* 52 (February 21, 1810): 213–214. The author was most likely the pro-French liberal José Marchena, and the *Gazeta* was the official mouthpiece of Joseph I's government. "Las mujeres y la guerra," 60 (February 11, 1811), in *Tertulia Patriótica de Cádiz*, ed. M. Angulo (Cádiz: Biblioteca de las Cortes de Cádiz, 2011), 397–398.

22. Álvaro Flórez Estrada, *Examen imparcial de las disensiones de América con la España* (Cádiz: Manuel Ximénez Carreño, 1812), 49–50. That from the very beginning this war was seen as a struggle for independence from French tyranny and was not construed as such after the fact, Demetrio Castro, "La nación en las Cortes: Ideas y cuestiones sobre la nación española en el periodo 1808–1814," *Cuadernos Dieciochistas* 12 (2011): 38–42.

23. *Diario de las Discusiones y Actas de las Cortes (DDAC) (*Cádiz: Imprenta Real, 1811-1813), 23 vols., Session 29, December 1810, vol. 2, 164, 172. On the use of the term *national independence* in this phase of the fight against the French and its meaning, Javier Fernández Santamaría, "La independencia de España y otras independencias," in *Las declaraciones de independencia*, ed. A. Ávila, J. Dym, and E. Pani (México: UNAM/El Colegio de México, 2013), 57–79.

24. *Instrucciones y memorias de los virreyes novohispanos*, ed. E. de la Torre (México: Editorial Porrua, 1991), vol. 1, 1474–1475, 1476. On this topic see Monica Ricketts, "Together or Separate in the Fight against Oppression? Liberals in Peru and Spain in the 1820s," *European History Quarterly* 41 (2011): 413–427.

25. *Semanario Patriótico*, 41, 17 January 1811, 217. Jeremy Adelman, "The Rites of Statehood: Violence and Sovereignty in Spanish America, 1789-1821," *Hispanic American Historical Review*, 90 (2010): 391-422.

26. For a general overview from a constitutional perspective, see José M. Portillo, *Crisis Atlántica* (Madrid: Marcial Pons Historia, 2006), 159–209.

27. Capmany, *Centinela contra franceses*, 17–18.

28. Elisa Martín-Valdepeñas et al., "Una traductora de Mably en el Cádiz de las Cortes: La Marquesa de Astorga," *Historia Constitucional* 10 (2009): 63–136; Marieta Cantos and Beatriz Sánchez, "Escritoras y periodistas ante la Constitución de 1812 (1808–1823), *Historia Constitucional* 10 (2009): 137–179.

29. Charles Esdaile, *Fighting Napoleon: Guerrillas, Bandits, and Adventurers in Spain, 1808–1814* (New Haven: Yale University Press, 2004); Fraser, *Napoleon's Cursed War.*

30. On the so-called "generation of 1808" and their experiences, ideologies, readings, and preoccupations, Manuel Moreno, *La generación española de 1808* (Madrid: Alianza Universidad, 1989).

31. Henry R. Bassall, Baron of Holland, *Foreign Reminiscences* (New York: Harper, 1851), 100. On the domestic roots of Spanish liberalism, Antonio Elorza, *La ideología liberal en la Ilustración española* (Madrid: Tecnos, 1970);

Antonio Elorza, "La excepción y la regla: reaccionarios y revolucionarios en torno a 1789," *Historia Contemporánea* 43 (2012): 547–583.

32. Salas, *Lecciones de derecho público constitucional*, vol. 1, v, viii, ix–x. On the political factions during this period, Ignacio Fernández Sarasola, *Los partidos políticos en el pensamiento español* (Madrid: Marcial Pons Historia, 2009), first part; a general study of the first liberalism in the Iberian world, *La aurora de la libertad. Los primeros liberalismos en el mundo iberoamericano*, ed. Javier Fernández Sebastián (Madrid: Marcial Pons Historia, 2012).

33. John Allen, *Suggestions on the Cortes* (1809), in Ignacio Fernández Sarasola, *Proyectos constitucionales en España (1786–1824)* (Madrid: CEPC, 2004), 591.

34. Quintín Casals, "El Parlamento de las Cortes de Cádiz," *Las Cortes de Cádiz y la historia parlamentaria*, ed. Diana Repeto García (Cádiz: Universidad de Cádiz, 2012), 52–63.

35. There are hundreds, perhaps thousands, of works on the Constitution of Cádiz in a variety of languages, and this number has quintupled in the past few years with the commemoration of the 200th anniversary of its proclamation in 2012. Among them are works of all types, from popular histories to scholarly ones, left- and right-leaning. Some of these works will be cited in the remainder of this chapter, but perhaps worth highlighting are Ignacio Fernández Sarasola, *La Constitución de Cádiz* (Madrid: CECP, 2011); and *Cortes y Constitución de Cádiz, 200 años*, ed. J. A. Escudero (Madrid: Espasa, 2011), 3 vols.

36. A fascinating analysis of constitutional traditions more generally, beyond the Spanish world, *Scripting Revolution*, ed. Keith Michael Baker and Dan Edelestein (Stanford: Stanford University Press, 2015), parts I and II.

37. Salas, *Lecciones de derecho público constitucional*, xiv–xv.

38. Spanish reformers from the late eighteenth century viewed the French constitution of 1791 as a potential model for Spain; Elorza, "La excepción y la regla," 179; Ignacio Fernández Sarasola, "El primer liberalismo en España (1808–1833)," *Historia Contemporánea* 43 (2012): 635–636.

39. An analysis of John Allen's *Suggestions*, with the English and Spanish versions in, Fernández Sarasola, *Proyectos constitucionales*, 587–641.

40. There are dozens of studies on the English influence, many of them gathered in *Il modelo constitutionale inglese e la sua recezione nell'area mediterránea tra la fine del 700 e la prima metà dell'800*, ed. A. Romano (Milan: Dott A. Giufrè Editore, 1998).

41. Gonzalo Martínez, "Viejo y nuevo orden constitucional: El 'Discurso preliminar' de nuestra primera constitución," *Cortes y Constitución de Cádiz, 200 años*, vol. 2, 593–594.

42. José Canga Arguelles, *Reflexiones sociales o idea para la constitución española que un patriota ofrece a los representantes de las Cortes* (Valencia: Imprenta de José Estevan, 1811), 3–4.

43. On the debates over Spanish constitutional traditions before Cádiz, Fernández Sarasola, *Proyectos constitucionales;* José Manuel Nieto Soria, *Medievo constitucional. Historia y mito político en los orígenes de la España contemporánea (ca. 1750–1814)* (Madrid: Akal, 2007).

44. Agustín de Arguelles, *Discurso preliminar leído en las Cortes al presentar la Comisión de Constitución el proyecto de ella*, ed. L. Sánchez (Madrid: CEPC, 2011), 67–69.

45. The impassioned debate on Article 3 took place during the sessions of August 27 and 29, 1811, DDAC, vol. 8, 47–63. On the question of the nation in the debates of the Cortes of Cádiz, Castro, "La nación en las Cortes."

46. *Instrucciones de la Junta Superior del principado de Cataluña*, August 13, 1809, cit. Jesús Fernández, "Uniformismo jurídico y reacción en Cataluña," in *Cortes y Constitución de Cádiz, 200 años*, vol. 2, 178. These instructions were drawn up by Felipe Aner de Esteve, who was one of the Catalan deputies in the Cortes.

47. DDAC, session of September 2, 1811, vol. 8, 116, 117–118.

48. DDAC, session of August 26, 1811, vol. 8, 16. Regarding the distinct conception of the "nation" championed by some American deputies, José Varela Suanzes-Carpegna, "Nación, representación y articulación territorial del estado en las Cortes de Cádiz," *Revista de Historia Jerónimo Zurita* 87 (2012): 14.

49. DDAC, session of September 27, 1811, vol. 9, 8, and 15.

50. Cit. Miguel Artola, *Los orígenes de la España contemporánea* (Madrid: Instituto Estudios Políticos, 1975), vol. 2, 659.

51. DDAC, session of September 2, 1811, vol. 8, 118

52. Felipe Bauzá, the engineer and geographer charged by the Cortes with designing the new territorial structure of the monarchy, reported in 1813 that although it was necessary to divide the country into equal provinces, it was not yet possible to abolish the kingdoms because the people "still preserve a certain affect and adherence to those territories," and to change everything now "would be a cause of resentment." Cit. María José Vilar, "El primer proyecto de division provincial de España. El propuesto por Felipe Bauzá y revisado por Miguel de Lastarría,"*Anales de Historia Contemporánea* 20 (2004): 31. The essential work on all these topics is Jesús Burgueño, *Geografía política de la España constitucional* (Madrid: Centro de Estudios Constitucionales, 1996).

53. DDAC, Vicente Terrero, deputy for Algeciras, priest, and Felipe Aner de Esteve, deputy for Catalonia, lawyer, session of September 2, 1811, vol. 8, 107, 108.

54. Arguelles, *Discurso preliminar*, 125.

55. Spaniards perfectly understood the new language of citizen and citizenship, but the word *citizen (ciudadano)* as the holder of citizenship rights *(ciudadanía)* did not enter the official dictionaries until the midlle of the nineteenth century, most probably due to the constitutional and political debates affecting Spain since the return of Ferdinand VII in 1813. On the evolution of the term *citizenship*, J. G. A. Pocock, "The Ideal of Citizenship since Classical Times," *Queens Quarterly* 99 (1999): 33–55; Peter Riesenberg, *Citizenship in the Western Tradition* (Chapel Hill: The University of North Carolina Press, 1992); and *Citoyens and citoyenneté sous la Révolution française*, ed. Raymonde Monnier (Paris: Societé des études robespierristes, 2006).

56. Javier Fernández Sebastián, "Ciudadanía," in *Diccionario político y social del siglo XIX español*, ed. J. Fernández and J. F. Fuentes (Madrid: Alianza Editorial, 2002), 139–143.

57. The only Spanish constitution—and there have been seven (1812, 1837, 1845, 1869, 1876, 1931, 1978)—that considered "Spaniards" and "Spanish citizens" as distinct categories is the Constitution of Cádiz.

58. On women's political and military activism during the War of Independence, Elena Fernández, *Mujeres en la Guerra de la Independencia* (Madrid: Silex, 2009); *Heroínas y patriotas. Mujeres de 1808*, ed. I. Castells, G. Espigado, and M. C. Romedo (Madrid: Cátedra, 2009). Juan Francisco Fuentes and Pilar Garí, *Amazonas de la libertad* (Madrid: Marcial Pons Historia, 2014).

59. John Adams to James Sullivan, May 26, 1776, in *The Founders' Constitution,* chap. 13, doc. 10, http://press-pubs.uchicago.edu/founders/documents/v1ch13s10.html. On the American case, see the classic study by Linda K. Kerber, *Women of the Republic: Intellect and Ideology in Revolutionary America* (Chapel Hill: University of North Carolina Press, 1980); and the more recent and equally compelling Rosemarie Zagarri, *Revolutionary Backlash: Women and Politics in the Early American Republic* (Philadelphia: University of Pennsylvania Press, 2008).

60. José Manuel Quintana, "Sobre las obras poéticas de Rosa Gálvez de Cabrera, publicadas en Madrid, 1804," *Variedades de Ciencias, Literatura y Artes,* Año II, vol. 1 (1805), 160.

61. DDAC, session of September 6, 1811, vol. 8, 205.

62. *Reglamento para el gobierno interno de las Cortes* (Cádiz: Imprenta Real, 1810), art. 3, 3; Bartolomé Clavero, "Cara oculta de la Constitución: sexo y trabajo," *Revista de las Cortes Generales* 10 (1987): 14–15.

63. DDAC, session of September 7, 1811, vol. 8 219.

64. Manuel Fernández Martín, *Derecho parlamentario español* (Madrid: Hijos de J. A. García, 1885), vol. 2, 599.

65. A good summary of deliberations on the American question in the Cortes of Cádiz is Carlos Martínez Shaw, "América en las Cortes de Cádiz," in *Cortes y constitución de Cádiz 200 años,* vol. 2, 165–183. But the essential work is still Manuel Chust, *La cuestión nacional americana en las Cortes de Cádiz (1810–1814)* (Valencia: UNED, 1999).

66. "Representación de la Diputación Americana a las Cortes de España, en primero de Agosto de 1811," in Manuel Calvillo, "México Cádiz 1811. Un documento y un debate," *Boletín del Instituto de Investigaciones Bibliográficas* 3 (1989): 129, 136. DDAC, Session of January 9, 1811, Francisco López Lisperguer, substitute deputy for Buenos Aires, vol. 2, 325, 326.

67. *Semanario Patriótico,* 46, 21 February 1811, 323–324.

68. Ibid., 299. On the Wars of Independences in Spanish America, perceived by many contemporaries as a "civil war" between Spaniards, see Jaime E. Rodríguez, *The Independence of Spanish America* (Cambridge: Cambridge University Press, 1998); David Brading, *The First America* (Cambridge: Cambridge University Press, 1993), chaps. 24–29; Jeremy Adelman, *Sovereignty and Revolution in the Iberian Atlantic* (Princeton: Princeton University Press, 2006), chaps. 5, 7.

69. Agustín de Arguelles, *Examen histórico de la reforma constitucional que hicieron las Cortes generales y extraordinarias.* (London: Carlos Wood e Hijo, 1835), vol. 2, chap. 6, 32, 33.

70. Arrámbari's report was read during the session of September 16, 1811, and although it was never included in the *DDAC,* the numerous speeches on

what to do with the text, and its author, were incorporated. The two representations of the Mexican *Consulado* (Merchants' Corporation), the ensuing debates in the Cortes, and the subsequent representation addressed to the Cortes, signed by all the American deputies, have been published together, with an introduction by Calvillo, "México Cádiz 1811," 7–141. The first representation, which was not read in the Cortes, is a petition requesting that European Spaniards be represented in the parliament by those of their own number. Cits. in 71–72, 66–67, 69.

71. The debates on the Representation of the *Consulado* of Mexico, one of the longest and most dramatic of the entire legislative session, in DDAC, sessions of September 16, 17, 18 and 19, 1811, vol. 8, 337–378.

72. DDAC, Session of 19 January 1811, vol. 3, 67.

73. Gregory Ablavsky, "The Savage Constitution," *Duke Law Journal* 63 (2014): 998–1089.

74. Alexander von Humboldt, *Ensayo político sobre la Isla de Cuba*, 2nd ed. (Paris: Librería de Lecointe, 1836), 270.

75. DDAC, Session of 25 January 1811, vol. 3, 87.

76. Ibid., Dionisio Inca Yupanqui, Session of 18 January 1811, vol. 3, 26.

77. Ibid., Session 9 January 1811, vol. 2, 316.

78. Ibid., Session of 19 January 1811, vol. 3, 75.

79. "Representación del Real Consulado de México a las Cortes de España," 54–76.

80. DDAC, José de Espiga y Gadea, Session of 9 January 1811, vol. 2, 327; Juan Pablo Valiente, Session 19 January 1811, vol. 3, 77; "Representación del Real Consulado de México a las Cortes de España," 65.

81. Upholding such principles did not signify a rejection of a more racialist theory about the Indians. Both theories—that the Indians' present state was the result of Spanish exploitation and negligence or the innate inferiority of the Indian—are present in the influential text by Alexander von Humboldt, *Ensayo politico sobre el reino de la Nueva-España*, bk. 2, chap. 6, vol. 1, 143–213. Parts of the text were published in French and Spanish between 1804 and 1811.

82. *El Español*, IV (30 July 1810), 279. This quote included precisely in an analysis of the French edition of Humboldt's work on New Spain, published in Paris between 1808–1809. Cit. Portillo, *Crisis atlántica*, 220–221. See also Flórez Estrada, *Examen imparcial de las disensiones*, 52–53.

83. Francisco Castillo et al., *Las Cortes de Cádiz y la imagen de América* (Cádiz: Universidad de Cádiz, 1994), questionnaire, October 1812, 75–78; responses, 99–169.

84. This topic has been more closely studied in recent years, so that we now have more sophisticated analyses of the situation. Worth consulting above all is *Los Indígenas en la Independencia y en la revolución mexicana*, ed. M. León-Portilla and A. Mayer (México: UNAM/INAH, 2010); Bartolomé Clavero, "Cádiz entre indígenas," in *Anuario de Historia del Derecho Español* 65 (1995): 931–1006; and Eva Sanz Jara, *Los indios de la nación* (Madrid: Iberoamericana, 2011), 21–102.

85. Humboldt, *Ensayo político sobre la Isla de Cuba*, 270.

86. Marcela Echeverri, *Indian and Slave Royalists in the Age of Revolution: Reform, Revolution, and Royalism in the Northern Andes, 1780-1825* (Cambridge: Cambridge University Press, 2016).

87. DDAC, Session of 25 January 1811, vol. 3, 90–91.

88. Christopher Brown, *Moral Capital: Foundations of British Abolitionism* (Chapel Hill: University of North Carolina Press, 2006).

89. David Waldstreicher, *Slavery's Constitution: From Revolution to Ratification* (New York: Hill and Wang, 2009).

90. DDAC, Session of 5 January 1811, vol. 2, 15.

91. The Constitution of Cádiz did not include a separate, specific declaration of rights like other contemporary constitutions, but under Article 4 a number of rights were mentioned, such as, for instance, that the nation was obliged to uphold "civil liberty, property, and other legitimate rights of all individuals who comprise it." On rights included in the Constitution of Cádiz, see Raúl Canosa, "Derechos y libertades en la Constitución de 1812," *Revista de Derecho Político* 82 (2011): 145–192.

92. "Representación de la Ciudad de la Habana a las Cortes, el 20 de julio de 1811," a series of documents prepared under the direction of Francisco de Arango, a member of the municipal government of Havana and one of the Cuban deputies in the Cortes. In Francisco de Arango, *Obras* (La Habana: Ministerio de Educación, 1952), vol. 2, 145–237, which, along with many relevant documents, also includes summaries of the Cortes debates.

93. José Blanco White, "Abolición de la esclavitud," *El Español* 14 (May 30, 1811): 149–154; see also his *Bosquejo del comercio de esclavos y reflexiones sobre este tráfico considerado moral, política y cristianamente* (London: Ellerton and Henderson, 1814). For the Spanish liberal perspective on these issues, see Antillón, *Disertación sobre el origen de la esclavitud de los negros*, which he delivered in 1802, in the Real Academia Matritense de Derecho Español y Público (Madrid Royal Academy of Spanish and Public Law) and published for the first time in 1811. Antillón was one of the liberal leaders in the Cortes of Cádiz. On the impact of the Haitian rebellion among the Spanish elites, see Ada Ferrer, *Freedom's Mirror: Cuba and Haiti in the Age of Revolution* (Cambridge: Cambridge University Press, 2015).

94. Guridi's proposal was added to the *Actas* of the Cortes after the one put forward by Arguelles had been discussed. DDAC, vol. 4, 447–448. Arguelles' proposal in DDAC, vol. 4, 439–440.

95. The Cuban historian Ramón Sagra claimed that between 1761 and 1812, the Spanish monarchy received more than $17 million in profits from the sale of Cuban tobacco, *Historia económica-política y estadística de la isla de Cuba* (Habana: Viudas de Arazoza y Soler, 1831), 266. The only decision taken by the Cortes was that Arguelles' and Guridi's proposals should be considered by a commission charged with implementing concrete proposals—although by the end of the Cortes in 1814, this commission had not presented a single concrete proposal. The commission nevertheless collected all the proposals, records of debates, and other documents related to the abolition of the slave trade in a volume titled *Documentos de que hasta ahora se compone el expediente que principiaron las Cortes extraordinarias sobre el tráfico y esclavitud de los negros* (Madrid: Imprenta de Repullés, 1814). On nineteenth-century abolitionism in the Spanish world, Robin Blackburn, *The American Crucible. Slavery, Emancipation, and Human Rights* (London: Verso, 2011), 251–273; *Esclavitud y derechos humanos: la lucha por la libertad del negro en el siglo XIX*, ed. F. Solano and A. Guimerá (CSIC: Madrid, 1990).

96. Thomas Holt, *The Problem of Freedom* (Baltimore: Johns Hopkins University Press, 1992); Fields, "Slavery, Race, and Ideology in the United States of America," *New Left Review* 181 (1990): 95–118.

97. Douglas Bradburn. "The Problem of Citizenship in the American Revolution," *History Compass* 8/9 (2010): 1100. On this topic see David Brion Davis, *The Problem of Slavery in the Age of Revolution* (Ithaca: Cornell University Press, 1975); and *The Problem of Slavery in the Age of Emancipation* (New York: Alfred A. Knopf, 2014); Ira Berlin, *Generations of Captivity* (Cambridge: Harvard University Press, 2003); and *Slaves without Masters* (New York: Pantheon Books, 1974).

98. Peter Blanchard, *Under the Flags of Freedom: Slave Soldiers and the Wars of Independence in Spanish South America* (Pittsburgh: University of Pittsburgh Press, 2008); and "The Language of Liberation: Slaves Voices in the Wards of Independence," *Hispanic American Historical Review* 82 (2020): 499–523; Marcela Echeverri, "Popular Royalists, Empire, and Politics in Southwestern New Granada, 1809–1819," *Hispanic American Historical Review* 91 (2011): 237–269. On conspiracies by free blacks in territories where no independence movements arose, see Matt D. Childs, *The 1812 Aponte Rebellion in Cuba and the Struggle against Atlantic Slavery* (Chapel Hill: University of North Carolina Press, 2006).

99. DDAC, José Calatrava, Session of 10 September 1811, vol. 8, 234.

100. DDAC, Antonio Larrazábal, Session of 6 September 1811, vol. 8, 199.

101. Josep M. Fradera, "Raza y ciudadanía. El factor racial en la delimitación de los derechos de los americanos," in Ibid., *Gobernar colonias.* (Barcelona: Península, 1999), 65; see also Josep Fradera, "Ciudadanía, ciudadanía congelada, y súbditos residuales," *Illes i Imperis*, 7 (2004), 113–134.

102. DDAC, Morales Duárez, Session of 7 February 1811, vol. 3, 382.

103. Ibid., Agustín Arguelles, Session of 4 September 1811, vol. 8, 155–157.

104. Ibid., 7 September 1811, vol. 8, 216

105. *Colección de los discursos que pronunciaron los señores diputados de América contra el artículo 22 del Proyecto de Constitución, ilustrados con algunas notas interesantes por los españoles pardos de esta capital* (Lima: Imprenta de los Huérfanos, 1812).

106. Salas, *Lecciones de derecho público constitucional*, 48–49.

107. Ibid.

Conclusion

1. *Spanish Constitution*, 1978, tit. VIII, chap. 3.

2. *Estatuto de Autonomía de Cataluña* (Barcelona: Parlament de Catalunya, 2013), art. 1.

3. *Spanish Constitution*, 1978, preliminary title.

4. Tony Judt, "The New Old Nationalism," *New York Review of Books* 42, no. 10 (May 26, 1994): 44.

5. Francisco Caja, *La raza catalana. El núcleo doctrinal del catalanismo* (Madrid: Ediciones Encuentro, 2010).

6. For an excellent analysis of this symposium and the controversies it provoked, see the commentaries by Valentian historian Pedro Ruiz Torres at http://usagespublicsdupasse.ehess.fr/pedro-ruiz-torres-espanya-contra-catalunya-una-mirada-historica-1714-2014/, accessed August 8, 2016. On the

history of Spain viewed from Catalonia and other parts of Spain, see Joan B. Culla and Borja de Riquer, "La enseñanza de la historia desde una perspectiva catalana," *Ayer* 30 (1998): 159–170.

7. Tomás Calvo Buezas, *Inmigración y racismo* (Madrid: Cauce Editorial, 2000), 187, 190–191.

8. José Manuel Pérez-Prendes, "El nuevo marco legal: de la Real Cédula de 1802 a los acuerdos de 1992," in *Los judíos en la España contemporánea*, ed. R. Izquierdo et al. (Cuenca: Universidad Castilla La Mancha, 2000), 75–92; Américo Castro, *España en su historia: cristianos, moros y judíos* (Buenos Aíres: Editorial Losada, 1948); Américo Castro, *La realidad histórica de España* (México: Editorial Porrúa, 1954); Rafael Valls, "La presencia del Islam en los actuales manuales españoles de historia," *Iber* 70 (2011).

9. Angel Rosenblat, *La población indígena y el mestizaje en América* (Buenos Aires: Editorial Nova, 1954), 13. See also Richard Konetzke, "El mestizaje y su importancia en el desarrollo de la población hispano-americana durante la época colonial," *Revista de Indias* 7 (1946): 36–37. The idea of *mestizaje* as representative of the lack of racial prejudices of Spaniards is in many ways the official theory of Spanish historiography. Hispanic scholars have not been alone in interpreting the early modern period in Spain as a time free of racial prejudices. Frank Tannenbaum, the Austrian American scholar, argued in his widely influential book *Slave and Citizen, the Negro in the Americas* (New York: A. A. Knopf, 1946), that the Iberian world had created a much more humane slave system than any other empire in the Americas, based on civil law rather than racist arguments. Because of this, he wrote, Spaniards always tended to justify their actions with less recourse to racist theories. Less known, and perhaps more interesting, is the case of the African American historian Carter G. Woodson, who in 1935, after evaluating the literature produced in Spain during the early modern and modern periods, concluded that "Spain evidently, then, is one of the countries that has been saved from the evils of race prejudice." Woodson saw this demonstrated by the works Spanish writers published but, most importantly, by Spain's policies and practices throughout history. C. G. Woodson, "Attitudes of the Iberian Península," *Journal of Negro History* 20 (1935): 190–243.

10. Enrique Krauze, "Nueve inexactitudes sobre la cuestión indígena," *El País*, March 8, 2001.

11. This idea of racial universalism was more fully developed by Spanish and Portuguese authors of the nineteenth and twentieth centuries and especially in the work of a Brazilian, Gilberto Freyre, and a Mexican, José Vasconcelos. Gilberto Freyre, *Casa-grande e senzala: formação da familia brasileira sob o regimen de economia patriarchal* (Rio de Janeiro: Maia e Schmidt, 1933), a work enormously influential and translated into Spanish, English, and German; José Vasconcelos, *La raza cósmica* (Madrid: Agencia Mundial de Libreria, 1925), also enormously influential and translated into English.

ACKNOWLEDGMENTS

In writing this book I have acquired many debts of gratitude toward mentors, colleagues, friends, and relatives. I owe perpetual gratitude to my editor at Harvard University Press, Joyce Seltzer. She has supported me without hesitation throughout the many years that it took me to complete this manuscript. Igor Knezevic, who was my doctoral student at the University of Pennsylvania but who became my friend, helped me with countless translations, wise analysis, and advice. Pamela Haag gave new life and sense to my manuscript, and saved me from many mistakes and embarrassments.

It is very difficult to express in words how much I, and this book, owe to Stephanie McCurry. Without her support, sense of humor, amazing mind, encouragement, and especially her advice and intellectual challenge this book, and I, would be infinitely less. I also owe special gratitude to my friend and colleague Fernando Bouza. Without his care, advice, and encouragement, this book would have been simply impossible.

Two anonymous readers for Harvard University Press, and a few colleagues and friends, James Amelang, Stuart Schwartz, Richard Kagan, and Daniel Richter, who read *Speaking of Spain*, offered constructive criticism that allowed me—I hope they see it this way—to improve what was a chaotic first draft of this book. I am responsible for all the errors and misunderstandings still remaining, but they saved me from committing many more. Roger Chartier, Pedro Cardim, and Mercedes García Arenal never read any of the drafts of this book, but their work has always inspired me, and their friendship has been a constant source of support.

There are many other friends, colleagues, and students to whom I owe gratitude—Irma Elo, who had done more for me and my career than almost anybody else; Sir John Elliott; Alexander Ponsen; Jeremy Adelman; Josep Fradera; Angel Loureiro; Xavier Gil Pujol; Carmiña Escrigas; María Jordán; María Luisa López Vidriero; Georgina Dopico; Michael Gilsenan; Linda Colley; David Bell; and the late Christopher Schmidt-Nowara. I would also like to thank many doctoral students at the universities of Pennsylvania and Princeton who had to listen to me talking about these topics for many years. My former mentor at the Johns Hopkins University, J. G. A. Pocock, read about *Speaking of Spain* when it was only a book proposal and, as always, helped me to center the topic and my approach.

I dedicate this book to my sisters, Pilar and Lourdes; my mother, Pilar; and especially to my late brother, Moncho. He was diagnosed with cancer precisely when I was starting to write *Speaking of Spain*, and unfortunately he died before I was able to finish it. I know he would had been very happy to see this book finished, and I am very sad he is not here with us to celebrate the occasion.

INDEX